DOMESDAY BOOK

Lincolnshire

History from the Sources

DOMESDAY BOOK

A Survey of the Counties of England

LIBER DE WINTONIA

Compiled by direction of

KING WILLIAM I

Winchester
1086

DOMESDAY BOOK

general editor

JOHN MORRIS

31

Lincolnshire

edited by

Philip Morgan and Caroline Thorn

from a draft translation prepared by
Sara Wood

(Part One)

PHILLIMORE
Chichester
1986

1986
Published by
PHILLIMORE & CO. LTD.
London and Chichester
Head Office: Shopwyke Hall,
Chichester, Sussex, England

ISBN 0 85033 598 1 (case)
ISBN 0 85033 599 X (limp)

*Printed in Great Britain by
Titus Wilson & Son Ltd.,
Kendal*

LINCOLNSHIRE

History from the Sources
General Editor: John Morris

The series aims to publish history
written directly from the sources
for all interested readers, both
specialists and others. The first
priority is to publish important
texts which should be widely
available, but are not.

DOMESDAY BOOK

The contents, with the folio on which each county begins, are:

Supplementary volume (35) BOLDON BOOK

Domesday Book is termed *Liber de Wintonia* (The Book of Winchester) in column 332c

INTRODUCTION

The Domesday Survey

In 1066 Duke William of Normandy conquered England. He was crowned King, and most of the lands of the English nobility were soon granted to his followers. Domesday Book was compiled 20 years later. The Saxon Chronicle records that in 1085

> at Gloucester at midwinter ... the King had deep speech with his counsellors ... and sent men all over England to each shire ... to find out ... what or how much each landholder held ... in land and livestock, and what it was worth ... The returns were brought to him.[1]

William was thorough. One of his Counsellors reports that he also sent a second set of Commissioners 'to shires they did not know, where they were themselves unknown, to check their predecessors' survey, and report culprits to the King.'[2]

The information was collected at Winchester, corrected, abridged, chiefly by omission of livestock and the 1066 population, and fair-copied by one writer into a single volume, now known as Domesday Book Volume I, or DB. The task of abridgement and codification was not complete by the time work stopped at the death of King William. The remaining material, the commissioners' circuit returns for Norfolk, Suffolk and Essex, which there had not been time to reduce, was left unabridged, copied by several writers, in a second volume, smaller than the first, usually now referred to as Domesday Book Volume II or Little Domesday Book or LDB, which states that 'the Survey was made in 1086'. The surveys of Durham and Northumberland, and of several towns, including London, were not transcribed, and most of Cumberland and Westmorland, not yet in England, was not surveyed. The whole undertaking was completed at speed, in less than 12 months, though the fair-copying of the main volume may have taken a little longer. Both volumes are now preserved at the Public Record Office. Some versions of regional returns also survive. One of them, from Ely Abbey,[3] copies out the Commissioners' brief. They were to ask

> The name of the place. Who held it, before 1066, and now?
> How many *hides*?[4] How many ploughs, both those in lordship and the men's?
> How many villagers, cottagers and slaves, how many free men and Freemen?[5]
> How much woodland, meadow and pasture? How many mills and fishponds?
> How much has been added or taken away? What the total value was and is?
> How much each free man or Freeman had or has? All threefold, before 1066,
>   when King William gave it, and now; and if more can be had than at present.

The Ely volume also describes the procedure. The Commissioners took evidence on oath 'from the Sheriff; from all the barons and their Frenchmen; and from the whole Hundred, the priests, the reeves and six villagers from each village'. It also names four Frenchmen and four Englishmen from each Hundred, who were sworn to verify the detail.

---

[1]Before he left England for the last time, late in 1086. [2]Robert Losinga, Bishop of Hereford 1079-1095 (see *E.H.R.* 22, 1907, 74). [3]*Inquisitio Eliensis*, first paragraph. [4]A land unit, reckoned as 120 acres. [5]*Quot Sochemani*.

The King wanted to know what he had, and who held it. The Commissioners therefore listed lands in dispute, for Domesday Book was not only a tax-assessment. To the King's grandson, Bishop Henry of Winchester, its purpose was that every 'man should know his right and not usurp another's'; and because it was the final authoritative register of rightful possession 'the natives called it Domesday Book, by analogy from the Day of Judgement'; that was why it was carefully arranged by Counties, and by landholders within Counties, 'numbered consecutively ... for easy reference'.[6]

Domesday Book describes Old English society under new management, in minute statistical detail. Foreign lords had taken over, but little else had yet changed. The chief landholders and those who held from them are named, and the rest of the population was counted. Most of them lived in villages, whose houses might be clustered together, or dispersed among their fields. Villages were grouped in administrative districts called Hundreds, which formed regions within Shires, or Counties, which survive today with minor boundary changes; the recent deformation of some ancient county identities is here disregarded, as are various short-lived modern changes. The local assemblies, though overshadowed by lords great and small, gave men a voice, which the Commissioners heeded. Very many holdings were described by the Norman term *manerium* (manor), greatly varied in size and structure, from tiny farmsteads to vast holdings; and many lords exercised their own jurisdiction and other rights, termed *soca*, whose meaning still eludes exact definition.

The Survey was unmatched in Europe for many centuries, the product of a sophisticated and experienced English administration, fully exploited by the Conqueror's commanding energy. But its unique assemblage of facts and figures has been hard to study, because the text has not been easily available, and abounds in technicalities. Investigation has therefore been chiefly confined to specialists; many questions cannot be tackled adequately without a cheap text and uniform translation available to a wider range of students, including local historians.

Previous Editions

The text has been printed once, in 1783, in an edition by Abraham Farley, probably of 1250 copies, at Government expense, said to have been £38,000; its preparation took 16 years. It was set in a specially designed type, here reproduced photographically, which was destroyed by fire in 1808. In 1811 and 1816 the Records Commissioners added an introduction, indices, and associated texts, edited by Sir Henry Ellis; and in 1861-1863 the Ordnance Survey issued zincograph facsimiles of the whole. Texts of individual counties have appeared since 1673, separate translations in the Victoria County Histories and elsewhere.

[6]*Dialogus de Scaccario* 1,16.

This Edition

Farley's text is used, because of its excellence, and because any worthy alternative would prove astronomically expensive. His text has been checked against the facsimile, and discrepancies observed have been verified against the manuscript, by the kindness of Miss Daphne Gifford of the Public Record Office. Farley's few errors are indicated in the notes.

The editor is responsible for the translation and lay-out. It aims at what the compiler would have written if his language had been modern English; though no translation can be exact, for even a simple word like 'free' nowadays means freedom from different restrictions. Bishop Henry emphasized that his grandfather preferred 'ordinary words'; the nearest ordinary modern English is therefore chosen whenever possible. Words that are now obsolete, or have changed their meaning, are avoided, but measurements have to be transliterated, since their extent is often unknown or arguable, and varied regionally. The terse inventory form of the original has been retained, as have the ambiguities of the Latin.

Modern English commands two main devices unknown to 11th century Latin, standardised punctuation and paragraphs; in the Latin, *ibi* ('there are') often does duty for a modern full stop, *et* ('and') for a comma or semi-colon. The entries normally answer the Commissioners' questions, arranged in five main groups, (i) the place and its holder, its hides, ploughs and lordship; (ii) people; (iii) resources; (iv) value; and (v) additional notes. The groups are usually given as separate paragraphs.

In both volumes of the MS, chapters were numbered 'for easy reference'. In the larger volume, sections within chapters are commonly marked, usually by initial capitals, often edged in red. In LDB (representing an earlier stage of the Inquiry's codification) sections are at first usually introduced by a paragraph mark, while red edging is reserved for chapter and Hundred headings; further on, however, the system of paragraphing the text becomes more haphazard and it is thus not always followed in the present translation. Owing to the less tabulated nature of the entries in LDB for Norfolk and Suffolk it is not possible to maintain throughout the translation of these two counties the sub-paragraphing that the late John Morris employed in the translation of other counties in the series. Maps, indices and an explanation of technical terms are also given. Later, it is hoped to publish analytical and explanatory volumes, and associated texts.

The editor is deeply indebted to the advice of many scholars, too numerous to name, and especially to the Public Record Office, and to the publisher's patience. The draft translations are the work of a team; they have been co-ordinated and corrected by the editor, and each has been checked by several people. It is therefore hoped that mistakes may be fewer than in versions published by single fallible individuals. But it would be Utopian to hope that the translation is altogether free from error; the editor would like to be informed of mistakes observed.

The maps are the work of Wendy Morgan.

The preparation of this volume has been greatly assisted by a generous grant from the Leverhulme Trust Fund.

This support, originally given to the late Dr. J. R. Morris, has been kindly extended to his successors. At the time of Dr. Morris's death in June 1977, he had completed volumes 2, 3, 11, 12, 19, 23, 24. He had more or less finished the preparation of volumes 13, 14, 20, 28. These and subsequent volumes in the series were brought out under the supervision of John Dodgson and Alison Hawkins, who have endeavoured to follow, as far as possible, the editorial principles established by John Morris.

Conventions

★   refers to note on discrepancy between MS and Farley text

[ ]   enclose words omitted in the MS   ( ) enclose editorial explanation

336 a

IN CIVITATE LINCOLIA. erant Tépore regis
Eduuardi nouies centũ 7 LXX. manfiones hos
pitatæ. Hic numer anglice cõputat. I. Centũ p. cxx.
In ipfa ciuitate erant. XII. Lageman. ideſt haben
tes facā 7 focā. Hardecnut. Suartin. f. griboldi. Vlf
fili Suertebrand. qui habuit thol 7 theim. Walra
uen. Aluuold. Britric. Guret. Vlbert. Godric. f. eddeue.
Siuuard. Leuuine. Aldene.

Modo funt ibi totidē. hñtes fimilit facā 7 focā.
Suardinc loco Hardecnut patris fui. Suartinc.
Sortebrand loco Vlf patris fui. Agemund loco Walra
uen patris fui. Aluuold. Goduin fili Brictric. Nor
mann craſſus loco Guret. Vlbert fr Vlf adhuc uiuit.
Petrus de ualonges loco Godric filij Eddeue. Vl
nod pbr loco Siuuard. p. Buruolt loco patris fui
Leuuine qui modo. ē monach. Leduuin fili reuene
loco Aldene pbri.

Tochi fili Outi habuit in ciuitate. xxx. manfiones
præter fuã Hallã. 7 II. æcclas 7 dimidiã. 7 fuã hallã
habuit quietã ab omi confuetudine. 7 fup alias
xxx. manfiones habuit locatione. 7 pter hoc de
una quaq unũ denariũ ideſt Landgable. Sup has
.xxx. manſ habebat rex theloneũ & forisfacturã. ut
burgenfes iurauer. Sed his iurantibᴣ contradicit
Vluiet pbr. 7 offert fe portaturũ iudiciũ qd non
ita eſt ficuti dicunt. Hanc aulã tenet Goisfrid
alfelin. 7 fuus nepos Radulf. Remigi eps tenet

★

LINCOLNSHIRE

[CITY OF LINCOLN]

1   In the City of LINCOLN there were 970 occupied residences before   336 a
1066. This number is reckoned by the English method, (that is)
100 for 120.

2   In the City itself there were 12 lawmen, that is those who have
full jurisdiction: Harthaknutr; Svertingr son of Grimbald; Ulfr's
son, Svartbrandr, who had market rights; Valhrafn; Alwold;
Beorhtric; Guthrothr; Wulfbert; Godric son of Eadgifu; Siward
the priest; Leofwine the priest; Halfdan the priest.

3   Now there are as many there who likewise have full jurisdiction:
1. Svertingr in place of his father Harthaknutr; 2. Svertingr;
3. Svartbrandr in place of his father Ulfr; 4. Agmundr in place of
his father Valhrafn; 5. Alwold; 6. Godwine son of Beorhtric;
7. Norman Crassus in place of Guthrothr; 8. Wulfbert, Ulfr's
brother, is still living; 9. Peter of Valognes in place of Godric son
of Eadgifu; 10. Wulfnoth the priest in place of Siward the priest;
11. Burgwald in place of his father Leofwine who is now a monk;
12. Leodwine son of Rafn in place of Halfdan the priest.

4   Toki son of Auti had 30 residences in the City besides his
Hall and 2½ churches. He had his Hall exempt from every
customary due. He had rent in respect of the 30 other
residences, and besides this 1d from each one, that is the
land tribute. In respect of these 30 residences the King had
toll and forfeiture, as the burgesses have sworn. But Wulfgeat
the priest contradicts their sworn testimony and offers to
undergo ordeal that it is not as they state. Geoffrey Alselin
and his nephew Ralph hold this Hall. Bishop Remigius holds

fup̃dictas . xxx . manfiones in æcclã S̃ MARIÆ . ita q̃d
Goisfrid alfelin nichil inde hr̃ . neq̃ fcangiũ neq̃
aliã redditionẽ . Ifdem Goisfrid hr̃ . ı . manfionẽ
extra murũ . unde hr̃ Landgable . fic habuit Tochi.

⌐Radulf⁹ pagenel hr̃ . ı . manſ quæ fuit Merlefuen.
quietã ab om̃i c̃fuetudine.

⌐Ernuin pb̃r hr̃.ı.manſ Morcari cõm̃ cũ faca 7 foca.7 fic
de rege tenet fic Morcar habuit . ut ipfe dicit.

⌐Gifleb̃t⁹ de gand hr̃.ı.manſ . Vlf.cũ faca 7 foca.
7 aliã manſ unde habeb̃.ı.den̄́.7 iterũ.ı.manſ.
Siuuard q̃etã ab om̃i confuetudine.

⌐Comes Hugo hr̃ . ı . manſ comitis Heroldi . cũ faca 7 foca.
7 ıı . manſ unde habet Landgable.   ⌐7 foca.

⌐Roger⁹ de bufli hr̃ . ı . manſ Suen .f.Suaue . cũ faca

⌐Judita comitiffa . hr̃ . ı . manſ Stori fine faca 7 foca.
7 hanc calũniat́ Iuo taillebofc p̃ burgenfes.

⌐Remigius eps̃ hr̃ . ı . maneriolũ cũ . ı . car̃ c̃t́iguũ in ciui
tate tiLincolia.æ cũ faca 7 foca 7 cũ Thol 7 Theim.7 fup
ııı . manſ fimilit́.7 fup . ıı . æcclas.7 fup . LXXVIII.
manſ fimilit́ . præt́ geldũ regis q̃d dant cũ þur
genfib̃ . Ex his fuñ́ . xx . manſ Waftæ . De trib̃ fupiorib̃
manſ eſt . ı . q̃eta . ab om̃ib reb.duæ ũ fuñ́ in geldo cũ þur
                                    ⌐genfib̃.⁹

I̊n cãpis Lincoliæ ext́ã ciuitatẽ funt xíı.
carucatæ tr̃æ 7 dimidia . p̃ter carucatã ep̃i ciuit́.
De hac tr̃a hũt Rex 7 comes . vııı . carucatas
in dñio . Ex his dedit unã rex Wills cuidã
Vlchel pro una naui quã ab eo emit . Ille ũ
qui uauí uendidit mortuus.c̃.7 hanc carucatã
tr̃e nullus hr̃ nifi rege c̃cedente . Præt́ has . vııı.
carucatas . hr̃ rex 7 comes cc 7 xxx.ı.ac̃s tr̃æ
arabilis inland.7 c . ac̃s p̃ti.

the said 30 residences among (the lands of) the church of St. Mary with the result that Geoffrey Alselin has nothing from them, neither (in) exchange nor other payment. Geoffrey also has 1 residence outside the wall from which he has the land tribute, as Toki had.

5 Ralph Pagnell has 1 residence, which was Merlesveinn's, exempt from every customary due.

6 Earnwine the priest has 1 residence of Earl Morcar's with full jurisdiction; he holds from the King in the same way as Morcar had it, as he states himself.

7 Gilbert of Ghent has 1 residence, Ulfr's, with full jurisdiction, another residence from which he had 1d, and a further 1 residence, Siward's, exempt from every customary due.

8 Earl Hugh has 1 residence, Earl Harold's, with full jurisdiction, and 2 residences from which he has the land tribute.

9 Roger of Bully has 1 residence, Sveinn son of Svafi's, with full jurisdiction.

10 Countess Judith has 1 residence, Stori's, without full jurisdiction. Ivo Tallboys claims it through the burgesses.

11 Bishop Remigius has 1 small manor with 1 carucate adjacent to the City of Lincoln, with full jurisdiction and market rights; likewise in respect of 3 residences, 2 churches and 78 residences except for the King's tax which they pay with the burgesses. Of these, 20 residences are unoccupied. Of the 3 residences above, 1 is exempt from everything, but 2 are taxed with the burgesses.

12 In the fields of Lincoln outside the City there are 12½ carucates   336 b
of land, besides the carucate of the Bishop of the City. Of this land the King and the Earl have 8 carucates in lordship. King William gave one of them to Ulfketill for a ship which he bought from him. But the man who sold the ship is dead and no one has this carucate of land except with the King's consent. Besides these 8 carucates the King and the Earl have 231 acres of arable land, *inland*, and 100 acres of meadow.

De reliq̃ tra ideſt . iiii . car̃ 7 dimidia . T.R.E
habuit Vlf . i . car̃ . nẽ ht̃ fili ej Sortebrand.

Aliã car̃ . T.R.E . habuer̃ Siuuard pbr̃ 7 Outi.
7 vi . acs træ quas tenet Vluiet pbr̃ . Nunc
ht̃ Alfnod medietatẽ huj carucatæ.

7 Norman fili Siuuard pbr̃i alterã medietatẽ.
Hanc ũ p̃dictã medietatẽ iſtius tre . 7 uxorem
Siuuardi pbr̃i inuaſit Vnlof pbr̃ dũ erat iɴ
ſaiſitione regis p̃pt . xl . ſolid quos ipſemet rex
impoſuerat ſup Siuuardũ pbr̃m.

Terciã caruc̃ ht̃ petr̃ de Valongies . q̃ ht̃ Godric̃
T.R.E.

Quarta caruc̃ adjacuit iɴ æccła omiũ ſcoʒ . T.R.E.
7 xir̃ . toftes . 7 iiii . croftes . Hanc æcclãm 7 trã æcclæ
7 quicq̃d ad eã p̃tin̄ . habuit Godric̃ fili Gareuinæ.
Sʒ eo facto monacho . abb̃ de Burg obtinet.
Burgenſes ũ om̃s Lincoliæ dñt q̃d injuſte habet.
q̃a nec Gareuin nec Godric̃ fili ej nec ullus alius
dare potuer̃ extra ciuitatẽ nec extra parentes
eoʒ . niſi conceſſu regis . Hanc æcclãm 7 q̃ ibi p̃tin̄
clam Ernuin pbr̃ hereditate Godrici c̃ſanguinei

Reſiduã dimidiã caruc̃ træ habuit 7 habet Sc̃a
Maria de Lincolia . iɴ qua nc̃ eſt epiſcopatus.
Inter æcclas Lincoliæ 7 burgenſes . habuer̃ . xxx.
vi . croftes in Lincolia . exceptis . xii . 7 dim̃ caruc̃
træ quæ. enumeratæ ſuɴ̃.

Ex p̃dictis mañs quæ T.R.E . fuer̃ hoſpitatæ.
ſunt m̃ Waſte . cc . anglico numero . i.cc.xl.
7 eod̃ numero ſepties centũ 7 lx . ſunt m̃ hoſpitatæ.

13   Of the remaining land, that is 4½ carucates, before 1066 Ulfr had 1 carucate, now his son Svartbrandr has it.

14   Before 1066 Siward the priest and Auti had another carucate, and 6 acres of meadow which Wulfgeat the priest holds. Now Alnoth has half of this carucate and Norman son of Siward the priest the other half. But Wulfnoth the priest seized the said half of that land — and the wife of Siward the priest — while it was in the King's possession because of (a fine of) 40s which the King himself had imposed on Siward the priest.

15   Peter of Valognes has the third carucate which Godric had before 1066.

16   The fourth carucate was attached to the church of All Saints before 1066, also 12 plots and 4 crofts. Godric son of Garwine had this church, the church's land and whatever belonged to it. But now that he has become a monk the Abbot of Peterborough holds them. But all the burgesses of Lincoln state that he has them wrongfully, because neither Garwine nor Godric his son nor anyone else could grant them outside the City or outside their family except with the King's consent. This church and what belongs to it Earnwine the priest claims by inheritance from his kinsman Godric.

17   St. Mary's of Lincoln, where the Bishopric is now, had and has the remaining ½ carucate of land.

18   Between them the churches of Lincoln and the burgesses had 36 crofts in Lincoln, besides the 12½ carucates of land which are listed above.

19   Of the said residences which were occupied before 1066, 200 are now unoccupied by the English reckoning, that is 240, and by the same reckoning 760 are now occupied.

⌐Hi fubfcripti n̄ deder̄ geldū regis fīc debuiſſeꝗ.

Terra S̱ MARIE in qua Tedbert manet in magno

uico. n̄ ded̄ geld́. neqᷠ tra eṕi ad S̄ Laurent́ poſita.

n̄ ded̄ geld́ de. I. domo.

Abƀ de burg de. I. domo 7 de. III. toftis n̄ ded̄ gld̄.

Hugo de om̄i t́ra fua n̄ ded̄ gld̄. neqᷠ Turald́

de greteuilla. neqᷠ Loſuard́ neqᷠ Chetelbert́.

Hugo. f. Baldrici n̄ ded̄ gld de. II. toftis. Neqᷠ

Goiſfrid́ alſelin. ſimil de. II. toftis.

Neqᷠ Gislebt́ de. III. domiƀ ded̄ geldū. Neqᷠ Petrus

de ualonges de ſua domo. Neqᷠ judita de ſua domo.

Neqᷠ Radulf́ pagenel de. I. domo. Neqᷠ Radulf́ de

badpalmas de ſua domo. Neqᷠ Ertald́ de ſua domo.

⌐Domū de qua abƀ de Burg ut dict̄ū. ē n̄ ded̄ gld̄.

ipſā clamat Norm̄ann de feuo regis. Ipſā enĩ

habuit Godred́ anteceſſor ſuus in uadimon̄

ꝓ tribᷦ mark̄ argenti 7 dimid́.

⌐Colſuen hr̄ in Lincolia ciuitate. IIII. toftes de

t́ra Cole nepotis ſui. 7 ext̄ ciuitat̄e hr̄ XXX.VI.

domos 7 II. æccłas in quibᷦ nichil adjacet. quas

hoſpitauit in Waſta t́ra quā rex ſibi dedit. 7 quæ

nunꝗ ante hoſpitata fuit. Modo hr̄ rex om̄s con

ſuetudines ex eis.

⌐Alured́ nepos Turoldi hr̄. III. toftes de t́ra Sẏbi.

q̄m rex ſibi ded́. in q̇bᷦ hr̄ om̄s c̄ſuetudines. p̄ter

gld̄ regis de monedagio.

⌐Abƀ de Elẏg hr̄ dimid́ mañs de t́ra Edſtan.

⌐Hugo. f. baldrici. hr̄. II. toftes q̄s rex ſibi dedit.

20 Those written below have not paid the King's tax as they ought
to have:
   The land of St. Mary's where Theodbert lives in the High Street
has not paid tax; nor has the Bishop's land situated at St.
Lawrence's paid tax on 1 house.
   The Abbot of Peterborough has not paid tax on 1 house and 3
plots.
   Earl Hugh has not paid tax on all his land, nor has Thoraldr of
Greetwell, nor Losoard nor Ketilbjorn.
   Hugh son of Baldric has not paid tax on 2 plots, nor has
Geoffrey Alselin, likewise on 2 plots.
   Nor has Gilbert paid tax on 3 houses; nor Peter of Valognes on
his house; nor Countess Judith on her house; nor Ralph Pagnell
on 1 house; nor Ralph of Bapaume on his house; nor Ertald on
his house.

21 The house on which the Abbot of Peterborough has not paid tax,
as has been stated (above), Norman Crassus claims as (part) of   336 c
the King's holding. For Guthrothr his predecessor had it in pledge
for 3½ marks of silver.

22 Kolsveinn has in the City of Lincoln 4 plots of his nephew Cola's
land. Outside the City he has 36 houses and 2 churches to which
nothing is attached, which he settled on waste land which the
King gave him and which had never been settled before. Now the
King has all the customary dues from them.

23 Alfred, Thoraldr's nephew, has 3 plots of Sibbi's land which the
King gave him, in which he has all the customary dues except for
the King's tax from the mint.

24 The Abbot of Ely has ½ residence from Aethelstan's land.

25 Hugh son of Baldric has 2 plots which the King gave him.

De p̄dictis Waſtis mans̄.ppt̄ caſtellū deſtructæ
fuer̄ c.lx.vi. Reliq̃.lxx.iiii. Waſtatæ ſunt
extra metā caſtelli. non ppt̄ oppreſſionē uico
mitū 7 miniſtroꝛ꞉ ſ; ppt̄ infortuniū 7 pauꝑta
tē.7 igniū exuſtionem.

T.R.E. reddebat ciuitas Lincolia regi.xx.libras.
7 comiti.x.liƀ. Modo redd̄.c.liƀ ad numerū.
int̄ regē 7 comitē. Moneta ū   redd̄.lxx.v.liƀ.

Conſuetudines regis 7 comitis in Sudlincolia꞉
redduꞃ.xxviii.liƀ.
In Norttreding c̄ſuetudines regis 7 comitis.
reddunt.xx.iiii.liƀ.
In Weſtreding c̄ſuetudines regis 7 comitis꞉
redduꞃ.xii.liƀ.
In Sudtreding c̄ſuetudines regis 7 comitis꞉
reddunt.xv.liƀ.

Pax manu regis uel Sigillo ej̄ data. ſi fuerit
infracta꞉ emendatur p xviii. hundrez.
Vnūqdq̃ hund̄ ſoluit.viii.liƀ. Duodeci hund̄
em̄dant regi.7 vi.comiti.
Siqs pro aliq̃ reatu exulat fuerit a rege 7 á comi
te 7 ab hominiƀ uicecomitat꞉ nullus niſi rex ſibi
dare pacē poterit.

26   Of the said unoccupied residences 166 were destroyed because of the castle; the remaining 74 are unoccupied outside the castle's perimeter, not because of the oppression of the Sheriffs and officers, but because of misfortune, poverty and the ravages of fire.

27   Before 1066 the City of Lincoln paid £20 to the King and £10 to the Earl. Now it pays £100 at face value between the King and the Earl, but the mint pays £75.

28   The customary dues of the King and the Earl in South Lincoln(shire) pay £28.

29   In the North Riding the customary dues of the King and the Earl pay £24.

30   In the West Riding the customary dues of the King and the Earl pay £12.

31   In the South Riding the customary dues of the King and the Earl pay £15.

32   If the peace, given by the King's hand or by his seal, is broken, a fine is paid throughout 18 hundreds. Each hundred pays £8. 12 hundreds pay the fine to the King and 6 to the Earl.

33   If anyone for any crime should be exiled by the King, the Earl and the men of the Shire, no one but the King can give him peace.

STANFORD BVRGV REGIS . dedit geldũ T.R.E.

pro . XII . hundrez 7 dimidio . In exercitu . 7 naui

gio . 7 in Danegeld . Ibi fuer 7 funt . VI . cuſtodie.

Quinq̷ in Lincoleſcŷre . 7 ſexta in Hantuneſcŷre . quæ

eſt ultra pontē . 7 tam ipſa reddebat oĩem cſuetudinē

cũ alijs . p̄ter gablũ 7 theloneũ . qd abb de Burg

habebat 7 habet.

In his . v . cuſtodijs T.R.E . fuer . CXL 7 I . mãs . 7 dimid

molend . quæ reddebaɴ oĩs eſuetudines . S; & m̃ totid

funt . p̄ter . v . quæ ꝓpt op caſtri fuɴ waſtæ.

In his cuſtodijs funt . VI . mãs quæ . T.R.E . dabant oĩs

cſuetudines . m̃ autē n̄ daɴ . Brand hr . IIII . 7 Vlchetel

fili Mereuuine . II.

In his cuſtodijs funt LXXVII . mãs ſochemanoɀ . qui

hn̄t tras ſuas in dñio . 7 qui petuɴ dños ubi uolunt.

ſuᵽ quos rex nichil aliud hr niſi emdationē foris

facturæ eoɀ . 7 heriete . 7 theloneũ . 7 I . moliñ de . XXX .

ſolid qd abſtulit de huntedune . Illud erat uni ſochi.

In Stanford . T.R.E . erant . XII . Lagemanni . qui ha

bebant infra domos ſuas ſacā 7 ſocā . 7 ſuᵽ hões ſuos .

p̄ter geld 7 heriete . 7 forisfacturā corpoɀ ſuoɀ de

XL . oris argenti . 7 p̄ter Latronē . Hoc idē m̃ habent.

S; non funt niſi noue . Vnus eoɀ hr XVII . mãs

ſub ſe . 7 dimid moliñ . XV . ſolidoɀ . Alt . XIIII . mãs.

una ex his . e Waſta . Terci . II . m: n̄s . Quart . II . 7 dimid.

Quint . qnq̷ Sext . IIII . Septim . III . Octauus . unā.

Nonus . III . ſ; Hugo muſard duas ei abſtulit.

In his cuſtodijs adhuc ſuɴ . XXII . mãs . 7 II . æcclæ

cũ . XII . acris træ de . XIIII . ſolid . quas habebat

Ernuin pbr . T.R.E . 7 Ezi habebat . I . mãs . has . XX.III .

mãs hr m̃ Eudo dapiſer . Sup eas habebat rex

oĩem cſuetudinē . modo n̄ hr.

[BOROUGH OF STAMFORD]

1 The King's Borough of STAMFORD paid tax before 1066 for 12½   336 d
hundreds for the army, ship service and for Danegeld. There were
and are six wards: five in Lincolnshire and the sixth in
Northamptonshire — it is across the bridge; however, it paid
every customary due with the others except for tribute and toll,
which the Abbot of Peterborough had and has.

2 In these five wards before 1066 there were 141 residences and ½
mill which paid all the customary dues; but now there are as
many except for 5 which are unoccupied because of the
construction of the castle.

3 In these wards there are 6 residences which before 1066 paid all
the customary dues, but now they do not pay them. Brandr has 4;
Ulfketill son of Merewine, 2.

4 In these wards there are 77 residences of Freemen who have their
lands in lordship and seek lords where they will. The King has
nothing over them except for a fine (consisting) of their forfeiture,
heriot and toll. 1 mill at 30s which Eustace of Huntingdon took
away; it was one of the Freemen's.

5 In Stamford before 1066 there were 12 lawmen who had full
jurisdiction within their houses and over their men, except for
tax, heriot, forfeiture involving their bodies at 40 *ora* of silver,
and robbery. They also have this now, but they are only nine;
one of them has 17 residences under him and ½ mill, 15s; the
second, 14 residences — one of these is unoccupied; the third, 2
residences; the fourth, 2½; the fifth, 5; the sixth, 4; the seventh,
3; the eighth, 1; the ninth, 3, but Hugh Musard has taken 2 away
from him.

6 In these wards there are still 22 residences and 2 churches with
12 acres of land at 14s which Earnwine the priest had before
1066; Eadsige had 1 residence. Eudo the Steward now has these
23 residences. The King had every customary due in respect of
them, now he does not.

In ead uilla ħƀ Azor, vii. mans 7 dimid moliñ. T.R.E,

ṁ ħ Gunfrid de ciocħes. Ad has ptiñ. lxx. acræ

extra uilla.

⌐ Eduuard cild ħƀ. xiiii. mans 7 lxx. acs. ext uilla. ṁ

ħ Judita comitiſſa.

⌐ Edded regina ħƀ. lxx. mans quæ jacueᵲ in Roteland

cū omibȝ c̄ſuetudinibȝ. ſine panificis. Ad has adjaceꝗ

ii. caᵲ træ 7 dimid. 7 i. caruca araꝗꝰ. 7 xlv. ac̄ p̄ti ext uilla,

Modo ħ Rex. W. 7 ualet vi. liƀ. T.R.E. uaſ. iiii. liƀ.

⌐ Abƀ de Burg ħƀ 7 ħ in Stanford x. mans ptiñ ad

Lincoleſȳre. 7 i. moliñ. xl. ſolid. 7 v. ſolid de domibȝ 7 de viii. ᶠᵃᶜʳⁱˢ.

⌐ Leuuiñꝰ ħƀ. ix. mans. ṁ Alured ħ. Ite Leuuiñꝰ. i. mans

ad omem c̄ſuetud. ſine geldo. quā ṁ ħ Wido de rēbudcurt.

⌐ Faſtolf ħƀ unā æcclam de rege ꝙeta cū. viii. acris.

⌐ Albᵗ unā æcclam S Petri cū. ii. mans. 7 dim caᵲ tre quæ

jacet in Rotelande in hemeldune. Vaſ. x. ſolid.

⌐ Terrā arabilē ext uilla in Lincoleſcire ħ rex. ꝺc. acs.

⌐ Lagemanni 7 burgenſes ħñt. cc. 7 lxxii. acs. ſine omi c̄ſuetud,

⌐ T.R.E. dabat Stanford. xv. liƀ. ṁ dat ad firmā. l. liƀ.

De omi c̄ſuetudine regis. ṁ dat. xxviii. liƀ,

337 a

In Torcheseᵲ. T.R.E. fueᵲ. cc. 7 xiii. burgenſes.

Eaſdē c̄ſuetudines habebant oms q̄s & Lincolienſes.

7 tantū plus qd ꝙcunqȝ eoȝ manſionē in ead uilla

habebat. neqȝ intrans neqȝ exiens theloneū dabat

nec c̄ſuetudinē. Hoc auᵗ eoȝ erat. ut ſi legati regis

illuc uenireꝗˑ hões ejd uici cū nauibȝ ſuis 7 alijs

inſtrumᵗis nauigationis uſqȝ eboracū eos conduce

reꝗ. 7 uicecomes uictū legatoȝ 7 nautarū ex firma

ſua inueniret. Qd ſi aliꝗs burgenſiū alibi uellet

abire. 7 domū quæ ēet in ead uilla uendereˑ ſine

ſcientia | ppoſiti ſi uellet poſſet facere.

7   Also in this town Atsurr had 7 residences and ½ mill before 1066; now Gunfrid of Chocques has them. To them belong 70 acres outside the town.

8   Edward Young had 14 residences and 70 acres outside the town; now Countess Judith has them.

9   Queen Edith had 70 residences which lay in Rutland, with all the customary dues, except the bakers'. Attached to them are 2½ carucates of land and 1 plough, which is ploughing, and 45 acres of meadow outside the town. Now King William has them. Value £6; value before 1066 £4.

10 In Stamford the Abbot of Peterborough had and has 10 residences which belong to Lincolnshire; 1 mill, 40s; 5s from houses and from 8 acres.

11 Leofwine had 9 residences; now Alfred has them. Leofwine also [had] 1 residence with every customary due except tax, which Guy of Raimbeaucourt has now.

12 Fastulfr had 1 church from the King, exempt, with 8 acres.

13 Albert [has?] 1 church, St. Peter's, with 2 residences and ½ carucate of land which lies in Rutland, in Hambleton. Value 10s.

14 The King has 600 acres of arable land outside the town in Lincolnshire.

15 The lawmen and burgesses have 272 acres without every customary due.

16 Before 1066 Stamford paid £15, now it pays £50 in revenue. It now pays £28 in respect of every customary due of the King's.

[T]   [TORKSEY]

1   In TORKSEY before 1066 there were 213 burgesses. They all had   337 a
    the same customary dues as the men of Lincoln, and so much
    more, since whoever of them had a residence in this town did not
    pay toll on entering or leaving nor a customary due. However,
    this was their (duty): if the King's officers should come there the
    men of this small town should conduct them with their ships and
    other equipment for navigation as far as York, and the Sheriff
    should find supplies for the officers and the sailors out of his
    revenue. But if any of the burgesses wished to go away anywhere
    and sell (his) house which was in this town, he could do it, if he
    wished, without the knowledge and permission of the reeve.

Hcc fuburbiū Torchefȳg 7 Harduic m̄ ei c̄tiguū
habuit Eddid regina in dñio.7 habeƀ foris urbē
.ii.car̄ træ fine geldo.Modo h̄t rex in dñio.7 fuɴ̄
ibi.c̄ii.burgenfes manentes.Waftæ fuɴ̄ u̇.c.xi.
manfiones.Ad hanc uiłłā ptiñ xx.ac̄ p̄ti.7 lx.ac̄
filuæ minutæ.7 xi.pifcariæ.Vna ex his.ē Bereng
de tcdeni.T.R.E.int regē.7 comitē.uał.xviii.liƀ.
m̄.xxx.liƀ.

T.R.E.reddeƀ Torchefȳ 7 Harduic in Lincolia
q̇ntū denariū de geldo ciuitatis.Ad hāc q̇ntā
partē dabat Torchefȳg.ii.den̄.7 Harduic tciū.
De hac Torchefig habebat Morcar tciū denariū
de omibȥ c̄fuetudiniƀ.

In Harduic̣ h̄ƀ Suen 7 Godric.i.car̄ træ.7 ibi ma
nebant.xii.hōes.Modo h̄t Roger de bufli me
dietatē.7 eps Lincolienfis aliā med.ad S maria
de Stou.Ibi cadit tcia pars geldi regis.qd rex
ñ h̄t de illa q̄ ptiñ ad Dorchefȳg.

Hic notant̄ qui habuer̄ in Lincolefcire facā 7 focā.
7 Tol 7 Thiam.Ep̄s Lincolie.Eddid regina.Abƀ de
Burg.Abƀ de Ramefȳ.Abƀ de Croiland.Haroldus.
Morcar.Waltef.Radulf.Vlffenifc.Merlefuen.
★ Turgot.Tochi.Stori.Radulfus.Siuuard barn.
Harold.Fȳach.Rolf.f.Sceldeware.Godricus.
Achi.f.Siuuardi 7 Wilac fr ej fup trā patris eoȥ.
Leuuine.Azer.Ailric.Outi.Adestan.Tori.
★ Toli.Azer.Wluuard.Vlf.Haminc.Bardi.
Suan.

2 Queen Edith had this small town of Torksey and the manor of Hardwick adjacent to it in lordship and she had 2 carucates of land without tax outside the town. Now the King has them in lordship; there are 102 burgesses who live there, but 111 residences are unoccupied. To this town belong 20 acres of meadow, 60 acres of underwood and 11 fisheries. One of them is Berengar of Tosny's.
Value before 1066, between the King and the Earl, £18; now £30.

3 Before 1066 Torksey and Hardwick paid in Lincoln the fifth penny from the City's tax. Towards this fifth part Torksey paid two pennies and Hardwick the third. Morcar had the third penny of all the customary dues of this (place called) Torksey.

4 In Hardwick Sveinn and Godric had 1 carucate of land; 12 men lived there. Now Roger of Bully had half and the Bishop of Lincoln the other half at Stow St. Mary. There falls to (Hardwick) the third part of the King's tax which the King does not have from that (part) which is due from Torksey.

5 Here are noted those who had full jurisdiction and market rights in Lincolnshire:

The Bishop of Lincoln	Rothulfr son of Skjaldvǫr
Queen Edith	Godric son of Thorfrothr
The Abbot of Peterborough	Aki son of Siward and Vigleikr
The Abbot of Ramsey	his brother over their
The Abbot of Crowland	father's land
Earl Harold	Leofwine son of Alwine
Earl Morcar	Atsurr son of Svala
Earl Waltheof	Aelfric son of Mergeat
Earl Ralph	Auti son of Atsurr
Ulfr Fenman	Aethelstan son of Godram
Merlesveinn	Thorir son of Roaldr
Thorgautr	Toli son of Alsige
Toki son of Auti	Atsurr son of Burg
Stori	Wulfweard White
Ralph the Constable	Ulfr
Siward Barn	Hemingr
Harold the Constable	Barthi
Fiacc	Sveinn son of Svafi

.I. TERRA REGIS

.II. Archiepi eboracūsis.
.III Epi Dunelmensis.
.IIII Epi Baiocensis.
.V. Epi Osmundi Sarisberiens.
.VI. Epi Constantiensis.
.VII. Epi Lincoliensis.
.VII. Abbatis de Burg.
.IX. Abbatis de Westmonast.
.X. Abbis de Ramesyge.
.XI. Abbis de Croilande.
.XII. Alani comitis.
.XIII. Hugonis comitis.
.XII. Iuonis taillebosc.
.XV. Willelmi de Warenna.
.XVI. Rogerij pictauensis.
.XVII Rogerij de busli.
.XVI. Robti de Todeni.
.XIX Berengerij de Todeni.
.XX. Ilbti de Laci.
.XXI. Henrici de ferrarijs.
.XXII. Willelmi de pci.
.XXIII Gisleberti Tison.
.XXII. Gislebti de gand.
.XXV. Hugonis filij Baldrici.
.XXVI. Colsuani.
.XXVII. Alueredi de Lincole.
.XXVI. Gozelini filij Lanbti.
.XXIX. Eudo filij Spireuuic.
.XXX. Drogonis de brurere.
.XXXI. Walterij de Aincurt.
.XXXII. Normanni de Adreci.
.XXXIII. Normanni crassi.
.XXXII. Ernegis de burun.
.XXXV. Radulfi pagenel.
.XXXVI. Radulfi de mortemer.
.XXXVII. Robti de Veci.
.XXXVI. Robti dispensatoris.
.XXXIX. Widonis de rebudcurt.
.XL. Raynerij de brimou.

.XLI. Osbni de arcis.
.XLII. Ogerij britonis.
.XLIII. Rannulfi de S Walarico.
.XLIIII. Durandi malet.
.XLV. Martini.
.XLVI. Waldini britonis.
.XLVII. Waldini ingeniosi.
.XLVIII Odonis balistarij.
.XLIX. Willelmi blundi.
.L. Restoldi.
.LI. Godefridi de cabrai.
.LII. Gunfridi de ciochis.
.LIII. Osberni pbri. 7
.LIIII. Radulfi dapiferi.
.LV. Ansgoti.
.LVI. Juditæ comitissæ.
.LVII. Widonis de Credun.
.LVIII. Robti malet.
.LIX. Robti de stadford.
.LX. Petri de Valonges.
.LXI. Hepponis balistarij.
.LXII. Radulfi filij Hubti.
.LXIII. Goisfridi de Wirce.
.LXII. Goisfridi Alselini.
.LXV. Balduini flandrensis.
.LXVI. Witti taillebosc.
.LXVII. Colegrim.
.LXVI. Sortebrand.
.LXIX. Chetelbern 7 alioz
.LXX. Tainoz regis.

[LIST OF LANDHOLDERS IN LINCOLNSHIRE]

1 LAND OF THE KING
2 of the Archbishop of York
3 of the Bishop of Durham
4 of the Bishop of Bayeux
5 of Bishop Osmund of Salisbury
6 of the Bishop of Coutances
7 of the Bishop of Lincoln
8 of the Abbot of Peterborough
9 of the Abbot of Westminster
10 of the Abbot of Ramsey
11 of the Abbot of Crowland
12 of Count Alan
13 of Earl Hugh
14 of Ivo Tallboys
15 of William of Warenne
16 of Roger of Poitou
17 of Roger of Bully
18 of Robert of Tosny
19 of Berengar of Tosny
20 of Ilbert of Lacy
21 of Henry of Ferrers
22 of William of Percy
23 of Gilbert Tison
24 of Gilbert of Ghent
25 of Hugh son of Baldric
26 of Kolsveinn
27 of Alfred of Lincoln
28 of Jocelyn son of Lambert
29 of Eudo son of Spirewic
30 of Drogo of La Beuvrière
31 of Walter of Aincourt
32 of Norman of Arcy
33 of Norman Crassus
34 of Erneis of Buron
35 of Ralph Pagnell
36 of Ralph of Mortimer
37 of Robert of Vessey
38 of Robert the Bursar
39 of Guy of Raimbeaucourt
40 of Rainer of Brimeux

41 of Osbern of Arques   337 b
42 of Odger the Breton
43 of Ranulf of St. Valéry
44 of Durand Malet
45 of Martin
46 of Waldin the Breton
47 of Waldin the Artificer
48 of Odo the Crossbowman
49 of William Blunt
50 of Restold
51 of Godfrey of Cambrai
52 of Gunfrid of Chocques
53 of Osbern the Priest and
54 of Ralph the Steward
55 of Asgautr
56 of Countess Judith
57 of Guy of Craon
58 of Robert Malet
59 of Robert of Stafford
60 of Peter of Valognes
61 of Heppo the Crossbowman
62 of Ralph son of Hubert
63 of Geoffrey of La Guerche
64 of Geoffrey Alselin
65 of Baldwin the Fleming
66 of William Tallboys
67 of Kolgrimr
68 of Svartbrandr
69 of Ketilbjorn and others
70 of the King's Thanes

TERRA REGIS.

ASWARDETIERNE WAPENTAC.

Ⓜ **I**N *CHERCHEBI* . habuit comes Morcar . v . caruc
træ ad gld . Tra ad iiii . car . Nc hr Rex ibi . i . car .
7 xiiii . foch . . . car . . v . uilt 7 v . bord . cu . i . car.
Ibi dimid æccła . T.R.E . uał . iiii . lib . m̄ viii . lib cu
pondere 7 arſione.

Ɓ Euedune jacet in ſupdicto Ⓜ . x . bou træ ad gld .
Tra ad . i . car . Ibi . ii . foch . . ii . uilt hn̄t . i . car . Ibi
mold . v . ſolidoʒ 7 iiii . den . 7 ſeđ . i . molđ . 7 vi . ac pti .
Ad eunđ Ⓜ ptiñ h̄ ſoca . Oustorp . Welle . Hechin
tone . Cornintone Simul ad gld . i . car 7 dim̄ . 7 dim̄
bou . Tra ad . i . car 7 dim̄ . In his hr rex . vii . foch .
hn̄tes . i . car . Ibi . i . m̄ld . xii . ſoł . 7 xiii . ac pti . 7 xi .
ac ſiluæ minute . 7 xx . ac mareſch.

Ⓜ **I**n *CHIME* . hɓ Morcar . iiii . car træ 7 ii . bou ad gld .
Tra ad . ii . car . Nc hr Rex ibi dim̄ car . 7 xii . uilt
7 iii . borđ cu . ii . car . Ibi . ii . æcclæ 7 i . pɓr . 7 ii . ac pti .
7 vi . piſcine . iiii . ſolidoʒ . Silua past p loca . ce .
7 x . ac . 7 ſepties . c . ac mareſc . T.R.E . uał xl . ſoł .
m̄ . lx . ſoł cu pondere 7 arſione.

Ⓜ **I**n *BODEBI* hɓ Morcar . viii . car træ ad gld . Tra
ad . ix . car . Rex hr ibi . ii . car . 7 xx . uilt 7 ii . bord .
hn̄tes . iiii . c . 7 xi . foch de . iii . carucatis . hn̄tes . iii . car .
Ibi æccła 7 pɓr . una caruc jacet in æccła . Ibi . i . mold
iii . ſolidoʒ . 7 cxx . ac pti . T.R.E . uał . xx . lib . m̄ ſim̄
xx . lib . cu penſione.

ASWARDHURN Wapentake

1 M. In KIRKBY (la Thorpe) Earl Morcar had 5 carucates of land taxable. Land for 4 ploughs. Now the King has 1 plough there.
  14 Freemen [with 2] ploughs [and] 5 villagers and 5 smallholders with 1 plough.
  ½ church.
  Value before 1066 £4; now £8 weighed and assayed.

2 B. EVEDON lies in the (lands of the) above manor. 10 bovates of land taxable. Land for 1 plough.
  2 Freemen [and] 2 villagers have 1 plough.
  A mill, 5s 4d; 1 mill site; meadow, 6 acres.

3 Also to this manor belongs this jurisdiction:
  EAST THORPE, 1 carucate; HOWELL, 2½ bovates; HECKINGTON, 1 bovate; QUARRINGTON, 1 bovate. Altogether, 1½ carucates and ½ bovate taxable. Land for 1½ ploughs. In these (lands) the King has
  7 Freemen who have 1 plough.
  1 mill, 12s; meadow, 13 acres; underwood, 11 acres; marsh, 20 acres.

4 M. In (South) KYME Earl Morcar had 4 carucates of land and 2 bovates taxable. Land for 2 ploughs. Now the King has ½ plough there.
  12 villagers and 3 smallholders with 2 ploughs.
  2 churches and 1 priest; meadow, 2 acres; 6 fish-ponds, 4s; woodland, pasture in places, 210 acres; marsh, 700 acres.
  Value before 1066, 40s; now 60s weighed and assayed.

5 M. In BOOTHBY (Graffoe) Earl Morcar had 8 carucates of land taxable. Land for 9 ploughs. The King has 2 ploughs there.
  20 villagers and 2 smallholders who have 4 ploughs; 11 Freemen on 3 carucates who have 3 ploughs.
  A church and a priest; 1 carucate of land lies·in the church (lands). 1 mill, 3s; meadow, 120 acres.
  Value before 1066 £20; now the same, £20 weighed.

M̄ In *WELLINGOVRE* . ħƀ Morcar . xviii . car̄ træ ad gld . Tr̄a ad totid̄ car̄ . Rex hī nc̄ ibi . ii . car̄ . 7 vii . uiłł 7 vii . bord . cū . i . car̄ . 7 xxviii . soch̄ cū . vii . car̄ . Ibi æccła 7 pb̄r . h̄ns . ii . car̄ 7 ii . bō de ead tr̄a . 7 Ipsa æccła ptinet ad æccłam S̄ petri in Lincolia . Ibi . cxxix . ac̄ p̄ti . 7 aliæ xiiii . ac̄ ptin̄ ad eccłā T.R.E . uał . xxx . lib̄ . m̊ xv . lib̄ cū pensione .

M̄ In *COLEBI* . ħƀ Siuuard . vii . car̄ træ ad gld . Tr̄a ad totid car̄ . Rex hī nc̄ ibi . i . car̄ . 7 v . uiłł 7 vi . bord cū . i . car̄ . 7 x . soch̄ cū . ii . car̄ . 7 xxx . ac̄s p̄ti . T.R.E . uał . iiii . lib̄ . Rex ů . W . apposuit hanc tr̄ā in Was hingeburg . 7 ibi app̄ciat̄ . Pb̄r 7 æccła . h̄ns . i . bou de hac tr̄a .

337 d

S̄ 7 B In ipsa Colebi sunt xii . car̄ træ ad gld . Tr̄a ad totid car̄ . Ex his . ē una car̄ inland in Washingeburg . undecī ů sunt in soca . Hanc tr̄a ħƀ Radulf stalre . Nc̄ hī rex ibi xiiii . soch̄ 7 vii . uiłł cū . ix . (viii.) car̄ . 7 lx . ac̄s p̄ti . Huj p̄ciū . ē in Washingeburg .

M̄ In *GRANTHAM* . habuit Edid regina . xii . car ad gld̄ . Non . ē ibi tr̄a arabił ext̄ uillā . Ibi n̄ habuit q̄sq̄ sacā 7 socā . p̄t Elsuid monialē . q̄ ded S̄ Petro de burg 7 ħ hī m̊ Colegrim . cū saca 7 soca . Regina Eddid habuit aulā . 7 ii . car̄ . 7 tr̄ā de . iii . car̄ . sine gld̄o . Burgenses . c . 7 xi . Toftes sochoꝝ teignoꝝ q̄ter xx . iii . min̄ . Nunc similit hī rex . Iuo inueñ . i . car̄ . 7 adhuc ē . 7 lxxii . bord . Æccłam . i . cū . viii . toftis . 7 iiii . mol de xii . sol . 7 viii . ac̄s p̄ti sine gld̄o . De supiorib; toftis . calūniat̄

6 M. In WELLINGORE Morcar had 18 carucates of land taxable. Land for
as many ploughs. The King now has 2 ploughs there;
> 7 villagers and 7 smallholders with 1 plough; 28 Freemen with
> 7 ploughs.
>
> A church and a priest, who has 2 carucates and 2 bovates of
> this land. This church belongs to St. Peter's Church in
> Lincoln. Meadow, 129 acres; another 14 acres belong to
> the Church.

Value before 1066 £30; now £15 weighed.

7 M. In COLEBY Siward had 7 carucates of land taxable. Land for as
many ploughs. The King now has 1 plough there.
> 5 villagers and 6 smallholders with 1 plough; 10 Freemen with
> 2 ploughs.
>
> Meadow, 30 acres.

Value before 1066 £4; but King William placed this land in
Washingborough; it is assessed there.
A priest and a church, which has 1 bovate of this land.

8 S. In COLEBY itself there are 12 carucates of land taxable. Land for
& B. as many ploughs. 1 carucate of these is *inland*, in Washingborough,
but 11 are in a jurisdiction. Ralph the Constable had this land.
Now the King has there
> 14 Freemen and 7 villagers with 8 ploughs; and
> meadow, 60 acres.

Its assessment is in Washingborough.

337 d

9 M. In GRANTHAM Queen Edith had 12 carucates taxable. No arable
land outside the town. No one had full jurisdiction except the
nun Alswith, who gave it to St. Peter's of Peterborough.
Kolgrimr has it now, with full jurisdiction. Queen Edith had a
Hall, 2 ploughs and land for 3 ploughs, without tax. 111 burgesses
[and?] 80, less 3, plots of the Freemen of the thanes. Now the
King has the same. Ivo found 1 plough — it is still there — and
> 72 smallholders and
> 1 church with 8 plots; 4 mills at 12s; meadow, 8 acres, without
> tax.

Of the above plots the Bishop of Durham claims 7 plots, which

eͬps dunelmenſis . vii . toftas . q̃s h̃t Ernuin⁹ p̃br . 7 hund̃
teſtim̃ portat ẽpo . T.R.E . tota Granhã fuit ſocá ad . lii .
liƀ . m̃ redd̃ . c . liƀ ad pond̃ . Æcc̃a fuit t̃c ad . viii . liƀ .
m̃ eſt ad . x . liƀ . ſed non ualet niſi . c . ſol

S̃⁷B In *Gvnfordebi* . ſunt vii . car̃ tre ad gld . T̃ra ad
.ix . car̃ . Tres car̃ ſuᵧ̃ inland . 7 iiii . ſoça in Grandhã .
Ibi h̃t rex m̃ . i . car̃ . 7 xxi . ſoch̃ . 7 i . uiłł 7 i . bord̃ .
hñtes . vi . car̃ . 7 c 7 v . ac̃ p̃ti .

S̃⁷B In *Herlavestvne* . ſunt xii . car̃ tre ad głd . T̃ra
ad . xvi . car̃ . Nouē ſunt in ſoca . 7 iii . in aula Granhã .
Rex h̃t ibi nc̃ x . uiłł . 7 ii . bord̃ . cū . ii . car̃ . 7 lviii .
ſoch̃ . hñtes . xiiii . car̃ . Ibi . ii . mold̃ . ii . ſolidoᷓ 7 lx .
ac̃ p̃ti . 7 lx . ſpineti .

S̃ In Sudſtoͮi̇ches 7 Nortſtoͥͥͥ̇ches ſunt . ix . car̃ træ ad gld .
T̃ra ad . xii . car̃ . Nc̃ h̃t rex ibi . i . car̃ . 7 xvi . uiłł .
cū . iii . car̃ . 7 x . ſoch̃ cū . ii . car̃ . 7 ii . mold̃ redd̃
xxi . ſol 7 iiii . den . P̃ti . ix . q̃ᷓ lg̃ . 7 iii . lat̃ . 7 xx . ac̃s .

S̃ In Nongtone . ſunt . iii . car̃ tre 7 v . bou ₁ ad gld . T̃ra
ad tñtd̃ . Soca in Grãhã . Ibi h̃t rex . xiii . ſoch̃ . 7 vi .
uiłł . cū . iiii . car̃ . 7 i . mold xiii . ſolidoᷓ 7 iiii . den̄ .
7 iii . ac̃s p̃ti .

m̃⁷S In magna *Paptvne* . h̃ƀ Edid reg̃ . xii . car̃ tre
ad gld . T̃ra ad . x . car̃ . Nc̃ . ē h̃ tra ſoca in Granhã .
Ibi ſunt m̃ . x . uiłł 7 iii . bord̃ . 7 xii . ſoch̃ . 7 dim̃ car̃ .
Tant̃i inuenit Iuõ iƀi.
Silua minuta . viii . q̃ᷓ lg̃ . 7 iii . lat̃ .

Ad Granhã ptiñ h̃ Soca . Sumerdebi Sapretone
7 Breizbi . Wellebi . Beltone . Herigerbi . Dunetorp .
Lundetorp . Barcheſtone . Dentone .

Simul ad głd . lv . carucatæ . T̃ra ad . lx . carucas .

H̃ tra ē tota in Aſuuardetierne *Wapentac* .

Earnwine the priest has; the hundred bears witness for the Bishop.

Before 1066 the whole of Grantham was a jurisdiction, at £52; it now pays £100 by weight. The church was then valued at £8; now it is at £10, but the value is only 100s.

10 S. & B. In GONERBY 7 carucates of land taxable. Land for 9 ploughs. 3 carucates are *inland* and 4 (are) a jurisdiction of Grantham. The King now has 1 plough.
21 Freemen, 1 villager and 1 smallholder who have 6 ploughs. Meadow, 105 acres.

11 S. & B. In HARLAXTON 12 carucates of land taxable. Land for 16 ploughs. 9 [carucates] are in a jurisdiction and (are) in the Hall of Grantham. The King now has
10 villagers and 2 smallholders with 2 ploughs; 58 Freemen who have 14 ploughs.
2 mills, 2s; meadow, 60 acres; spinney, 60 [acres].

12 S. In SOUTH STOKE 6 and NORTH STOKE 3 — 9 carucates of land taxable. Land for 12 ploughs. Now the King has 1 plough there.
16 villagers with 3 ploughs; 10 Freemen with 2 ploughs.
2 mills which pay 21s 4d; meadow, 9 furlongs long and 3 wide and 20 acres.

13 S. In *NONGTONE* 3 carucates of land and 5½ bovates taxable. Land for as much. A jurisdiction of Grantham. The King has
13 Freemen and 6 villagers with 4 ploughs.
1 mill, 13s 4d; meadow, 3 acres.

14 M. & S. In GREAT PONTON Queen Edith had 12 carucates of land taxable. Land for 10 ploughs. This land is now a jurisdiction of Grantham.
Now 10 villagers, 3 smallholders, 12 Freemen and ½ plough.
Underwood 8 furlongs long and 3 wide.
So much Ivo found there.

15 To GRANTHAM belongs this jurisdiction:
(Old) SOMERBY, 2 carucates and 2 bovates; SAPPERTON, 5 carucates; BRACEBY, 5 carucates; WELBY, 8 carucates; BELTON, 5 carucates; HARROWBY, 4 carucates; 'DUNSTHORPE', 2 carucates; LONDONTHORPE, 5 carucates and 6 bovates; BARKSTON, 8 carucates; DENTON, 10 carucates.
Altogether 55 carucates taxable. Land for 60 ploughs. The whole of this land is in Aswardhurn Wapentake.

In Sũmerdebi . hĩ rex . ~~II . car̃ 7 dim . 7~~ VIII . ſoch cũ . II . car

In Sapretone 7 Brezbi . ſunt XXIIII . ſoch . 7 v . uilt

7 II . bord . cũ . IX . car̃ . 7 CXL . ac̃ p̃ti . 7 XLVI . ac̃ ſiluę

paſt . 7 LXIIII . ac̃ ſiluæ minutæ . 7 I . æccla

In Wellebi . ſunt XXXVII . ſoch . 7 VII . uilt 7 IIII . bord .

cũ . X . car̃ . 7 CLX . ac̃ p̃ti . 7 CL . ac̃ ſiluæ minutæ . 7 eccla

In Beltone . ſunt XVIII . ſoch . 7 XIIII . bord   cũ p̃bro

cũ . IIII . car̃ . 7 LXVIII . ac̃ p̃ti .

In Herigerbi . ſuɴ XVI . ſoch cũ . IIII . car̃ . 7 XXX.IIII . ac̃ p̃ti .

In Dunetorp . ſuɴ . v . uilt 7 I . bord . 7 VIII . ſoch . cũ . II . car̃ .

In Lundertorp . ſunt XXI . ſoch . 7 VI . uilt   7 XX . ac̃ p̃ti .

cũ . v . car̃ . 7 XLIIII . ac̃ p̃ti . 7 I . mold . x . ſolidoʒ .

In Barcheſtone . ſunt . XXX.v . ſoch . 7 X . bord . cũ . VI . car̃ .

7 LXX . ac̃ p̃ti . 7 II . mold . q̃s habuit Turued . SOCA eoʒ in

In Dentone ſunt | XX . ac̃ p̃ti .   .F. Vlued   granhã .

In Schillintune ſoca de granhã . III . car̃ tre ad gld .

Tra ad . III . car̃ . Ibi . XIIII . uilt . 7 II . bord . 7 I . ſoch . hñt . III .

car̃ . 7 X . ac̃s p̃ti . 7 CXL . ac̃s ſiluæ minutæ . p̃ciũ ej in Grãhã .

In BASINGEHã . lĩb com̃ Morcar . XX.IIII . car̃ tre ad

gld . Tra ad XVI . car̃ . Ibi hĩ rex . II . car̃ . 7 XXX.v . uilt .

7 VIII . bord . 7 I . ſoch . hñtes . VI . car̃ . 7 II . mold redd

XXX.II . ſol . Ibi eccla 7 p̃br . 7 CCCC . 7 XX ac̃ p̃ti . Toĩ

XVI . q̃ʒ 7 dim̃ lg̃ . 7 XV . q̃ʒ lat̃ . T.R.E. ual XXV . lib .

m̃ XVI . lib

16   In (Old) SOMERBY the King has *2½ carucates and 2 bovates.*
     8 Freemen with 2½ ploughs.

17   In SAPPERTON and BRACEBY there are
     24 Freemen, 5 villagers and 2 smallholders with 9 ploughs.
     Meadow, 140 acres; woodland pasture, 46 acres; underwood,
        64 acres; 1 church.

18   In WELBY there are
     37 Freemen, 7 villagers and 4 smallholders with 10 ploughs.
     Meadow, 160 acres; underwood, 150 acres; a church with a
        priest.

19   In BELTON there are
     18 Freemen and 14 smallholders with 4 ploughs.
     Meadow, 68 acres.

20   In HARROWBY there are
     16 Freemen with 4 ploughs.
     Meadow, 34 acres.

21   In 'DUNSTHORPE' there are
     5 villagers, 1 smallholder and 8 Freemen with 2 ploughs.
     Meadow, 20 acres.

22   In LONDONTHORPE there are
     21 Freemen and 6 villagers with 5 ploughs.
     Meadow, 44 acres; 1 mill, 10s.

23   In BARKSTON there are
     35 Freemen and 10 smallholders with 6 ploughs.
     Meadow, 70 acres. 2 mills, which Thorfrothr son of Wulffrith
        had. Their jurisdiction [is] in Grantham.

24   In DENTON there are
     meadow, 80 acres.

25   In SKILLINGTON, a jurisdiction of Grantham, 3 carucates of land
     taxable. Land for 3 ploughs.
        14 villagers, 2 smallholders and 1 Freeman have 3 ploughs and
        meadow, 10 acres and underwood, 140 acres.
     Its assessment is in Grantham.

26 M. In BASSINGHAM Earl Morcar had 24 carucates of land taxable.
     Land for 16 ploughs. The King has 2 ploughs.
        35 villagers, 8 smallholders and 1 Freeman who have 6 ploughs.
        2 mills which pay 32s. A church and a priest; meadow, 420
           acres.
        The whole [is] 16½ furlongs long and 15 furlongs wide.
     Value before 1066 £25; now £16.

In Torp.ē ſoca huj ꝯ M.vi.boū træ ad gld.Tra ad.v.boueſ꞉
Ibi.ē.i.ſocħ cū dim car.7 v.ac̄ p̄ti.

M In TITE.ħƀ Algar.v.car tre 7 i.boū ad gld.Tra ad
iiii.car.Ibi h̄r rex.i.car.⁊ xvi.uill 7 v.bord.7 i.ſocħ.
h̄ntes.viii.car.7 q̄ter xx.ac̄s p̄ti.T.R.E.ual.viii.liƀ
7 i.piſcaria cū ſilua reddeƀ.lxx.ſol.iiii.den min.
m̄ ualet tot.xv.liƀ.

M In LVCTONE.ħƀ Algar.iiii.car tre ad gld.Tra ad
ii.car.Ibi h̄r rex.vi.boū.7 xvi.uill cū.iiii.car.
7 i.piſcar.xii.den.7 lx.ac̄s p̄ti.T.R.E.ual.viii.liƀ.
m̄ ſimilit.
In Tite.ē Berew huj ꝯ M.ii.car 7 i.boū tre ad gld.
Ibi ſunt m̄.viii.uill 7 i.ſocħ.h̄ntes.i.car 7 iios.boues.
7 xxx.ac̄ p̄ti.

M In GADENAI.ħƀ Algar.viii.car træ ad gld.Tra
ad iiii.car.Ibi h̄r rex.vi.boues.7 xviii.uill cū.iii.
car.7 xxx.ac̄s p̄ti.7 piſcar.xii.den.lg.xx.q̄ꝛ 7 lat xii.
T.R.E.ual.viii.liƀ.m̄.vi.liƀ.

338 b

In Holebech.ē ſoca huj ꝯ M.viii.car træ 7 vi.bō ad gld
Ibi h̄r rex.xx.vi.ſocħ 7 v.bord cū xi.car.7 q̄ter xx.
ac̄s p̄ti.Iſta ſoca.ē ap̄pciata ext numer̄ ſup̄dictū.
xvii.liƀ.
In ead holebech 7 Copelade ſunt.v.car træ ad gld.
quas comes alan tenebat.m̄ ſunt in manu regis.

In FLeot ħƀ Algar.vi.car tre ad gld.Tra ad.iiii.c.
Ibi h̄r rex.vi.boues.7 viii.uill cū.ii.car 7 dim.
7 i.piſcar.xvi.den.7 ii.ſalinas.ii.ſolidoꝛ.7 q̄ngent
ac̄ p̄ti.Vna lev lg.7 i.lat.T.R.E.ual.iiii.liƀ.
m̄.ɫ.ſol

27 In THORPE (on the Hill) is a jurisdiction of this manor, 6 bovates of land taxable. Land for 5 oxen.
    1 Freeman with ½ plough.
    Meadow, 5 acres.

28 In TYDD (St. Mary) Earl Algar had 5 carucates of land and 1 bovate taxable. Land for 3 ploughs. The King has 1 plough.
    16 villagers, 5 smallholders and 1 Freeman who have 8 ploughs.
    Meadow, 80 acres.
Value before 1066 £8; 1 fishery with woodland paid 70s, less 4d.
Value of the whole now £15.

29 M. In LUTTON Earl Algar had 4 carucates of land taxable. Land for 2 ploughs. The King has 6 oxen.
    16 villagers with 4 ploughs.
    1 fishery, 12d; meadow, 60 acres.
Value before 1066 £8; now the same.

30 In TYDD (St. Mary) there is an outlier of this manor: 2 carucates and 1 bovate of land taxable. There are now
    8 villagers and 1 Freeman who have 1 plough and 2 oxen.
    Meadow, 30 acres.

31 M. In GEDNEY Earl Algar had 8 carucates of land taxable. Land for 4 ploughs. The King has 6 oxen.
    18 villagers with 3 ploughs.
    Meadow, 30 acres; a fishery, 12d.
    [It is] 20 furlongs long and 12 wide.
Value before 1066 £8; now £6.

32 In HOLBEACH there is a jurisdiction of this manor; 8 carucates of   338 b
land and 6 bovates taxable. The King has
    26 Freemen and 5 smallholders with 11 ploughs; and
    meadow, 80 acres.
This jurisdiction is assessed at £17 (and this is) in addition to the above sum.

33 In HOLBEACH also and WHAPLODE there are 5 carucates of land taxable, which Count Alan held; now they are in the King's hands.

34 In FLEET Earl Algar had 6 carucates of land taxable. Land for 4 ploughs. The King has 6 oxen and
    8 villagers with 2½ ploughs; and
    1 fishery, 16d; 2 salt-houses, 2s; meadow, 500 acres.
    [It is] 1 league long and 1 wide.
Value before 1066 £4; now 50s.

ᴍ In *NETELHAM*. hȝ Edid̃ xii . car̃ træ ad glđ.

Tra ad xvi . car̃ . Ibi hȝ rex . iii . car̃ . 7 xxviii ; uilłi

7 xii . borđ . 7 i . focħ . hñtes . xi . car̃ . Toŧ xx . q̃ƶ

lg̃ . 7 xx . laŧ . T.R.E . uał . xx . iiii . liƀ . m̃ . xxx . liƀ.

In Dvnehā . ē foca huj̃ ᴍ . viii . car̃ træ ad glđ.

Tra ad totiđ car̃ . Ibi funt . xviii . focħ cū . vi . car̃.

7 ʟ . ac̃ p̃ti . De hac tra hȝ Odo balist̃ . ii . car̃ 7 dim̃.

In Sonetorp 7 Wichingebi . Soca in Netelhā . In Rerefbi . foca ibiđ.

ᴍ In *CHIRCHETONE* . hȝ Eduiñ . viii . car̃ træ ad glđ.

Tra ad . xvi . car̃ . Ibi hȝ rex m̃ . iiii . car̃ in dñio.

7 q̃ter xx . uilł . 7 xxx . vii . borđ . cū xviii . car̃.

7 i . mold . xii . deñ . 7 cc . ac̃s p̃ti . Duas leṽ lg̃ . 7 xx .

q̃ƶ laŧ . T.R.E . uał xx . iiii . liƀ . m̃ q̃ter xx . liƀ.

Ad ipfū ᴍ p̃tiñ foca H̄ . Glenteuurde . Helmes

welle . Herpefwelle . Esnetrebi . Saffebi . Grangehā.

Coringehā . Asebi . Jopeham . Springetorp 7 corin

gehã . Sumerdebi . Blitone . Pileham . Torp.

Aschebi . Hiboldestone . Staintone . Reburne.

Brunebi . Aschebi . Budiesforde . Jadulfeftorp.

Witrintone . Escumetorp .   Simul ad glđ

ʟ . viiii . carucatæ tre .   Tra . ē ad . ʟx . viii . car̃.

ix . bȝ

Mortuū

338 c

In Glenteuurde . funt xx . iiii . focħ 7 vi . borđ . cū . v .

car̃ . 7 cc . 7 xii . ac̃ p̃ti.

In Helmefwelle . funt xvii . focħ . 7 i . uilł 7 vii . borđ

cū . iii . car̃ . 7 cʟxxiii . ac̃ p̃ti .   ⌐7 cʟ . ac̃ p̃ti.

In Herpefwelle . funt vi . focħ cū . ii . car̃ 7 dimiđ

35 M. In NETTLEHAM Queen Edith had 12 carucates of land taxable. Land for 16 ploughs. The King has 3 ploughs.
    28 villagers, 12 smallholders and 1 Freeman who have 11 ploughs.
    The whole [is] 20 furlongs long and 20 wide.
Value before 1066 £24; now £30.

36 In DUNHOLME there is a jurisdiction of this manor; 8 carucates of land taxable. Land for as many ploughs.
    18 Freemen with 6 ploughs.
    Meadow, 50 acres.
    Odo the Crossbowman has 2½ carucates of this land.

37 In SWINTHORPE, 6 bovates, and WICKENBY, 1 carucate. A jurisdiction of Nettleham. In REASBY, 2 bovates. A jurisdiction also there.

38 M. In KIRTON (in Lindsey) Earl Edwin had 8 carucates of land taxable. Land for 16 ploughs. Now the King has 4 ploughs in lordship.
    80 villagers and 37 smallholders with 18 ploughs.
    1 mill, 12d; meadow, 200 acres.
    [It is] 2 leagues long and 20 furlongs wide.
Value before 1066 £24; now £80.

39 To this manor belongs this jurisdiction:
GLENTWORTH, 6 carucates and 2½ bovates; HEMSWELL, 4 carucates and 2 bovates; HARPSWELL, 2 carucates and 6½ bovates; SNITTERBY, 4 bovates; SAXBY, 1 carucate; GRAYINGHAM, 4 carucates; CORRINGHAM, 1 carucate; AISBY, 1 carucate; HEAPHAM, 2½ carucates; SPRINGTHORPE and CORRINGHAM, 6 carucates; MORTON, 9 bovates; SOMERBY, 2 carucates; BLYTON, 3 carucates; PILHAM, 1 carucate; NORTHORPE, 2 carucates; ASHBY, 1 carucate; HIBALDSTOW, 2½ carucates; STAINTON, 6 bovates; REDBOURNE, 9 bovates; BRUMBY, 5 carucates; ASHBY, 13 bovates; BOTTESFORD, 2 carucates; YADDLETHORPE, 1 carucate; WINTERTON, 4 carucates; SCUNTHORPE, 3 carucates, 6 bovates and 2 parts of 1 bovate.
Altogether 59 carucates of land taxable. Land for 69 ploughs.

40 In GLENTWORTH there are   338 c
    24 Freemen and 6 smallholders with 5 ploughs.
    Meadow, 212 acres.

41 In HEMSWELL there are
    17 Freemen, 1 villager and 7 smallholders with 3 ploughs.
    Meadow, 173 acres.

42 In HARPSWELL there are
    6 Freemen with 2½ ploughs.
    Meadow, 150 acres.

In Efnetrebi . fuɴ . ɪx . foch cū . ɪɪ . car.

In Saffebi . funt . ɪɪɪɪ . foch cū . ɪ . car . 7 vɪ . ač ṗti.

In Grangehā funt vɪɪ . foch 7 xɪɪɪɪ . uiłł cū . ɪɪɪɪ . car

In Coringhā funt . ɪɪɪɪ . foch 7 ɪ . bord cū . ɪɪ . car

In Afeby funt vɪɪ . foch 7 ɪ . bord . cū . ɪɪ . car

In Lopehā . funt xvɪ . foch cū . ɪɪɪɪ . car . 7 cxx . ač ṗti

_{7 Coringehā}

In Springetorp fuɴ . xʟ.ɪ . foch cū x . car . æccła 7 pƀr.

In Sūmerdebi . fuɴ . vɪ . foch cū . ɪ . car 7 dɪm . 7 xʟv.

In Blittone . nihił ⌠ač ṗti.

In Pileham . vɪɪɪ . foch cū . ɪɪ . car 7 xvɪ . ač ṗti.

In Torp . vɪ . foch cū . ɪɪ . car . 7 dɪm . 7 ʟx . ač ṗti.

In Afchebi . ɪx . foch cū . ɪ . car 7 dɪm.

In Hiboldeſton . ē . ɪ . car in dñio . 7 xvɪ . uiłł 7 ɪɪ . bord cū . ɪɪ . car . 7 cc . 7 xx.ɪɪ . ač ṗti . 7 cxx . ač filuæ min.

_{7 Wadinghā}

In Staintone funt . ɪɪɪ . foch hñtes . v . ƀo . 7 xvɪ . ač ṗti.

In Reburne . funt . ɪɪɪɪ . foch cū . ɪ . car . 7 xxx . ač ṗti.

43   In SNITTERBY there are
         9 Freemen with 2 ploughs.

44   In SAXBY there are
         4 Freemen with 1 plough.
         Meadow, 6 acres.

45   In GRAYINGHAM there are
         7 Freemen and 14 villagers with 4 ploughs.

46   In CORRINGHAM there are
         4 Freemen and 1 smallholder with 2 ploughs.

47   In AISBY there are
         7 Freemen and 1 smallholder with 2 ploughs.

48   In HEAPHAM there are
         16 Freemen with 4 ploughs.
         Meadow, 120 acres.

49   In SPRINGTHORPE and CORRINGHAM there are
         41 Freemen with 10 ploughs.
         A church and a priest.

50   In SOMERBY there are
         6 Freemen with 1½ ploughs.
         Meadow, 45 acres.

51   In BLYTON, nothing.

52   In PILHAM
         8 Freemen with 2 ploughs.
         Meadow, 16 acres.

53   In (Nor)THORPE
         6 Freemen with 2½ ploughs.
         Meadow, 60 acres.

54   In ASHBY
         9 Freemen with 1½ ploughs.

55   In HIBALDSTOW there is 1 plough in lordship;
         16 villagers and 2 smallholders with 2 ploughs.
         Meadow, 222 acres; underwood, 120 acres.

56   In STAINTON and WADDINGHAM there are
         3 Freemen who have 5 oxen.
         Meadow, 16 acres.

57   In REDBOURNE there are
         4 Freemen with 1 plough.
         Meadow, 30 acres.

In Brunebi . XIIII . foch cū . III . car̄ .7 q̄t xx . ac̄ p̄ti.

In Afchebi . VII . foch cū . I . car̄ 7 dīm

In Budlesforde . II . foch eū . II . bob 7 xxx . ac̄ p̄ti.

★ In Ladulftorp . nichil . nifi xv . ac̄ p̄ti .7 XII . ac̄ filuæ

In Wintretune . IX . foch 7 I . bord . cū . v . bob . ⌐mīm

In Efcumetorp . xx . foch cū . II . car̄ 7 II . bob .7 LXXX . ac̄ p̄ti.

Int oīns cc .7 XXIII . foch . XVI . bord . XV . uill . cū . L . car̄.

In Tedulbi 7 Derbi .7 Burtone . h̄t rex . VI . toftas .7 dimid

mercatū ad Chirchetone p̄tiñ.

Hiboldefton . ē Bereuuita n̄ foca .7 in Grangehā fu√

. II . car̄ inland .7 in fpringetorp . dīm car̄ . ē inland.

Reliq̄ oīnis . ē foca.

ω̄ ⁊ In CASTRE 7 Humendone . h̄b Morcar . III . car̄
7 B ⁊
tre ad gld . Tra ad . VI . car̄ . Ibi h̄t Rex in dn̄io . I . car̄.

7 XL . uill .7 XII . foch . cū . III . car̄ . Ibi eccla 7 p̄br

q̄ ep̄s Lincoliæ clamat . Ibi . IIII . mold . XIII . folidoz̄

7 IIII . den̄ .7 LX . ac̄ p̄ti . T.R.E. ual xxx . lib . m̊ . L . lib.

Ad huj ω̄ aulā p̄tiñ Catenai 7 Vfun . IIII . car̄ tre

ad gld . Tra ad . VIII . car̄ . Ibi . in dn̄io . II . car̄ .7 xx uill

7 xv . foch .7 x . bord . h̄ntes . IX . car̄ . Ibi ccc .7 LX . ac̄

⌐p̄ti.

338 d

Ad eund ω̄ iacet H Soca.

In Linberge . IIII . car̄ tre 7 dīm .7 dīm bou . Ibi in dn̄io

. I . car̄ .7 xxx . III . foch .7 v . uill . cū . III . car̄ .7 xxx . ac̄ p̄ti.

In Norchelfei . v . car̄ tre . Ibi funt . L . foch .7 II . uill

cū . VI . car̄ .7 DCC . ac̄ p̄ti.

58   In BRUMBY
       14 Freemen with 3 ploughs.
       Meadow, 80 acres.

59   In ASHBY
       7 Freemen with 1½ ploughs.

60   In BOTTESFORD
       2 Freemen with 2 oxen.
       Meadow, 30 acres.

61   In YADDLETHORPE nothing except
       meadow, 15 acres; underwood, 12 acres.

62   In WINTERTON
       9 Freemen and 1 smallholder with 5 oxen.

63   In SCUNTHORPE
       20 Freemen with 2 ploughs and 2 oxen.
       Meadow, 80 acres.
  Between them all, 223 Freemen, 16 smallholders and 15 villagers
with 50 ploughs.

64   In THEALBY, DERBY and BURTON (upon Stather) the King has 6
plots and ½ market which belong to Kirton (in Lindsey).
       HIBALDSTOW is an outlier not a jurisdiction; in GRAYINGHAM
there are 2 carucates *inland*; in SPRINGTHORPE ½ carucate is
inland. All the rest is a jurisdiction.

65 M.   In CAISTOR and HUNDON Earl Morcar had 3 carucates of land
  & B. taxable. Land for 6 ploughs. The King has 1 plough in lordship;
       40 villagers and 12 Freemen with 3 ploughs.
       A church and a priest, which the Bishop of Lincoln claims.
       4 mills, 13s 4d; meadow, 60 acres.
  Value before 1066 £30; now £50.

66   To the Hall of this manor belong CADNEY and HOWSHAM; 4
carucates of land taxable. Land for 8 ploughs. In lordship 2
ploughs;
       20 villagers, 15 Freemen and 10 smallholders who have 9
         ploughs.
       Meadow, 360 acres.

  Also to this manor belongs this jurisdiction: 338 d
67   In (Great) LIMBER 4½ carucates of land and ½ bovate. In lordship
1 plough;
       33 Freemen and 5 villagers with 3 ploughs.
       Meadow, 30 acres.

68   In NORTH KELSEY 5 carucates of land.
       50 Freemen and 2 villagers with 6 ploughs.
       Meadow, 700 acres.

In Fuldenebi.I.cař tre 7 dim̃.Ibi.xvIIII.foch cū.III,

In Clifbi.I.cař tre 7 dim̃.inland 7 foca.Ibi.I.cař

in dñio.7 xIIII.uilł.7 II.foch eū.III.cař.7 xxx.ač p̃ti.

In Chernitone.IIII.cař tre 7 vI.boũ.Ibi fuŋ.xx.foch

7 I.uilł 7 xlIIII.borđ.cū.III.cař 7 dim̃.

In Crocheftune.II.boũ tre.Ibi.III.foch eū dim̃ cař.

In Linberge.III.boũ tre.Ibi funt.III.foch.

In Grofebi.dim̃ cař tre p̃tin ad ecclam de Caftre.

eū.I.uillo.hñte.I.boũe.ħ app̃ciat.vI.fol 7 vIIII.deñ.

In Odenebi.v.boũ tre.inland.Ibi nichil.nifi.x.ač p̃ti.

In Sourebi.I.boũ tre inland.Ibi.ē.I.uilłs eū.II.bob.

In Haburne 7 Neuhufe.II.cař tre.7 II.boũ.7 II.part

uni bõ.Ibi funt.vIII.foch 7 II.borđ cū.I.cař 7 dim̃.

7 I.falina.xII.denař.7 cc.ač p̃ti.

In Chelebi.xv.boũ tre ad glđ.Ibi xIII.foch 7 III.

borđ.hñt.II.cař.

In Colefi.III.cař tre.Ibi xxxv.foch 7 xII.borđ

hñt.v.cař 7 dim̃.p̃tũ.I.lev lg̃.7 II.q̃ɫ 7 dim̃ lať.

In Hoctune.II.cař tre 7 dim̃.Ibi xxvI.foch hñt

III.cař 7 dim̃.7 lx.ač p̃ti.De hac foca.ħ Iuo.I.cař

Simul ad glđ.xxvIII.caruc tre.7 I.boũ.

Tra ad.lvIIII.carucas.   Int tot.cc.7 xI.foch.

7 xxIIII.uilł.7 xxvIII.borđ.cū xxx.cař.

ꝳIn GETTUNE.ħɓ Edid.III.cař tre ad glđ.Tra ađ

IIII.cař.Ibi ht Rex in dñio.I.cař 7 dim̃.7 xvIIII.

foch 7 IIII.borđ cū.v.cař.Ibi æccła 7 l.ač p̃ti.

vII.q̃ɫ 7 dim̃ lg̃.7 vII.lať T.R.E.uał xv.liɓ.m̃.

69   In FONABY 1½ carucates of land.
        18 Freemen with 3 ploughs.
        Meadow, 3 acres.

70   In CLIXBY 1½ carucates of land, *inland*; a jurisdiction. 1 plough in lordship;
        14 villagers and 2 Freemen with 3 ploughs.
        Meadow, 30 acres.

71   In KIRMINGTON 4 carucates of land and 6 bovates.
        20 Freemen, 1 villager and 14 smallholders with 3½ ploughs.

72   In CROXTON 2 bovates of land.
        3 Freemen with ½ plough.

73   In (Little) LIMBER 3 bovates of land.
        3 Freemen.

74   In GRASBY ½ carucate of land belongs to the church of Caistor with
        1 villager who has 1 ox.
      This is assessed at 6s 8d.

75   In OWMBY 5 bovates of land, *inland*. Nothing except
        meadow, 10 acres.

76   In SEARBY 1 bovate of land, *inland*.
        1 villager with 2 oxen.

77   In HABROUGH and NEWSHAM 2 carucates of land, 2 bovates and 2 parts of 1 bovate.
        8 Freemen and 2 smallholders with 1½ ploughs.
        1 salt-house, 12d; meadow, 200 acres.

78   In KEELBY 15 bovates of land taxable.
        13 Freemen and 3 smallholders have 2 ploughs.

79   In (South) KELSEY 3 carucates of land.
        35 Freemen and 12 smallholders have 5½ ploughs.
        Meadow 1 league long and 2½ furlongs wide.

80   In HOLTON (le Moor) 2½ carucates of land.
        26 Freemen have 3½ ploughs.
        Meadow, 60 acres.
        Ivo Tallboys has 1 carucate of this jurisdiction.
      Altogether 28 carucates of land and 1 bovate taxable. Land for 58 ploughs. In total, 211 Freemen, 24 villagers and 28 smallholders with 30 ploughs.

81 M. In GAYTON (le Wold) Queen Edith had 3 carucates of land taxable.
        Land for 4 ploughs. The King has 1½ ploughs in lordship;
        18 Freemen and 4 smallholders with 5 ploughs.
        A church; meadow, 50 acres.
        [It is] 7½ furlongs long and 7 wide.
      Value before 1066 £15; now £45.

Soca huj⁹ Manerij.

In Salflatebi . ii . car̄ tre . Ibi funt xl . foch 7 ix.

borđ.hn̄tes . iiii . car̄.7 cxx . ac̄ p̄ti.   ⌐car̄.

In Mannebi . iii . car̄ tre . Ibi funt xx . foch . cū . iiii.

In Grimaɪbi . iiii . car̄ tre . Ibi . vi . foch 7 v . borđ

hn̄t . iii . car̄.7 c . ac̄ p̄ti.

In Germundſtorp . ii . car̄ træ . Ibi . xiii . foch 7 vi.

uiɫɫ hn̄t . ii . car̄.7 vi . faliñ . vi . folidoʒ.

In Sūmercotes . iii . car̄ tre . Ibi xxx . foch 7 vii . uiɫɫ

7 viii . borđ.hn̄t . vi . car̄.7 q̄t xx . ac̄ p̄ti.

In Gereburg . ii . car̄ tre 7 dim̄.7 i . bō.7 iii . pars . i . bō.

In Aluinghā . i . car̄ tre . Ibi . xiiii . foch 7 vii . uiɫɫ

7 v . borđ cū . ii . car̄.7 xl . ac̄ p̄ti

In Schitebroc . iii . car̄ tre . Ibi . xxiiii . foch 7 iii . uiɫɫ

hn̄t . viii . car̄ 7 dim̄.7 lx . ac̄ p̄ti.

In Welletone . iiii . car̄ tre . Ibi . xx . foch 7 xiiii . uiɫɫ

hn̄t . v . car̄ 7 dim̄.7 xl . ac̄ p̄ti.

Simul ad gld . xxv . carucate 7 dim̄.7 i . bō.7 iii . pars . bō.

Tra ad xxxviii . car̄.   ⌐hn̄tes xxxiiii . car̄.

In his funt . clxvii . foch.7 xxxvii . uiɫɫ.7 xxvii . borđ.

Ⓜ In HORNECASTRE . h̄b regiñ Edid . iii . car̄ træ fine glđo.

Tra ad . iiii . car̄ . Ibi|. Rex h̄r. ii . car̄ in dn̄io.7 xxix . viɫɫ.

7 xii . borđ . hn̄tes , iii . car̄ . Ibi . ii . molđ . xxvi . foliđ.

7 c . ac̄ p̄ti . T.R.E. uaɫ xx . lib̄ . m̄ . xl . iiii . lib̄.

Soca hvjvs Manerij.

In Stimblebi . iiii . car̄ tre

Ibi xxii . foch.7 xviii . uiɫɫ.hn̄t . iiii . car̄ 7 dimiđ.

7 cc . xl . ac̄ p̄ti.

Jurisdiction of this manor:

82   In SALTFLEETBY 2 carucates of land.
        40 Freemen and 9 smallholders who have 4 ploughs.
        Meadow, 120 acres.

83   In MANBY 3 carucates of land.
        20 Freemen with 4 ploughs.

84   In GRIMOLDBY 4 carucates of land.
        6 Freemen and 5 smallholders have 3 ploughs.
        Meadow, 100 acres.

85   In GRAINTHORPE 2 carucates of land.
        13 Freemen and 6 villagers have 2 ploughs.
        6 salt-houses, 6s.

86   In SOMERCOTES 3 carucates of land.
        30 Freemen, 7 villagers and 8 smallholders have 6 ploughs.
        Meadow, 80 acres.

87   In YARBURGH 2½ carucates of land, 1 bovate and the third part of
        1 bovate.

88   In ALVINGHAM 1 carucate of land.   339 a
        14 Freemen, 7 villagers and 5 smallholders with 2 ploughs.
        Meadow, 40 acres.

89   In SKIDBROOKE 3 carucates of land.
        24 Freemen and 3 villagers have 8½ ploughs.
        Meadow, 60 acres.

90   In WELTON (le Wold) 4 carucates of land.
        20 Freemen and 14 villagers have 5½ ploughs.
        Meadow, 40 acres.
    Altogether 25½ carucates, 1 bovate and the third part of a bovate
    taxable. Land for 38 ploughs. 167 Freemen, 37 villagers and 27
    smallholders who have 34 ploughs.

91 M. In HORNCASTLE Queen Edith had 3 carucates of land without tax.
        Land for 4 ploughs. The King has 2 ploughs in lordship;
        29 villagers and 12 smallholders who have 3 ploughs.
        2 mills, 26s; meadow, 100 acres.
    Value before 1066 £20; now £44.

Jurisdiction of this manor:

92   In THIMBLEBY 4 carucates of land.
        22 Freemen and 18 villagers have 4½ ploughs.
        Meadow, 240 acres.

In Todintune.iii.car tre.Ibi xxiii.focħ 7 ii.uiħi.

7 vii.borđ.hñt.iiii.caɼ.7 ccc.acs p̃ti.

In Langetone 7 Torp.iii.car tre.Ibi xiii.focħ 7 xxii

uiħ hñt.iiii.caɼ.7 i.molđ ix.foliđ.7 cxx.acs p̃ti.

7 ccl.acs filue paſtilis.

In Folefbi.dim car tre.Ibi.iii.focħ hñt dim caɼ.

7 viii.acs p̃ti.7 cxx.acs filuæ past p loca.

In Cuningefbi.i.car tre 7 dim jnland.Ibi.viii.uiħ

7 iii.borđ cū.i.caɼ 7 dim.7 v.pifcariæ.v.foliđ.7 xii.

ac p̃ti.7 lx ac filuæ minutæ.

In Holthā.ii.caɼ 7 vi.boū tre.Ibi.vii.focħ hñt

i.caɼ 7 dim.7 xxx.ii.acs p̃ti.7 xx.acs filuæ paſtilis.

In Folefbi.i.car tre.Ibi.i.focħ hĩ.i.caɼ.

In Rocſtune.xii.boū træ.Ibi.viii.focħ hñt.i.caɼ

7 dim.7 xv.acs p̃ti.7 xl.acs filuæ past.

In Scriuelefbi.iii.caɼ 7 vii.boū tre.Ibi.xx.focħ.7 xii.

borđ.hñt.vi.caɼ.7 cc.ac p̃ti.7 vi.acs filuæ minutæ.

In Morebi.iii.caɼ tre.Ibi.viii.focħ.7 x.borđ hñt

iiii.caɼ.Ibi æccła.7 ccxl.ac p̃ti.7 vi.acs filue miñ.

In Marun.iii.car tre.Ibi xxi.focħ 7 xi.borđ.hñt

iiii.caɼ.Ibi æccła 7 pbr.7 lx.ac p̃ti.7 ccc.acs filuæ miñ.

In Endrebi.iii.caɼ tre.Ibi.xvi.focħ 7 vi.borđ hñt

iiii.caɼ.7 lx.acs p̃ti.7 cccc.l.ac filuæ past.

In Wilchesbi.i.car træ 7 dim.Ibi.iiii.focħ 7 v.borđ.

hñt.i.caɼ.7 xx.acs filuæ minutæ.

In Afchebi.vi.caɼ tre.Ibi.xlv.focħ.7 v.uiħ 7 xiii.borđ

hñt.viii.caɼ.7 qngentæ ac p̃ti 7 paſture.

93 In TOYNTON 3 carucates of land.
23 Freemen, 2 villagers and 7 smallholders have 4 ploughs and
meadow, 300 acres.

94 In LANGTON and *TORP* 3 carucates of land.
13 Freemen and 24 villagers have 4 ploughs.
1 mill, 9s; meadow, 120 acres; woodland pasture, 250 acres.

95 In FULSBY ½ carucate of land.
3 Freemen have ½ plough and
meadow, 8 acres; woodland, pasture in places, 120 acres.

96 In CONINGSBY 1½ carucates of land, *inland*.
8 villagers and 3 smallholders with 1½ ploughs.
5 fisheries, 5s; meadow, 12 acres; underwood, 60 acres.

97 In HALTHAM 2 carucates and 6 bovates of land.
7 Freemen have 1½ ploughs and
meadow, 32 acres; woodland pasture, 20 acres.

98 In FULSBY 1 carucate of land.
1 Freeman has 1 plough.

99 In ROUGHTON 12 bovates of land.
8 Freemen have 1½ ploughs and
meadow, 15 acres; woodland pasture, 40 acres.

100 In SCRIVELSBY 3 carucates and 7 bovates of land.
20 Freemen and 12 smallholders have 6 ploughs.
Meadow, 200 acres; underwood, 6 acres.

101 In MOORBY 3 carucates of land.
8 Freemen and 10 smallholders have 4 ploughs.
A church; meadow, 240 acres; underwood, 6 acres.

102 In MAREHAM (le Fen) 3 carucates of land.
21 Freemen and 11 smallholders have 4 ploughs.
A church and a priest; meadow, 60 acres; underwood, 300 acres.

103 In (Wood) ENDERBY 3 carucates of land.
16 Freemen and 6 smallholders have 4 ploughs and
meadow, 60 acres; woodland pasture, 450 acres.

104 In WILKSBY 1½ carucates of land.
4 Freemen and 5 smallholders have 1 plough and
underwood, 20 acres.

105 In (West) ASHBY 6 carucates of land.
45 Freemen, 5 villagers and 13 smallholders have 8 ploughs.   339 b
Meadow and pasture, 500 acres.

In Tedlintune . IIII . car̃ træ . Ibi xx . I . foch . 7 VIII . uilt

7 III . borđ . hñt . VIII . car̃ . 7 cccc . ac̃ p̃ti .

Int̃ totũ ad glđ . XLII . carucate tre . T

Tra ad . LVIII . carucas .

In his ſunt . ccxII . foch . 7 LXVI . uilt . 7 LXX . borđ .

hñtes . LV . carucas .

.II. ̈ **I**TERRA ARCHIEP̃I EBORACENSIS.

In *VLINGEHAM* . habuit Elmær . III . car̃ tre ad glđ .

Tra . ē ad . IIII . car̃ . Nc̃ hr̃ Thomas archiep̃s . 7 Witts

de eo . In dñio . II . car̃ 7 dim̃ . 7 XI . uilt 7 II . bord . hñtes

II . car̃ . 7 LXX . VII . ac̃s p̃ti . T.R.E . uat . IIII . lib . 7 x . fot .

m̃ fimilit .

In Barcuurde . ē foca huj ꝯ ꝏ . VI . boũ tre ad gld . Tra

ad . I . car̃ 7 dim̃ . Ibi . VII . foch . 7 I . bord . hñt . I . car̃ . Ibi

XIII . ac̃ p̃ti .

In *PANTONE* . hb̃ Aluric . II . car̃ tre ad gld . Tra ad

III . car̃ . Nc̃ hr̃ Gifleb̃t ꝯ hõ arch in dñio . I . car̃ 7 dim̃ .

7 I . uilt . 7 XII . foch . cũ . I . car̃ 7 dim̃ . 7 XVII . ac̃s p̃ti .

T.R.E . uat xxx . fot . m̃ . XL . fot .

In Barcuurde . ē foca huj ꝯ ꝏ . VI . boũ tre ad gld . Tra

ad . I . car̃ . Wafta . ē . Ibi . xv . ac̃ p̃ti .

In *GRISEBI* . hb̃ Ælmar . II . car̃ tre 7 II . boũ ad gld .

Tra ad . IIII . car̃ 7 dim̃ . Nc̃ hr̃ Witts hõ arch in dñio

II . car̃ . 7 VIII . uilt 7 VII . bord . 7 XVIII . foch . hñtes

IIII . car̃ 7 dimid . 7 xx . ac̃s p̃ti . T.R.E . uat . III . lib .

m̃ fimilit . 7 tailgia . xx . fot .

In *STALINGEBVRG* . hb̃ Elaf . I . car̃ tre 7 II . boũ

ad gld . Tra ad . II . car̃ 7 dim̃ . Ibi Herb̃t hõ arch

hr̃ in dñio . I . car̃ . 7 v . uilt 7 III . foch . 7 I . bord . cũ

una car̃ . Ibi molđ dimidiũ . xxx . II . den . 7 II . falinæ .

7 q̃ter xx . ac̃ p̃ti . T.R.E . uat xxx . fot . m̃ . L . fot .

106   In TOYNTON 4 carucates of land.
           21 Freemen, 8 villagers and 3 smallholders have 8 ploughs.
           Meadow, 400 acres.
       In total, 42 carucates of land taxable. Land for 58 ploughs. In them
       212 Freemen, 66 villagers and 70 smallholders who have 55 ploughs.

2   LAND OF THE ARCHBISHOP OF YORK   339 c

1 2 In (South) WILLINGHAM Aelmer had 3 carucates of land taxable.
  M. Land for 4 ploughs. Now Archbishop Thomas has it, and William
       from him. In lordship 2½ ploughs;
           11 villagers and 2 smallholders who have 2 ploughs and
           meadow, 77 acres.
       Value before 1066 £4 10s; now the same.

2   In BARKWITH there is a jurisdiction of this manor; 6 bovates of
       land taxable. Land for 1½ ploughs.
           7 Freemen and 1 smallholder have 1 plough.
           Meadow, 13 acres.

3 M. In PANTON Aelfric had 2 carucates of land taxable. Land for 3
       ploughs. Now Gilbert, the Archbishop's man, has in lordship 1½
       ploughs;
           1 villager and 12 Freemen with 1½ ploughs.
           Meadow, 17 acres.
       Value before 1066, 30s; now 40s.

4   In BARKWITH there is a jurisdiction of this manor; 6 bovates of
       land taxable. Land for 1 plough. It is waste.
           Meadow, 15 acres.

5 M. In GIRSBY Aelmer had 2 carucates of land and 2 bovates taxable.
       Land for 4½ ploughs. Now William, the Archbishop's man, has in
       lordship 2 ploughs;
           8 villagers, 7 smallholders and 18 Freemen who have 4½
               ploughs and
           meadow, 20 acres.
       Value before 1066 £3; now the same. Exactions 20s.

6 2 In STALLINGBOROUGH Eilafr had 1 carucate of land and 2 bovates
  M. taxable. Land for 2½ ploughs. Herbert, the Archbishop's man,
       has in lordship 1 plough;
           5 villagers, 3 Freemen and 1 smallholder with 1 plough.
           ½ mill, 32d; 2 salt-houses; meadow, 80 acres.
       Value before 1066, 30s; now 50s.

Soca hvj Ⓜ.Heg%helinge.Cleia.Ternescou.

Idest vi.bov%træ ad gld.Tra ad.i.car 7 ii.bou.

Ibi.v.foch 7 iii.uilt hñt.i.car.7 xx.v.ac pti.

Ⓜ In *Chelebi*.ħb Elaf.iiii.bou% træ 7 dim ad gld.

Tra ad.i.car 7 i.boue.Ibi Wilts hõ arch ħ dim

car.7 ii.foch 7 ii.borđ.7 dim molđ.iii.folidoʒ.

7 iiii.den.T.R.E.uat.x.fot.m similit.

Ⓜ In *Cvcvalt*.ħb.Fulchri.vii.bõ tre ad glđ.Tra ad.i.

car 7 vi.bou.Ibi Wilts hõ arch ħ.i.car.7 i.uilt

7 i.borđ.7 i.foch.Ipfi.i.car.T.R.E.uat.xx.fot.m simit.

In Svalun.e soca huj Ⓜ.i.car tre ad gld.Tra ad.ii.

car.Ibi funt.iii.foch 7 i.borđ.cũ dim car.

Ⓜ In *Lessintone*.ħb Lanbecarle.iiii.car tre ad gld.

Tra ad.x.car.Ibi Herbt hõ arch ħ in dñio.ii.car.

7 xvi.uilt 7 viii.borđ.7 iiii.foch.hñtes.v.car.Ibi

ǫter xx.ac pti.7 qt xx.ac filuæ minutæ.T.R.E.uat.iiii.

liħ.m.vii.liħ 7 x.fot.Tailla.xl.fot.

Inland

7 Soca huj Ⓜ.In Sonetorp.i.car tre 7 dim.Tra ad.ii.car.

Ibi in dñio.i.car.7 ii.uilt.7 xii.ac 7 dim pti.Ibi.iii.ac pti.

In Efnelẽt.ii.bõ tre ad gld.Tra ad dim car.Wafta.e.

In Houtune.i.car tre ad gld.Tra ad.ii.car.Ibi.v.foch

7 v.uilt hñt.iii.car.7 xiii.ac pti.

S In Bechelinge.ii.bõ tre ad gld.Tra ad dim car.Ibi.iiii.

foch hñt.i.car 7 vi.boues arantes.

Jurisdiction of this manor:

7   HEALING, 1 bovate; CLEE, 3 bovates; THRUNSCOE, 2 bovates. That is, 6 bovates of land taxable. Land for 1 plough and 2 oxen.
  5 Freemen and 3 villagers have 1 plough.
  Meadow, 25 acres.

8 M. In KEELBY Eilafr had 4½ bovates of land taxable. Land for 1 plough and 1 ox. William, the Archbishop's man, has ½ plough.
  2 Freemen and 2 smallholders.
  ½ mill, 3s 4d.
Value before 1066, 10s; now the same.

9 M. In CUXWOLD Fulcric had 7 bovates of land and 3 parts of 1 bovate taxable. Land for 1 plough and 6 oxen. William, the Archbishop's man, has 1 plough.
  1 villager, 1 smallholder and 1 Freeman; they (have) 1 plough.
Value before 1066, 20s; now the same.

10   In SWALLOW there is a jurisdiction and *inland* of this manor; 1 carucate of land taxable. Land for 2 ploughs.
  3 Freemen and 1 smallholder with ½ plough.

11   In LISSINGTON Lambakarl had 4 carucates of land taxable. Land for 10 ploughs. Herbert, the Archbishop's man, has in lordship 2 ploughs;
  16 villagers, 8 smallholders and 4 Freemen who have 5 ploughs.
  Meadow, 80 acres; underwood, 80 acres.
Value before 1066 £4; now £7 10s. Exactions 40s.

Inland and jurisdiction of this manor: 339 d
12   In SWINTHORPE 1½ carucates of land taxable. Land for 2 ploughs.
  In lordship 1 plough;
  2 villagers.
  Meadow, 12½ acres.

13   In SNELLAND 2 bovates of land taxable. Land for ½ plough. It is waste.
  Meadow, 3 acres.

14   In HOLTON (cum Beckering) 1 carucate of land taxable. Land for 2 ploughs.
  5 Freemen and 5 villagers have 3 ploughs.
  Meadow, 13 acres.

15 S. In BECKERING 2 bovates of land taxable. Land for ½ plough.
  4 Freemen have 1 plough and 6 ploughing oxen.

M̄ In *Beningvrde*. hb̄ Goduin᷒. II. car' tre 7 dim̃ ad gld.
Tra ad. III. car' 7 dim̃. Nc̄ Osbn᷒ pb̄r hr̄ de archiepo.
In dnio. II. car̄. 7 VII. uilt. 7 II. bord. 7 VI. soch. hn̄tes
. I. car' 7 dim̃. Ibi æccła. 7 sedes. I. mold. 7 LX. ac̄ p̄ti.
T.R.E. uał xxx. sol. m̃. LXX. sol.

M̄ In *Agetorne*. hb̄ Aluuin᷒. I. car' 7 V. bō tre ad gld.
M̄ 7 Auti. III. boū tre ad gld. Tra ad. III. car̄ 7 dim.
Ibi Wills hō arch hr̄. I. car'. 7 VI. uilt 7 VII. bord.
7 II. soch hn̄t. III. car'. 7 V. boues. Ibi dimid æccła
7 II. mold. IIII. solidoꝝ. 7 LX. ac̄ p̄ti. T.R.E. uał
LX. sol. m̃. XL. sol.
In Soca huj᷒ M̄ hr̄ archieps. T. III. boū ad gld.

M̄ In *Rigesbi*. hb̄ Aldene. VI. bō tre ad gld. Tra
Tra ad. I. car' 7 II. bou. Ibi Herbt᷒ hō arch hr̄. I. car.
7 III. uilt 7 IIII. bord. cū. II. bobꝝ. Ibi æccła 7 pb̄r.
7 q̄ter xx 7 x. ac̄ silue past'. 7 LX. ac̄ siluæ minutæ.
T.R.E. uał. LX. sol. m̃ similir̄.
* In Sudtune 7 Dreuistorp 7 Herdetorp. ē inland
huj᷒ M̄. dimid car' tre ad gld. Tra ad. I. carucā.
Ibi. VI. uilt. hn̄t dim car̄. 7 XL. ac̄ p̄ti.
Soca ejdē᷒ M̄. Righesbi [IIII. bō]. Halebi [III. bō]. Tatebi [Lc' hoc M̄ fuit]. Idest
ad gld. XV. bou' tre. Tra ad. III. car' 7 dimidiā.
In eis. VII. soch 7 II. uilt 7 I. bord. hn̄t. I. car̄ 7 dimid.
7 XX. acs p̄ti. 7 XII. ac̄ siluæ. 7 XX. ac̄ minutæ.
h Soca T.R.E. uał. IIII. lib. m̃ XL. sol.

II. M̄ In *Tesforde*. hb̄r Elmer 7 Arnui. III. car̄ træ ad gld.
Tra ad. IIII. car̄. Ibi Gislebt᷒ hō arch hr̄. II. car'. 7 I. boū.

16 M. In BENNIWORTH Godwine had 2½ carucates of land taxable. Land for 3½ ploughs. Now Osbern the priest has it from the Archbishop.
In lordship 2 ploughs;
7 villagers, 2 smallholders and 6 Freemen who have 1½ ploughs.
A church; 1 mill site; meadow, 60 acres.
Value before 1066, 30s; now 70s.

17 M. In HACKTHORN Alwine had 1 carucate and 5 bovates of land
M. taxable, and Auti 3 bovates of land taxable. Land for 3½ ploughs.
William, the Archbishop's man, has 1 plough.
6 villagers, 7 smallholders and 2 Freemen have 3 ploughs
and 5 oxen.
½ church; 2 mills, 4s; meadow, 60 acres.
Value before 1066, 60s; now 40s.
In the jurisdiction of this manor Archbishop Thomas has 3
bovates taxable.

18 M. In RIGSBY Halfdan had 6 bovates of land taxable. Land for 1
plough and 2 oxen. Herbert, the Archbishop's man, has 1 plough.
3 villagers and 4 smallholders with 2 oxen.
A church and a priest; woodland pasture, 90 acres;
underwood, 60 acres.
Value before 1066, 60s; now the same.

19 In SUTTON (le Marsh), TRUSTHORPE and ADDLETHORPE there is *inland* of
this manor; ½ carucate of land taxable. Land for 1 plough.
6 villagers have ½ plough.
Meadow, 40 acres.

Jurisdiction also of this manor:
20 RIGSBY, 4 bovates; AILBY, 3 bovates; *TATEBI*, 1 carucate: this was a
manor. That is 15 bovates of land taxable. Land for 3½ ploughs.
In them
7 Freemen, 2 villagers and 1 smallholder have 1½ ploughs and
meadow, 20 acres; woodland, 12 acres; under[wood], 20 acres.
Value of this jurisdiction before 1066 £4; now 40s.

21 2 In TETFORD Aelmer and Earnwine had 3 carucates of land taxable.
M. Land for 4 ploughs. Gilbert, the Archbishop's man, has 2 ploughs
and 1 ox.

7 VIII . uilt . 7 VII . foch cū . II . car . Ibi æccła . 7 I . molđ .

IIII . folidoʒ . 7 cxx . acs p̄ti . 7 VI . ac̄ filuæ minutæ .

T.R.E . uał xxx . fol . m̄ . IIII . lib̄ .

In Ormesbi . ē foca huj M̄ dim̄ car tre ad gld .

Tra ad . VI . boū . Ibi . I . foch 7 I . uilt cū dim̄ car .

7 xx . ac̄ p̄ti .

In Haintone . ē Soca de Torp . I . car tre 7 dim̄ ad gld .

Tra ad . III . car̄ . Ibi . III . foch 7 III . borđ hn̄t . v . boues .

arantes . 7 q̄ter . xx . ac̄ p̄ti . Elmer hb̄ . Wilts hr̄ de ARC .

In SOCA de Linberge hr̄ arch . III . boū tre ad glđ .

Tra ad . I . car̄ .

In Stalinburg . ē inland de Linberge . dim̄ bō tre

ad gld . Tra ad . I . bouē . Ibi arch . I . uilt cū . I . bouē

arans . 7 feđ molđ . 7 dim̄ Laninā .   ⋆

In Neutone hr̄ arch . c . acs p̄ti p̄tin ad Lanun .

M̄ In HERPESWELLE . hb̄ Aluuin . v . boū tre 7 dim̄

ad glđ . Tra ad . I . car̄ . Ibi Wilts hō arch hr̄ . I . uilt

7 v . foch . cū . VI . bob arantes . 7 xxxix . acs p̄ti .

T.R.E . uał . xvi . fol . m̄ . x . fol .

M̄ In WLVRICESBI . hb̄ Aluric . II . car tre 7 II . bō .

ad gld . Tra ad . III . car̄ . Nc̄ arch hr̄ ibi . I . car̄ .

7 I . uilt . 7 x . foch cū : I . car̄ . 7 xx . acs p̄ti : T.R.E : uał

III . lib̄ . m̄ . xL . fol .

M̄ In DVSEBI . hb̄ Aldene . III . car træ ad gld . Tra ad

. III . car̄ . Nc̄ hugo hō arch hr̄ ibi . I . car̄ . 7 ix . uilt

7 III . borđ . 7 I . foch . hn̄tes . II . car̄ . 7 I . molđ . III . folidoʒ .

7 xxx . II . ac̄ p̄ti . 7 xx . ac̄ filue minutæ . T.R.E . uał

III . lib̄ . m̄ . IIII . lib̄ . Tailla . xx . fol .

In Bichere . ē inland huj M̄ . I . bō tre 7 dim̄ ad glđ .

Tra ad tntđ . Wafta . ē . lbi . ē . I . falina . Wafta .

8 villagers and 7 Freemen with 2 ploughs.
A church; 1 mill, 4s; meadow, 120 acres; underwood, 6 acres.
Value before 1066, 30s; now £4.

22 In (South) ORMSBY there is a jurisdiction of this manor; ½
carucate of land taxable. Land for 6 oxen.
1 Freeman and 1 villager with ½ plough.
Meadow, 20 acres.

23 In HAINTON there is a jurisdiction of *Torp*; 1½ carucates of land   340 a
taxable. Land for 3 ploughs.
3 Freemen and 3 smallholders have 5 ploughing oxen.
Meadow, 80 acres.
Aelmer had it; William has it from the Archbishop.

24 In the jurisdiction of (Great) LIMBER the Archbishop has 3 bovates
of land taxable. Land for 1 plough.

25 In STALLINGBOROUGH there is *inland* of (Great) Limber; ½ bovate of
land taxable. Land for 1 ox. The Archbishop [has]
1 villager with 1 ploughing ox; and
a mill site; ½ wool-house.

26 In NEWTON (on Trent) the Archbishop has 100 acres of meadow
which belong to Laneham.

27 M. In HARPSWELL Alwine had 5½ bovates of land taxable. Land for 1
plough. William, the Archbishop's man, has
1 villager and 5 Freemen with 6 ploughing oxen; and
meadow, 39 acres.
Value before 1066, 16s; now 10s.

28 M. In WORLABY Aelfric had 2 carucates of land and 2 bovates taxable.
Land for 3 ploughs. Now the Archbishop has 1 plough there.
1 villager and 10 Freemen with 1 plough.
Meadow, 20 acres.
Value before 1066 £3; now 40s.

29 M. In DOWSBY Halfdan had 3 carucates of land taxable. Land for 3
ploughs. Now Hugh, the Archbishop's man, has 1 plough there.
9 villagers, 3 smallholders and 1 Freeman who have 2 ploughs.
1 mill, 3s; meadow, 32 acres; underwood, 20 acres.
Value before 1066 £3; now £4. Exactions 20s.

30 In BICKER there is *inland* of this manor; 1½ bovates of land
taxable. Land for as much. It is waste.
1 salt-house; waste.

In GREIBI.ē Soca ejdē M̅.1.caruc̄ tre.Tra ad.1.
car̄.Ibi.vi.ſoch hn̄t.1.car̄ 7 1.bouē.

M̅In BILLINGEBVRG.hb Turchil.v.bou tre ad gld.
Tra ad.v.boues.Nc̄ Walter⁹ de arch.ht.Ibi dim̅
car̄.7 1.uilt 7 1.bord.7 vii.ac̄s p̄ti.7 1.ſed molđ.Val.x.ſot.

M̅In HORBELINGE.hb Turchil.iiii.car̄ træ ad gld.
Tra ad totiđ car̄.Nc̄ Walter de Arch ht.In dn̄io
.1.car̄.7 ix.uilt 7 1.bord.7 viii.ſoch.hn̄tes iii.car̄.
Ibi æccla.7 xx.ac̄ p̄ti.Tra arabit.1.lev lg̅.7 1.lat.
T.R.E.ual.vi.lib.m̅ xL.ſot.Tailla.xx.ſot.

M̅In WIME.hb B˖co.1.car̄ træ ad gld.Tra ad.1.car̄.
M̅ 7 Vluuine.1.car̄ ad gld.Tra ad.1.car̄.Nc̄ Walchelin
hō arch ht ibi.11.car̄.7 iiii.uilt 7 11.bord cū.1.car̄.
Ibi æccla.de qua Eduuard ht tcia parte.7 1.ſed
molđ.7 xxvii.ac̄ p̄ti.T.R.E.ual xL.ſot.m̅.L.ſot.
Tailla.xi.ſot.

In Tuiforde.ē ſoca de Nortuuine.dim̅ car̄ træ ad
gld.Tra ad dim̅ car̄.Ibi.11.bord cū.11.bob arantes.

340 b

Ibi.iii.ac̄ p̄ti.7 xxvii.ac̄ ſiluæ minutæ.
M̅In WIME.hb Aluuin.11.car̄ tre ad gld.Tra
ad.11.car̄.Ibi Walchelin hō arch.11.car̄.7 vi.
uilt 7 11.ſoch.7 1.cenſore.Ibi q̄ter xx.ac̄ p̄ti.7 ix.
7 cxx.ac̄ ſiluæ in Warnode drogonis.7 xL.acre
ſiluæ minutæ.T.R.E.ual xx.ſot.m̅ xx.v.ſot.
Tailla.v.ſot.

In SCHILLINTVNE.hb Morcar.iii.car̄ tre ad gld.
7 Friguiſt 7 Bridmer.1.car̄ tre ad gld Tra ad.v.car̄
7 dim̅.Frigeſoca in Schillintune.Ibi Walchelin
hō arch.11.car̄.7 xiii.uilt 7 v.ſoch.hn̄tes.iiii.car̄.
Ibi cxxi.ac̄ 7 dim̅ p̄ti.7 Lx.ac̄ ſilue paſt in Wat
node ep̄i.Remigii.T.R.E.ual.iiii.lib.m̅ ſimilit.
Tailla.xx.ſot.

340 a, b

31   In (East) GRABY there is a jurisdiction also of this manor; 1
carucate of land. Land for 1 plough.
      6 Freemen have 1 plough and 1 ox.

32 M. In BILLINGBOROUGH Thorketill had 5 bovates of land taxable.
Land for 5 oxen. Now Walter of Aincourt has them from the
Archbishop. ½ plough.
      1 villager and 1 smallholder.
      Meadow, 7 acres; 1 mill site.
Value 10s.

33 M. In HORBLING Thorketill had 4 carucates of land taxable. Land for
as many ploughs. Now Walter has them from the Archbishop. In
lordship 1 plough;
      9 villagers, 1 smallholder and 8 Freemen who have 3 ploughs.
      A church; meadow, 20 acres; arable land 1 league long and
        1 wide.
Value before 1066 £6; now 40s. Exactions 20s.

34 M. In (North) WITHAM Baca had 1 carucate of land taxable. Land for 1
M. plough. And Wulfwine (had) 1 carucate taxable. Land for 1 plough.
Now Walchelin, the Archbishop's man, has 2 ploughs there.
      4 villagers and 2 smallholders with 1 plough.
      A church of which Edward Young has the third part; 1 mill
        site; meadow, 27 acres.
Value before 1066, 40s; now 50s. Exactions 11s.

35   In 'TWYFORD' there is a jurisdiction of North Witham; ½ carucate
of land taxable. Land for ½ plough.
      2 smallholders who plough with 2 oxen.
      Meadow, 3 acres; underwood, 27 acres.   340 b

36 M. In (North) WITHAM Alwine had 2 carucates of land taxable. Land
for 2 ploughs. Walchelin, the Archbishop's man, [has] 2 ploughs
and
      6 villagers, 2 Freemen and 1 tributary.
      Meadow, 89 acres; woodland in Drogo's *warnode*, 120 acres;
        underwood, 40 acres.
Value before 1066, 20s; now 25s. Exactions 5s.

37   In SKILLINGTON Earl Morcar had 3 carucates of land taxable and
Frithgestr and Beorhtmaer 1 carucate of land taxable. Land for 5½
ploughs. A free jurisdiction of Skillington. Walchelin, the
Archbishop's man, [has] 2 ploughs.
      13 villagers and 5 Freemen who have 4 ploughs.
      Meadow, 121½ acres; woodland pasture in Bishop Remigius'
        warnode, 60 acres.
Value before 1066 £4; now the same. Exactions 20s.

Ꝏ Ibidē jn *Estone* . h̅b Siuuard . III . caꝛ́ træ ad gld.

Tra ad . III . caꝛ́ 7 VI . boū . Ibi Osbn h̅o arch h̅t . I . caꝛ́.

7 XII . uilł 7 VI . borđ . Ibi dimiđ æccła . 7 I . molđ . VIII.

ſolidoᵹ . 7 X . a̅c p̅ti . 7 CC . a̅c ſiluæ paſt . 7 CCXL . a̅c

ſiluæ minutæ . T.R.E . uał XL . ſoł . m̅ XL . ſoł.

§ In *Colstewrde* h̅b Morcar . III . cař tre ad gld.

Tra ad . III . caꝛ́ . Soca in Schellintune . Ibi . IIII . ſoc̅h

7 IIII . uilł h̅nt . II . caꝛ́ . 7 ɔxx . a̅c ſiluæ paſt p̄ loca.

Ꝏ In *Belingei* . h̅b Suuen . XII . caꝛ tre ad gld.

Tra ad . IIII . caꝛ́ . Ibi Walchel h̅o arch 7 II . filij Suuen.

II . caꝛ́ . 7 III . uilł . 7 XV . ſoc̅h h̅ntes . IIII . caꝛ́ . Ibi

XVI . a̅c p̅ti . 7 III . ſed piſcaꝛ́.

T.R.E . uał IIII . lib̅ . m̅ ſimilit̅ . 7 V . ſoł plus.

In Walecote . ē inland huj Ꝏ . VIII . caꝛ træ ad glđ.

Tra ad . VI . caꝛ́ . Ibi . XV . ſoc̅h 7 I . uilłs h̅nt . VI . caꝛ́

7 IIII . ac̅s p̅ti . 7 XLVI . a̅c ſiluæ minutæ.

Ꝏ In *Lavintone* . h̅b Vlf . IIII . caꝛ́ træ ad gld . Tra ad . V . caꝛ́.

Ibi Rannulf cleric arch . II . caꝛ́ h̅t

in d̅nio . 7 XII . uilł 7 I . ſoc̅h 7 IIII . borđ . h̅ntes . VI . caꝛ́.

Ibi XXX . VI . a̅c p̅ti . 7 CX . a̅c ſiluæ minutæ . In War

ńode Widonis de credun . Tra arabił 7 paſcuæ.

II . leꝟ łg̅ . 7 VI . q̄ᵹ lat̅ . T.R.E . uał . IIII . lib̅ . m̅ . LX . ſoł.

340 c

.III. TERRA EP̅I DUNELMENSIS.

Ꝏ In *Brotvlbi* . habuit Stepiot . V . boū træ ad glđ. Soca ibiđ

Tra ad . VI . boucs . Nꝺ eꝑs dunelm̅ . 7 colſuuen de eo.

h̅t hanc tꝛ́a 7 colit eā . T.R.E . III . ſoł . m̅ . IIII . ſoł.

Ꝏ In Snardesforde . h̅b Siuuard . II . caꝛ́ træ 7 II . bo̅ ad

glđ . Tra ad . II . caꝛ́ 7 VI . boū . Nꝺ eꝑs dunelm̅ 7 Colſuan

de eo h̅t . I . caꝛ́ . 7 XIIII . ſoc̅h cū . II . caꝛ́ . 7 LX . ac̅s p̅ti.

T.R.E . XX . ſoł . m̅ . XXX . ſoł . 7 tailla . X . ſoł.

38 M. There also [and] in EASTON Siward had 3 carucates of land taxable. Land for 3 ploughs and 6 oxen. Osbern, the Archbishop's man, has 1 plough.

> 12 villagers and 6 smallholders.
> ½ church; 1 mill, 8s; meadow, 10 acres; woodland pasture, 200 acres; underwood, 240 acres.

Value before 1066, 40s; now 40s.

39 S. In COLSTERWORTH Earl Morcar had 3 carucates of land taxable. Land for 3 ploughs. A jurisdiction of Skillington.

> 4 Freemen and 4 villagers have 2 ploughs.
> Woodland, pasture in places, 120 acres.

40 M. In BILLINGHAY Sveinn had 12 carucates of land taxable. Land for 4 ploughs. Walchelin, the Archbishop's man, and the two sons of Sveinn [have] 2 ploughs.

> 3 villagers and 15 Freemen who have 4 ploughs.
> Meadow, 16 acres; 3 sites for fisheries.

Value before 1066 £4; now the same and 5s more.

41 In WALCOT there is *inland* of this manor; 8 carucates of land taxable. Land for 6 ploughs.

> 15 Freemen and 1 villager have 6 ploughs and
> meadow, 4 acres; underwood, 46 acres.

42 M. In 'LAVINGTON' Ulfr had 4 carucates of land taxable. Land for 5 ploughs. Ranulf, a clerk of the Archbishop's, has 2 ploughs in lordship;

> 12 villagers, 1 Freeman and 4 smallholders who have 6 ploughs.
> Meadow, 36 acres; underwood, 110 acres. In the *warnode* of Guy of Craon. Arable land and pastureland 2 leagues long and 6 furlongs wide.

Value before 1066 £4; now 60s.

3   LAND OF THE BISHOP OF DURHAM   340 c

1 M. In BRATTLEBY Stjupi had 5 bovates of land taxable. A jurisdiction also there. Land for 6 oxen. Now the Bishop of Durham, and Kolsveinn from him, has this land and cultivates it. [Value] before 1066, 3s; now 4s.

2 M. In SNARFORD Siward had 2 carucates of land and 2 bovates taxable. Land for 2 ploughs and 6 oxen. Now the Bishop of Durham, and Kolsveinn from him, has 1 plough.

> 14 Freemen with 2 ploughs.
> Meadow, 60 acres.

[Value] before 1066, 20s; now 30s. Exactions 10s.

㋒ In _Berlinge_ . hb Dane . ix . bou ꝛre ad glꝺ . Tra ad
1 . car 7 dim . Nc Colſuan de epo . In dnio . 1 . car . 7 ii . uilt
7 1 . borꝺ cu . 1 . car . 7 xx . ac p̃ti . 7 xx . ac ſiluæ minutæ .
T.R.E . ual xvi . ſot . m̃ . xx . ſot .

㋒ In _Bliburg_ . hb Redulf . vii . bo ꞇræ ad gld . Tra ad . ii .
car . Nc monachi dunelmi hn̄t ibi . ii . car . 7 iii . uilt
7 1 . borꝺ . 7 1 . ſoch cu . 1 . car . 7 xx . acs p̃ti . 7 dimiꝺ æccta
int epm 7 Gozet . T.R.E . ual xx . ſot . m̃ xxx . ſot .
f. Lanbt

NORTREDING.

㋒ In _Brachelesbi_ . hb Goduin . 1 . car ꞇræ ad glꝺ . Tra
ad . ii . car . Ibi Nigel ho epi h̄ꞇ . iii . uilt cu . 1 . boue .
7 xxx . acs p̃ti . T.R.E . ual . xl . ſot . m̃ x . ſot .

㋒ In _Fvgelestov_ . hbr Aldene 7 Elmar . 1 . car ꞇræ
7 ii . bou ad gld . Tra ad . ii . car 7 dim . Ibi Walbt ho
epi h̄ꞇ xvi . uilt 7 x . borꝺ cu dim car . 7 1 . car in dnio
7 xi . ſalin . ii . ſolidoƶ . 7 lx . acs p̃ti . T.R.E . ual . lx .
ſot . m̃ . iiii . lib .

㋒ In _Nevtone_ hb Grinchel . xi . bou ꞇre ad glꝺ .
Tra ad . ii . car . Ibi Walbt ho epi h̄ꞇ . 1 . car . 7 ii .
uilt 7 ii . borꝺ cu dim car . Ibi æccta 7 xl . acs p̃ti .
7 In Turgribi . 1 . molꝺ . qꝺ Norman de Areci tenet
7 x . ac p̃ti.
injuſte . T.R.E . ual . c . ſot . m̃ xxx . ſot . Ibi halla cu
tofta 7 ſoca 7 ſaca.

SVD REDING.

㋒ In _Bolintone_ . hb Aluric . iii . bou ꞇræ 7 dim ad glꝺ .
Tra ad . 1 . car . Ibi Nigel ho epi h̄ꞇ dim car . 7 vi . uilt
cu . 1 . car . 7 x . acs p̃ti . 7 clx . ac ſiluæ minutæ . T.R.E .
ual . xx . ſot . m̃ x . ſot .

3 M. In BARLINGS Dena had 9 bovates of land taxable. Land for 1½ ploughs. Now Kolsveinn [holds] from the Bishop. In lordship 1 plough;
 2 villagers and 1 smallholder with 1 plough.
 Meadow, 20 acres; underwood, 20 acres.
Value before 1066, 16s; now 20s.

4 M. In BLYBOROUGH Ralph had 7 bovates of land taxable. Land for 2 ploughs. Now the monks of Durham have 2 ploughs there and
 3 villagers, 1 smallholder and 1 Freeman with 1 plough; and
 meadow, 20 acres; ½ church between the Bishop and Jocelyn
 son of Lambert.
Value before 1066, 20s; now 30s.

NORTH RIDING

5 M. In BROCKLESBY Godwine had 1 carucate of land taxable. Land for 2 ploughs. Nigel, the Bishop's man, has
 3 villagers with 1 ox and
 meadow, 30 acres.
Value before 1066, 40s; now 10s.

6 2 In FULSTOW Halfdan and Aelmer had 1 carucate of land and 2
M. bovates taxable. Land for 2½ ploughs. Walbert, the Bishop's man, has
 16 villagers and 10 smallholders with ½ plough. 1 plough in
 lordship.
 11 salt-houses, 2s; meadow, 60 acres.
Value before 1066, 60s; now £4.

7 2 In (Wold) NEWTON Grimketill had 11 bovates of land taxable.
M. Land for 2 ploughs. Walbert, the Bishop's man, has 1 plough.
 2 villagers and 2 smallholders with ½ plough.
 A church; meadow, 40 acres. In Thorganby 1 mill which
 Norman of Arcy holds wrongfully; meadow, 10 acres.
Value before 1066, 100s; now 30s.
 A Hall with a plot and full jurisdiction.

SOUTH RIDING

8 M. In BULLINGTON Aelfric had 3½ bovates of land taxable. Land for 1 plough. Nigel, the Bishop's man, has ½ plough.
 6 villagers with 1 plough.
 Meadow, 10 acres; underwood, 160 acres.
Value before 1066, 20s; now 10s.

ᴁ In *HARDVVIC*. ħƀ Aluric. ii. boū tre 7 tciã partē
uni bov ad glđ. Tra ad. v. bou. Nigel hŧ de eƥo 7 Wasŧ. ē.
Ibi xxvii. aᷓ ƥti. T.R.E. ual. x. fol. m̃ iii. fol.

★ In Langetone. fuᷤ. iii. bou tre ad glđ. Tra ad vi. bõ
Soca. ē in Stratone. 7 lxv. aᷓ filuæ minutæ ibi.

Ŝ In Wifpinctune. ii. caɼ træ ad glđ. Tra ad. iiii.
7 ᴮcaɼ. Inland 7 Soca. in Stratone 7 Cherchebi. Ibi ix.
focħ 7 vi. borđ. cū. iii. caɼ.

340 d
Ŝ In Waldingurde. vi. caɼ tre ad glđ. Tra ad. vi. caɼ.
Soca. ē in Stratone 7 in Cherchebi. Ibi xx. focħ cū iiii.
caɼ. 7 xx. aᷓ ƥti. 7 xxv. aᷓ filuæ minutæ

ᴁ In *CHIRCHEBI*. ħƀ Harold. x. bou træ ad glđ. Tra ad
xiii. bõ. Ibi hŧ eƥs duñ. iii. uiŧ 7 ii. borđ cū dim̃ caɼ.
7 xii. aᷓ ƥti. 7 clxx. aᷓ filuæ paſt ƥ loca. T.R.E. ual
c. fol. m̃ fimiliŧ.
In Martone. ē foca huj ᴁ. xii. bou ad glđ. Tra ad. ii.
caɼ. Ibi. iii. focħ 7 ii. borđ hñt. i. caɼ. 7 xxx. iiii. aᷓ
ƥti. 7 xxx. iii. aᷓ filue paſt. 7 lx. aᷓ filuæ minutæ.
In Torp. ē inland 7 foca ejđ ᴁ. ii. car tre ad glđ.
Tra ad. ii. caɼ. Ibi xvi. uiŧ 7 i. focħ 7 iiii. borđ
hñt. i. caɼ. 7 tciã parte. ii. mold. de. viii. fol. 7 iii.
k pifcaɼ de. vii. fol 7 vi. deñ. 7 xv. aᷓ ƥti. 7 cxx. aᷓ
filuæ paſt. Eudo caluñ.

ᴁ In *COVENHA*. ħƀ Efbern. ii. car tre 7 dim̃ ad glđ.
Tra ad. iii. caɼ 7 vi. bõ. Nc̄|hŧ Ŝ Karilef ibi. ii. caɼ.
7 dim̃. 7 xii. uiŧ. 7 vi. focħ cū. i. caɼ 7 dim̃. Ibi æccła.
7 lx. aᷓ ƥti. 7 ii. faline. iii. fol. T.R.E. ual. lx. fol.

✝ m̃. iiii. liƀ. Tailla. xx. fol.
In Grimefbi. ē foca huj ᴁ. ii. bõ tre ad glđ. Tra
ad. iii. bõ. Wafta f̊. m̃ coliŧ.

340 c, d

9 M. In 'HARDWICK' Aelfric had 2 bovates of land and the third part of 1 bovate taxable. Land for 5 oxen. Nigel has it from the Bishop. It is waste.
> Meadow, 27 acres.
Value before 1066, 10s; now 3s.

10 In LANGTON (by Wragby) 3 bovates of land taxable. Land for 6 oxen. It is a jurisdiction of (Little) Sturton.
> Underwood, 65 acres there.

11 S. In WISPINGTON 2 carucates of land taxable. Land for 4 ploughs.
& B. *Inland* and a jurisdiction of (Little) Sturton and Kirkby (on Bain).
> 9 Freemen and 6 smallholders with 3 ploughs.

12 S. In WADDINGWORTH 6 carucates of land taxable. Land for 6 ploughs. 340 d
It is a jurisdiction of (Little) Sturton and of Kirkby (on Bain).
> 20 Freemen with 4 ploughs.
> Meadow, 20 acres; underwood, 25 acres.

13 M. In KIRKBY (on Bain) Harold had 10 bovates of land taxable. Land for 13 oxen. The Bishop of Durham has
> 3 villagers and 2 smallholders with ½ plough.
> Meadow, 12 acres; woodland, pasture in places, 170 acres.
Value before 1066, 100s; now the same.

14 In MARTIN there is a jurisdiction of this manor; 12 bovates taxable. Land for 2 ploughs.
> 3 Freemen and 2 smallholders have 1 plough.
> Meadow, 34 acres; woodland pasture, 33 acres; underwood,
>> 60 acres.

15 In (Tattershall) THORPE there is *inland* and a jurisdiction also of this manor; 2 carucates of land taxable. Land for 2 ploughs.
K
> 16 villagers, 1 Freeman and 4 smallholders have 1 plough and the third part of 2 mills at 8s; 3 fisheries at 7s 6d; meadow,
>> 15 acres; woodland pasture, 120 acres.
> Eudo claims it.

16 M. In COVENHAM Esbjorn had 2½ carucates of land taxable. Land for 3 ploughs and 6 oxen. Now St. Karilef's has 2½ ploughs there from the Bishop.
> 12 villagers and 6 Freemen with 1½ ploughs.
> A church; meadow, 60 acres; 2 salt-houses, 3s.
£ Value before 1066, 60s; now £4. Exactions 20s.

3,17–18 are added at the foot of col. 340d (after 3,26), their correct place in the text being indicated by transposition signs.

19 In (Little) GRIMSBY there is a jurisdiction of this manor, 2 bovates of land taxable. Land for 3 oxen. It was waste; it is now cultivated.

ᴍ̊ᴵᴵ In *FOREBI*.ħƀr Sūmerled 7 Archil vii.bõ ad glđ.
Ťra ad.ii.cař 7 v.bõ.Ibi Turſtin̉ hõ epi hť.i.ſocħ.
vi.uiłł hñtes.i.cař.7 xlii.aċ p̃ti.T.R.E.uał.iiii.
liƀ.m̃.xx.ſoł.

ᴍ̊ In *ENDREBI* 7 Radebi ħƀ Elnod.iiii.bõ 7 dīm ad
glđ.Ťra ad.v.bõ.Nċ.ē dīm cař ibi.7 i,uiłł.7 dīm
ſeđ molđ.7 x.aċ p̃ti.T.R.E.uał.x.ſoł.m̃ ſimil.

ᴍ̊ In *SPILESBI* 7 Ireſbi 7 Torp.ħƀ Aſchil.vi.cař̉
tre ad glđ.Ťra ad.vi.cař.Ibi hť eꝑs.i.cař.7 v.
uiłł 7 v.ſocħ.7 i.borđ.hñtes.i.cař.7 ii.molđ.ix
k ſolidoꝫ.7 xii.aċ p̃ti.T.R.E.uał.xx.ſoł.m̃ ſimiliť.Eudo clam̃.
Ibidē.ē ſoca.de Gredbi.7 Eſtrecale.ii.cař̉ træ̉
ad glđ.Ťra ad.iii.cař.Ibi xii.ſocħ hñt.ii.cař.

ᴍ̊ In *ESTRECALE*.ħƀ Elnod.vi.bõ tře ad gld.Ťra
ad.vi.boū.Ibi.ii.uiłł arant.ii.boƀꝫ.Ibi.v.aċ
k p̃ti.T.R.E.uał x.ſoł.m̃ ſimiliť.Eudo clam̃ ſocā.
In Totintune.ē ſoca de Spileſbi.ii.boū tře ad glđ.
Ťra ad.ii.bõ.Ibi.i.ſocħ.7 vi.aċ p̃ti.

✝In Scitebroc ē inland de Couenhā.vii.boū tře ad
glđ.Ťra ad.ix.boū.Ibi S̃ Karilef̉ hť.vi.hões cū.ii.
cař.7 ix.aċs p̃ti.ꝛ ad glđ.Ibi.vi.uiłł hñt.i.cař 7 ii.boū.

In Germundtorp.ē ſoca de Couenhā.iiii.bõ tře 7 dīm
£7 ʟ.aċ p̃ti.

340 d

20 2 In FOTHERBY Sumarlithi and Arnketill had 7 bovates taxable.
M. Land for 2 ploughs and 5 oxen. Thorsteinn, the Bishop's man, has
  1 Freeman; 6 villagers who have 1 plough.
  Meadow, 42 acres.
Value before 1066 £4; now 20s.

21 M. In (Mavis) ENDERBY and RAITHBY Alnoth had 4½ bovates taxable.
Land for 5 oxen. Now ½ plough there.
  1 villager.
  ½ mill site; meadow, 10 acres.
Value before 1066, 10s; now the same.

22 M. In SPILSBY, ERESBY and THORPE (St. Peter) Asketill had 6 carucates
of land taxable. Land for 6 ploughs. The Bishop has 1 plough.
  5 villagers, 5 Freemen and 1 smallholder who have 1 plough.
  2 mills, 9s; meadow, 12 acres.
Value before 1066, 20s; now the same.
K   Eudo claims it.

23 There also is a jurisdiction of Grebby and East Keal; 2 carucates
of land taxable. Land for 3 ploughs.
  12 Freemen have 2 ploughs.

24 In HUNDLEBY 4 acres of land.

25 M. In EAST KEAL Alnoth had 6 bovates of land taxable. Land for 6
oxen.
  2 villagers plough with 2 oxen.
  Meadow, 5 acres.
Value before 1066, 10s; now the same.
K   Eudo claims the jurisdiction.

26 In TOYNTON there is a jurisdiction of Spilsby; 2 bovates of land
taxable. Land for 2 oxen.
  1 Freeman.
  Meadow, 6 acres.

3,17–18, added at the foot of col. 340d and directed by transposition signs to their correct
place in the text.

17 In SKIDBROOKE there is *inland* of Covenham; 7 bovates of land
taxable. Land for 9 oxen. St. Karilef has
  6 men with 2 ploughs and
  meadow, 9 acres.

LOUTHESK Wapentake
18 In GRAINTHORPE there is a jurisdiction of Covenham; 4½ bovates
of land taxable.
  6 villagers have 1 plough and 2 oxen.
  Meadow, 50 acres.

SVDKEDING.

ↄↄ In *CADITON* . h̄br Harold 7 Artor . ıx bō tre 7 dim̄
ad glđ . Tra ad . ı . car̄ 7 dim̄ . Ibi Turſtin hō epi h̄t
. ı . car̄ . 7 xv . ſoch 7 xɪɪ . uiłł cū . ɪɪɪɪ . car̄ . 7 ɪɪɪ . molđ
7 dim̄ . xx . ſoł . 7 xɪɪ . ac̄s p̄ti . T.R.E . uał xʟ . ſoł .
m̄ . ʟx . ſoł .

✝ Iɳ Salflatebi . ē ſoca huj ↄↄ . ı . boū tre ad glđ . Tra
ɪɪ . bō . Ibi . ɪɪɪ . ſoch 7 ı . uiłł . cū . ɪɪɪɪ . bob .
In Crochinton . ē alia ſoca . dimiđ boū tre ad glđ .
Tra ad . ı . boū . Ibi . ı . uiłłs arans . ı . boue .

WINEGEBRIGE WAPENȾ.

ↄↄ In *GVNFORDEBI* . h̄b Morcar . ı . car̄ træ 7 dim̄ ad
glđ . Tra ad . ɪɪ . car̄ . Ibi Lanbt hō epi h̄t . ı . car̄ .
7 v . uiłł 7 ɪɪ . borđ . cū . ı . car̄ . 7 ɪɪ . molđ . xvɪ . ſoliđ .
7 xxɪɪ . ac̄s p̄ti 7 dim̄ . T.R.E . uał . xʟ . ſoł . m̄ ſimilit .

AVELVNT WAPENȾ.

In *NEVTONE* . h̄b Vluric Wilde . vɪɪ . bō træ ad glđ .
Tra ad . ɪɪ . car̄ . Eps dunelm̄ h̄t medietatē . 7 Vluiet
7 uxor ej alia . de rege h̄nt . Tota h̄ tra fuit matris
uxoris ej . Ibi h̄t eps dim̄ car̄ . 7 ɪɪɪ . uiłł cū dim̄ car̄ .
7 vɪ . ac̄s p̄ti . 7 xxxv . ac̄s ſilue minute .
Vluiet h̄t dim̄ car̄ . 7 ɪɪɪ . uiłł cū dim̄ car̄ . 7 vɪ . ac̄s
p̄ti . 7 xxx.v . ac̄s ſiluæ min . Tot . T.R.E . uał . xʟ . ſoł .
m̄ pars epi . xxv . ſoł . 7 pars Eps clamat. Vluiet xxv . ſoł .

HAZEBI HVND.

ↄↄ In *PICHEVRDE* h̄br Suuen 7 Agemund . ı . car̄
7 v . boū tre ad gld . Tra ad . ɪɪ . car̄ 7 ɪɪ . boū .
N̄c Goiſlan hō epi h̄t ibi . ı . car̄ . 7 v . uiłł . 7 ɪɪɪ . borđ .
arantes . v . bob . Ibi dim̄ æccła 7 xvɪ . ac̄ p̄ti . 7 xxx
ɪɪɪ . ac̄s ſiluæ paſtił p loca . T.R.E . uał xʟ . ſoł . m̄ ſimilit .

27 2 In KEDDINGTON Harold and Arnthorr had 9½ bovates of land
M. taxable. Land for 1½ ploughs. Thorsteinn, the Bishop's man, has
1 plough.
    15 Freemen and 12 villagers with 4 ploughs.
    3½ mills, 20s; meadow, 12 acres.
Value before 1066, 40s; now 60s.

28 In SALTFLEETBY there is a jurisdiction of this manor; 1 bovate of
land taxable. Land for 2 oxen.
    3 Freemen and 1 villager with 4 oxen.

*3,29 is added at the foot of col. 341b (in the middle of 3,48) with a transposition sign to
indicate its correct place in the text.*

30 In COCKERINGTON there is another jurisdiction; ½ bovate of land
taxable. Land for 1 ox.
    1 villager who ploughs with 1 ox.

WINNIBRIGGS Wapentake
31 M. In GONERBY Morcar had 1½ carucates of land taxable. Land for 2
ploughs. Lambert, the Bishop's man, has 1 plough.
    5 villagers and 2 smallholders with 1 plough.
    2 mills, 16s; meadow, 22½ acres.
Value before 1066, 40s; now the same.

AVELAND Wapentake
32 In NEWTON Wulfric Wilde had 7 bovates of land taxable. Land for
2 ploughs. The Bishop of Durham has half and Wulfgeat and his
wife have the other (half) from the King. The whole of this land
was his wife's mother's. The Bishop has ½ plough.
    3 villagers with ½ plough.
    Meadow, 6 acres; underwood, 35 acres.
Wulfgeat has ½ plough.
    3 villagers with ½ plough.
    Meadow, 6 acres; underwood, 35 acres.
Value of the whole before 1066, 40s; now of the Bishop's part,
25s; of Wulfgeat's part, 25s: the Bishop claims it.

HACEBY hundred
33 2 In PICKWORTH Sveinn and Agmundr had 1 carucate and 5 bovates
M. of land taxable. Land for 2 ploughs and 2 oxen. Now Jocelyn,
the Bishop's man, has 1 plough there.
    5 villagers and 3 smallholders who plough with 5 oxen.
    ½ church; meadow, 16 acres; woodland, pasture in places,
       33 acres.
Value before 1066, 40s; now the same.

KEHOS WAPENT.

In Brezbi. ē ſoca huj M̃. I. car̃ tre ad glđ. Tra ad. I. car̃. Ibi. I. ſoch. hr̃ dim car̃.7 xxx. ac̃ pti.7 xxi. ac̃ ſiluæ paſt p loca.

ASWARDETIERNE WAPENT. LEDVLFTORP HVND

.III.
M̃ In CHELEBI. hbr Aſlac Brictric 7 Archil vi. car̃ tre 7 III. bou ad glđ. Tra ad. vIII. car̃. Nc̃ Almod hõ epi hr̃ ibi. II. car̃.7 vII. uiłł.7 III. ſoch.7 III. borđ. cũ. II. car̃. T.R.E. ual. Lxx. ſol. m̃. vi. liƀ. Ibi Lxx. ac̃ pti.7 q̃t xx.7 x ac̃ ſiluæ minutæ. q̃s. R. eƥs 7 Colegri 7 eoɀ ſocij teneſ. eƥs hr̃ ſocã.

FLAXEWELLE WAPENT. HASCHEBI HĐ.

M̃ In EVEDVNE. hƀ Turuert. II. car̃ 7 dim ad glđ. Tra ad III. car̃. Ibi Colſuan hõ epi hr̃. I. car̃.7 IIII. uiłł.7 II. borđ. cũ. I. car̃.7 II. bob.7 xx. ac̃s pti. T.R.E. ual. IIII. liƀ.

Γ m̃. xx. ſol.

341 b

In Roſbi 7 altero Roſbi. ē ſoca in Wilgebi ł Chir chebi. III. car̃ tre 7 I. bou ad glđ. Tra ad IIII. car̃. Ibi Almod hõ epi hr̃. xv. ſoch 7 vi. borđ. hñtes v. car̃.7 dim æcclã. H appciant in M̃ ſupdict. In Euedune. ē ſoca de Cherchebi. I. bou træ ad glđ. Ibi. I. uiłł.7 II. borđ.7 II. ac̃ pti.

NORTREDING. BRADELAI WAPENT. ALESBI HĐ.

M̃ In ALESBI. hƀ Aben. vi. bou træ 7 tcia parte. uni bou ad glđ. Tra ad. I. car̃. Ibi Nigel hõ epi hr̃ dim car̃.7 III. ſoch.7 I. uiłł 7 I. borđ. cũ dim ear̃.7 ſeđ uni molđ. T.R.E. ual. xL. ſol. m̃ xx. ſol.

THREO Wapentake

34   In BRACEBY hundred there is a jurisdiction of this manor; 1 carucate of land taxable. Land for 1 plough.
      1 Freeman has ½ plough.
      Meadow, 30 acres; woodland, pasture in places, 21 acres.

ASWARDHURN Wapentake
LAYTHORPE hundred

35 3 In KELBY Aslakr, Beorhtric and Arnketill had 6 carucates of land
M. and 3 bovates taxable. Land for 8 ploughs. Now Alnoth, the Bishop's man, has 2 ploughs there.
      7 villagers, 3 Freemen and 3 smallholders with 2 ploughs.
      Value before 1066, 70s; now £6.
      Meadow, 70 acres; underwood, 90 acres, which Bishop
         Remigius, Kolgrimr and their companions hold. The Bishop
         has the jurisdiction.

FLAXWELL Wapentake
ASHBY hundred

36 M. In EVEDON Thorfrothr had 2½ carucates taxable. Land for 3 ploughs. Kolsveinn, the Bishop's man, has 1 plough.
      4 villagers and 2 smallholders with 1 plough and 2 oxen.
      Meadow, 20 acres.
Value before 1066 £4; now 20s.

37   In RAUCEBY hundred and the other RAUCEBY hundred there is a
jurisdiction of (Silk) Willoughby or Kirkby (la Thorpe); 3 carucates of land and 1 bovate taxable. Land for 4 ploughs.
Alnoth, the Bishop's man, has
      15 Freemen and 6 smallholders who have 5 ploughs.
      ½ church.
These are assessed in the above manor.

341 b

38   In EVEDON there is a jurisdiction of Kirkby (la Thorpe); 1 bovate of land taxable.
      1 villager and 2 smallholders.
      Meadow, 2 acres.

NORTH RIDING

BRADLEY Wapentake
AYLESBY hundred

39 M. In AYLESBY Habeinn had 6 bovates of land and the third part of 1 bovate taxable. Land for 1 plough. Nigel, the Bishop's man, has ½ plough.
      3 Freemen, 1 villager and 1 smallholder with ½ plough.
      1 mill site.
Value before 1066, 40s; now 20s.

HAWARDESHOV WAPENT̃.   *FENBI HD̃.*

ⓂIn *RAVENEDAL*. ħb Grinchel. II. bou tre ad gld. Tra
ad dim̃ car̃. Walbt̃ hō eρ̃i. arat eā. III. bob. T.R.E.
ual. xx. ſol. m̃. v. ſol.

SVDREDING. WARAGEHOV WAPENT̃.

ⓂIn *BISCOPETORP*. ħbr Godric 7 II. frs ej. III. car̃
træ ad gld. Duo ſeruiebant tcio. Nc̃: II. hōes eρ̃i. Tra. vi. c̃.
hn̄t ibi. II. car̃. 7 III. uilt 7 VII. bord̃. 7 IX. ſoch.
cū. II. car̃ 7 dim̃. 7 II. mold̃. v. ſolid. 7 XXIIII. ac̃ ρ̃ti.
T.R.E. ual. LX. ſol. m̃ ſimilit̃.

ⓂIn *TORP* ħbr Goduine 7 Gunnewate. v. bou tre
7 tciā parte uni bou ad gld̃. Tra ad. vi. boues.
Ibi hт̃ eρ̃s. I. car̃. 7 v. uilt 7 I. bord̃. cū. I. car̃. 7 IIII.
parte uni mold̃. XII. deñ. 7 I. piſcar̃ 7 dim̃. III. ſol.
7 tciā parte æcclæ. 7 VIII. ac̃s ρ̃ti. 7 XLVI. ac̃s ſiluæ
paſt̃. T.R.E. ual. III. lib̃. m̃ XXX.III. ſol. 7 IIII. deñ.

CALNODESHOV WAPENT̃.

ⓂIn *SCRENBI*. ħb Fenchel. I. car̃ træ ad gld. Tra ad. I. c̃.
Nc̃ iſde hт̃ de eρ̃o. Ibi. I. car̃. 7 IIII. uilt. v. bob arant̃.
T.R.E. ual. XL. ſol. m̃ xx. ſol.

In Aſchebi. ē ſoca huj Ⓜ. I. car̃ tre ad gld. Tra
ad. I. car̃. Ibi. II. uilt. 7 v. ac̃ ρ̃ti.

In Screnbi. ē ſoca de Eſtrecale. II. bou træ ad gld̃.

In Heretorp. ē inland de Eſtrecale 7 Hereſbi 7 Greibi.
VI. bou træ ad gld̃. Tra ad. vi. bou. Ibi. vi. uilt
7 I. ſoch. hn̄t. I. car̃. 7 I. bouē arant̃. 7 cxx. ac̃s ρ̃ti.

ⒷIn *WENFLET*. ħbr. III. frs. VII. bou tre| ad gld.
Tra ad. I. car̃. Ħ ē inland in ſuρ̃dict̃ Ⓜ.

Nc̃ Bundo 7 Radulf hn̄t ibi. x. uilt 7 I. bord̃
cū. I. car̃. 7 II. bob.   7 II. ſat. VIII. deñ.
7 qt xx. ac̃s ρ̃ti. 7 III. ac̃s.

HAVERSTOE Wapentake
FENBY hundred

40 M. In RAVENDALE Grimketill had 2 bovates of land taxable. Land for ½ plough. Walbert, the Bishop's man, ploughs it with 3 oxen. Value before 1066, 20s; now 5s.

SOUTH RIDING

WRAGGOE Wapentake

41 3 In BISCATHORPE Godric and his two brothers had 3 carucates of
M. land taxable. Two served the third. Land for 6 ploughs. Now two of the Bishop's men have 2 ploughs there.
   3 villagers, 7 smallholders and 9 Freemen with 2½ ploughs.
   2 mills, 5s; meadow, 24 acres.
Value before 1066, 60s; now the same.

42 M. In (Tattershall) THORPE Godwine and Gunnhvatr had 5 bovates of land and the third part of 1 bovate taxable. Land for 6 oxen. The Bishop has 1 plough and
   5 villagers and 1 smallholder with 1 plough; and
   the fourth part of 1 mill, 12d; 1½ fisheries, 3s; the third part
     of a church; meadow, 8 acres; woodland pasture, 46 acres.
Value before 1066 £3; now 33s 4d.

CANDLESHOE Wapentake

43 M. In SCREMBY Fenkell had 1 carucate of land taxable. Land for 1 plough. Now he also has it from the Bishop. 1 plough.
   4 villagers who plough with 5 oxen.
Value before 1066, 40s; now 20s.

44 In ASHBY (by Partney) there is a jurisdiction of this manor; 1 carucate of land taxable. Land for 1 plough.
   2 villagers.
   Meadow, 5 acres.

45 In SCREMBY there is a jurisdiction of East Keal; 2 bovates of land taxable.

46 In ADDLETHORPE there is *inland* of East Keal, Orby and Grebby; 6 bovates of land taxable. Land for 6 oxen.
   6 villagers and 1 Freeman have 1 plough and 1 ploughing ox and
   meadow, 120 acres.

47 B. In WAINFLEET 3 brothers had 7½ bovates of land taxable. Land for 1 plough. It is *inland* of the above manor. Now Bondi and Ralph have there
   10 villagers and 1 smallholder with 1 plough and 2 oxen; and
   2 salt-houses, 8d; meadow, 83 acres.

LUDES WAPENT.

☩ In CATEBI . ħbr Sūmerde 7 Ofgot . IIII . boū træ 7 dim̄

☩ In Salflatebi . I . boū ad glđ.　　　　　　　　　　ad glđ.

341 c

Tra ad . I . car 7 II . boū . Ibi Turſtin hō eƥi ħ ibi . I . car.

7 III . uilt 7 I . borđ . cū . II . bob arantes . 7 x . ac̄s ƥti . T.R.E.

ual xx . fot . m̄ xvIII . fot.　　　　　　　　　acras ƥti.

In Welletone . ē foca huj . ☩ . I . car tre ad glđ . Tra ad . I . c.

Ibi . II . foch hūt dim̄ car . 7 tciā part fedis . I . molđ . 7 x.

CALSUAD WAPENT.

☩ In HAGE 7 Calefbi . ħ Aldene . II . boū tre ad glđ.

Tra ad . III . boū . Nc Wilts hō eƥi ħ ibi . dim̄ car . 7 I . borđ.

T.R.E . ual . x . fot . m̄ x . fot.

☩ In BRVNETORP . ħ Tori . I . car træ ad glđ . Tra ad . II . car.

Ibi Nigell hō eƥi ħ . I . car . 7 VI . uilt 7 IIII . borđ . cū . I . car.

7 IX . ac̄ ƥti . T.R.E . ual . LX . fot . m̄ . LX . fot . cū dim̄ car . 7 xx . ac̄ ƥti.

B In Slodebi . dim̄ car tre ad glđ . Tra . VII . boū . Ibi VI . uilt . 7 II . borđ.

☩ In FVLLOBI . ħbr Siuuard 7 Edric . III . car tre 7 VI.

boū ad glđ . Tra ad . v . car . Ibi Wilts hō eƥi ħ . II . car.

7 v . uilt . 7 XIX . foch . hntes . II . car . 7 II . boues . Ibi . L . ac̄

ƥti . T.R.E . ual . IIII . lib . m̄ c . fot

In Oxetune . ē foca huj ☩ . I . car tre 7 dim̄ ad glđ.

Tra ad . II . car . Ibi . XI . foch hūt . II . car . 7 LX . ac̄s ƥti.

LOUTHESK Wapentake

48 2 In (South) 'CADEBY' Sumarlithi and Asgautr had 4½ bovates of
M. land taxable.

3,48 continues after 3,29.

3,29, added at the foot of col. 341b and directed by transposition signs to its correct place in the text.

29 In SALTFLEETBY 1 bovate taxable.

3,48 continued

(48) Land for 1 plough and 2 oxen. Thorsteinn, the Bishop's man,   341 c
has 1 plough there.
3 villagers and 1 smallholder who plough with 2 oxen.
Meadow, 10 acres.
Value before 1066, 20s; now 18s.

49 In WELTON (le Wold) there is a jurisdiction of this manor, 1
carucate of land taxable. Land for 1 plough.
2 Freemen have ½ plough and
the third part of 1 mill site; meadow, 10 acres.

CALCEWATH Wapentake

50 M. In HAUGH and CALCEBY Halfdan had 2 bovates of land taxable.
Land for 3 oxen. Now William, the Bishop's man, has ½ plough
there.
1 smallholder.
Value before 1066, 10s; now 10s.

51 M. In BONTHORPE Thorr had 1 carucate of land taxable. Land for 2
ploughs. Nigel, the Bishop's man, has 1 plough.
6 villagers and 4 smallholders with 1 plough.
Meadow, 9 acres.
Value before 1066, 60s; now 60s.

52 B. In SLOOTHBY, *inland*, ½ carucate of land taxable. Land for 7 oxen.
6 villagers and 2 smallholders with ½ plough.
Meadow, 20 acres.

53 2 In FULLETBY Siward and Eadric had 3 carucates of land and 6
M. bovates taxable. Land for 5 ploughs. William, the Bishop's man,
has 2 ploughs.
5 villagers and 19 Freemen who have 2 ploughs and 2 oxen.
Meadow, 50 acres.
Value before 1066 £4; now 100s.

54 In OXCOMBE and WORLABY there is a jurisdiction of this manor;
1½ carucates of land taxable. Land for 2 ploughs.
11 Freemen have 2 ploughs and
meadow, 60 acres.

ƀ In Ƙichinghehã.ẽ inland de Neutone . v . boũ træ

7 vɪ pars . ɪɪ . bouat ad glđ . Ibi . ɪ . focħ 7 ɪɪɪ . uiłł hũtes

dimiđ car̃ . Ibi hƭ eƥs dun̆ . xɪɪ . parte ũni æcclæ

Ƨ Petri . 7 vɪ . parte uni æcclæ Ƨ Mariæ . 7 vɪ . parte

de . ɪɪɪɪ . boũ træ q̆ jacent in æccła ƨ MAR.

In eođ ħđ 7 in hac eađ uilla hƭ q̆đã Vluiet de

elemofina regis . tantđ træ 7 æcclarũ partes.

7 caruc̆ 7 hõum . quanƭ fuƥdićƭũ eſt habe eƥm.

partiunƭ eni Neutone 7 quæ ibi ƥtineƭ ƥ mediũ.

⁣TERRA EƤI BAIOCENſIS.

.ɪɪɪɪ. ꝏ In CARLENTONE . ħƀ Aldremán . ɪ . car̃ ƭre ad glđ.
Ƭra ad . ɪ . car̃ . Ibi eƥs baiocenſis . ɪɪɪɪ . focħ hƭ cũ . ɪ.

car̃ 7 dim̃ . 7 ɪ . æcclam . T.R.E. uał . x . foł . 7 vɪɪɪ . den̆.

m̆ fimiliƭ . Tailla . xɪɪɪ . foł . 7 ɪɪɪɪ . den̆.

Hanc ƭra hñt Radulf̆ dapifer 7 Gisłebƭ de ganđ

ƥ figillũ eƥi baiocenſis . Ernuin̆ ƥƀr dicit eã regis . ee.

⎰ debeƭe.

.ɪɪ. ꝏ In ENGLEBI ħƀr Cħetel 7 Vlcħil . ɪɪɪ . car̃ ƭre 7 vɪ . bǒ

ad glđ . Ƭra ad . ɪɪɪɪ . car̃ . Ibi Colſuan 7 Wadarđ hǒes

eƥi Baioc̆ hñt . ɪɪ . car̃ . 7 xɪɪ . uiłł . 7 ɪɪ . focħ . 7 ɪɪɪɪ . borđ.

hũtes . ɪ . car̃ 7 dim̃ . 7 q̆ter xx . ac̃s ƥti . 7 x . 7 cx ac̃s

filuæ minutæ . T.R.E. uał xxx . foł . m̆ . ʟ . foł.

Tailla . xx foliđ.

ꝏ In STRATONE Vlcħil Asfort Reſtelf 7 Vlmer

ħƀr . vɪɪɪ . car̃ ƭre ad glđ . Ƭra ad . vɪɪɪ . car̃ . Ibi Ilƀƭ

hǒ eƥi hƭ . ɪɪɪɪ . car̃ . 7 xvɪ . uiłł cũ . ɪɪ . car̃ . 7 xxx . ac̃s

ƥti . 7 q̆ter xx . ac̃s filue minute . T.R.E. uał vɪɪ . liƀ.

m̆ . ɪɪɪɪ . liƀ . Tailla . xʟ . foł.

55 B. In THREEKINGHAM there is *inland* of Newton; 5 bovates of land and the sixth part of 2 bovates taxable.

1 Freeman and 3 villagers who have ½ plough.

The Bishop of Durham has the twelfth part of one church of St. Peter, the sixth part of one church of St. Mary and the sixth part of 4 bovates of land which lie in (the lands of) the church of St. Mary.

56 Also in this hundred and in this village a certain Wulfgeat has in alms from the King as much land and (as many) parts of churches, ploughs and men as it is said above that the Bishop has. For they divide Newton and what belongs to it, in half.

4   LAND OF THE BISHOP OF BAYEUX   342 a

1 M. In (South) CARLTON Ealdormann had 1 carucate of land taxable. Land for 1 plough. The Bishop of Bayeux has

4 Freemen with 1½ ploughs and
1 church.

Value before 1066, 10s 8d; now the same. Exactions 13s 4d.

Ralph the Steward and Gilbert of Ghent have this land by the Bishop of Bayeux' seal. Earnwine the priest states that it ought to be the King's.

2 2 In INGLEBY Ketill and Ulfketill had 3 carucates of land and 6
M. bovates taxable. Land for 4 ploughs. Kolsveinn and Wadard, the Bishop of Bayeux' men, have 2 ploughs.

12 villagers, 2 Freemen and 4 smallholders who have 1½ ploughs.

Meadow, 90 acres; underwood, 110 acres.

Value before 1066, 30s; now 50s. Exactions 20s.

3 M. In STURTON (by Stow) Ulfketill, Asfrothr, Restelf and Wulfmaer had 8 carucates of land taxable. Land for 8 ploughs. Ilbert, the Bishop's man, has 4 ploughs.

16 villagers with 2 ploughs.

Meadow, 30 acres; underwood, 80 acres.

Value before 1066 £7; now £4. Exactions 40s.

꙼ In *WELINGEHA*. hb Archil . I . car͛ 7 dm̄ ad gld͛ . T͛ra
ad XII . bō . Nc̄ Ilbt̄ hō epī ht̄ ibi . I . car͛ . 7 II . uilt . 7 III .
foch cū . I . car͛ . T.R.E . uat . xx . fot . m̄ fimilit.

꙼ In *INGEHA*. hb Gamel . I . car͛ tre ad gld͛ . T͛ra ad . XII . bō .
Nc̄ Ilbt̄ ht̄ ibi . II . car͛ . 7 II . uilt 7 III . bord͛ . 7 III . foch
hn̄tes . I . car͛ . 7 x . ac̄s p̄ti . T.R.E . uat . v . fot . m̄ xx . fot . Tailla

★ ꙼ In *GLENTEWRDE* . hb Eftan . VII . bou͛ tre͛   ʃx . fot . ✠
ad gld͛ . Ibid͛ . IIII . bou tre ad gld͛ . Soca in Glandham.
T͛ra ad . x . car͛ . Nc̄ Wadard hō epī ht̄ dm̄ car͛ . 7 VI . ⊖
foch 7 I . uilt dm̄ car͛ . 7 xxx . ac̄s p̄ti . 7 xx . T . R . E . uat xv .
fot . 7 IIII . den̄ . m̄ . XL . fot . 7 VIII . den̄ .

꙼ In *HELMESWELLE* . hb Elriod . IIII . bou͛ tre ad gld͛ . T͛ra
ad . I . car͛ . Nc̄ Lofoard hō epī ht̄ ibi . I . uilt 7 II . bord͛
cū . I . car͛ . 7 XXVII . ac̄s p̄ti . 7 dm̄ . T.R.E . uat . xx . fot . m̄ . x . s͛

꙼ In *GLANDHAM* . hbr Adeftan 7 Vlmær . x . bou͛ træ
ad gld͛ . T͛ra ad . x . bou . Ibi | Wadard . II . uilt 7 II . foch   ★
cū . I . car͛ . Ipfe . I . car͛ . 7 XL . ac̄s p̄ti . T.R.E . uat . xv . fot
7 IIII . den̄ . m̄ . LX . fot .

꙼ In *NORMANESTOV* . hb Tor . I . car͛ tre ad gld͛ . T͛ra ad . II .
car͛ . Nc̄ Ilbt̄ hō epī ht̄ . II . foch cū . I . car͛ . 7 x . ac̄s p̄ti .
T.R.E . uat x . fot m̄ XII . fot .

4 M. In WILLINGHAM (by Stow) Arnketill had 1½ carucates taxable. Land for 12 oxen. Now Ilbert, the Bishop's man, has 1 plough there.
> 2 villagers and 3 Freemen with 1 plough.
> Value before 1066, 20s; now the same.

5 M. In INGHAM Gamall had 1 carucate of land taxable. Land for 12 oxen. Now Ilbert has 2 ploughs there.
> 2 villagers, 3 smallholders and 3 Freemen who have 1 plough.
> Meadow, 10 acres.
> Value before 1066, 5s; now 20s. Exactions 10s.

4,6 is entered after 4,21 in the opposite column and directed by transposition signs to its correct place in the text.

7 S. In GLENTWORTH Steinn had 7 bovates of land taxable. Also there 4 bovates of land taxable. A jurisdiction of Glentham. Land for 10 ploughs. Now Wadard, the Bishop's man, has ½ plough.
> 6 Freemen and 1 villager [with] ½ plough.
> Meadow, 30 acres; 20 [......].
> Value before 1066, 15s 4d; now 40s 8d.

8 M. In HEMSWELL Alnoth had 4 bovates of land taxable. Land for 1 plough. Now Losoard, the Bishop's man, has there
> 1 villager and 2 smallholders with 1 plough; and
> meadow, 27½ acres.
> Value before 1066, 20s; now 10s.

9 M. In GLENTHAM Aethelstan and Wulfmaer had 10 bovates of land taxable. Land for 10 oxen. Wadard has
> 2 villagers and 1(?) Freeman with 1 plough.
> He [has] 1 plough himself and
> meadow, 40 acres.
> Value before 1066, 15s 4d; now 60s.

10 M. In NORMANBY (-by-Spital) Thorr had 1 carucate of land taxable. Land for 2 ploughs. Now Ilbert, the Bishop's man, has
> 2 Freemen with 1 plough; and
> meadow, 10 acres.
> Value before 1066, 10s; now 12s.

꤮ .II.
In *FRISEBI*.hƀr Aluui 7 Afchil.III.car tre.7 v.boū ad
glđ.Nc̄ llƀt hō eƥi kt ibi.II.caꝛ.7 VIII.uiƚƚ.7 VIII.borđ.

342 b
7 VI.foch cū.II.caꝛ.Ibi æccƚa.7 xxx.ac̄s ƥti.T.R.E.uaƚ
LX.foƚ.m̄ fimiliꞇ.Taiƚƚa.x.foƚ.

꤮ In *TORP*.hƀ Afchil x.boū ad glđ.Tra ad.II.caꝛ.
Nc̄ llƀt hō eƥi.ht ibi.I.car.7 v.uiƚƚ.7 III.borđ.cū.I.caꝛꞇ
7 x.ac̄s ƥti.T.R.E.uaƚ.xx.foƚ.m̄.xx.foƚ.

꤮ In *CLETHAM*.hƀ Afchil.VI.boū tre ad glđ.Tra ađ
XII.boū.llƀt hō eƥi ht.I.caꝛ.7 III.uiƚƚ.7 II.borđ.
cū.I.caꝛ.7 VI.ac̄s ƥti.T.R.E.uaƚ xxx.foƚ.m̄ xL.foƚ.

꤮ In *STANTONE* 7 Widingehā.hƀ Ardegrip.VI.boū
tre ad glđ.Tra ad.I.car.Ipfe.I.car. llƀt hō eƥi ht ibi.VI.uiƚƚ.
7 II.borđ cū.I.caꝛ| 7 xvi. ac̄ ƥti. T.R.E.uaƚ xx.foƚ.m̄.xI.foƚ. ★

꤮ In *ELESHAM*.hƀ Chetelbern.VII.boū tre ad glđ.
Tra ad.II.caꝛ.llƀt hō eƥi ht ibi.VI.uiƚƚ.7.I.borđ
.III. cū.I.caꝛ.7 xLVII.ac̄ ƥti.T.R.E.uaƚ xx.foƚ.m̄.xv.foƚ.

꤮ In *ALDVLVEBI*.hƀr Tofti Turuet 7 Ernui.x.boū
træ ad glđ.Tra ad.III.caꝛ.Nc̄ in dn̄io.III.caꝛ.7 xv.
uiƚƚ.7 III.foch 7 VI.borđ cū.II.caꝛ.7 LX.ac̄s ƥti.
T.R.E.uaƚ.c.foƚ.m̄ VIII.liƀ.Toꞇ xv.q̃ꝝ lg̃.7 VI.laꞇ.
Soca hvɉ ꤮.In Neutone.x.boū tre ad glđ.Tra
ad.III.car.Ibi.x.foch hn̄t.III.caꝛ.
In Sv̄merlede.v.boū tre ad gld.Tra ad.I.caꝛ 7 dim̄.
Ibi.VIII.foch hn̄t.I.car 7 II.boū arantes.

342 a, b

ᚳᛏ

11 2 In FIRSBY Alwige and Asketill had 3 carucates of land and 5
M. bovates taxable. Now Ilbert, the Bishop's man, has 2 ploughs
there.

    8 villagers, 8 smallholders and 6 Freemen with 2 ploughs.   342 b
    A church; meadow, 30 acres.

Value before 1066, 60s; now the same. Exactions 10s.

4,12 is entered at the foot of col. 342b (after 4,25), directed by transposition signs to its correct place in the text.

13 M. In (Nor)THORPE Asketill had 10 bovates taxable. Land for 2
ploughs. Now Ilbert, the Bishop's man, has 1 plough there.
    5 villagers and 3 smallholders with 1 plough.
    Meadow, 10 acres.

Value before 1066, 20s; now 20s.

14 M. In CLEATHAM Asketill had 6 bovates of land taxable. Land for 12
oxen. Ilbert, the Bishop's man, has 1 plough.
    3 villagers and 2 smallholders with 1 plough.
    Meadow, 6 acres.

Value before 1066, 30s; now 40s.

15 M. In STAINTON and WADDINGHAM Harthgripr had 6 bovates of land
taxable. Land for 1 plough. Ilbert, the Bishop's man, has 1 plough
there himself.
    6 villagers and 2 smallholders with 1 plough.
    Meadow, 16 acres.

Value before 1066, 20s; now 11(?)s.

16 M. In ELSHAM Ketilbjorn had 7 bovates of land taxable. Land for 2
ploughs. Ilbert, the Bishop's man, has there
    6 villagers and 1 smallholder with 1 plough.
    Meadow, 47 acres.

Value before 1066, 20s; now 15s.

17 3 In AUDLEBY Tosti, Thorfrothr and Earnwine had 10 bovates of
M. land taxable. Land for 3 ploughs. Now in lordship 3 ploughs;
    15 villagers, 3 Freemen and 6 smallholders with 2 ploughs.
    Meadow, 60 acres.

Value before 1066, 100s; now £8.

The whole [is] 15 furlongs long and 6 wide.

Jurisdiction of this manor:

18 In NEWTON (by Toft) 10 bovates of land taxable. Land for 3
ploughs.
    10 Freemen have 3 ploughs.

19 In *SUMERLEDE* 5 bovates of land taxable. Land for 1½ ploughs.
    8 Freemen have 1 plough and 2 ploughing oxen.

In Rifebi . i . caᵘ tre ad glð . Tra ad . ii . caᵘ . Ibi . xiiii.

foch 7 iiii . uitt hñt . iii . caᵘ . 7 xxx . i . aᶜ pᵗi 7 xii . aᶜ

filuæ minutæ . Tres lev lḡ . 7 iii . q̃⅖ laᵗ

In Chenebi . v . boū tre ad glð . Tra ad . ii . caᵘ . Ibi . viii.

foch hñt . i . caᵘ . 7 ii . boū arantes. ☞

Ƀ In *COTES* . ē inland de Ingehā . dim car tre ad glð.

✝ Tra . ad dim caᵘ . Ibi Ilƀt hᵗ . iii . uitt 7 ii . bord . hñt . i . c.

☞ In Ofgotebi . v . boū tre ad glð . Tra ad . x . boū . Ibi

ix . foch hñt . i . caᵘ 7 ii . boū arantes . Soca in Alduluebi.

ꝏ̇̇ In *NETELTONE* . ħƀr Chetelber 7 Gamel . i . caᵘ 7 vi.

boū træ ad gld . Tra ad . iii . caᵘ 7 dim . Nᷓ Ernegis

7 Wadard hoēs epi hñt ibi . ii . caᵘ . 7 xiii . uitt . 7 v.

bord . cū . i . caᵘ 7 ii . bob . 7 ii . molð . iii . foliđ . 7 lx . aᶜs

pᵗi . T.R.E. uat . lx . fot . m̂ . iiii . liƀ.

In Torefbi 7 Aluuoldebi . ē foca huj ꝏ̃ . ii . boū træ ad gld.

Ibi . fuᶮ . iiii . uitt . 7 iii . faline . 7 xx . aᶜ pᵗi.

In Rodowelle . i . boū træ ad gld . Ibi . i . foch hᵗ . i . bouē.

◐ In Neutone . ē foca de Frifebi . vi . boū tre ad gld.

Tra ad . ii . caᵘ . Ibi hᵗ Ilƀt . v . foch   cū . i . caᵘ

7 dimið . 7 xx . aᶜs pᵗi.

342 c

ꝏ̃ In *GROSBI* . ħƀ Vlchil . ii . car tre ad glð . Tra ad

iiii . caᵘ . Ibi m̂ in dñio . ii . caᵘ . 7 vi . uitt 7 vi . bord.

7 xi . foch hñtes . ii . caᵘ . Ibi æccta 7 pƀr . 7 i . molð

iii . foliđ . 7 xl . aᶜ pᵗi . T.R.E. uat . lx . fot . m̂ . c . fot.

In Sualun . ē foca huj ꝏ̃ . i . caᵘ tre ad glð.

Tra ad . ii . caᵘ . Ibi . viii . foch cū . i . caᵘ.

20   In RISBY 1 carucate of land taxable. Land for 2 ploughs.
        14 Freemen and 4 villagers have 3 ploughs.
        Meadow, 31 acres; underwood, 12 acres.
        [It is] 3 leagues long and 3 furlongs wide.

21   In KINGERBY 5 bovates of land taxable. Land for 2 ploughs.
        8 Freemen have 1 plough and 2 ploughing oxen.

4,22 is entered after the inserted 4,6.

4,6, directed by transposition signs to its correct place in the text.
6 B.   In COATES there is *inland* of Ingham; ½ carucate of land taxable.
        Land for ½ plough. Ilbert has
        3 villagers and 2 smallholders [who] have 1 plough.

22   In OSGODBY 5 bovates of land taxable. Land for 10 oxen.
        9 Freemen have 1 plough and 2 ploughing oxen.
        A jurisdiction of Audleby.

23 2   In NETTLETON Ketilbjorn and Gamall had 1 carucate and 6 bovates
   M.   of land taxable. Land for 3½ ploughs. Now Erneis and Wadard,
        the Bishop's men, have 2 ploughs there.
        13 villagers and 5 smallholders with 1 plough and 2 oxen.
        2 mills, 3s; meadow, 60 acres.
      Value before 1066, 60s; now £4.

24   In (North) THORESBY and 'AUDBY' there is a jurisdiction of this
        manor; 2 bovates of land taxable.
        4 villagers.
        3 salt-houses; meadow, 20 acres.

25   In ROTHWELL 1 bovate of land taxable.
        1 Freeman has 1 ox.

4,12, entered at the foot of col. 342b and directed by transposition signs to its correct place in the text.
12   In NEWTON (by Toft) there is a jurisdiction of Firsby; 6 bovates of
        land taxable. Land for 2 ploughs. Ilbert has
        5 Freemen with 1½ ploughs; and
        meadow, 20 acres.

26 M.   In GRASBY Ulfketill had 2 carucates of land taxable. Land for 4   342 c
        ploughs. Now in lordship 2 ploughs;
        6 villagers, 6 smallholders and 11 Freemen who have 2 ploughs.
        A church and a priest; 1 mill, 3s; meadow, 40 acres.
      Value before 1066, 60s; now 100s.

27   In SWALLOW there is a jurisdiction of this manor; 1 carucate of
        land taxable. Land for 2 ploughs.
        8 Freemen with 1 plough.

℧ In *CHELEBI*. ħb Sigar . IIII . boú træ 7 dim̃ ad glđ.
T̃ra ad . IX . bou . Ibi Wadard ħõ epĩ ħt . I . cař.
7 II . uiłł . 7 III . focħ . cũ . II . bob arantes . T.R.E. uał
xxx . foł . m̃ fimił . In Wenflet . II . bõ ad gł . T̃ra . II . boú.
In Stalinburg e͡| <u>Inland</u> soca huj ℧ . v . bou tre 7 dim̃ ad glđ.
T̃ra ad XI . bou . Ibi VIII . uiłł 7 II . focħ ħñt . I . cař.
7 c 7 q̃t xx . aćs p̃ti . 7 dim̃ mold . III . folid.

℧ In *HEGELINGE* . ħb Sigar . VII . boú tre ad glđ.
T̃ra ad . I . cař 7 VI . bou . Ibi Wadard ħõ epĩ ħt . I .
cař . 7 III . uiłł 7 v . borđ 7 II . focħ cũ . I . cař . 7 v . aćs p̃ti.
T.R.E. uał xxx . foł . m̃ XL . foł . Tailla . xx . foł.
In Cleia . e̅ foca huj ℧ , III . bouate tre ad glđ . T̃ra
ad dim̃ cař . Ibi . IIII . focħ 7 II . uiłł 7 I . borđ . ħñt . v .
boues arantes . 7 xxv . aćs p̃ti.
In Ternefco . II . boú tre ad glđ . T̃ra ad dim̃ cař . Ibi
. I . uiłł 7 III . focħ ħñt dim̃ cař.

℧ In *SVDCOTES* ħb Azor . xv . boú tre ad glđ . T̃ra
ad . IIII . cař . Nc̃ funt ibi xvI . focħ ħñtes . III . cař.
7 XL . aćs p̃ti . T.R.E. uał . xx . foł . m̃ . XL . foł.
In Cotes . v̇I . boú tre ad glđ . T̃ra ad vI . boues . Soca
in Sudcotes . Ibi . II . focħ ħñt . II . boues arañt . 7 c . aćs

℧ In *CLEIA* . ħb Algar . dim̃ cař tre ad glđ.   ⌐ p̃ti.
T̃ra ad . I . cař . Nc̃ Ilbt̃ ħt de epõ . 7 Wafta . e̅ . Ibi fuṅt
XL . ać p̃ti . T.R.E. uał x . foł . m̃ xx . foł.
In Itrebi . e̅ <u>foca</u> inland huj . ℧ . <u>na</u> I . cař tre ad glđ . T̃ra
ad . I . cař 7 dim̃ . Ibi ħt Ilbt̃ . v . focħ 7 II . uiłł . ħñtes
I . cař 7 dim̃.

28 M. In KEELBY Sigarr had 4½ bovates of land taxable. Land for 9
oxen. Wadard, the Bishop's man, has 1 plough.
2 villagers and 3 Freemen who plough with 2 oxen.
Value before 1066, 30s; now the same.

29 In *WENFLET* 2 bovates taxable. Land for 2 oxen.

30 In STALLINGBOROUGH there is *inland* of this manor; 5½ bovates of
land taxable. Land for 11 oxen.
8 villagers and 2 Freemen have 1 plough and
meadow, 180 acres; ½ mill, 3s.

31 M. In HEALING Sigarr had 7 bovates of land taxable. Land for 1
plough and 6 oxen. Wadard, the Bishop's man, has 1 plough.
3 villagers, 5 smallholders and 2 Freemen with 1 plough.
Meadow, 5 acres.
Value before 1066, 30s; now 40s. Exactions 20s.

32 In CLEE there is a jurisdiction of this manor; 3 bovates of land
taxable. Land for ½ plough.
4 Freemen, 2 villagers and 1 smallholder have 5 ploughing
oxen and
meadow, 25 acres.

33 In THRUNSCOE 2 bovates of land taxable. Land for ½ plough.
1 villager and 3 Freemen have ½ plough.

34 M. In SOUTH COATES Atsurr had 15 bovates of land taxable. Land
for 4 ploughs.
Now 16 Freemen there who have 3 ploughs and
meadow, 40 acres.
Value before 1066, 20s; now 40s.

35 In (Great) COATES 6, or 3, bovates of land taxable. Land for 6
oxen. A jurisdiction of South Coates.
2 Freemen have 2 ploughing oxen and
meadow, 100 acres.

36 M. In CLEE Algar had ½ carucate of land taxable. Land for 1 plough.
Now Ilbert has it from the Bishop. It is waste.
Meadow, 40 acres.
Value before 1066, 10s; now 20s.

37 In ITTERBY there is *inland* and a jurisdiction of this manor; 1
carucate of land taxable. Land for 1½ ploughs. Ilbert has
5 Freemen and 2 villagers who have 1½ ploughs.

ⓂIn *RASE*. ħƀ Rolf. v. boů ꞇre ad gld. 7 ɪɪɪ. partes   ★
uni bouatæ. Ꞇ'ra ad. ɪ. caꞃ 7 dim̃. Ibi Wimund hõ
eꝑi hꞇ. ɪ. caꞃ. 7 vɪɪ. uilꞇ. 7 ɪɪɪ. bord cũ. ɪ. caꞃ. 7 ɪɪ. molđ
vɪ. ſol. 7 ʟxɪ. ač ꝑti. T.R.E. ual xx. ſol. m̃. xxx. ſol

ⓂIn *RASA*. ħƀr Vlgrin. Brodos. Vlf. Goduin. Aluuin   ★
7 Leuric. ɪɪ. caꞃ 7 ɪ. boů ꞇre ad gld'. Ꞇra ad. v. caꞃ. Ibi ⹀
Wadard hõ eꝑi hꞇ xvɪɪɪ. uilꞇ. 7 xɪ. bord hñtes. v. caꞃ.
Ibi æccła 7 pƀr cũ. ɪɪ. bord. Vna boů ꞇræ huj ꝑtinet æcclæ.
Ibi. c. xx. ač ꝑti. T.R.E. ual. ʟxx. ſol. m̃. ɪɪɪɪ. liƀ.

342 d

ⓂIn *TOFTE*. ħƀ Azor. xɪɪɪɪ. boů ꞇre 7 ꞇciã parꞇe uni
bouatæ ad gld. Ꞇra ad. ɪɪɪɪ. caꞃ. Ibi Wadard hõ eꝑi
hꞇ. ɪ. caꞃ. 7 ɪɪɪ. uilꞇ 7 xɪ. ſocħ. hñtes. v. caꞃ. 7 ʟx. ačs
ꝑti. T.R.E. ual. x. ſol. m̃. ʟx. ſol. Tailla. xx. ſol.

ⓂIn *TAVELESBI*. ħƀ Rolf dim̃ caꞃ ꞇræ ad gld. Ꞇra
ad. ɪ. caꞃ. Ibi Loſoard hõ eꝑi hꞇ. ɪ. caꞃ. 7 ɪɪɪ. uilꞇ.
cũ. ɪɪɪ. boƀ arantes. 7 ɪ. molđ. ɪɪ. ſolid. 7 aliũ molđ.
qđ ꝑtin ad Groſbi. T.R.E. ual. xx. ſol. m̃ similiꞇ.

ⓂIn *TORESBI* 7 *ALWOLDEBI*. ħƀ Toruet. ɪɪɪɪ. caꞃ ꞇre
7 ɪɪɪ. bouatas. 7 vɪ. parꞇe boů. ad gld. Ꞇra ad. vɪ. caꞃ.
Ibi Ilƀt hõ eꝑi hꞇ. ɪɪ. caꞃ. 7 xx. ɪɪɪ. uilꞇ. 7 v. bord
cũ. ɪɪ. caꞃ 7 v. boƀ. 7 xxvɪɪ. ſocħ hñtes. v. caruc
. ɪɪ. boues min̄. Ibi q̃ter xx. ač ꝑti. 7 toruelande redđ
x. ſol. 7 xvɪ. ſalinæ redđ xvɪ. ſol. T.R.E. ual
vɪɪɪ. liƀ. m̃ similiꞇ. Tailla. xʟ. ſol
Hanc ꞇra cãbiauit Eduuard eꝑo baioc'.

ⓂIn *STRATONE*. ħƀ Grinchel. ɪɪɪ. caꞃ ꞇre 7 ɪɪ. boů
7 ɪɪ. partes. ɪ. boů ad gld. Ibi Ilƀt⁹ hõ eꝑi hꞇ nc̃. ɪ. caꞃ. Ꞇra. ɪɪɪɪ. caꞃ.
7 ɪɪɪ. uilꞇ 7 ɪɪɪ. borđ. 7 xxɪɪɪ. ſocħ. hñtes ɪɪɪɪ. caꞃ.
Ibi æccła. 7 ɪ. molđ. vɪɪɪ. ſol. 7 cxx. ačs ꝑti. T.R.E.
ual xʟ. ſol. m̃. ʟ. ſol. Tailla. x. ſol.

38 M. In (West) RASEN Rothulfr had 5 bovates of land taxable and 2 parts of 1 bovate. Land for 1½ ploughs. Wigmund, the Bishop's man, has 1 plough.
 7 villagers and 3 smallholders with 1 plough.
 2 mills, 6s; meadow, 61 acres.
Value before 1066, 20s; now 30s.

39 M. In (Middle) RASEN Wulfgrim, Broklauss, Ulfr, Godwine, Alwine and Leofric had 2 carucates and 1 bovate of land taxable. Land for 5 ploughs. Wadard, the Bishop's man, has
 18 villagers and 11 smallholders who have 5 ploughs.
 A church and a priest with 2 smallholders. 1 bovate of this land belongs to the church. Meadow, 120 acres.
Value before 1066, 70s; now £4.

40 M. In TOFT (next Newton) Atsurr had 14 bovates of land and the third part of 1 bovate taxable. Land for 4 ploughs. Wadard, the Bishop's man, has 1 plough.
 3 villagers and 11 Freemen who have 5 ploughs and meadow, 60 acres.
Value before 1066, 10s; now 60s. Exactions 20s.

342 d

41 M. In TEALBY Rothulfr had ½ carucate of land taxable. Land for 1 plough. Losoard, the Bishop's man, has 1 plough.
 3 villagers who plough with 3 oxen.
 1 mill, 2s; another mill which belongs to Grasby.
Value before 1066, 20s; now the same.

42 M. In (North) THORESBY and 'AUDBY' Thorfrothr had 4 carucates of land, 3 bovates and the sixth part of 1 bovate taxable. Land for 6 ploughs. Ilbert the Bishop's man, has 2 ploughs.
 23 villagers and 5 smallholders with 2 ploughs and 5 oxen.
  27 Freemen who have 5 ploughs, less 2 oxen.
 Meadow, 80 acres; turf-land which pays 10s; 16 salt-houses which pay 16s.
Value before 1066 £8; now the same. Exactions 40s.
 Edward exchanged this land with the Bishop of Bayeux.

43 M. In (Great) STURTON Grimketill had 3 carucates of land, 2 bovates and 2 parts of 1 bovate taxable. Land for 4 ploughs. Now Ilbert, the Bishop's man, has 1 plough.
 3 villagers, 3 smallholders and 23 Freemen who have 4 ploughs.
 A church; 1 mill, 8s; meadow, 120 acres.
Value before 1066, 40s; now 50s. Exactions 10s.

In Randebi . ē inland 7 ſoca huǰ ⊙̃ . Nouē boū

trǽ ad glđ . Ťra ad . ɪɪ . caŕ . Ibi nē in dñio . ɪ . caŕ.

7 ɪɪɪ . uiłł 7 ɪ . borđ . 7 ɪɪɪɪ . ſocħ hñtes . ɪ . caŕ . 7 cc . ac̃

p̃ti . Ibi æccła ad quā ptiñ xʟ . ac̃ trǽ . 7 v . ac̃ p̃ti.

Ibi p̄r hñs dim̃ caŕ.

In Burgrede . ē ſoca . ɪɪɪ . boū trǽ ad glđ . Ťra ad dim̃

caŕ . Ibi . ē un uiłłſ 7 ɪ . borđ . hñtes . ɪ . boū arantē.

7 xv . ac̃ p̃ti . 7 cxx . ac̃ ſilue paſt . 7 c . ac̃ ſilue miñ.

⊙̃ In HAINTONE . ħb Rolf xv . boū trǽ ad glđ . Ťra

ad . ɪɪɪ . caŕ 7 vɪ . boū : Ibi Ilbt̃ hō ep̃i hē dim̃ caŕ.

7 ɪx . uiłł 7 ɪɪ . borđ . 7 ɪ . ſocħ . hñtes . ɪɪ . caŕ . 7 c . ac̃ p̃ti.

T.R.E. uał xʟ . ſoł . m̊ ſimiliŧ . ✕

In Strubi . ɪɪ . boū tre ad glđ . Ťra ad dim̃ caŕ . Ibi ^{Soca.ē}

ɪɪɪ . ſocħ hñt dim̃ caŕ.

In Bacuurde . ɪɪɪ . boū tre ad glđ . Ťra ad . vɪ . boū.

Ibi . ɪɪɪ . ſocħ . hñt dim̃ caŕ.

⊙̃ In SOTEBI . ħb Vlnod . ɪɪɪɪ . caŕ trǽ ad glđ . Ťra

ad . vɪ . caŕ . Ibi Radulf hō ep̃i hē xvɪ . ſocħ.

7 ɪɪɪ . uiłł cū . ɪɪɪɪ . caŕ . In dñio nihil . Ibi æccła.

7 cʟ . ac̃ p̃ti . T.R.E. uał . ɪɪɪ . lib̃ . m̊ . ɪɪɪɪ . lib̃.

In LANGETONE . 7 in TORP . ħb Lepſi . ɪ . caŕ trǽ

ad glđ . Ťra ad . ɪ . caŕ 7 dimiđ . Ibi un hō ep̃i hē

✕ In Sutreie . jnland in Haintone . ɪɪ . boū tre ad glđ . Ťra ad

dim̃ caŕ . Ibi . ɪɪ . uiłł hñt dim̃ caŕ . 7 ɪɪɪɪ . ac̃ p̃ti . 7 xx . ac̃ ſiluæ.

. ɪ . caŕ . 7 xxvɪ . uiłł . 7 ɪɪɪ . ſocħ hñtes . v . boū arantes.

7 ʟx . ac̃s p̃ti . 7 q̃ter xx . ac̃s ſiluæ paſt p̄ loca . T.R.E.

uał . xʟ . ſoł . m̊ ſimiliŧ.

44 In RANBY there is *inland* and a jurisdiction of this manor; 9
bovates of land taxable. Land for 2 ploughs. Now in lordship
1 plough;
> 3 villagers, 1 smallholder and 4 Freemen who have 1 plough.
> Meadow, 200 acres. A church to which belong 40 acres of
> land and meadow, 5 acres. A priest who has ½ plough.

45 In 'BURRETH' there is a jurisdiction; 3 bovates of land taxable.
Land for ½ plough.
> 1 villager and 1 smallholder who have 1 ploughing ox.
> Meadow, 15 acres; woodland pasture, 120 acres; underwood,
> 100 acres.

46 M. In HAINTON Rothulfr had 15 bovates of land taxable. Land for 3
ploughs and 6 oxen. Ilbert, the Bishop's man, has ½ plough.
> 9 villagers, 2 smallholders and 1 Freeman who have 2 ploughs.
> Meadow, 100 acres.

Value before 1066, 40s; now the same.

4,47 is entered at the foot of col. 342d (in the middle of 4,51), directed by transposition
signs to its correct place in the text.

48 In STRUBBY 2 bovates of land taxable. Land for ½ plough. It is a
jurisdiction.
> 3 Freemen have ½ plough.

49 In BARKWITH 3 bovates of land taxable. Land for 6 oxen.
> 3 Freemen have ½ plough.

50 M. In SOTBY Wulfnoth had 4 carucates of land taxable. Land for 6
ploughs. Ralph, the Bishop's man, has
> 16 Freemen and 3 villagers with 4 ploughs.
> In lordship nothing.
> A church; meadow, 150 acres.

Value before 1066 £3; now £4.

51 In LANGTON and *TORP* Leofsige had 1 carucate of land taxable.
Land for 1½ ploughs. A man of the Bishop's has

4,51 continues at the top of col. 343a (after 4,47).

4,47, entered at the foot of col. 342d and directed by transposition signs to its correct place
in the text.

47 In SOUTHREY, *inland* of Hainton, 2 bovates of land taxable. Land
for ½ plough.
> 2 villagers have ½ plough.
> Meadow, 4 acres; woodland 20 acres.

4,51 continued

(51) 1 plough.

> 26 villagers and 3 Freemen who have 5 ploughing oxen and
> meadow, 60 acres; woodland, pasture in places, 80 acres.

Value before 1066, 40s; now the same.

In Stinblebi . ē inland 7 ſoca hujꝰ . ꝏ̄ . Decē bou̅ tr̄æ
ad glđ . Tra ad . XIIII . bou̅ . Ibi . v . uilli 7 III . ſocħ hn̅t
II . caꞃ̄ . 7 XII . ac̄ p̄ti . 7 xxx . ac̄ ſilue minutæ.

ꝏ̄ In *VLINGEHĀ* . hb̄ Aſchil . vi . bou̅ tre 7 dimiđ ad glđ.
Tra ad . XIII . bou̅ . Ibi Wadard hꞇ̄ . I . caꞃ̄ . 7 IIII . uilt
7 I . borđ cū . I . caꞃ̄ . 7 xxxvi . ac̄ p̄ti . T . R . E . ual . xx . ſol.
m̊ XL . ſol.

ꝏ̄ In *CHIRCHEBI* . hb̄ Wlmar . x . bou̅ tr̄æ ad glđ.
Tra ad . I . caꞃ̄ 7 dim̄ . Ibi Ilb̄t hō ep̄i hꞇ̄ . I . caꞃ̄ . 7 xꝛ
uilt . 7 IIII . borđ cū . I . caꞃ̄ . 7 ſedē molđ . 7 XII . ac̄s
p̄ti . 7 CLX ac̄s ſiluæ paſt p̄ loca . T . R . E . ual . XL . ſol
m̊ . xx . ſol.

♀ ꝏ̄ In *SISSE* . hb̄ Gudmunt . vi . bou̅ tre|ad glđ . Tra ad
IX . boues . Ibi Ilb̄t hō ep̄i hꞇ̄ . I . caꞃ̄ . 7 III . uilt . 7 I . borđ
7 II . ſocħ hn̅tes dim̄ caꞃ̄ . Ibi eccła 7 xẍ . ac̄ p̄ti . T . R . E .
ual . xx . ſol . m̊ xx . ſol.

ꝏ̄ In *COCRINTONE* . hb̄r Aſchil 7 Vlgrin . III . caꞃ̄ tre|
ad glđ . Tra ad . vi . caꞃ̄ . Ibi Ilb̄t hō ep̄i hꞇ̄ . II . caꞃ̄ .
7 vii . uilt 7 IIII . borđ . 7 xxvii . ſocħ hn̅tes . III . caꞃ̄ .
Ibi q̊t xx . ac̄ p̄ti . 7 LX . ac̄ ſilue minute . 7 II . partes
uni̊ molđ . II . ſolidoꝛ . T . R . E . ual . LX . ſol . m̊ ſimilitꝛ.
Tailla . xx . ſol.

In Aluingehā . IIII . bou̅ tr̄æ 7 II . partes uni̊ bou̅ ad glđ.
Tra ad . I . caꞃ̄ . Soca de Cocrinꞇ̄ . Ibi . IIII . ſocħ hn̅t . I . caꞃ̄ .
7 vii . ac̄ p̄ti.

ꝏ̄ In *ABI* . hb̄r Vlſtan 7 Aſchil . XIIII . bou̅ tre ad glđ.
Tra ad . II . caꞃ̄ 7 vi . boues . Ibi Wadard hō ep̄i hꞇ̄
. I . caꞃ̄ . 7 7 XII . uilt 7 IIII . ſocħ . 7 II . borđ . hntes . II . caꞃ̄
7 dim̄ . 7 q̊t xx . ac̄ p̄ti . 7 xxvii . ac̄ ſilue paſt . 7 CCC .
ac̄s ſiluæ minutæ . T . R . E . ual . III . liƀ . m̊ . IIII . liƀ.

52 In THIMBLEBY there is *inland* and a jurisdiction of this manor; 10 bovates of land taxable. Land for 14 oxen.
   5 villagers and 3 Freemen have 2 ploughs.
   Meadow, 12 acres; underwood, 30 acres.

53 M. In (South) WILLINGHAM Asketill had 6½ bovates of land taxable. Land for 13 oxen. Wadard has 1 plough.
   4 villagers and 1 smallholder with 1 plough.
   Meadow, 36 acres.
   Value before 1066, 20s; now 40s.

54 M. In KIRKBY (on Bain) Wulfmaer had 10 bovates of land taxable. Land for 1½ ploughs. Ilbert, the Bishop's man, has 1 plough and
   10 villagers and 4 smallholders with 1 plough; and
   a mill site; meadow, 12 acres; woodland, pasture in places, 160 acres.
   Value before 1066, 40s; now 20s.

Ψ *4,55 is added at the foot of col. 343a (in the middle of 4,63) and is directed by transposition signs to its correct place in the text.*

56 M. In SIXHILLS Guthmundr had 6½ bovates of land taxable. Land for 9 oxen. Ilbert, the Bishop's man, has 1 plough.
   3 villagers, 1 smallholder and 2 Freemen who have ½ plough.
   A church; meadow, 25 acres.
   Value before 1066, 20s; now 20s.

57 M. In COCKERINGTON Asketill and Wulfgrim had 3 carucates of land and 1 bovate taxable. Land for 6 ploughs. Ilbert, the Bishop's man, has 2 ploughs.
   7 villagers, 4 smallholders and 27 Freemen who have 3 ploughs.
   Meadow, 80 acres; underwood, 60 acres; 2 parts of 1 mill, 2s.
   Value before 1066, 60s; now the same. Exactions 20s.

58 In ALVINGHAM 4 bovates of land and 2 parts of 1 bovate taxable. Land for 1 plough. A jurisdiction of Cockerington.
   4 Freemen have 1 plough.
   Meadow, 7 acres.

59 M. In ABY Wulfstan and Asketill had 14 bovates of land taxable. Land for 2 ploughs and 6 oxen. Wadard, the Bishop's man, has 1 plough.
   12 villagers, 4 Freemen and 2 smallholders who have 2½ ploughs.
   Meadow, 80 acres; woodland pasture, 27 acres; underwood, 300 acres.
   Value before 1066 £3; now £4.

In Strobi.ı.car̄ 7 ıı.bou̇̇ træ ad glđ.Ťra ad.ıı.car̄
7 dı̄m.Ibi.v.focħ 7 ıııı.uiłł hn̄t.ıı.car̄.Soca in Abi.

ᴔ In *Rigesbi*.ħƀr Turulf 7 Outƀt.x.bou̇ ťre ad glđ.
Ťra ad.ıı.car̄.Ibi Lofoard hō epı̄ hƚ.ı.car̄.7 v.uiłł.
7 ııı.borđ.cū dimiđ car̄.7 cxx aꝯ̄ filue paſt̛.7 ʟx.aꝯ̄
filuæ minutæ.T.R.E.uał.ʟx.fot.m̄ fimilit̛.
In Welle.ı.bou̇ ťre ad glđ.Ťra ad.ııı.bou̇.Soca in Ri
gefbi.Ibi.ı.focħ 7 ı̊ı.uiłłı.
In Alebi.v.bou̇̇ ťre ad glđ.Ťra ad.x.bou̇.Soca in Rigefbi.
⳨ In *Torp*.ħ̄ƀ Vlmar.ıı.car̄ ťre ad glđ ꝑ ᴔ.Ťra.ıı.ꝯ.Ibi ſƚ.xvııı.
uiłłı 7 ıʟıı.borđ cū.ı.ꝯ.7 xvı.aꝯ̄ p̄ti.7 cxx.aꝯ̄ filue paſtit̛.7 ťcia pars
xıı.molinoꝝ de.vıı.fot.7 ııı.pifcarie de.xxx.den̄ Valuit 7 uał.xx.fot.
Eudo ten̄ de rege.

343 b
Ibi.ııı.focħ.7 ıı.borđ hn̄t.ı.car̄.7 xıı.aꝯ̄s p̄ti.7 xıı.aꝯ̄s
filuæ paſt.7 xʟ.aꝯ̄s filue minute.
In Touedebi.dı̄m car̄ ťre ad glđ.Ťra ad.x.bou̇.Soca Rigefbi.
Ibi.ııı.focħ.ıııı.bo̊b arant.7 xx.aꝯ̄ p̄ti.7 xıı.aꝯ̄ filuæ.

ᴔ In *Aschebi* ħƀr Odincarle^{7 Chiluert}.ıııı.car̄ ťræ ad glđ.Ťra
ad.v.car̄.Nꝯ̄ in dn̄io ep̄s hƚ ibi.ı.car̄.7 ıx.uiłł.
7 ıı.borđ.7 xıııı.focħ.hn̄tes.ııı.car̄.7 ıı.molđ.ıııı.
foliđ 7 vı.den̄.7 xxxı.aꝯ̄ p̄ti.T.R.E.uał.ııı.lib.m̄.vıı.łƀ.
In Andrebi 7 Marchebi vıı.bou̇̇ ťre ad gld.Ťra ad.ı.car̄.
Soca Afchebi.Ibi.xııı.focħ 7 x.uiłł 7 ı.borđ.hn̄t.ıı.car̄.
7 xıı.aꝯ̄ p̄ti.

60 In STRUBBY 1 carucate and 2 bovates of land taxable. Land for
2½ ploughs.
> 5 Freemen and 4 villagers have 2 ploughs.
A jurisdiction of Aby.

61 M. In RIGSBY Thorulfr and Authbjorn had 10 bovates of land
taxable. Land for 2 ploughs. Losoard, the Bishop's man, has 1
plough.
> 5 villagers and 3 smallholders with ½ plough.
Woodland pasture, 120 acres; underwood, 60 acres.
Value before 1066, 60s; now the same.

62 In WELL 1 bovate of land taxable. Land for 3 oxen. A jurisdiction
of Rigsby.
> 1 Freeman and 2 villagers.

63 In AILBY 5 bovates of land taxable. Land for 10 oxen. A
jurisdiction of Rigsby.

4,63 continues at the top of col. 343b (after 4,55).

*4,55, entered at the foot of col. 343a and directed by transposition signs to its correct place
in the text.*

55 In (Tattershall) THORPE Wulfmaer had 2 carucates of land taxable
as a manor. Land for 2 ploughs.
> 18 villagers and 4 smallholders with 1 plough.
Meadow, 16 acres; woodland pasture, 120 acres; the third part
of 2 mills at 7s; 3 fisheries at 30d.
The value was and is 20s.
Eudo holds from the King.

4,63 continued

(63) 3 Freemen and 2 smallholders have 1 plough and   343 b
meadow, 12 acres; woodland pasture, 12 acres; underwood,
40 acres.

64 In TOTHBY ½ carucate of land taxable. Land for 10 oxen.
A jurisdiction [of] Rigsby.
> 3 Freemen plough with 3 oxen.
Meadow, 20 acres; woodland, 12 acres.

65 M. In ASHBY (Puerorum) Othenkarl and Ketilbjorn had 4 carucates of
land taxable. Land for 5 ploughs. Now the Bishop has in lordship
1 plough;
> 9 villagers, 2 smallholders and 14 Freemen who have 3 ploughs.
2 mills, 3s 6d; meadow, 31 acres.
Value before 1066 £3; now £7.

66 In (Bag) ENDERBY, 3 bovates, and MARKBY, 4 bovates: 7 bovates of
land taxable. Land for 1 plough. A jurisdiction [of] Ashby.
> 14 Freemen, 10 villagers and 1 smallholder have 2 ploughs.
Meadow, 12 acres.

Ⓜ In *Aschebi* ħɓ Algar . ix . bou tre ad glđ . Tra ad . ii . car
7 ii . bou . Ibi Ilɓt hō epi ħt dim car . 7 ii . uilt . 7 ii . borđ.
7 viii . focħ cū . i . car . 7 i . molđ . iii . folid . 7 xxx . acs p̃ti.
7 vi . acs filue min . T.R.E . ual xxx . fot . m̃ xl . fot . Tailla . xx . s.
In Brigeflai . 7 Wade . 7 Rauenedal . ii . car tre 7 v . bou
7 dim̃ ad glđ . Tra ad . iiii . car 7 vi . bou . Soca in Afchebi.
Ibi xiii . focħ 7 x . uilt hn̄t . iiii . car . 7 xxv . ac̃ p̃ti.

Ⓜ In *Levesbi* 7 Bredelou 7 Scarhou ħɓr Suuen Arich
7 Tofti . ix . car tre ad glđ . Tra ad . xvi . car . Ibi eps Baioc̃
in dn̄io ħt . iii . car . 7 iiii . uilt . 7 v . borđ . 7 lxxxv.
focħ . hn̄tes xiii . car 7 dim̃ . Ibi . iii . æcclæ cū pɓris.
7 ii . molđ . viii . folid . 7 ccc.lx . ac̃ p̃ti . 7 c . ac̃ filuæ min.
In Grimefbi c̃fuetudines 7 paffagiū redđ . xl . fot.
T.R.E . ual . xii . liɓ . m̃ xxx . liɓ.
In Grimefbi 7 Cleia 7 Itrebi 7 Ternescou . Soca huj Ⓜ.
ad glđ iii . car 7 i . bou tre ad gld . Tra ad . v . car 7 vii . bou.
Ibi . lv . focħ 7 i . uilt hn̄t . vi . car . 7 liiii . acs p̃ti.

Ⓜ In *Wichale* . ħɓr Afchil 7 Outgrim . iii . car træ 7 dim̃ . tcia
parte . i . bō min ad glđ . Tra ad . vi . car . Ibi Ilɓt hō epi ħt
. i . car . 7 iiii . uilt . 7 xl . ii . focħ . hn̄tes vi . car . 7 ii . partes
molđ . xxvi . denar . 7 lvi . acs p̃ti . T.R.E . ual . iiii . liɓ.
m̃ similit . Tailla . xx . fot.
Ⓜ In *Stivetone* . ħɓ Afchil . iii . bou tre ad glđ . Tra ad . vi.
bou . Ibi Ilɓt ħt . i . car . 7 i . borđ . 7 iii . acs p̃ti . 7 lx acs
filuæ paft . T.R.E . ual . xx . fot . m̃ xv . fot.
Ⓜ In *Aresbi* . ħɓ Gamel . ii . car træ ad glđ . Tra ad . iiii.
car . Ibi Wadard hō epi ħt . i . car . 7 v . uilt 7 iiii . borđ
7 xx . vi . focħ hn̄tes . v . car . 7 cxxx . acs p̃ti . T.R.E . ual
xl . fot . m̃ . lx . fot . Tailla . xx . fot.

67 M. In ASHBY Algar had 9 bovates of land taxable. Land for 2 ploughs and 2 oxen. Ilbert, the Bishop's man, has ½ plough.
2 villagers, 2 smallholders and 8 Freemen with 1 plough.
1 mill, 3s; meadow, 30 acres; underwood, 6 acres.
Value before 1066, 30s; now 40s. Exactions 20s.

68 In BRIGSLEY, WAITHE and RAVENDALE 2 carucates of land and 5½ bovates taxable. Land for 4 ploughs and 6 oxen. A jurisdiction of Ashby.
13 Freemen and 10 villagers have 4 ploughs.
Meadow, 25 acres.

69 3 In LACEBY, BRADLEY and SCARTHO Sveinn, Eirikr and Tosti had 9
M. carucates of land taxable. Land for 16 ploughs. The Bishop of Bayeux has in lordship 3 ploughs;
4 villagers, 5 smallholders and 85 Freemen who have 13½ ploughs.
3 churches with priests; 2 mills, 8s; meadow, 360 acres; underwood, 100 acres.

70 In (Great) GRIMSBY customary dues and the ferry pay 40s.
Value before 1066 £12; now £30.

71 In (Great) GRIMSBY 11 bovates, CLEE 3 bovates and the third part of 1 bovate, ITTERBY 4 bovates and THRUNSCOE 7 bovates. A jurisdiction of this manor. 3 carucates and 1 bovate of land taxable. Land for 5 ploughs and 7 oxen.
55 Freemen and 1 villager have 6 ploughs and meadow, 54 acres.

72 2 In WITHCALL Asketill and Authgrimr had 3½ carucates of land,
M. less the third part of 1 bovate, taxable. Land for 6 ploughs.
Ilbert, the Bishop's man, has 1 plough.
4 villagers and 42 Freemen who have 6 ploughs and 2 parts of a mill, 26d; meadow, 56 acres.
Value before 1066 £4; now the same. Exactions 20s.

73 M. In STEWTON Asketill had 3 bovates of land taxable. Land for 6 oxen. Ilbert has 1 plough.
1 smallholder.
Meadow, 3 acres; woodland pasture, 60 acres.
Value before 1066, 20s; now 15s.

74 M. In OWERSBY Gamall had 2 carucates of land taxable. Land for 4 ploughs. Wadard, the Bishop's man, has 1 plough.
5 villagers, 4 smallholders and 26 Freemen who have 5 ploughs and meadow, 130 acres.
Value before 1066, 40s; now 60s. Exactions 20s.

ᴥ In *TORGREBI* . ħƀ Aluric xv . boᷘ træ ad glđ.

Tra ad . iii . caᷞ 7 vi . boᷘ . Ibi eᵱs . i . caᷞ . hᷓ . 7 viii . aᷗs ᵱti.
T.R.E. uaƚ . xl . foƚ . ᷙ . xx . foƚ.

ᴥ In *DODINTVNE* . ħƀ Gladuine . vi . boᷘ tre ad glđ.
Tra ad . vi . boᷘ . Ibi Baldric ᷘ hō eᵱi . ii . uiƚt 7 ii . borđ.
cᷘ . i . caᷞ . 7 dimiđ molđ . iii . foliđ . 7 x . aᷗs ᵱti . Valet

ᴥ In *CLAIPOL* . ħƀ Turuert . iii . caᷞ træ ⌐x . foƚ.
7 i . boᷘ ad glđ . Tra ad . iii . caᷞ . Ibi eᵱs hᷓ . i . caᷞ.
7 vi . uiƚt . 7 iii . borđ . cᷘ . i . caᷞ 7 diᷙ . 7 xv . aᷗ ᵱti.
T.R.E . xl . foƚ . ᷙ xxx . foƚ.

ᴥ In *KASCHINGETORP* . ħƀ Turuert . i . caᷞ træ 7 diᷙ
ad glđ . Tra ad xiiii . boᷘ . Ibi Suuen hō eᵱi hᷓ . v . uiƚt
7 i . borđ . cᷘ . i . caᷞ . 7 x . aᷗs ᵱti . T.R.E . uaƚ xl . foƚ . ᷙ . xxx.

ᴥ In *STAPLEFORDE* . ħƀ Turuert . ii . caᷞ tre ad glđ . Tra
ad . i . caᷞ . Ibi Tor hō eᵱi hᷓ . i . caᷞ . 7 iii . uiƚt 7 i . borđ
arantes . vi . boᷘƀ . Vna q̃ᷔ ᵱti . 7 dimiđ . T.R.E . uaƚ . xx.
foƚ . ᷙ fimiliᷓ.

In *CANVIC* . ħƀ Efcule . i . caᷞ 7 diᷙ ad glđ . Tra ad xii . bō.
.ii. Ibi Ilƀt hᷓ . ii . caᷞ . 7 ii . 7 i . borđ . 7 xxvii . aᷗs ᵱti.

ᴥ In *OVNEBI* . ħƀr Rolf 7 Siuuard . v . boᷘ træ ad glđ.
Tra ad . v . boᷘ . Ibi Ilƀt ᷘ 7 Wadard ᷘ hñt . v . boᷘ iɴ
carruca . 7 ix . aᷗs ᵱti . T.R.E . uaƚ . xv . foƚ . ᷙ xx . foƚ.
⌐7 . viii . deɴ.

TERRA OSMVNDI EᵱI.

.V. In *LVNDETORP* . funt xv . bouatæ træ ad glđ . Tra . ii.
carucarᷘ . Ħ tra ᵱtiñ ad æccƚam de Granthā . 7 ē đeta
ab oᷙibᷔ feruitijs . Ibi hᷓ Ofmund ᷘ eᵱs . vii . uiƚt cᷘ . i.
caᷞ . 7 xiii . aᷗs ᵱti.

75 M. In THORGANBY Aelfric had 15 bovates of land taxable. Land for 3   343 c
ploughs and 6 oxen. The Bishop has 1 plough and
    meadow, 8 acres.
Value before 1066, 40s; now 20s.

76 M. In (Dry) DODDINGTON Gladwine had 6 bovates of land taxable.
Land for 6 oxen. Baldric, the Bishop's man, has
    2 villagers and 2 smallholders with 1 plough.
    ½ mill, 3s; meadow, 10 acres.
Value 10s.

77 M. In CLAYPOLE Thorfrothr had 3 carucates of land and 1 bovate
taxable. Land for 3 ploughs. The Bishop has 1 plough.
    6 villagers and 3 smallholders with 1½ ploughs.
    Meadow, 15 acres.
[Value] before 1066, 40s; now 30s.

78 M. In 'CASTHORPE' Thorfrothr had 1½ carucates of land taxable. Land
for 14 oxen. Sveinn, the Bishop's man, has
    5 villagers and 1 smallholder with 1 plough.
    Meadow, 10 acres.
Value before 1066, 40s; now 30[s].

79 M. In STAPLEFORD Thorfrothr had 2 carucates of land taxable. Land
for 1 plough. Thorr, the Bishop's man, has 1 plough.
    3 villagers and 1 smallholder who plough with 6 oxen.
    Meadow, 1½ furlongs.
Value before 1066, 20s; now the same.

80   In CANWICK Skuli had 1½ carucates taxable. Land for 12 oxen.
Ilbert has 2 ploughs and
    2 .... and 1 smallholder.
    Meadow, 27 acres.

81 2 In OWMBY (-by-Spital) Rothulfr and Siward had 5 bovates of land
M. taxable. Land for 5 oxen. Ilbert and Wadard have 5 oxen in a
plough and
    meadow, 9 acres.
Value before 1066, 15s; now 20s 8d.

5   LAND OF BISHOP OSMUND   343 d

1   In LONDONTHORPE 15 bovates of land taxable. Land for 2 ploughs.
This land belongs to the Church of Grantham and is exempt
from all services. Bishop Osmund has
    7 villagers with 1 plough.
    Meadow, 13 acres.

In Nongetune h� S̃ Wlfrann de Granthā dim̃ car̃ træ
ad gld̃ . T̃ra . iiii . bob . Ibi . i . uiłłs arat . ii . bob.
In Gunfordebi hͭ S̃ Wlfrann de Grāħ . i . car̃ træ ad gld̃.
cū ſaca 7 ſoca . Tra . xii . boū.
p̄ciū huj̃ træ cōputat̃ cū æccła de Granthā.

GOISFRIDI EṔI.

.VI. ꟷ **I**n CANVIC 7 Brachebrige . ħb̃ Vlf . vi . car̃ tre
ad gld̃ . T̃ra totid̃ car̃ . Ibi hͭ Goisfrid eṕs . i . car̃ 7 dim.
7 ii· . ſoch de . xi . bou huj̃ tre . 7 xii . uiłł 7 xi . bord̃
hͤntes . ii . car̃ 7 dimid̃ . 7 iii . piſcar̃ de . iii . ſolid̃ . 7 q̃t̃ xx.
ac̃s ṕti . T.R.E. 7 m̃ uał . lx . ſoł . Tailla . x . ſoł.

344 a

TERRA EṔI LINCOLIENSIS.

.VII. **I**n SC̃Æ MARIÆ STOV . ſunt . iiii . carucate træ ad gld̃ .
T̃ra . ē ad . iiii . car̃ . Ibi eṕs Remigius . in dño . i.
car̃ . 7 xx . uiłł 7 iii . ſoch hͤntes . iii . car̃ 7 dimidiā.
Ibi æccła 7 pb̃r 7 iii . ferrariæ . T.R.E. uał . xxx.ii . lib̃.
m̃ xxx . lib̃ . Ex ea tra hñt . ii . milites qd̃ ualet . xxx . ſoł.
In Welingehā . ē inland huj̃ ꟷ . Decē bouatæ træ.
7 iii . pars duar̃ bou . T̃ra ad tntd̃ . Due bouate ſuᶰ
de q̃b꜔ Gozeł ħt ſocā.
In Couenebi . Inland de Stou . iiii . car̃ tre ad gld̃ . T̃ra
ad . iiii . car̃ . Ibi . xx . ſoch 7 xv . bord̃ . hñt . v . car̃ . Ibi
æccła . 7 i . mołd̃ . iiii . ſolid̃ . 7 xx . ac̃ ṕti.
In Nortune . vi . car̃ tre ad gld . T̃ra ad . vi . car̃ . Inland
7 Soca in Stou . Ibi in dño . iii . car̃ . 7 xxv . ſoch . 7 iiii·
uiłł . 7 xxi . bord̃ . hñt . v . car̃ . Ibi uñ hō eṕi hͭ . i . car̃.
Ibi ſed mołd̃ . 7 cccc.xxx : ac̃ ṕti.

2　In *NONGETUNE* St. Wulfram's of Grantham has ½ carucate of land taxable. Land for 4 oxen.
　　1 villager ploughs with 2 oxen.

3　In GONERBY St. Wulfram's of Grantham has 1 carucate of land taxable with full jurisdiction. Land for 12 oxen.

The assessment of this land is accounted for with the Church of Grantham.

6　　　[LAND] OF BISHOP GEOFFREY

1 2　In CANWICK and BRACEBRIDGE Ulfr had 6 carucates of land taxable.
M.　Land for as many ploughs. Bishop Geoffrey has 1½ ploughs.
　　　2 Freemen on 11 bovates of this land; 12 villagers and
　　　　11 smallholders who have 2½ ploughs.
　　　3 fisheries at 3s; meadow, 80 acres.
Value before 1066 and now, 60s. Exactions 10s.

7　　　LAND OF THE BISHOP OF LINCOLN　　344 a

1　In STOW ST. MARY 4 carucates of land taxable. Land for 4 ploughs.
Bishop Remigius [has] in lordship 1 plough;
　　　20 villagers and 3 Freemen who have 3½ ploughs.
　　　A church and a priest; 3 smithies.
　　Value before 1066 £32; now £30.
　　Of this land 2 men-at-arms have what is valued at 30s.

2　In WILLINGHAM (by Stow) there is *inland* of this manor; 10 bovates of land and the third part of 2 bovates. Land for as much.
　　2 bovates of which Jocelyn has the jurisdiction.

3　In CAENBY, *inland* of Stow, 4 carucates of land taxable. Land for 4 ploughs.
　　　20 Freemen and 15 smallholders have 5 ploughs.
　　　A church; 1 mill, 4s; meadow, 20 acres.

4　In (Bishop) NORTON 6 carucates of land taxable. Land for 6 ploughs. *Inland* and a jurisdiction of Stow. In lordship 3 ploughs.
　　　25 Freemen, 4 villagers and 21 smallholders have 5 ploughs.
　　　One of the Bishop's men has 1 plough.
　　　A mill site; meadow, 430 acres.

In Glenthā . III . car̃ tre 7 VI . boũ ad glð . Tra ad . III .

car̃ . 7 VI . boũ . Soca in Stou . Ibi . XVI . foch̃ . 7 XI . borð

hñt . V . car̃ . 7 cx . ac̃ p̃ti .

In Ounebi . IIII . car̃ tre 7 III . boũ ad glð . Tra ad tntð .

Ibi XVII . foch̃ hñt . V . car̃ 7 dim̃ . 7 XXI . ac̃ p̃ti .

In Opetune 7 Cheftefbi 7 Normanebi . Soca de Stou .

XI . car̃ træ . 7 VI . boũ 7 IIII . part . II . bouat . 7 II . part̃ dim̃ bõ

ad glð . Tra ad . X . car̃

Ibi XX . foch̃ 7 VII . borð . hñt . VI . car̃ 7 dimið .

7 CLXXI . ac̃ p̃ti . 7 CLXII . ac̃s filuæ minutæ .

ⓂIn WELLETONE h̃b Suuen XII . car̃ tre ad glð . Tra ad

XVI . car̃ . Nc̃ hñt| .VI . canonici de lincole . V . car̃ in dñio .

7 XLVIII . fock̃ 7 IIII . borð hñtes XI . car̃ . 7 V . molð XL .

folið . 7 CL . ac̃s p̃ti . 7 XL . ac̃s filuæ minutæ . T.R.E . uaĩ

XVI . liɓ . m̃ XI . liɓ . Tailla . XL . foĩ . Tres lev lg̃ . 7 I . laĩ .

In Burton foca huj Ⓜ . I . car̃ tre ad gld . Tra ad . I . car̃ .

Ibi . VI . foch̃ hñt . I . car̃ .

ⓂIn BRANTVNE . h̃b S̃ MAR̃ Stou . IIII . car̃ træ ad glð .

Tra ad . IIII . car̃ . Ibi nc̃ in dñio . IIII . car̃ . 7 IIII . uiĩĩ 7 I .

foch̃ cũ . II . car̃ . 7 XL . ac̃s p̃ti . 7 filuæ minutæ . X . q̃z̃ lg̃ .

7 IIII . laĩ . Tot Ⓜ . XVI . q̃z̃ lg̃ . 7 IX . laĩ . T.R.E . uaĩ XII . liɓ .

m̃ fimiliĩ .

In CHENEIDE . XII . bou| ad gld . Tra ad XIII . boũ . S̃ MAz̃

hĩ ibi . III . foch̃ cũ . II . car̃ . 7 XX . V . ac̃s p̃ti . 7 XX . VI . ac̃s filuæ .

In STOV . Soca de Brantune . I . car̃ . 7 II . part̃ de . II . bõ ad glð .

Ibið Alfi . I . toftã in foca Remigij ep̃i . W . de pci ten⟍ Tra ad tntð .

f̃ð ⓂIn INGEHA . h̃b Acum̃ . VI . boũ tre ad glð . Tra ad . I . car̃ .

Ibi Erchenold hõ ep̃i hĩ . V . boũ arantes . 7 I . uiĩĩ . 7 I . foch̃

cũ . VI . boɓ arantes . 7 XII . ac̃s p̃ti . T.R.E . uaĩ XX . foĩ .

m̃ XXV . foĩ . Tailla . V . foĩ .

5   In GLENTHAM 3 carucates of land and 6 bovates taxable. Land for
    3 ploughs and 6 oxen. A jurisdiction of Stow.
        16 Freemen and 11 smallholders have 5 ploughs.
        Meadow, 110 acres.

6   In OWMBY (-by-Spital) 4 carucates of land and 3 bovates taxable.
    Land for as much.
        17 Freemen have 5½ ploughs.
        Meadow, 21 acres.

7   In UPTON, KEXBY and NORMANBY (by Stow), a jurisdiction of Stow,
    11 carucates of land *and 6 bovates* and 4 parts of 2 bovates and 2
    parts of ½ bovate taxable. Land for 10 ploughs.
        20 Freemen and 7 smallholders have 6½ ploughs.
        Meadow, 171 acres; underwood, 162 acres.

8 M. In WELTON Sveinn had 12 carucates of land taxable. Land for 16
    ploughs. Now 6 Canons of Lincoln have 5 ploughs in lordship
    there;
        48 Freemen and 4 smallholders who have 11 ploughs.
        5 mills, 40s; meadow, 150 acres; underwood, 40 acres.
    Value before 1066 £16; now £11. Exactions 40s.
    [It is] 3 leagues long and 1 wide.

9   In BURTON, a jurisdiction of this manor, 1 carucate of land
    taxable. Land for 1 plough.
        6 Freemen have 1 plough.

10 M. In BRAMPTON St. Mary's, Stow, had 4 carucates of land taxable.
    Land for 4 ploughs. Now in lordship 4 ploughs;
        4 villagers and 1 Freeman with 2 ploughs.
        Meadow, 40 acres; underwood 10 furlongs long and 4 wide.
        The whole manor [is] 16 furlongs long and 9 wide.
    Value before 1066 £12; now the same.

11 In KNAITH 12 bovates and 2 parts of 1 bovate taxable. Land for
    13 oxen. St. Mary's has there
        3 Freemen with 2 ploughs; and
        meadow, 25 acres; woodland, 26 acres.

12 In STOW, a jurisdiction of Brampton, 1 carucate and 2 parts of 2
    bovates taxable. Land for as much.

13 There also Alsige [had] 1 plot in the jurisdiction of Bishop
    Remigius. William of Percy holds it.

14 M. In INGHAM Hakon had 6 bovates of land taxable. Land for 1   344 b
    plough. Erchenold, the Bishop's man, has 5 ploughing oxen.
        1 villager and 1 Freeman who plough with 6 oxen.
        Meadow, 12 acres.
    Value before 1066, 20s; now 25s. Exactions 5s.

f♂ ⓜ **In** *Cotes* . h̄b Acum dim̄ car̄ t̄re ad gld̄ . T̄ra ad tn̄td̄.

Ibi Erch̄enold h̄t . ɪ . car̄ . T.R.E. ual̄ xx . fot . m̄ xxx . fot.

ⓜ **In** Graingeh̄a . h̄b Aldene . ɪ . car̄ t̄re ad gld̄ . T̄ra

ad . ɪ . car̄ 7 dim̄ . Ibi Malger h̄o ēpi h̄t . ɪ . car̄ . 7 vɪɪɪ .

uilt cū . ɪ . car̄ . 7 xx . ac̄s p̄ti . T.R.E. ual̄ xʟ . fot . m̄ xxx . fot.

f♂ ⓜ **In** *Messingeh̄a* . h̄b Rolf . ɪɪ . car̄ t̄ræ 7 ɪɪ . boū ad gld̄ .

T̄ra ad tn̄td̄ . Ibi Malger h̄t . ɪ . car̄ . 7 ɪ . uilt . 7 ɪ . mold .

v . folid . 7 x . ac̄s p̄ti . T.R.E. ual̄ xʟ . fot . m̄ xv . fot.

ⓜ **In** *Bechebi* . h̄b Aldene . ɪ . car̄ t̄ræ ⌐ Tailla . v . fot.

ad gld̄ . T̄ra ad . ɪɪ . car̄ . Ibi Rannulf h̄o ēpi h̄t .

. ɪ . car̄ 7 dim̄ . 7 xɪ . uilt 7 ɪ . foch̄ cū . ɪ . car̄ 7 dimid̄ .

Ibi p̄br 7 æccta . T.R.E. ual̄ . ʟ . fot . m̄ xʟ . fot . Tailla . x . s̄.

ⓜ **In** *Eleham* . h̄b Vlmar . ɪɪ . car̄ t̄ræ 7 ɪɪ . boū ad

gld̄ . T̄ra ad . ɪx . car̄ . Ibi Goiflan h̄o ēpi h̄t . ɪɪɪ . car̄ .

7 x . uilt . 7 v . bord̄ . 7 ɪɪ . foch̄ h̄ntes . ɪɪ . car̄ . 7 c . ac̄s

m̄ p̄ti . 7 fed molini . T.R.E. ual̄ vɪ . lib̄ . m̄ . ʟxx . fot . Tailla . x . s̄.

f♂ ⓜ **In** *Vluricebi* . h̄br Vlmar 7 Alden . ɪɪ . car̄ t̄re

7 dim̄ ad gld̄ . T̄ra ad . v . car̄ . Ibi Goiflan h̄t . ɪɪɪɪ . car̄ .

7 x . uilt . 7 v . bord̄ . cū . ɪɪ . car̄ . T.R.E. ual̄ . c . fot .

ɪɪɪ . lib̄ . 7 x . fot . Tailla . x . fot.

ⓜ **In** *Vdetone* . h̄b Vlmar . ɪɪ . car̄ t̄ræ ad gld̄ . T̄ra

ad . ɪɪɪɪ . car̄ . Ibi Roger h̄o ēpi h̄t . ɪɪ . car̄ . 7 ɪɪɪɪ . uilt

7 vɪ . foch̄ . cū . ɪ . car̄ 7 dim̄ . T.R.E. ual̄ xʟ . fot . m̄ fimilit.

f♂ ⓜ **In** *Vlvesbi* . h̄b Alden . vɪ . boū t̄ræ ⌐ Tailla . x . fot.

ad gld̄ . T̄ra ad . ɪɪ . car̄ . Ibi Rannulf h̄o ēpi h̄t . ɪ . car̄ .

T.R.E. ual̄ x . fot . m̄ fimilit.

f♂ ⓜ **In** *Golse* . h̄b Auti . ɪ . car̄ t̄ræ ad gld̄ . T̄ra ad . ɪɪ . car̄ .

Ibi Roger h̄o ēpi h̄t . ɪɪ . car̄ . 7 vɪɪɪ . uilt . 7 vɪɪɪ . foch̄ .

cū . ɪ . car̄ . 7 qt xx . ac̄s p̄ti . T.R.E. ual̄ xxx . ɪɪ . fot .

m̄ . xʟ . fot . Tailla . x . fot.

ʄ 15 M. In COATES Hakon had ½ carucate of land taxable. Land for as
much. Erchenold has 1 plough.
Value before 1066, 20s; now 30s.

16 M. In GRAYINGHAM Halfdan had 1 carucate of land taxable. Land
for 1½ ploughs. Mauger, the Bishop's man, has 1 plough.
7 villagers with 1 plough.
Meadow, 20 acres.
Value before 1066, 40s; now 30s.

ʄ 17 M. In MESSINGHAM Rothulfr had 2 carucates of land and 2 bovates
taxable. Land for as much. Mauger has 1 plough.
1 villager.
1 mill, 5s; meadow, 10 acres.
Value before 1066, 40s; now 15s. Exactions 5s.

18 M. In BIGBY Halfdan [son of] Topi had 1 carucate of land taxable.
Land for 2 ploughs. Ranulf, the Bishop's man, has 1½ ploughs.
11 villagers and 1 Freeman with 1½ ploughs.
A priest and a church.
Value before 1066, 50s; now 40s. Exactions 10s.

19 M. In ELSHAM Wulfmaer had 2 carucates of land and 2 bovates
taxable. Land for 9 ploughs. Jocelyn, the Bishop's man, has 3
ploughs.
10 villagers, 5 smallholders and 2 Freemen who have 2 ploughs.
Meadow, 100 acres; a mill site.
Value before 1066 £6; now 70s. Exactions 10s.

ʄ 20 2 In WORLABY Wulfmaer and Halfdan had 2½ carucates of land
M. taxable. Land for 5 ploughs. Jocelyn has 4 ploughs.
10 villagers and 5 smallholders with 2 ploughs.
Value before 1066, 100s; [now] £3 10s. Exactions 10s.

21 M. In WOOTTON Wulfmaer had 2 carucates of land taxable. Land for
4 ploughs. Roger, the Bishop's man, has 2 ploughs.
4 villagers and 6 Freemen with 1½ ploughs.
Value before 1066, 40s; now the same. Exactions 10s.

ʄ 22 M. In ULCEBY Halfdan had 6 bovates of land taxable. Land for 2
ploughs. Ranulf, the Bishop's man, has 1 plough.
Value before 1066, 10s; now the same.

ʄ 23 M. In GOXHILL Auti had 1 carucate of land taxable. Land for 2
ploughs. Roger, the Bishop's man, has 2 ploughs.
8 villagers and 8 Freemen with 1 plough.
Meadow, 80 acres.
Value before 1066, 32s; now 40s. Exactions 10s.

ꝼð ⏁ **I**n *WIDVN* . ħƀ Rolf . II . caꞧ tꞃæ ad glđ . Tꞃa ad
III . caꞧ . Ibi Malger ħꞇ . I . caꞧ . 7 I . uiłł . 7 I . borđ .
7 XI . ſoch hūtes . II . caꞧ . 7 IIII . aćs p̄ti . 7 X . aćs ſiluę
minute . T.R.E . uał . xxx . ſoł . m̄ xL . ſoł . Tailla xx . ſoł .

§ **I**n Ormeſbi Soca hui ⏁ XIII . bou tꞃe ad glđ .
Tꞃa ad . III . caꞧ . Ibi . v . ſoch hūt . I . caꞧ . 7 VIII . aćs
p̄ti . 7 IIII . aćs ſiluæ minutæ .

⏁ **I**n *CROCHESTONE* . ħƀ Auti . II . bou tꞃæ ad glđ . de Soca^Grinchil.
Tꞃa ad dim̄ caꞧ . Ibi ħꞇ Goiſlan . I . caꞧ . 7 II . uiłł .
T.R.E . uałł . xx . ſoł . m̄ . v . ſoł .

344 c

⏁ **I**n *CHELEBI* . ħƀ Aldene . v . bou tꞃæ 7 tcia parte
uni bou ad glđ . Tꞃa ad XI . bō . Ibi Rannulf hō ep̄i
ħꞇ . I . caꞧ . 7 IIII . uiłł 7 I . borđ cū . II . bob . 7 I . molđ . VI .
ſoł . 7 VIII . deñ . 7 VI . ać p̄ti . T.R.E . uał xxx . ſoł . m̄
ſimiliꞇ . Tailla . x . ſoł .

⏁ **I**n *ARESBI* . ħƀ Outi . II . caꞧ tꞃe ad glđ . Tꞃa ad . IIII .
caꞧ . Ibi Goiſlan hō ep̄i ħꞇ . II . caꞧ . 7 III . uiłł . 7 VI .
borđ . 7 xx . ſoch cū . III . caꞧ . 7 I . molđ . III . ſoł . 7 cx .
aćs p̄ti . T.R.E . uał . III . liƀ . m̄ xL . ſoł . Tailla . xx . ſoł .

ꝼð ƀ **I**n *SVDtrie* . Inland de Vlingehā . II . bou tꞃæ ad glđ .
Tꞃa ad dim̄ caꞧ . Ibi Osƀñ^cleri̓ ep̄i ħꞇ . II . uiłł cū dim̄ caꞧ .

⏁ **I**n *DVNESBI* . ħƀ Aldene . v . caꞧ tre ad glđ . Tꞃa
ad totid caꞧ . Ibi Radulf hō ep̄i ħꞇ . II . caꞧ . 7 VI . uiłł
7 VI . borđ . 7 XIII . ſoch hūtes . VII . caꞧ . Ibi pƀr 7 æcctła .
7 c . aćs p̄ti . 7 c . ać ſiluæ paſt p . loca . T.R.E . uał . Lx .
ſoł . m̄ . IIII . liƀ . Tailla . xx . ſoł . .

§ **I**n Hacuneſbi . Soca hui ⏁ . 7 IIII . bou 7 dim̄ ad glđ .
Tꞃa at tn̄td . Ibi . v . ſoch hūt . I . caꞧ . 7 x . aćs p̄ti . 7 x .
aćs ſiluæ minutæ .

344 b, c

f∂ 24 M. In WYHAM Rothulfr had 2 carucates of land taxable. Land for 3 ploughs. Mauger has 1 plough.
 1 villager, 1 smallholder and 11 Freemen who have 2 ploughs and meadow, 4 acres; underwood, 10 acres.
Value before 1066, 30s; now 40s. Exactions 20s.

25 S. In (North) ORMSBY, a jurisdiction of this manor, 13 bovates of land taxable. Land for 3 ploughs.
 5 Freemen have 1 plough and meadow, 8 acres; underwood, 4 acres.

26 M. In CROXTON Auti had 2 bovates of land taxable, of Grimketill's jurisdiction. Land for ½ plough. Jocelyn has 1 plough.
 2 villagers.
Value before 1066, 20s; now 5s.

27 M. In KEELBY Halfdan had 5 bovates of land and the third part of 1 bovate taxable. Land for 11 oxen. Ranulf, the Bishop's man, has 1 plough.   344 c
 4 villagers and 1 smallholder with 2 oxen.
 1 mill, 6s 8d; meadow, 6 acres.
Value before 1066, 30s; now the same. Exactions 10s.

28 M. In OWERSBY Auti had 2 carucates of land taxable. Land for 4 ploughs. Jocelyn, the Bishop's man, has 2 ploughs.
 3 villagers, 6 smallholders and 20 Freemen with 3 ploughs.
 1 mill, 3s; meadow, 110 acres.
Value before 1066 £3; now 40s. Exactions 20s.

f∂ 29 B. In SOUTHREY, *inland* of (Cherry) Willingham, 2 bovates of land taxable. Land for ½ plough. Osbern, a clerk of the Bishop's, has 2 villagers with ½ plough.

30 M. In DUNSBY Halfdan had 5 carucates of land taxable. Land for as many ploughs. Ralph, the Bishop's man, has 2 ploughs.
 6 villagers, 6 smallholders and 13 Freemen who have 7 ploughs.
 A priest and a church; meadow, 100 acres; woodland, pasture in places, 100 acres.
Value before 1066, 60s; now £4. Exactions 20s.

31 S. In HACONBY, a jurisdiction of this manor, 4½ bovates taxable. Land for as much.
 5 Freemen have 1 plough and meadow, 10 acres; underwood, 10 acres.

ᛗ In *RINGESDVNE* . h̄b Aldene . ii . car̃ tre 7 ii . bou
ad gl̄d . Tra ad tnt̄d . Ibi Adā hō ep̄i h̄t . i . car̃ . 7 x .
uitt . 7 vi . bord . cū . ii . car̃ . Ibi p̄br 7 tcia pars æcctæ.
7 xx . ac̃s p̄ti . 7 lx . ac̃s siluæ minutæ . T.R.E . iii . lib̄.
m̄ . xl . sot . Tailla . xx . sot.

B In Dunesbi jnland huj᷑ ᛗ . i . car̃ tre ad gl̄d . Tra ad . i .
car̃ . Ibi . ii . uitt h̄nt dimid̄ car̃ . 7 xx . ac̃s p̄ti . 7 xl .ac̃s

ᛗ In *CEILA* h̄br Azor 7 frs ej᷑ . ii . car̃ træ 7 ii . bou / siluæ
ad gl̄d . Tra ad tnt̄d . Ibi Malger hō ep̄i h̄t . i . car̃.
7 vi . uitt cū . ii . car̃ 7 dimid . 7 viii . ac̃s p̄ti . 7 i . salina
viii . den̄ . P̄ciū ej᷑ in Gozeberdecherca.

In Quadheueringe . Inland huj᷑ ᛗ . i . car̃ tre ad gl̄d .
Tra ad . i . car̃ . Ibi h̄t Malger viii . uitt cū . i . car̃.

ᛗ In *GOZEBERDECHERCA* h̄b Asti . i . car̃ tre 7 vi . bou
ad gl̄d . Tra ad . i . car̃ 7 vi . boues . Ibi h̄t Malger . i . car̃.
7 xii . uitt 7 ix . bord cū . iii . car̃ . 7 i . salina . iiii . den̄.
7 xii . ac̃s p̄ti . 7 i . soch de suo orto . T.R.E . uat . vi . lib̄.
m̄ . iiii . lib̄ . Tailla . xx . sot . In Quadheueringe . i . car̃ 7 dim ad gl̄d.

ᛗ In *CARLEBI* . h̄b Bardi . i . car̃ tre 7 dimid̄ bou ad gl̄d.
Tra ad tnt̄d . Ibi Erchenold h̄t . i . car̃ . 7 x . uitt . 7 xi .
bord cū . ii . car̃ 7 x . ac̃s p̄ti . 7 xl . ac̃s siluæ pastit
p̄ loca . T.R.E . uat xxx . sot . m̄ . l . sot . Tailla . x . sot.

ᛗ In *CORBI* . h̄b Bardi . viii . car̃ tre ad gl̄d . Tra ad
viii . car̃ . Ibi Walt hō ep̄i h̄t . ii . car̃ . 7 xvii . uitt

344 d
7 xvii . uitt . xii . bord . 7 xxii . soch . h̄ntes . v . car̃.
7 mille . c . ac̃s siluæ pastit . T.R.E . uat vii . lib̄ . m̄ . vii .
lib̄ . Tailla . xl . sot.

32 M. In 'RINGSTONE' Halfdan had 2 carucates of land and 2 bovates taxable. Land for as much. Adam, the Bishop's man, has 1 plough.
   10 villagers and 6 smallholders with 2 ploughs.
   A priest and the third part of a church; meadow, 20 acres; underwood, 60 acres.
   [Value] before 1066 £3; now 40s. Exactions 20s.

33 B. In DUNSBY, *inland* of this manor, 1 carucate of land taxable. Land for 1 plough.
   2 villagers have ½ plough and
   meadow, 20 acres; woodland, 43 acres.

34 M. In CHEAL Atsurr and his brothers had 2 carucates of land and 2 bovates taxable. Land for as much. Mauger, the Bishop's man, has 1 plough.
   6 villagers with 2½ ploughs.
   Meadow, 8 acres; 1 salt-house, 8d.
   Its assessment is in Gosberton.

35 In QUADRING, *inland* of this manor, 1 carucate of land taxable. Land for 1 plough. Mauger has
   8 villagers with 1 plough.

36 M. In GOSBERTON Asli had 1 carucate of land and 6 bovates taxable. Land for 1 plough and 6 oxen. Mauger has 1 plough.
   12 villagers and 9 smallholders with 3 ploughs.
   1 salt-house, 4d; meadow, 12 acres.
   1 Freeman on his garden.
   Value before 1066 £6; now £4. Exactions 20s.

37 In QUADRING, *inland*, 1½ carucates taxable.

38 M. In CARLBY Barthi had 1 carucate of land and ½ bovate taxable. Land for as much. Erchenold, the Bishop's man, has 1 plough.
   10 villagers and 11 smallholders with 2 ploughs.
   Meadow, 10 acres; woodland, pasture in places, 40 acres.
   Value before 1066, 30s; now 50s. Exactions 10s.

39 M. In CORBY (Glen) Barthi had 8 carucates of land taxable. Land for 8 ploughs. Walter, the Bishop's man, has 2 ploughs.
   17 villagers, 12 smallholders and 22 Freemen who have   344 d
      5 ploughs and
   woodland pasture, 1100 acres.
   Value before 1066 £7; now £7. Exactions 40s.

In Billesfelt Soca huj M̄.ii.car̄ tre 7 ii.bō ad glđ.Tra
ad.iii.car̄.Ibi hȳ Walter hō epi.ii.car̄.7 iii.uitł
7 viii.borđ 7 vi.focħ.hn̄tes.iii.car̄.Ibi æccła 7 pbr.
7 i.molđ.xii.den.7 xiii.ac̄s p̄ti.7 feptingentas
ac̄s filuæ paſt p̄ loca.T.R.E.uat xx.fot.m̄ lx.fot.
m̄.xx.fot.

In Suafeld.Soca in corbi.ii.car̄ ad glđ.Tra ad.ii.
car̄.Ibi.x.focħ hn̄t.iii.car̄.7 viii.ac̄s filuæ.
In Suinhā.ii.car̄ ad glđ.Tra.ii.car̄.

M̄ In ESLAFORDE.ħb Bardi.xi.car̄ træ ad glđ.Tra
ad xi.car̄.Ibi hȳ ep̄s in dn̄io.iii.car̄.7 xxix.uitł.
7 vi.focħ.7 xi.borđ.hn̄tes.xiiii.car̄.Ibi pbr 7 æccła.
7 viii.molin̄ de.x.lib.7 ccc.7 xx.ac̄s p̄ti.7 i.ac̄ filuæ
minutæ.Marefc.ccc.7 xxx.ac̄.T.R.E.uat xx.lib.
m̄ xxv.lib.In Lōpintorp.ii.c̄ ad glđ.Tra.ii.c̄.Vat.xx.fot.
In Gerefbi.xiii.boū træ ad glđ.Tra ad x.boū.Soca
in Eflaforde.Ibi.ii.focħ cū.ii.bob araȳ.7 xvi.ac̄ p̄ti.
7 xiii.ac̄ filuæ minutæ.

In Welle.v.car̄ træ 7 iii.bō ad glđ.Tra ad.iiii.car̄.
Soca fimilit.Ibi funt.x.focħ 7 vii.borđ.hn̄tes.iiii.car̄
7 dim̄.Ibi pbr 7 æccła.7 xxx.ii.ac̄ p̄ti.   7 iii.ac̄s p̄ti.
In Echintune.ii.boū træ ad glđ.Ibi.i.uitłs hn̄s.ii.boū.

In Cornińtune.ħb Bardi.viiii.car̄ tre 7 ii.bou 7 dim̄
Tra ad.ix.car̄ 7 totiđ bou.Ibi funt.xxxii.focħ.7 xv.borđ.
cū.vii.car̄ 7 dimiđ.7.ii.molđ.xvi.fot.7 lx.ac̄s p̄ti.
In iſta Soca hȳ Ofmund.ii.car̄ in dn̄io.7 valet.lx.fot.
Iȳ in iſta foca hȳ Hugo rufus.i.car̄ træ.7 i.car̄ in dn̄io.
7 valet.xxv.fot.

40 In BITCHFIELD, a jurisdiction of this manor, 2 carucates of land and 2 bovates taxable. Land for 3 ploughs. Walter, the Bishop's man, has 2 ploughs.

    3 villagers, 8 smallholders and 6 Freemen who have 3 ploughs.
    A church and a priest; 1 mill, 12d; meadow, 13 acres;
        woodland, pasture in places, 700 acres.

Value before 1066, 20s; now 60s; now 20s.

41 In SWAYFIELD, a jurisdiction of Corby (Glen), 2 carucates taxable. Land for 2 ploughs.

    10 Freemen have 3 ploughs and
    woodland, 8 acres.

42 In SWINSTEAD 2 carucates taxable. Land for 2 ploughs.

43 M. In (New) SLEAFORD Barthi had 11 carucates of land taxable. Land for 11 ploughs. The Bishop has in lordship 3 ploughs;

    29 villagers, 6 Freemen and 11 smallholders who have 14 ploughs.
    A priest and a church; 8 mills at £10; meadow, 320 acres;
        underwood, 1 acre; marsh, 330 acres.

Value before 1066 £20; now £25.

44 M. In LOBTHORPE 2 carucates taxable. Land for 2 ploughs.
Value 20s.

45 In EWERBY 13 bovates of land taxable. Land for 10 oxen. A jurisdiction of (Old) Sleaford.

    2 Freemen plough with 2 oxen.
    Meadow, 16 acres; underwood, 13 acres.

46 In HOWELL 5 carucates of land and 3 bovates taxable. Land for 4 ploughs. A jurisdiction likewise.

    10 Freemen and 7 smallholders who have 4½ ploughs.
    A priest and a church; meadow, 32 acres.

47 In HECKINGTON, a jurisdiction, 2 bovates of land taxable.

    1 villager who has 2 oxen and
    meadow, 3 acres.

48 In QUARRINGTON Barthi had 9 carucates of land and 2½ bovates. Land for 9 ploughs and as many oxen.

    32 Freemen and 15 smallholders with 7½ ploughs.
    2 mills, 16s; meadow, 60 acres.
    In this jurisdiction Osmund has 2 ploughs in lordship.

Value 60s.

    Also in this jurisdiction Hugh Rufus has 1 carucate of land and 1 plough in lordship.

Value 25s.

In Leduluetorp.ıı.car̄ træ ad glđ.7 xı.boū Terra.

Ibi.v.focħ 7 ıı.borđ cū.ıı.car̄.

In Euedune.ıııı.car̄ tre 7 ııı.boū ad glđ.Tra ad.ıııı.car̄.

Ibi hт̄ ep̄s.xııı.focħ cū.v.car̄.7 xx.ac̄ p̄ti.7 c.ac̄ marefc.

7 xvı.ac̄ filuæ minutæ.

De ifta foca hт̄ Ofmund xı.boū tre.7 ı.car̄ 7 dim̄ in

dn̄io.Valet.xxx.fot.

In CANVIC ħƀ Welrauen.ıı.car̄ tre.7 ı.boū 7 dim̄

ad glđ.Tra ad.ıı.car̄ 7 ı.boū 7 dim̄.Ibi Witts ħo ep̄i

hт̄.ı.car̄.7 ııı.uitt.7 ııı.borđ.cū.ı.car̄.7 Lv.ac̄s p̄ti.

T.R.E.uat.Lx.fot.m̄ xx.fot.

Ꝋ In LESSINGHA.ħƀ Barne.vı.car̄ træ ad glđ.Tra

ad.vı.car̄.Ibi Ada ħo ep̄i hт̄.ıı.car̄.7 xvı.uitt.

345 a

7 ı.focħ 7 ıııı.borđ.hn̄tes.ıııı.car̄.7 xxx.ac̄s p̄ti.

T.R.E.uat.vı.liƀ.m̄.c.fot.

Ꝋ In WILGEBI.ħƀ Archel.ı.car̄ tre ad glđ.Tra ad.ıı.

car̄.Ibi Radulf ħo ep̄i hт̄.ıı.car̄.7 v.uitt 7 ıı.focħ.

hn̄tes.ıı.car̄.7 xxx.ac̄s p̄ti.T.R.E.uat xxx.fot.m̄.L.s

fƍ Ꝋ In HACAM.ħƀ Tori xıııı.car̄ tre ad glđ.Tra

ad.ıx.car̄ 7 dim̄.Ibi Hugo ħo ep̄i hт̄.ıı.car̄.7 xxı.

uitt.7 ıııı.focħ 7 ı.borđ.hn̄t.ıx.car̄.Ibi æccta 7 pƀr.

7 ıı.molđ.xııı.fot 7 ıııı.den.7 xL.ac̄s p̄ti.T.R.E.

uat.ıııı.liƀ.m̄ vıı.liƀ.

In hac uilla ħƀ Roƀt pƀr.ı.car̄ tre de rege in

elemofina.7 m̄ cū eadē tra effect eft | in S MARIÆ

Stou.Sed n̄ licet tra alicui habere nifi regis

conceffu.T.R.E.uat x.fot.m̄ fimit.

49 In 'LAYTHORPE', a jurisdiction, 2 carucates of land taxable. Land for 11 oxen.
5 Freemen and 2 smallholders with 2 ploughs.

50 In EVEDON 4 carucates of land and 3 bovates taxable. Land for 4 ploughs. The Bishop has
13 Freemen with 5 ploughs.
Meadow, 20 acres; marsh, 100 acres; underwood, 16 acres.
Of this jurisdiction Osmund has 11 bovates of land and 1½ ploughs in lordship.
Value 30s.

51 In CANWICK, a jurisdiction, Valhrafn had 2 carucates of land and 1½ bovates taxable. Land for 2 ploughs and 1½ oxen. William, the Bishop's man, has 1 plough.
3 villagers and 3 smallholders with 1 plough.
Meadow, 55 acres.
Value before 1066, 60s; now 20s.

52 M. In LEASINGHAM Barn had 6 carucates of land taxable. Land for 6 ploughs. Adam, the Bishop's man, has 2 ploughs.
16 villagers, 1 Freeman and 4 smallholders who have 4 ploughs   345 a
and
meadow, 30 acres.
Value before 1066 £6; now 100s.

53 M. In (Silk) WILLOUGHBY Arnketill had 1 carucate of land taxable. Land for 2 ploughs. Ralph, the Bishop's man, has 2 ploughs.
5 villagers and 2 Freemen who have 2 ploughs and
meadow, 30 acres.
Value before 1066, 30s; now 50s.

54 M. In HOUGHAM Thorir had 14 carucates of land taxable. Land for 9½ ploughs. Hugh, the Bishop's man, has 2 ploughs.
21 villagers, 4 Freemen and 1 smallholder have 9 ploughs.
A church and a priest; 2 mills, 13s 4d; meadow, 40 acres.
Value before 1066 £4; now £7.

55 In this village Robert the priest had 1 carucate of land from the King in alms. Now he has become a monk in St. Mary's, Stow, with this land, but no one may have the land except with the King's consent.
Value before 1066, 10s; now the same.

★ ⋈ In *Ludes* h̅b Ep̅s lincolie . xii . car̄ ꞌ ꞌ træ ad gld̄ .

Tra ad . xii . car̄ . Ibi h̅t m̊ ep̅s in dn̄io . iii . car̄ .

⁊ q̄ter xx . burgenſes . ⁊ i . mercatū de xx.ix . ſot .

⁊ xl . ſoch ⁊ ii . uitt . Int̄ om̅s hn̄t . xiii . car̄ . ⁊ xiii .

molin̄ redd̄ . lx . ſot . Ibi hn̄t . ii . milites . ii . car̄ .

⁊ xx.i . ać p̊ti . ⁊ cccc . ać s ſilue paſt p̄ loca . Vna

leū ⁊ viii . q̊ʓ lḡ . ⁊ x . q̊ʓ lat̄ . T.R.E . uat xii . lib̅ .

m̊ . xxii . lib̅ . Tailla . iii . lib̅ .

⋈ In *Rebvrne* . h̅b Archil . i . car̄ ꞌ ꞌ tre ad gld̄ . Tra ad

ii . car̄ . Nc̄ ep̅s Remigi ⁊ canonici . in S̅ Maria

hn̄t ii . uitt . cū . iii . bob arantes . ⁊ xx.iiii . ać s p̊ti .

T.R.E . uat . xx . ſot . m̊ . x . ſot .

In *Chenebi* . ten̄ Goiſlan de ep̄o . ii . car̄ ꞌ ꞌ tre ad gld̄ . Tra . vi .

car̄ . Outi tenuit . T.R.E . Ibi ſt̄ . ii . car̄ . p̊br ⁊ æccta . ⁊ xx . uitti

⁊ v . bord̄ cū . v . car̄ . ⁊ molin̄ . iiii . ſot . ⁊ cccc . ać p̊ti .

Valuit ⁊ uat . iiii . lib̅ .

In *Gvllingha* . x . bō ꞌ træ ad gld̄ . Tra . x . bō . Ibi . viii . uitti . ⁊ i . ſoch

cū . i . c̄ ⁊ dim̄ . ⁊ xx . ać p̊ti . Oli . xx . ſot . Modo . xxx . ſot uat .

VIII. Terra Sc̄i Petri De Bvrg.

⋈ In *Fiscartvne* . iii . car̄ træ ad gld̄ . Tra ad . iii . car̄ .

Hoc ⋈ fuit ⁊ eſt S̅ petri de Burg . Ibi in dn̄io . iii . car̄ .

⁊ xviii . uitt . ⁊ iii . bord̄ . hn̄tes . iiii . car̄ . Ibi æccta ⁊ p̊br .

⁊ iii . piſcar̄ ⁊ dim̄ redd̄ xx.i . denar̄ . ⁊ cxx . ać s p̊ti .

Silua paſt . x . q̊ʓ lḡ . ⁊ ix . lat̄ . Tot xx . q̊ʓ lḡ . ⁊ ix . lat̄ .

T.R.E . uat . xiiii . lib̅ . m̊ xvii . lib̅ . Tailla . iii . lib̅ .

Soca huj ⋈ In Scoltorne ⁊ Holme ⁊ Sutbroc

v . car̄ ꞌ ꞌ tre ⁊ dim̄ ad gld̄ . Tra ad . vi . car̄ . Ibi h̅t

S̅ Petr xxx.ii . ſoch hn̄tes viii . car̄ .

56 M. In LOUTH the Bishop of Lincoln had 12 carucates of land taxable. Land for 12 ploughs. The Bishop now has in lordship 3 ploughs;
> 80 burgesses, 1 market at 29s, 40 Freemen and 2 villagers; between them they have 13 ploughs.
> 13 mills which pay 60s.
> 2 men-at-arms have 2 ploughs.
> Meadow, 21 acres; woodland, pasture in places, 400 acres.
> [It is] 1 league and 8 furlongs long and 10 furlongs wide.

Value before 1066 £12; now £22. Exactions £3.

57 M. In REDBOURNE Arnketill had 1 carucate of land taxable. Land for 2 ploughs. Now Bishop Remigius and the Canons in St. Mary's have
> 2 villagers who plough with 3 oxen; and
> meadow, 24 acres.

Value before 1066, 20s; now 10s.

58 In KINGERBY Jocelyn holds from the Bishop 2 carucates of land taxable. Land for 6 ploughs. Auti held them before 1066. 2 ploughs.
> A priest and a church; 20 villagers and 5 smallholders with 5 ploughs.
> A mill, 4s; meadow, 400 acres.

The value was and is £4.

59 In (Cherry) WILLINGHAM 10 bovates of land taxable. Land for 10 oxen.
> 8 villagers and 1 Freeman with 1½ ploughs.
> Meadow, 20 acres.

Formerly 20s; value now 30s.

8   LAND OF ST. PETER'S OF PETERBOROUGH   345 c

1 M. In FISKERTON 3 carucates of land taxable. Land for 3 ploughs. This manor was and is St. Peter's of Peterborough. In lordship 3 ploughs;
> 18 villagers and 3 smallholders who have 4 ploughs.
> A church and a priest; 3½ fisheries which pay 21d; meadow, 120 acres; woodland pasture 10 furlongs long and 9 wide.
> The whole [is] 20 furlongs long and 9 wide.

Value before 1066 £14; now £17. Exactions £3.

2 Jurisdiction of this manor in SCOTHERN, 'HOLME' and SUDBROOKE;
> 5½ carucates of land taxable. Land for 6 ploughs. St. Peter's has 32 Freemen who have 8 ploughs.

Inland huj͜ ⊙ In Refaim . iiii . car|t̄re ad gld̄ . T́ra
ad . iiii . car̄ . Ibi xii . uilt 7 ii . bord h̄nt . iiii . car̄.
7 lx . aćs p̃ti . Silua minuta . viii . q̃ɉ lḡ . 7 iiii . lat̄.

⊙ In *TVROLVEBI* . h̄b 7 h̄t S̄ Petr͗ de Burg . iii . car̄ t́re
7 v . boú ad gld̄ . T́ra ad tntd̄ car̄ 7 boú . Ibi . ē in dñio
i . car̄ . 7 x . uilt 7 ii . foch h̄nt . i . car̄ 7 dim . De hac
t́ra h̄nt . ii . hoēs abb̄is . ii . carucat́ . 7 ibi . i . car̄ 7 dim̄
7 vii . uilt 7 ii . foch cū . i . car̄ . Ibi xx . aċ p̃ti . 7 q̃t xx .
aċ filuæ paftit p̄ loca . T.R.E . uat . lx . fot . m̄ fimilit̄ . Tailla
x . fot.

⊙ In *ADEWELLE* . h̄b 7 h̄t S̄ petr͗ de Burg . v . car̄ t́re ad
gld̄ . T́ra ad . v . car̄ . Ibi nc̄ in dñio . ii . car̄ . 7 x . uilt . 7 ii .
bord . 7 ii . foch . h̄ntes . iii . car̄ 7 dim̄ . 7 xviii . aċ p̃ti .
Siluæ paſt c 7 q̃t xx . aćs . 7 minute filuæ . lx : aćs .
T.R.E . uat . lx . fot . m̄ fimit . Tailla . xii . fot.

In *WITHA* 7 Mannetor . 7 Toftlund . ē Bereuuita
dim̄ car t́ræ ad gld̄ . T́ra ad . iiii . boú . Ibi . ii . uilt h̄nt
dim̄ car̄ . 7 viii . aćs p̃ti . 7 xl . aćs filuæ minutæ .
T.R.E . uat . v . fot 7 iiii . den̄ . m̄ fimilit͗ . Ansfrid tenet.

Berewita de Bergeftorp . ē in Bintha̅ . iiii . car̄ t́ræ
ad gld̄ . T́ra ad . iiii . car̄ . H́ t́ra ē S̄ petri Burg dñica.
Ibi nc̄ . vi . uilt h̄nt . ii . car̄ 7 ii . boú . Ibi Safuualo
ho̅ abb̄is h̄t de ipfa t́ra . ii . carucat́ t́ræ . 7 in dñio
dim̄ car̄ . 7 iii . uilt cū . i . car̄ . 7 xxv . aćs p̃ti . 7 c . aćs
filue minutæ . T.R.E . uat h̄ foch t́ra . xxx . fot . m̄ xx . fot.

3   *Inland* of this manor in REEPHAM; 4 carucates and 6 bovates of land taxable. Land for 4 ploughs and 6 oxen.

12 villagers and 2 smallholders have 4 ploughs and meadow, 60 acres; underwood 8 furlongs long and 4 wide.

4 M. In THURLBY St. Peter's of Peterborough had and has 3 carucates of land and 5 bovates taxable. Land for as many ploughs and oxen. In lordship 1 plough.

10 villagers and 2 Freemen have 1½ ploughs.

Two of the Abbot's men have 2 carucates of this land; 1½ ploughs there;

7 villagers and 2 Freemen with 1 plough.

Meadow, 20 acres; woodland, pasture in places, 80 acres.

Value before 1066, 60s; now the same. Exactions 10s.

5 M. In *ADEWELLE* St. Peter's of Peterborough had and has 5 carucates of land taxable. Land for 5 ploughs. Now in lordship 2 ploughs;

10 villagers, 2 smallholders and 2 Freemen who have 3½ ploughs.

Meadow, 18 acres; woodland pasture, 180 acres; underwood, 60 acres.

Value before 1066, 60s; now the same. Exactions 12s.

6   In WITHAM (on the Hill), MANTHORPE, TOFT and LOUND there is an outlier; ½ carucate of land taxable. Land for 4 oxen.

2 villagers have ½ plough and meadow, 8 acres; underwood, 40 acres.

Value before 1066, 5s 4d; now the same.

Ansfrid holds it.

7   There is an outlier of *Bergestorp* in BYTHAM; 4 carucates of land taxable. Land for 4 ploughs. The land is lordship (land) of St. Peter's [of] Peterborough.

Now 6 villagers have 2 ploughs and 2 oxen.

Of this land Saswalo, the Abbot's man, has 2 carucates of land. In lordship ½ plough;

3 villagers with 1 plough.

Meadow, 25 acres; underwood, 100 acres.

Value before 1066 of this jurisdiction, 30s; now 20s.

Ⓜ In *OSGOTEBI* ħɓ 7 ħт S petr⁹ de burg.v.caῖ tre
ad glđ.Tra ad.v.caῖ.Nc Anſchitillus hõ aɓɓis
ħт ibi.11.caῖ.7 XIII.uiłł cũ.IIII.caῖ.7 XIIII.acs
p̃ti.Siluæ paſt.XIII.q̃ɀ lg̃.7 IIII.laῖ.T.R.E.ual

345 d
LX.ſoł.m̃.c.ſoł.Tailla.XX.ſoł.
Tra arabił.XIIII.q̃ɀ lg̃.7 VI.laῖ.Duæ carucatæ
iſtius Ⓜ.jacent in Lauintone ħđ

Ⓜ In *WALECOTE*.ħɓ 7 ħт S petrus de Burg.v.caῖ
tre ad glđ.Tra ad.VI.caῖ.Nc Giſleɓt hõ aɓɓis
ħт ibi.1.caῖ.7 VI.uiłł.7 v.borđ.cũ.11.caῖ.7 Eccła.
7 XIIII.ſocħ de.11.carucatis.ħntes.IIII.caῖ.Vna
medietas de ſoca.ē S petri.7 altera Giſleɓti de gant
p̃tiñ in Folchingehã.Ibi.XXX.ac̃ p̃ti.T.R.E.ual.VIII.
liɓ.m̃.IIII.liɓ. ✝

Ⓜ In *DVNINCTVNE*.ħɓ 7 ħт S petr⁹ de Burg.III.caῖ tre
ad glđ.Tra ad.III.caῖ.Ibi nc̃.1.caῖ in dñio.7 XII.uiłł
7 XX.borđ cũ.11.caῖ.7 XVI.ſaline.XX.ſoliđ.7 XII.
ac̃ p̃ti.T.R.E.ual LX.ſoł.m̃ ſimiliῖ.

✝ SOCA de Walecote.In hodebi.11.bou træ ad gld.
Tra ad.1.bou 7 dim̃.Ibi.1.ſocħs arat.II°ᵇ.boɓɀ.Iuo tenet.

In *HOCTVNE* ħт S petr⁹ de Burg dimiđ caῖ tre ad
glđ.cũ ſaca 7 ſoca.Ibi.III.uiłł ħ̃nt.1.caῖ.Colegrĩ tenet.

Ⓜ In *RISVN*.ħɓ Elnod.IIII.bõ tre ad glđ.Tra ad dim̃
caῖ.Nc̃ ħт Colſuan de aɓɓ.T.7 ipſe ibi.11.borđ.
T.R.E.ual dim̃ marcã argenti.7 m̃ ſimiliῖ.

345 c, d

8 M. In OSGODBY St. Peter's of Peterborough had and has 5 carucates of land taxable. Land for 5 ploughs. Now Asketill, the Abbot's man, has 2 ploughs there.

    13 villagers with 4 ploughs.

    Meadow, 14 acres; woodland pasture, 13 furlongs long and 4 wide.

Value before 1066, 60s; now 100s. Exactions 20s.   345 d

    Arable land 14 furlongs long and 6 wide.

    2 carucates of this manor lie in 'Lavington' hundred.

9 M. In WALCOT St. Peter's of Peterborough had and has 5 carucates of land taxable. Land for 6 ploughs. Now Gilbert, the Abbot's man, has 1 plough there.

    6 villagers and 5 smallholders with 2 ploughs.

    A church; 14 Freemen on 2 carucates who have 4 ploughs.

    Half of the jurisdiction is St. Peter's, the other (half) [is] Gilbert of Ghent's [and] belongs in Folkingham.

    Meadow, 30 acres.

Value before 1066 £8; now £4.   Ψ

8,10 is added after 8,11, directed by transposition signs to its correct place in the text.

11 M. In DONINGTON St. Peter's of Peterborough had and has 3 carucates of land taxable. Land for 3 ploughs. Now 1 plough in lordship;

    12 villagers and 20 smallholders with 2 ploughs.

    16 salt-houses, 20s; meadow, 12 acres.

Value before 1066, 60s; now the same.

8,10, misplaced but directed to its correct position by transposition signs.

Ψ 10   A jurisdiction of Walcot in 'HAYTHBY'; 2 bovates of land taxable. Land for 1½ oxen.

    1 Freeman ploughs with 2 oxen.

    Ivo holds it.

12   In 'HOUGHTON' St. Peter's of Peterborough has ½ carucate of land taxable with full jurisdiction.

    3 villagers have 1 plough.

    Kolgrimr holds it.

13 M. In RISEHOLME Alnoth had 4 bovates of land taxable. Land for ½ plough. Now Kolsveinn has it from Abbot Thoraldr and himself (has) there

    2 smallholders.

Value before 1066, ½ mark of silver; now the same.

f ⓂIn *LOLESTORP* ħɓ Rolft dim̅ car̅ træ ad glð.T̊ra ad
iiii.bou̅.Ibi.T.abɓ hr̅.i.car̅.7 iii.ac̊s p̊ti.T.R.E.ual
xii.fol.m̊.v.fol.

ⓂIn *SCOTONE* ħɓ Afchil.vi.car̊ tre ad glð.T̊ra ad.vi.
car̅.Ibi Ricard ho̊ abɓis hr̅ fub_abɓe.iii.car̅.
7 xxii.uiłł 7 v.borð.7 xvii.focħ.hn̅tes.ii.car̅.In
Lincolia.iii.burgenſes.v.fol reddentes.7 L.ac̊s p̊ti.
7 xxx.vi.ac̊s filuæ minutæ.T.R.E.ual.c.fol.m̊.iiii.
liɓ.Tailla.xl.fol.
Soca hůj Ⓜ in Torp.i.car̊ tre ad glð.T̊ra ad.i.car̅
.ıı. 7 dim̊.Ibi.iiii.focħ hn̅t.ii.uiłł 7 i.borð.cu̅.i.car̅.

ⓂIn *SCOTERE*.ħɓr Alnod 7 Afchil.viii.car̊ tre ad glð.
T̊ra ad.xii.car̅.Ibi Turold abɓ hr̅ nc̅.iiii.car̅.
7 xxx.ii.uiłł.7 xiii.borð.cu̅.iiii.car̅.7 xv.focħ cu̅.iii.
or
car̅.7 i.molin̅ 7 medietate̅ duoʒ redð.viii.folið.7 ii.
piſcar̊.xv.folið.7 cxx.ac̊s p̊ti.7 xxviii.ac̅ filuæ
paſt̊.T.R.E.xi.liɓ.m̊ x.liɓ.Tres lev̊ lg̅.7 i.lar̅.

f Soca hůj Ⓜ eſt in Scaltorp.iii.car̊ tre ad glð.
T̊ra ad.ii.car̅.Ibi.viii.focħ 7 iiii.uiłł hn̅t.iiii.car̅.
346 a
7 xxx.ac̊s p̊ti.

f ⓂIn *CLETHAM*.ħɓ Ælnod.vii.boů tre ad glð.T̊ra
ad i.car̅ 7 dim̅.Ibi Roger ho̊ abɓ hr̅.i.car̅.7 iiii.
uiłł arant.s cu̅.v.boɓ.7 vii.ac̊s p̊ti.T.R.E.ual
xl.fol.m̊ xxx.fol.

f ⓂIn *MAMELTVNE*.ħɓ Rolft.ii.car̊ tre ad glð.T̊ra
ad.iiii.car̅.Ibi Radulf̊ ho̊ abɓ hr̅.i.car̅.7 v.uiłł.
7 iiii.borð cu̅.i.car̅.7 xx.ac̊s p̊ti.T.R.E.ual xii.
liɓ.m̊.lx.fol.Tailla.xx.fol.Duas lev̊ lg̅.7 i.lar̅.
Soca hůj Ⓜ in Cletha̅.i.boů tre ad glð.Ibi.i.
focħ arans.i.bou̅.

f 14 M. In YAWTHORPE Rothulfr had ½ carucate of land taxable. Land for
4 oxen. Abbot Thoraldr has 1 plough and
    meadow, 3 acres.
Value before 1066, 12s; now 5s.

15 M. In SCOTTON Asketill had 6 carucates of land taxable. Land for 6
ploughs. Richard, the Abbot's man, has under the Abbot 3 ploughs.
    22 villagers, 5 smallholders and 17 Freemen who have 2 ploughs.
    In Lincoln 3 burgesses who pay 5s.
    Meadow, 50 acres; underwood, 36 acres.
Value before 1066, 100s; now £4. Exactions 40s.

16 A jurisdiction of this manor in (Nor)THORPE; 1 carucate of land
taxable. Land for 1½ ploughs.
    4 Freemen have 2 villagers and 1 smallholder with 1 plough.

17 2 In SCOTTER Alnoth and Asketill had 8 carucates of land taxable.
   M. Land for 12 ploughs. Now Abbot Thoraldr has 4 ploughs and
    32 villagers and 13 smallholders with 4 ploughs;
        15 Freemen with 3 ploughs; and
        1 mill and a half of 2 [mills] which pay 8s; 2 fisheries, 15s;
        meadow, 120 acres; woodland pasture, 28 acres.
Value before 1066 £11; now £10.
[It is] 3 leagues long and 1 wide.

f 18 There is a jurisdiction of this manor in SCOTTERTHORPE; 3
carucates of land taxable. Land for 2 ploughs.
    8 Freemen and 4 villagers have 4 ploughs and
    meadow, 30 acres.

346 a

f 19 M. In CLEATHAM Alnoth had 7 bovates of land taxable. Land for 1½
ploughs. Roger, the Abbot's man, has 1 plough.
    4 villagers who plough with 5 oxen.
    Meadow, 7 acres.
Value before 1066, 40s; now 30s.

f 20 M. In MANTON Rothulfr had 2 carucates of land taxable. Land for 4
ploughs. Ralph, the Abbot's man, has 1 plough.
    5 villagers and 4 smallholders with 1 plough.
    Meadow, 20 acres.
Value before 1066 £12; now 60s. Exactions 20s.
[It is] 2 leagues long and 1 wide.

21 A jurisdiction of this manor in CLEATHAM; 1 bovate of land
taxable.
    1 Freeman who ploughs with 1 ox.

ꝏ **I**n *HIBOLDESTOV*.h̄ɓ Rolſt.x.boú træ ad glđ.

Ꞇra ad.iii.car̄.Ibi Giſleɓꞇ hō aɓɓis h̄ꞇ.ii.car̄.

7 xi.uiłł 7 i.ſocħ 7 iii.borđ hn̄t.ii.car̄ 7 dim̄.7 i.mo

lenđ.iiii.ſoliđ.7 cxi.ac̄s p̄ti.7 lx.ac̄s ſiluæ minutæ.

T.R.E.uał.vi.liɓ.m̄.lxx.ſoł.Tailla.xx.ſoł.

f ꝏ **I**n *RAGENELTORP*.h̄ɓ Aſchil.ii.car̄ tre ad glđ.

Ꞇra ad.iiii.car̄.Ibi Radulf hō aɓɓis h̄ꞇ.i.car̄.7 v.

uiłł.7 iiii.borđ.cū.i.car̄.7 xii.ac̄s p̄ti.T.R:E.uał

vi.liɓ.m̄.xxx.ſoł.Tailla.x.ſoł. In *CLETHA*.ii.bō ad glđ.

f **S**ocA huj ꝏ in Holm.iii.car̄ tre ad gld.Ꞇra ad

iii.car̄.Ibi.vi.ſocħ hn̄t.ii.car̄.7 i.molin̄.iiii.ſoliđ.

7 xii.ac̄ ſiluæ minuꞇæ.

SocA alia in Aſchebi.iii:boú tre ad gld.Ꞇra ad.iii.

boú.Ibi.i.ſocħ h̄ꞇ.i.car̄.7 iii.ac̄ ſilue minute.

f ꝏ **I**n *APLEBI* 7 *RISEBI* 7 *SALECLIF*.h̄ɓ Aſchil.iii boū

tre ad glđ.Ꞇra ad.vi.boú.Ibi Radulf hō aɓɓis h̄ꞇ

.i.car̄.7 xii.ac̄s p̄ti.T.R.E. uał xx.ſoł.m̄ xvi.ſoł.

f ꝏ **I**n *WALECOTE*.h̄ɓ Aſchil.vi.car̄ tre 7 v.boú ad glđ.

Ꞇra ad totiđ car̄ 7 boú. N̄c Iuo h̄ꞇ de aɓɓe.Ibi.i.car̄.

7 vii.uiłł 7 ii.borđ 7 x.ſocħ cū.ii.car̄.7 ccc.7 q̂ꞇ xx.

ac̄ p̄ti.7 lx.ac̄s ſiluæ minuꞇæ.T.R.E.uał vi.liɓ.m̄ xl.

ſoł.Tailla.x.ſoł.

f **B**erew̄ huj ꝏ in Alchebarge.i.car̄ tre ad gld.

Ꞇra ad.i.car̄ 7 dim̄. Ibi.iii.uiłł arant.iii.boɓʒ.

SocA in Hedebi.ii.boú tre ad glđ.Ꞇra ad.i.boú

7 dim̄.Ibi.i.ſocħ arat.ii.bob.

ꝏ **I**n *MESSINGEHA*.h̄ɓ Elnod.v.car̄ tre ad gld.

Ꞇra ad.v.car̄ 7 ii.boú.Ibi Wiłłs hō aɓɓis h̄ꞇ.ii.

car̄.7 v.uiłł 7 iiii.borđ.7 xviii.ſocħ.hn̄tes.iii.car̄.

7 xx.ac̄s p̄ti.T.R.E.uał.iiii.liɓ.m̄ ſimił.Tailla.xx.ſoł.

22 M. In HIBALDSTOW Rothulfr had 10 bovates of land taxable. Land for 3 ploughs. Gilbert, the Abbot's man, has 2 ploughs.
11 villagers, 1 Freeman and 3 smallholders have 2½ ploughs.
1 mill, 4s; meadow, 111 acres; underwood, 60 acres.
Value before 1066 £6; now 70s. Exactions 20s.

f 23 M. In 'RAVENTHORPE' Asketill had 2 carucates of land taxable. Land for 4 ploughs. Ralph, the Abbot's man, has 1 plough.
5 villagers and 4 smallholders with 1 plough.
Meadow, 12 acres.
Value before 1066 £6; now 30s. Exactions 10s.

24 In CLEATHAM 2 bovates taxable.

f 25 A jurisdiction of this manor in HOLME; 3 carucates of land taxable. Land for 3 ploughs.
6 Freemen have 2 ploughs.
1 mill, 4s; underwood, 12 acres.

26 Another jurisdiction in ASHBY; 3 bovates of land taxable. Land for 3 oxen.
1 Freeman has 1 plough.
Underwood, 3 acres.

f 27 M. In APPLEBY, RISBY and 'SAWCLIFFE' Asketill had 3 bovates of land taxable. Land for 6 oxen. Ralph, the Abbot's man, has 1 plough and
meadow, 12 acres.
Value before 1066, 20s; now 16s.

f 28 M. In WALCOT Asketill had 6 carucates of land and 5 bovates taxable. Land for as many ploughs and oxen. Now Ivo has them from the Abbot. 1 plough.
7 villagers, 2 smallholders and 10 Freemen with 2 ploughs.
Meadow, 380 acres; underwood, 60 acres.
Value before 1066 £6; now 40s. Exactions 10s.

f 29 An outlier of this manor in ALKBOROUGH; 1 carucate of land taxable. Land for 1½ ploughs.
3 villagers plough with 3 oxen.

30 A jurisdiction in 'HAYTHBY'; 2 bovates of land taxable. Land for 1½ oxen.
1 Freeman ploughs with 2 oxen.

31 M. In MESSINGHAM Alnoth had 5 carucates of land taxable. Land for 5 ploughs and 2 oxen. William, the Abbot's man, has 2 ploughs.
5 villagers, 4 smallholders and 18 Freemen who have 3 ploughs and
meadow, 20 acres.
Value before 1066 £4; now the same. Exactions 20s.

Berew huj ō̃ in Efcumetorp.una bou͛ tra͛e 7 ͛tcia
pars.i.bou͛ ad gld̄.Tra ad.i.bou͛.Ibi un͡ uiłłs h̄r.ii.
bou͡ in carruca.

In Offintone h̄r S petrus de Burg.xlviii.ac͛s p̄ti
fine gld̄.Hos tenet Goisfrid͡.7 uiłł aƀƀis.T.R.E.uał.xx.
foł.m̊ fimiłi͛t.

ō̃In *Witham* 7 Mannetorp 7 Toftlund.ħƀ Hereuuard
xii.bou͛ ͛tre ad gld̄.Tra ad.i.car̄ 7͛ dim̄.Ibi Afuert hō
aƀƀis Turoldi h̄r.vi.uiłł 7 iiii.bord 7 ii.focħ cū.ii.car̄.
7 xx.ac͛s p̄ti.7 xl.ac͛s filuae.T.R.E.uał.xl.foł.m̊ fimiłi͛t.
Berew huj ō̃ in Bercaħa 7 Eftou.i.car̄ ͛trae ad gld̄.T͛ra
ad.i.car̄.Ibi Asford h̄r.ii.uiłł 7 ii.bord cū.i.car̄.
Ibide͛.i.carucata ͛trae ad gld̄.Tra ad.i.car̄.Soca in Burg.
Nc̄ Godefrid͡ hō aƀƀis h̄r ix.focħ.7 i.uiłł.7 ii.bord.cū
ii.car̄.Roƀt tenet dimid͡.T.R.E.uał xx.foł.m̊.xx.fimił.
In *Estov* Soca in Witħā.iiii.bou͛ ͛tre 7 dim̄ ad gld̄.
T͛ra ad tntd̄.Ibi Asfort de aƀƀe h̄r.i.uiłł 7 ii.focħ cū
dim̄ car̄.
Ibide͛.ii.bou͛ ͛trae ad gld͛.Tra ad.ii.bou͛.Soca in Werche
S petri de Burg.Ibi h̄r Godefr͛ de aƀƀe.i.uiłł 7 ii.focħ
cū dim̄ car̄.T.R.E.uał.iii.foł.m̊ fimiłi͛t.
ō̃In *Tvroldebi*.ħƀ Elnod.i.caruc͛ 7 dim̄ ad gld̄.Tra ad
i.car̄ 7 dim̄.Frigfoca fub Aflac.Ibi Goisfrid͡ fub aƀƀe.
h̄r.i.car̄.7 i.uiłł 7 iiii.bord.7 xxx.ac͛s filuae minutae.
T.R.E.uał.xx.foł.m̊ xx.foł fimił.

.IX. Terra Sc̄i Petri De Westmon͛.
ō̃In *Dodinctone*.ħƀ Ailric.vi.car̄ ͛trae ad gld̄.
T͛ra.iiii.car̄.Ibi S Petr̄ de Weftmonaft͛ h̄r.i.car̄.

32 An outlier of this manor in SCUNTHORPE; 1 bovate of land and the third part of 1 bovate taxable. Land for 1 ox.
　　1 villager has 2 oxen in a plough.

33 In UFFINGTON St. Peter's of Peterborough has 48 acres of meadow without tax. Geoffrey holds them and the Abbot's villagers.
　　Value before 1066, 20s; now the same.

34 M. In WITHAM (on the Hill), MANTHORPE and TOFT and LOUND Hereweard had 12 bovates of land taxable. Land for 1½ ploughs. Asfrothr, Abbot Thoraldr's man, has
　　6 villagers, 4 smallholders and 2 Freemen with 2 ploughs; and meadow, 20 acres; woodland, 40 acres.
　　Value before 1066, 40s; now the same.

35 Outliers of this manor in BARHOLM and 'STOWE'; 1 carucate of land taxable. Land for 1 plough. Asfrothr has
　　2 villagers and 2 smallholders with 1 plough.

36 There also 1 carucate of land taxable. Land for 1 plough. A jurisdiction of Peterborough. Now Godfrey, the Abbot's man, has
　　9 Freemen, 1 villager and 2 smallholders with 2 ploughs. Robert holds half.
　　Value before 1066, 20s; now 20[s] likewise.

37 In 'STOWE', a jurisdiction of Witham, 4½ bovates of land taxable. Land for as much. Asfrothr has from the Abbot
　　1 villager and 2 Freemen with ½ plough.

38 There also 2 bovates of land taxable. Land for 2 oxen. A jurisdiction of St. Peter's of Peterborough's work.
　　Godfrey has from the Abbot
　　1 villager and 2 Freemen with ½ plough.
　　Value before 1066, 3s; now the same.

39 M. In THURLBY Alnoth had 1½ carucates of land taxable. Land for 1½ ploughs. [It is] a free jurisdiction under Aslakr. Geoffrey has under the Abbot 1 plough.
　　1 villager and 4 smallholders.
　　Underwood, 30 acres.
　　Value before 1066, 20s; now 20s likewise.

9　　LAND OF ST. PETER'S OF WESTMINSTER

1 M. In DODDINGTON Aelfric had 6 carucates of land taxable. Land for 4 ploughs. St. Peter's of Westminster has 1 plough.

7 xiiii . uiłł 7 vi . borđ . cū . iiii . cař . Ibi pbr 7 æccła.
p̃tū dim̃ leṽ lg̃.7 dim̃ łat . Silua past . i . leṽ 7 dim̃ lg̃.
7 dim̃ leṽ łat . T.R.E . cū om̃ibȝ ad ħ m̃ ptinentibȝ.
uał . xx . lib̃ . Modo ualet qđ S̃ petř ħt . iiii . lib̃.

B̃ In Torp . vi . cař træ 7 ii . bou ad glđ . Tra . vi . cař . Soca
ejđ m̃ . Ibi . xxx . focħ hn̄t . vii . cař 7 dim̃ . p̃ti . ii . q̃ȝ lg̃.
£7 ii . łat.

346 c

.X. TERRA SC̃I BENEDICTI DE RAMESIG.

m̃ In CORNINCTVNE ħb 7 ħt S̃ Benedc̃ de Rameſỹ
i . cař tre 7 vi . bõ ad glđ . Tra ad totđ cař 7 bou.
Ibi nc̄ in dn̄io . i . cař . 7 iii . uiłł 7 i . borđ . 7 i . focħ cū
. i . cař . Ibi . ii . æccłæ 7 i . molin xxi . folid 7 iiii . den.
7 xiiii . ac̃ p̃ti . T.R.E . uał xl . fot . m̃ iiii . lib̃.
Soca huj m̃ in Eſlaforde . i . cař tre . Tra ad . i.
cař . Ibi . i . focħ 7 ii . uiłł hn̄t . i . cař . 7 xxvii . ac̃ p̃ti.
Soca alia in Dunneſbi . vi . cař tre ad glđ . Tra
ad totiđ cař . Ibi m̃ . xi . focħ 7 iii . borđ . hn̄t . iii . cař.
7 vi . ac̃s p̃ti.

★ m̃ In K̃RICHINGHA̅ ħb 7 ħt S̃ Beneđ de Rameſỹ.
dim̃ cař tre ad glđ . Tra ad . iiii . bou . Ibi . i . uiłłs
ħt dim̃ cař . T.R.E . uał . v . fot . m̃ fimilit.
In Coteland ħt S̃ Beneđ . dim̃ cař p̃ti ad glđ . in
Craneuuelle.

346 d

.XI. TERRA SC̃I GUTHLACI DE CRVILA̅ND.

m̃ In HOLEBEN 7 COPELADE ħb 7 ħt S̃ Gutlac . i . cař tre
ad glđ . Tra ad . vi . bou . Ibi nc̄ . i . cař in dn̄io . 7 iii . uiłł
cū dim̃ cař . 7 xii . ac̃ p̃ti . T.R.E . uał xx . fot . m̃ fimił.

14 villagers and 6 smallholders with 4 ploughs.
A priest and a church; meadow ½ league long and ½ wide;
    woodland pasture 1½ leagues long and ½ league wide.
Value before 1066, with everything belonging to this manor, £20;
now value of what St. Peter's has, £4.

2 B. In THORPE (on the Hill) 6 carucates of land and 2 bovates taxable.
Land for 6 ploughs. A jurisdiction also of this manor.
    30 Freemen have 7½ ploughs.
    Meadow, 2 furlongs long and 2 wide.

10   LAND OF ST. BENEDICT'S OF RAMSEY   346 c

1 M. In QUARRINGTON St. Benedict's of Ramsey had and has 1 carucate
of land and 6 bovates taxable. Land for as many ploughs and oxen.
Now in lordship 1 plough;
    3 villagers, 1 smallholder and 1 Freeman with 1 plough.
    2 churches; 1 mill, 21s 4d; meadow, 14 acres.
Value before 1066, 40s; now £4.

2   A jurisdiction of this manor in (Old) SLEAFORD; 1 carucate of
land taxable. Land for 1 plough.
    1 Freeman and 2 villagers have 1 plough.
    Meadow, 27 acres.

3   Another jurisdiction in 'DUNSBY'; 6 carucates of land taxable.
Land for as many ploughs.
    Now 11 Freemen and 3 smallholders have 3 ploughs and
    meadow, 6 acres.

4 M. In THREEKINGHAM St. Benedict's of Ramsey had and has ½
carucate of land taxable. Land for 4 oxen.
    1 villager has ½ plough.
Value before 1066, 5s; now the same.

In *COTELAND* St. Benedict's has ½ carucate of meadow taxable
in Cranwell.

11   LAND OF ST. GUTHLAC'S OF CROWLAND   346 d

1 M. In HOLBEACH and WHAPLODE St. Guthlac's had and has 1 carucate
of land taxable. Land for 6 oxen. Now 1 plough in lordship;
    3 villagers with ½ plough.
    Meadow, 12 acres.
Value before 1066, 20s; now the same.

In Spallinge BEREW de Croiland . II . car̄ tre ad glđ.
Tra ad . I . car̄ 7 dim̄ . Ibi . VII . uilt 7 IIII . borđ . hn̄t . III . car̄.
T.R.E. uat . xx . fot . m̄ fimilit.

ᵹⁱIn LANGETOF . hƀ 7 hē S̄ Gutlac . VI . car̄ træ ad glđ.
Tra ad . VI . car̄ . Ibi nē in dn̄io . I . car̄ . 7 VIII . uilt . 7 IIII .
borđ . 7 xx . foch hn̄tes . V . car̄ . 7 c . ac̄ p̄ti . Silua . II . fot.
Marefc . II . leu lḡ . 7 II . lat̄ . Tra araƀ . xv . q̄ʒ lḡ . 7 IX . lat̄.
T.R.E. uat . IIII . liƀ . m̄ Lx . fot . Tailla . x . fot.

ᵹⁱIn BASTVNE hƀ 7 hē S̄ Gutlac . I.I.I . car̄ træ ad glđ.
Tra ad . IIII . car̄ . Ibi nē in dn̄io . I . car̄ . 7 v . uilt . 7 II .
borđ . 7 VII . foch cū . II . car̄ . Ibi æccta 7 dim̄ molin̄.
7 xLv . ac̄ p̄ti . Marefc . xvi . q̄ʒ lḡ . 7 VIII . lat̄ . Tra
araƀ VIII . q̄ʒ lḡ . 7 VIII . lat̄ . T.R.E. uat . xL . fot . m̄ fimit.

ᵹⁱIn DVVEDIC . hƀ 7 hē S̄ Gutlac . II . car̄ tre ad glđ.
Tra ad . II . car̄ . cū facca 7 foca . Ibi nē . I . car̄ in dn̄io.
7 xIII . uilt cū . I . car̄ . 7 xx . ac̄ p̄ti . T.R.E. uat . xL.
fot . m̄ fimilit . Colegr̄i tenet
BEREW huᵹⁱ ᵹⁱ in Draitone . I . car̄ tre ad glđ.
Tra ad . I . car̄ . Ibi . v . uilt . n̄ arant . Ibi . IIII . falinæ
v . foliđ 7 IIII . den̄ . 7 vI . ac̄ p̄ti.
In Alfgare BEREW alia . xII . bou tre ad glđ . Tra
ad . x . bou . Nē Wafta . ē . Colegr̄i tenet de abƀe.
In Burtoft hƀ 7 hē S̄ Gutlac . I . bou tre quæ jacet
in Duuedic . Inde hē rex foca.

ᵹⁱIn BUCHEHALE . hƀ Gamel . x . bou træ ad glđ . Tra
Ibiđē SOCA de Badesford . x . bou tre   ⌠ad x . bou.
ad glđ . Tra ad x . bou . Ibi hē nē S̄ Gutlac . I . car̄
in dn̄io . 7 v . uilt 7 II . borđ . 7 VIII . foch hn̄tes . I . car̄.
Ibi . cxx . ac̄ p̄ti . 7 L . ac̄s filuæ past . 7 Lxx . ac̄s filuæ min̄.
T.R.E. uat xxx . fot . m̄ fimilit . Hanc tra dedit
Turold S̄ Gutlaco p̄ anima fua.

2   In SPALDING, an outlier of Crowland, 2 carucates of land taxable.
Land for 1½ ploughs.
> 7 villagers and 4 smallholders have 3 ploughs.

Value before 1066, 20s; now the same.

3 M. In LANGTOFT St. Guthlac's had and has 6 carucates of land
taxable. Land for 6 ploughs. Now in lordship 1 plough;
> 8 villagers, 4 smallholders and 20 Freemen who have 5 ploughs.
> Meadow, 100 acres; woodland, 2s; marsh 2 leagues long and
> > 2 wide; arable land 15 furlongs long and 9 wide.

Value before 1066 £4; now 60s. Exactions 10s.

4 M. In BASTON St. Guthlac's had and has 4 carucates of land taxable.
Land for 4 ploughs. Now in lordship 1 plough;
> 5 villagers, 2 smallholders and 7 Freemen with 2 ploughs.
> A church and ½ mill; meadow, 45 acres; marsh 16 furlongs
> > long and 8 wide; arable land 8 furlongs long and 8 wide.

Value before 1066, 40s; now the same.

5 M. In DOWDYKE St. Guthlac's had and has 2 carucates of land taxable.
Land for 2 ploughs with full jurisdiction. Now 1 plough in lordship;
> 13 villagers with 1 plough.
> Meadow, 20 acres.

Value before 1066, 40s; now the same.
> Kolgrimr holds it.

6   An outlier of this manor in DRAYTON; 1 carucate of land taxable.
Land for 1 plough.
> 5 villagers do not plough.
> 4 salt-houses, 5s 4d; meadow, 6 acres.

7   In ALGAR(kirk), another outlier, 12 bovates of land taxable. Land
for 10 oxen. Now it is waste. Kolgrimr holds it from the Abbot.

8   In BURTOFT St. Guthlac's had and has 1 bovate of land which lies
in Dowdyke. The King has jurisdiction over it.

9 M. In BUCKNALL Gamall had 10 bovates of land taxable. Land for 10
oxen. There also a jurisdiction of Belchford, 10 bovates of land
taxable. Land for 10 oxen. Now St. Guthlac's has 1 plough in
lordship;
> 5 villagers, 2 smallholders and 8 Freemen who have 1 plough.
> Meadow, 120 acres; woodland pasture, 50 acres; underwood,
> > 70 acres.

Value before 1066, 30s; now the same.
> Thoraldr the Sheriff gave this land to St. Guthlac's for his soul.

.XII. TERRA ALANI COMITIS.

Ⓜ .II. In *BORTONE* . ħbr Gonneuuate 7 Godric
iiii . car̄ træ 7 vi . boū ad glđ . Tra ad . v . car̄.
Nc̄ ħt comes Alan ibi . i . car̄. 7 x . focħ hn̄tes
.iii : car̄. 7 xl . ac̄s p̄ti . 7 lxx . ac̄s broce . T.R.E.
uat . iii . lib . m̄ xxx . fot . Tailla . x . fot.
Soca huj Ⓜ in Martone . vi . bō træ ad glđ.
Tra ad . i . car̄ . Wafta . e.

Ⓜ In *WELINGEHĀ* . ħb Staigri xii . bō tre ad glđ.

Ⓜ Tra ad xii . boū . Ibidē ħb Gunneuuate . vi . boū
tre 7 iii . partē . ii . bouat . ad glđ . Tra ad tntđ bǫū.
Ibi ħt com̄ Alan in dñio . i . car̄. 7 v . uitt 7 ii . focħ
cū . i . car̄. T.R.E. uat . xl . fot . m̄ xx . fot.

Ⓜ .IIII. In *LEA* . ħbr Fulcheri 7 ii . fr̄s ej̄ . iii . car̄ tre 7 dim̄
ad glđ . Ibidē ħb Vlchil dim̄ car̄ tre ad glđ.
Tra ad . v . car̄ . Ibi Robt̄ hō comitis ħt nc̄ . i . car̄.
7 xvi . uitt 7 ii . focħ cū . iii . car̄. 7 dimid piícariā
de . x . den̄ . 7 i . paffagiū de . xii . den̄ . 7 c . ac̄s p̄ti.
7 c . ac̄s filuæ minutæ . T.R.E. uat . c . fot . m̄ xxx . fot.
Tailla . xx . fot.
Berew̄ huj Ⓜ 7 Soca . iiii . bou træ ad glđ . In
Lopehā . Tra ad dim̄ car̄ . Ibi . iiii . fochi m̄ arant
ii . bob . Ibi . xx . ac̄ p̄ti.
Soca alia in Sumerdebi : dim̄ car̄ træ ad glđ.
Tra ad . iiii . boū . Ibi . ii . focħ arant̄ . iii . bob . Ibi . x .
ac̄ p̄ti . 7 x . ac̄ filue minutæ.

Ⓜ .VI. In *CHELVINGEHOLM* Radolf Welgrim . Afchil
Archel Sagrim . 7 Ernuin ħbr . ii . car̄ tre 7 dim̄
ad glđ . Tra ad . vi . car̄ . Ibi Landric hō com̄ ħt
nc̄ . ii . car̄. 7 xi . uitt cū . i . car̄. 7 c . ac̄s p̄ti . T.R.E.
uat . iiii . lib . m̄ xxx . fot . Tailla . x . fot.

1 2 In (Gate) BURTON Gunnhvatr and Godric had 4 carucates of land
M. and 6 bovates taxable. Land for 5 ploughs. Now Count Alan has
1 plough there.
   10 Freemen who have 3 ploughs and
   meadow, 40 acres; water-meadow, 70 acres.
Value before 1066 £3; now 30s. Exactions 10s.

2 A jurisdiction of this manor in MARTON; 6 bovates of land taxable.
Land for 1 plough. It is waste.

3 M. In WILLINGHAM (by Stow) Steingrimr had 12 bovates of land
taxable. Land for 12 oxen.
M. There also Gunnhvatr had 6 bovates of land and the third part of
2 bovates taxable. Land for as many oxen. Count Alan has in
lordship 1 plough;
   5 villagers and 2 Freemen with 1 plough.
Value before 1066, 40s; now 20s.

4 4 In LEA Fulcric and his 2 brothers had 3½ carucates of land taxable.
M. There also Ulfketill had ½ carucate of land taxable. Land for 5
ploughs. Robert, the Count's man, now has 1 plough and
   16 villagers and 2 Freemen with 3 ploughs; and
   ½ fishery at 10d; 1 ferry at 12d; meadow, 115 acres;
      underwood, 100 acres.
Value before 1066, 100s; now 30s. Exactions 20s.

5 An outlier of this manor and a jurisdiction in HEAPHAM; 4 bovates
of land taxable. Land for ½ plough.
   4 Freemen now plough with 2 oxen.
   Meadow, 20 acres.

6 Another jurisdiction in SOMERBY; ½ carucate of land taxable.
Land for 4 oxen.
   2 Freemen plough with 3 oxen.
   Meadow, 10 acres; underwood, 10 acres.

7 6 In KILLINGHOLME Ralph, Wilgrim, Asketill, Arnketill, Saegrimr and
M. Earnwine the priest had 2½ carucates of land taxable. Land for 6
ploughs. Landric, the Count's man, now has 2 ploughs.
   11 villagers with 1 plough.
   Meadow, 100 acres.
Value before 1066 £4; now 30s. Exactions 10s.

ꝏ In *CHERNITONE* . ħb . Afchilbar . iiii . bou trǽ ad glđ

Tra ad . i . car 7 dim̃ . Ibi nc̃ . i . car in dñio . 7 i . uilt . 7 iiii.

foch cu̅ . i . car . T.R.E . uat . xl . fot . m̃ xx . fot.

ꝏ In *NORTCHELESEI* . ħb Grimbold crac . i . car trǽ ad glđ.

Tra ad . ii . car . Ibi nc̃ . i . uilts cu̅ . vi . bob . 7 i . molin̄ . vii.

folid . T.R.E . uat xx . fot . m̃ fimilit.

Berew̃ huj ꝏ . in Seurebi . iii ꞏbou tre ad glđ . Tra ad . vi.

bou̅ . Ibi . i . uilts arat . iii . bobʒ.

Berew̃ alia in Catenafe 7 Vfun . v . bou trǽ ad glđ . 7 tcia

347 b

pars . i . bouate ad glđ . 7 tñtd ad arand . Ibi . v . uilt

hñt . ii . car . 7 c . ac̃ p̃ti . Vt . xl . fot . •

Berew̃ alia in Odenebi . iii . bou tre ad glđ . Ibi un̅

uilts arat . iii ꞉ bobʒ . Ibi . viii . ac̃ p̃ti.

ꝏ In *CATENASE* 7 *VSVN* . ħb Grimbold crac . v . bou

trǽ . 7 tciã parte bouatæ ad glđ . Tra ad totid boues.

Ibi . vi ꞉ cu̅ dño hñt . iii . car 7 dimid . T.R.E . uat . lx.

fot . m̃ xl . fot.

ꝏ In *ALESBI* . ħb Orm . ii . car trǽ 7 vi . bou꞉ 7 ii . partes

uni bouate ad glđ . Tra ad . v . car . Ibi Picot hō

comitis ht nc̃ . ii . car . 7 vi . uilt 7 iii . borđ . 7 xx . foch

hñtes . ii . car 7 ii . boues . Ibi eccta 7 p̃br . 7 i . molin̄

7 dimid . ix . folid . T.R.E . uat . v . lib . m̃ . iiii . lib . Tailla

Soca huj ꝏ in Sualun . iii . bou trǽ   £xx . fot.

ad glđ . Tra ad . vi . bou . Ibi m̃ un̅ borđ.

Soca alia in Cotes . una bouata tre ad glđ . Wafta . ē.

ꝏ In *SVALVN* . ħb Sbern . i . car 7 dim̃ ad glđ . Tra ad . iii.

car . Ibi ht Picot dim̃ car . 7 v . uilt 7 i . borđ . 7 ix.

foch cu̅ . i . car 7 dimid . T.R.E . uat . xx . fot . m̃ . lx . fot.

          £ Tailla . xx . fot.

8 M. In KIRMINGTON Asketill Barn had 4 bovates of land taxable. Land
 for 1½ ploughs. Now 1 plough in lordship;
    1 villager and 4 Freemen with 1 plough.
 Value before 1066, 40s; now 20s.

9 M. In NORTH KELSEY Grimbald Krakr had 1 carucate of land taxable.
 Land for 2 ploughs.
    Now 1 villager with 6 oxen.
    1 mill, 7s.
 Value before 1066, 20s; now the same.

10 An outlier of this manor in SEARBY; 3 bovates of land taxable.
 Land for 6 oxen.
    1 villager ploughs with 3 oxen.

11 Another outlier in CADNEY and HOWSHAM; 5 bovates of land
 taxable and the third part of 1 bovate taxable. As much land for   347 b
 ploughing.
    5 villagers have 2 ploughs.
    Meadow, 100 acres.
 Value 40s.

12 Another outlier in OWMBY; 3 bovates of land taxable.
    1 villager ploughs with 3 oxen.
    Meadow, 8 acres.

13 M. In CADNEY and HOWSHAM Grimbald Krakr had 5 bovates of land
 and the third part of a bovate taxable. Land for as many
 oxen.
    6 [villagers?] with the lord have 3½ ploughs.
 Value before 1066, 60s; now 40s.

14 M. In AYLESBY Ormr had 2 carucates of land and 6 bovates and 2
 parts of 1 bovate taxable. Land for 5 ploughs. Picot, the Count's
 man, now has 2 ploughs.
    6 villagers, 3 smallholders and 20 Freemen who have 2 ploughs
     and 2 oxen.
    A church and a priest; 1½ mills, 9s.
 Value before 1066 £5; now £4. Exactions 20s.

15 A jurisdiction of this manor in SWALLOW; 3 bovates of land
 taxable. Land for 6 oxen.
    Now 1 smallholder.

16 Another jurisdiction in (Great) COATES; 1 bovate of land taxable.
 It is waste.

17 M. In SWALLOW Esbjorn had 1½ carucates taxable. Land for 3 ploughs.
 Picot has ½ plough.
    5 villagers, 1 smallholder and 9 Freemen with 1½ ploughs.
 Value before 1066, 20s; now 60s. Exactions 20s.

M In *HOLTVN*. hb̄ Turgot. II. bou̓ t̓re 7. II. vrg' 7 V. acs ad gld̓. Ibi Wimund hō com̄. ht̄. II. uilt. cū V. bob3 arantes. 7 V. acs p̄ti. T.R.E. ual. III. sol. m̄. VIII. s.

.II. M In *FVGELESTOV*. hb̄r Rolf 7 Sbern. II. car̄ t̓re 7 II. bou̓ ad gld̓. T̓ra ad. III. car̄ 7 dim̄. Ibi Picot de comite ht̄. II. car̄. 7 XIIII. uilt. 7 VII. bord̓. 7 II. soch̄ cū. II. car̄. 7 VIII. salinas de. VIII. sol. 7 CC. LX. acs p̄ti. T.R.E. ual XL. sol. m̄. IIII. lib̄. Tailla. XX. sol.

.III. M In *GRENESBI*. Spille. Adestan. 7 Lepsi. hb̄r. III. car̄ t̓re ad gld̓. T̓ra ad. V. car̄. Ibi Wimund hō comitis ht̄. I. car̄ 7 dim̄. 7 XII. uilt 7 IIII. bord̓. 7 XIII. soch̄ hn̄tes. III. car̄ 7 dim̄ 7 LI. ac̄ p̄ti. 7 Toruelande V. solid̓ 7 IIII. den̓. T.R.E. ual LXX. sol. m̄. IIII. lib̄ Tailla. XX. sol.

M In *WALTHAM*. hb̄ Radulf stalre. VI. car̄ t̓re ad gld̓. T̓ra ad. XII. car̄. Ibi ht̄ nc̄ comes Alan. IIII. car̄. 7 XII. uilt. 7 I. bord̓. 7 XVIII. soch̄ hn̄tes. IX. car̄ 7 dimid̓. Ibi æccl̄a 7 pb̄r. 7 LX. VIII. ac̄ p̄ti. T.R.E. ual XX. lib̄. m̄ XL. V. lib̄. Tailla. XV. lib̄. Tot̄. XV. qz lḡ. 7 IX. lat̄.

SOCA huj M In Wade. XI. bou̓ t̓re ad gld̓. T̓ra ad XI. boues. Ibi. XII. soch̄ hn̄t. I. car̄ 7 dim̄. 7 XX. acs p̄ti.

SOCA alia In Aschebi. VI. bou̓ t̓re ad gld̓. T̓ra ad. XII. car̄. Ibi. V. soch̄ hn̄t. I. car̄. 7 XX. V. acs p̄ti. 7 V. ac̄ silue min̄.

In Bernulfbi SOCA. VI. car̄ t̓ræ ad gld. T̓ra ad. XII. car̄.

347 c

Ibi. XXVI. soch̄ 7 IX. bord̓. hn̄tes. IX. car̄ 7 dimid̓. 7 CC. ac̄ p̄ti.

S In *FENDEBI* Soca. III. car̄ t̓ræ ad gld̓. T̓ra ad. VI. car̄. Ibi XV. soch̄ 7 II. bord̓ hn̄tes. III. car̄ 7 dim̓. 7 XL. acs p̄ti.

18 M. In HOLTON (le Clay) Thorgautr had 2 bovates of land and 5 acres and 2 virgates taxable. Wigmund, the Count's man, has
> 2 villagers who plough with 5 oxen; and
> meadow, 5 acres.
Value before 1066, 3s; now 8s.

19 2 In FULSTOW Rothulfr and Esbjorn had 2 carucates of land and 2
M. bovates taxable. Land for 3½ ploughs. Picot has 2 ploughs from the Count and
> 14 villagers, 7 smallholders and 2 Freemen with 2 ploughs; and
> 8 salt-houses at 8s; meadow, 260 acres.
Value before 1066, 40s; now £4. Exactions 20s.

20 3 In GRAINSBY Spillir, Aethelstan and Leofsige had 3 carucates of
M. land taxable. Land for 5 ploughs. Wigmund, the Count's man, has 1½ ploughs.
> 12 villagers, 4 smallholders and 13 Freemen who have 3½ ploughs.
> Meadow, 51 acres; turf-land, 5s 4d.
Value before 1066, 70s; now £4. Exactions 20s.

21 M. In WALTHAM Ralph the Constable had 6 carucates of land taxable. Land for 12 ploughs. Now Count Alan has 4 ploughs.
> 12 villagers, 1 smallholder and 18 Freemen who have 9½ ploughs.
> A church and a priest; meadow, 68 acres.
Value before 1066 £20; now £45. Exactions £15.
The whole [is] 15 furlongs long and 9 wide.

22 A jurisdiction of this manor in WAITHE; 11 bovates of land taxable. Land for 11 oxen.
> 12 Freemen have 1½ ploughs and
> meadow, 20 acres.

23 Another jurisdiction in ASHBY; 6 bovates of land taxable. Land for 12 ploughs.
> 5 Freemen have 1 plough and
> meadow, 25 acres; underwood, 5 acres.

24 In BARNOLDBY (le Beck), a jurisdiction, 6 carucates of land taxable. Land for 12 ploughs.
> 26 Freemen and 9 smallholders who have 9½ ploughs. 347 c
> Meadow, 200 acres.

25 S. In FENBY, a jurisdiction, 3 carucates of land taxable. Land for 6 ploughs.
> 15 Freemen and 2 smallholders who have 3½ ploughs and
> meadow, 40 acres.

ꝶ In Rauenedal 7 altera Rauenedale.Soca.III.caꝛ traͤ
ad glđ.Tra ad.VI.caꝛ.Ibi XIIII.ſocħ hñt.II.caꝛ.

ꝶ In Cadebi Soca.III.caꝛ tre ad glđ.Tra ad.IIII.caꝛ.
Ibi XIIII.ſocħ hñt.III.caꝛ.

ꝶ In Beſebi Soca.III.caꝛ tre ad glđ.Tra ad.IIII.caꝛ.
Ibi hɫ comes Alan.I.caꝛ.7 I.ſocħ.7 XVI.aĉs p̄ti.
7 VI.aĉs ſiluaͤ minutaͤ.

ꝳ In| *BASEBI*.ħɓr Ingemund 7 Oune Edric 7 Eculf
III.caꝛ 7 III.bou traͤ 7 III.partes.uni bouate.7 itĕ
tciã partĕ uni bou.Tra ad.IIII.caꝛ.
Ibi hɫ nĉ cõm.I.ſocħ 7 VIII.uiɫɫ cū.I.caꝛ 7 dim̃.
7 XVI.aĉ p̄ti.7 VI.aĉ ſiluaͤ minutaͤ.T.R.E. XX.ſoɫ.
m̃.XXX.ſoɫ.Terrã Eculf.habebat Wiɫɫs blund
eo die quó Ernuin p̄br capt fuit.& ante.

ꝶ In Neutone Soca.III.caꝛ tre 7 dim̃ bou ad glđ.Tra
ad.V.caꝛ.Ibi XX.ſocħ 7 II.borđ.hñt.IIII.caꝛ.

ꝳ In eađ *NEVTONE*.ħɓr Ingemund 7 III.frs ej.III
bou tre ad glđ.Tra ad.I.caꝛ.Ibi Wimund ħo cõm
hɫ.I.caꝛ. SOCA IN WALTHAM.

ꝶ In Hauuardebi Soca.II.caꝛ tre 7 III.bou ad glđ.
Tra ad.IIII.caꝛ.Ibi XIIII.ſocħ.7 I.uiɫɫ 7 I.borđ.
cū.III.caꝛ.

ꝶ In Suinhope Soca XV.bou traͤ 7 q̃rta pars.I.bõ
ad glđ.Tra ad.IIII.caꝛ.Ibi XVI.ſocħ hñt.II.caꝛ.

ꝶ In Gunreſbi Soca.II.caꝛ tre ad glđ.Tra ad.IIII.caꝛ.
Ibi.VI.ſocħ 7 V.borđ hñt.IIII.caꝛ.7 I.moliñ.VI.ſoɫ.
7 X.aĉs p̄ti

ꝶ In Hadecliue Soca.IIII.caꝛ tre ad glđ.Tra ad.VII.caꝛ.
Ibi.IX.ſocħ 7 IX borđ hñt.IIII caꝛ.7 II.molinos
VIII.ſoɫ.7 XX.aĉs p̄ti.

ꝶ In Beleſbi Soca.IIII.caꝛ tre ad glđ.Tra ad.VIII.caꝛ.

347 c

26 S. In RAVENDALE and the other RAVENDALE, a jurisdiction, 3 carucates of land taxable. Land for 6 ploughs.
14 Freemen have 2 ploughs.

27 S. In (North) CADEBY, a jurisdiction, 3 carucates of land taxable. Land for 4 ploughs.
14 Freemen have 3 ploughs.

28 S. In BEESBY, a jurisdiction, 3 carucates of land taxable. Land for 4 ploughs. Count Alan has 1 plough.
1 Freeman.
Meadow, 16 acres; underwood, 6 acres.

29 M. Also in BEESBY Ingimundr, Authunn, Eadric and Ecgwulf had 3 carucates and 3 bovates of land and 3 parts of 1 bovate and also the third part of 1 bovate. Land for 4 ploughs. Now the Count has
1 Freeman and 8 villagers with 1½ ploughs.
Meadow, 16 acres; underwood, 6 acres.
Value before 1066, 20s; now 30s.
William Blunt had Ecgwulf's land, 5½ bovates, on the day on which Earnwine the priest was taken, and before.

30 S. In (Wold) NEWTON, a jurisdiction, 3 carucates of land and ½ bovate taxable. Land for 5 ploughs.
20 Freemen and 2 smallholders have 4 ploughs.

31 4 M. Also in (Wold) NEWTON Ingimundr and his 3 brothers had 3 bovates of land taxable. Land for 1 plough.
Wigmund, the Count's man, has 1 plough.

Jurisdiction of Waltham:

32 S. In HAWERBY, a jurisdiction, 2 carucates of land and 3 bovates taxable. Land for 4 ploughs.
14 Freemen, 1 villager and 1 smallholder with 3 ploughs.

33 S. In SWINHOPE, a jurisdiction, 15 bovates of land and the fourth part of 1 bovate taxable. Land for 4 ploughs.
16 Freemen have 2 ploughs.

34 S. In GUNNERBY, a jurisdiction, 2 carucates of land taxable. Land for 4 ploughs.
6 Freemen and 5 smallholders have 4 ploughs.
1 mill, 6s; meadow, 10 acres.

35 S. In HATCLIFFE, a jurisdiction, 4 carucates of land taxable. Land for 7 ploughs.
9 Freemen and 9 smallholders have 4 ploughs and
2 mills, 8s; meadow, 20 acres.

36 S. In BEELSBY, a jurisdiction, 4 carucates of land taxable. Land for 8 ploughs.

Ibi xx.iiii.foch 7 vii.bord hn̄t vii.car̄.7 ii.mol

7 dim̄.xii.fol.7 xxx.ac̄ p̄ti.

ꝯ In WELLETVNE ħɓ Siuuard.i.car̄ tre ad glđ.

Tra ad.ii.car̄.Ibi Landric ho comitis ħt.ii.car̄.

7 xi.uiłł 7 ii.foch cū.i.car̄ 7 dim̄.7 i.molin̄.x.fol.

HAWARDES 7 xx.ac̄s p̄ti.7 iiii.parte.æcclæ.T.R.E.uał.iiii.liɓ.m̄.iii.liɓ.

HOV WAP ꟗIn Torefbi Soc̄a de Walthā.ix.bou tre 7 dim ad glđ.

Tra ad.xiiii.bou.Ibi xiiii.foch 7 ii.bord hn̄t.ii.car̄.

347 d

7 ii.falin 7 ii.folidoꝝ.7 xvi.ac̄s p̄ti.

ꟗ In Brigeflai.Soca de Walthā.i.car̄ træ 7 dimiđ

ad glđ.Tra ad.iii.car̄.Ibi xvii.foch 7 i.bord hn̄t

iii.car̄.7 x.ac̄ p̄ti.   BOLIBROC WAP

ꝯ In HALTVN 7 Stepi.ħɓ Ælric.iii.bou træ ad glđ.

Tra ad.iii.car̄.Ibi Eudo ho comitis ħt.i.car̄.

WELLE 7 qt xx.ac̄s p̄ti.T.R.E.uał x.fol.m̄ fimiłt.

WAP ꟗ In STOV ħt Alan com dimiđ car̄ tre ad glđ.Soca ē

Tra ad dim̄ car̄.Ibi.ii.foch hn̄t dim̄ car̄.

ASLACHESHOV.

WAP ꝯ In SPREDELINTONE ħɓ Cnut.ii.car̄ træ 7 i.bou

7 dim̄ ad glđ.Tra ad.iii.car̄ 7 ii.bou.Ibi ħt com

.i.car̄ in dn̄io.7 vi.uiłł 7 vi.bord.7 vi.foch.hn̄tes

iii.car̄ 7 ii.boues.7 viii.ac̄s p̄ti.T.R.E.uał.xxx.fol.

m̄ fimiłt.Tailla.x.fol.

LOVEDVNE WAPENTAC.   HAG Hꝺ.

ꝯ In HACHE.ħɓ Radulf.vii.car̄ 7 vi.bou ad

glđ.Tra ad xii.car̄.Ibi ħt Alan com.iiii.car̄.

7 xvii.uiłł.7 xiiii.foch.7 vii.bord.hn̄tes xii.

car̄.Ibi p̄br 7 æccła.7 iiii.molin̄.xxx.folidoꝝ.

7 c.ac̄s p̄ti.T.R.E.uał xii.liɓ.m̄ xvi.liɓ.

Tailla.iiii.liɓ.Ad uic̄tu equoꝝ.L.fol.

24 Freemen and 7 smallholders have 7 ploughs.
2½ mills, 12s; meadow, 30 acres.

37 M. In WELTON (le Wold) Siward had 1 carucate of land taxable. Land
for 2 ploughs. Landric, the Count's man, has 2 ploughs and
11 villagers and 2 Freemen with 1½ ploughs; and
1 mill, 10s; meadow, 20 acres; the fourth part of a church.
Value before 1066 £4; now £3.

HAVERSTOE Wapentake

38 S. In (North) THORESBY, a jurisdiction of Waltham, 9½ bovates of
land taxable. Land for 14 oxen.
14 Freemen and 2 smallholders have 2 ploughs.
2 salt-houses, 2s; meadow, 16 acres.   347 d

39 S. In BRIGSLEY, a jurisdiction of Waltham, 1½ carucates of land
taxable. Land for 3 ploughs.
17 Freemen and 1 smallholder have 3 ploughs.
Meadow, 10 acres.

BOLINGBROKE Wapentake

40 M. In HALTON (Holegate) hundred and (Little) STEEPING Aelfric had 3
bovates of land taxable. Land for 3 ploughs. Eudo, the Count's
man, has 1 plough and
meadow, 80 acres.
Value before 1066, 10s; now the same.

WELL Wapentake

41 S. In STOW (St. Mary) Count Alan has ½ carucate of land taxable. It
is a jurisdiction. Land for ½ plough.
2 Freemen have ½ plough.

ASLACOE Wapentake

42 M. In SPRIDLINGTON Knutr had 2 carucates of land and 1½ bovates
taxable. Land for 3 ploughs and 2 oxen. The Count has 1 plough
in lordship;
6 villagers, 6 smallholders and 6 Freemen who have 3 ploughs
and 2 oxen and
meadow, 8 acres.
Value before 1066, 30s; now the same. Exactions 10s.

LOVEDEN Wapentake
HOUGH (on the Hill) hundred

43 M. In HOUGH (on the Hill) Ralph the Constable had 7 carucates and 6
bovates taxable. Land for 12 ploughs. Count Alan has 4 ploughs.
17 villagers, 14 Freemen and 7 smallholders who have 12
ploughs.
A priest and a church; 4 mills, 30s; meadow, 100 acres.
Value before 1066 £12; now £16. Exactions £4.
For the supplies of horses, 50s.

In Cheueleſtune BEREW huj ⏑M̃.XII.car̃ tre
ad glð.Tra ad.XVI.car̃.Ibi m̃ XVIII.uiłł 7 VI.
borð 7 II.ſocħ hñt.VI.car̃.7 CXLVI.ac̃s p̃ti.
7 cc.ac̃ ſilue minute.7 Warenna Lepoȝ.   ⟩—
In Carletune ẽ.I.car̃ tre ad glð.SOCA DE HACH.
⏑M̃ In *HVNDRET* *ſtalre* .hb Radulf XIII.car̃ tre ad glð
BVRTVNE
in dñio 7 V.car̃ tre ad glð de ſoca.Tra ad XVIII.
car̃.Ibi hr̃.A.com̃ in dñio.III.car̃.7 XXXVI.uiłł.
7 IX.borð 7 XV.ſocħ 7 alios XI.borð.Simul hñtes
XV.car̃.Ibi pbr 7 æcc̃ła.7 I.molı̃ñ.XII.ſolidoȝ.
7 cc.ac̃ p̃ti.De ſup̃dic̃ta ſoca tenet Cadiou.VI.
bou tre.7 hr̃ Ibi.VI.boues arantes.T.R.E.uał
XV.lıb.m̃ XVIII.lıb.Tailla.c.ſoł.Ad uic̃tu eq̃.
.L.ſoł.   .IIII. *HVNDRET.*
In *FVLEBEC* 7 *LEDENEHA* hb Radulf Stalre
XXIIII.car̃ tre ~~ad.glð in dñio 7 XV.car̃ ad glð de Soca.~~
Tra ad.XXIIII.car̃.Ibi hr̃.A.com̃ in dñio.VI.car̃.
7 LXIX.uiłł 7 II.borð 7 XLIV.ſocħ.Simul hñtes
XXVIII.car̃.Ibi.II.æcc̃łæ 7 II.pbri.7 dim̃ molı̃ñ.X.ſoł.
De hac tra hñt Colegri 7 Derinc.V.car̃ 7 VI.bou.
7 ibi hñt.II.car̃ 7 dim̃.T.R.E.uał XXX.lıb.m̃ XXXII.
lıb.Tailla.VIII.lıb.Ad uic̃tu equoȝ.c.ſoł.

⟩—In Mereſtune.I.car̃ tre ad glð.SOCA de Hach.Tra ad XII.b.

348 a
⏑M̃ In *BENINCTVN* hb Radulf XIIII.car̃ tre ad
glð.in dñio.7 VII.car̃ 7 VI.bõ tre ad glð de SOCA.
Ibi hr̃.A.com̃ in dñio.V.car̃.7 XIX.uiłł.7 V.
borð.7 XX.ſocħ.Simul hñtes.XII.car̃.Ibi pbr
7 æcc̃ła 7 ccc.ac̃ p̃ti.De hac tra tenet Herueus.
.I.carucatã 7 III.bou.7 hr̃ ibi.I.car̃.T.R.E.uał
XXVI.lıb.m̃ XXX.II.lıb.Tailla.VIII.lıb.Ad uic̃tu
equoȝ.c.ſoł.Ibi ſuŋ.IIII.molini.redð.IIII.lıb.

44   In GELSTON hundred, an outlier of this manor, 12 carucates of land taxable. Land for 16 ploughs.
> Now 18 villagers, 6 smallholders and 2 Freemen have 6 ploughs and
> Meadow, 146 acres; underwood, 200 acres; a warren of hares. $\longrightarrow$

12,45 is added at the foot of col. 347d (after 12,48) and is directed by transposition signs to its correct place in the text.

46   In CARLTON (Scroop) 1 carucate of land taxable. A jurisdiction of Hough (on the Hill).

47 M. In (Brant) BROUGHTON hundred Ralph the Constable had 13 carucates of land taxable in lordship and 5 carucates of land taxable of the jurisdiction. Land for 18 ploughs. Count Alan has in lordship 3 ploughs and
> 36 villagers, 9 smallholders, 15 Freemen and another 11 smallholders who together have 15 ploughs.
> A priest and a church; 1 mill, 12s; meadow, 200 acres.
> Of the above jurisdiction Cadiou holds 6 bovates of land and has 6 ploughing oxen there.

Value before 1066 £15; now £18. Exactions 100s.
> For the supplies of horses, 50s.

48   In FULBECK and LEADENHAM, four hundreds, Ralph the Constable had 24 carucates of land taxable *in lordship and 15 carucates taxable of the jurisdiction*. Land for 24 ploughs. Count Alan has in lordship 6 ploughs;
> 69 villagers, 4 smallholders and 44 Freemen who together have 28 ploughs.
> 2 churches and 2 priests; ½ mill, 10s.
> Of this land Kolgrimr and Dering have 5 carucates and 6 bovates. They have 2½ ploughs.

Value before 1066 £30; now £32. Exactions £8.
> For the supplies of horses, 100s.

12,45, added at the foot of col. 347d and directed by transposition signs to its correct place in the text.

$\longrightarrow$ 45   In MARSTON 1 carucate of land taxable. A jurisdiction of Hough (on the Hill). Land for 12 oxen.

49 M. In the two hundreds of (Long) BENNINGTON Ralph the Constable had 14 carucates of land taxable in lordship and 7 carucates and 6 bovates of land taxable of the jurisdiction. Count Alan has in lordship 5 ploughs;
> 19 villagers, 5 smallholders and 20 Freemen who together have 12 ploughs.
> A priest and a church; meadow, 300 acres.
> Of this land Hervey holds 1 carucate and 3 bovates and has 1 plough there.

348 a

Value before 1066 £26; now £32. Exactions £8.
> For the supplies of horses, 100s.
> 4 mills which pay £4.

In F̄oꞳtune Berēw̄ huj ꟽ . xii . caꞃ tre ad glꝺ .

~~in dn̄io . 7 vii . caꞃ tre ad glꝺ de Soca~~ . Ibi hꞇ m̄

com̄ . ii . caꞃ . 7 x . uiłł 7 v . borꝺ xlvi . focħ hn̄tes

ſimul . xi . caꞃ . 7 c . ac̄s p̄ti . Ꞇra arabił . ad xii . caꞃ

ꟽ In ead FoꞳꞇvn . ħƀ Turuert . i . caꞃ tre ad glꝺ .

Ꞇra ad . ii . caꞃ . Ibi Herueus hō comitis hꞇ . i . caꞃ .

7 ii . uiłł 7 i . borꝺ cū dimiꝺ caꞃ . T . R . E . uał . xvi .

ſoł . m̄ x . ſoł . BELTESLAVVE WAPEN꞊ . BERꞱVN . H .

ꟽ In WesꞱbi . ħƀ Carle . vi . boū tre ad glꝺ . Ꞇra

ad . vi . boū . Ibi Colegꞃi hō comitis hꞇ . i . uiłł .

7 i . borꝺ cū . i . caꞃ . 7 vii . ac̄s 7 dimiꝺ p̄ti . 7 xxix

AvelvnꞱ ac̄s ſiluæ minutæ . T . R . E . uał . x . ſoł . m̄ . xii . ſoł .

Wap ꟽ In Cherchebi . ħƀ Wider . v . boū tre ad glꝺ .

Ꞇra ad . v . boū . Ibi Godric hō comitis hꞇ . ii . uiłłos

7 i . borꝺ cū . ii . boƀ arantes . 7 iiii . ac̄s p̄ti . 7 lx . ac̄s ſiluæ

minutæ . T . R . E . uał . xx . ſoł . m̄ . x . ſoł . HVNꝺ .

In Pochinton Soca ħuj ꟽ dim̄ caꞃ tre ad glꝺ .

Ꞇra ad . iiii . boū . Ibi . i . focħ 7 ii . borꝺ hn̄t dim̄ caꞃ .

★ ꟽ In Bilinge . vrg ħƀ Carle . i . caꞃ tre ad glꝺ . Ꞇra

ad . i . caꞃ . Ɓbi Colegꞃi hō comitis hꞇ . i . caꞃ in dn̄io .

★ . . . uiłłos 7 ii . borꝺ . cū dim̄ caꞃ . 7 xv . ac̄s p̄ti . T . R . E .

uał xx . ſoł . m̄ ſimiliꞇ . HVNꝺ .

ꟽ In Horbelinge . ħƀ Greꝺe . iiii . caꞃ tre ad glꝺ .

Ꞇra ad . iiii . caꞃ . Ibi Stefan hō comitis hꞇ . ii . caꞃ .

7 ix . uiłł 7 i . borꝺ 7 iii . focħ hn̄tes . iii . caꞃ . 7 xx . ac̄

p̄ti . T . R . E . uał xl . ſoł . m̄ ſimiliꞇ .

50 In FOSTON hundred, an outlier of this manor, 12 carucates of land taxable *in lordship and 7 carucates of land taxable of the jurisdiction*. Now the Count has 2 ploughs.

    10 villagers, 5 smallholders and 46 Freemen who together have 11 ploughs.

    Meadow, 100 acres; arable land for 14 ploughs.

51 M. Also in FOSTON Thorfrothr had 1 carucate of land taxable. Land for 2 ploughs. Hervey, the Count's man, has 1 plough.

    2 villagers and 1 smallholder with ½ plough.

Value before 1066, 16s; now 10s.

BELTISLOE Wapentake
BURTON (Coggles) hundred

52 M. In WESTBY Karli had 6 bovates of land taxable. Land for 6 oxen. Kolgrimr, the Count's man, has

    1 villager and 1 smallholder with 1 plough; and

    meadow, 7½ acres; underwood, 29 acres.

Value before 1066, 10s; now 12s.

AVELAND Wapentake

53 M. In KIRKBY (Underwood) Vitharr had 5 bovates of land taxable. Land for 5 oxen. Godric, the Count's man, has

    2 villagers and 1 smallholder who plough with 2 oxen; and

    meadow, 4 acres; underwood, 60 acres.

Value before 1066, 20s; now 10s.

54 In POINTON hundred, a jurisdiction of this manor, ½ carucate of land taxable. Land for 4 oxen.

    1 Freeman and 2 smallholders have ½ plough.

55 M. In BILLINGBOROUGH hundred, Karli had 1 carucate of land taxable. Land for 1 plough. Kolgrimr, the Count's man, has 1 plough in lordship and

    ..... villagers and 2 smallholders with ½ plough; and

    meadow, 15 acres.

Value before 1066, 20s; now the same.

56 M. In HORBLING hundred Greifi had 4 carucates of land taxable. Land for 4 ploughs. Stephen, the Count's man, has 2 ploughs.

    9 villagers, 1 smallholder and 3 Freemen who have 3 ploughs.

    Meadow, 20 acres.

Value before 1066, 40s; now the same.

ꝝ In *ORBELINGE.* HERIGERBI. ħƀ Wider . I . car tre ad glđ . Tra
ad . I . car 7 II . bou . Ibi Godric hō cõm hŧ dim car
in dñio . 7 IIII . uiłł hñtes v . bou arant . 7 II . moliñ
x . folid . 7 x . acs p̄ti . T.R.E. uał xII . fol . m̄ . xvI . fol

ꝝ In *HUNDRET* DRAITONE . ħƀ Greue vI . bou træ ad glđ .
Tra ad . vI . bou . Ibi Toli hō cõm hŧ . I . car in dñio .
7 IIII . uiłł 7 IIII . borđ cū . I . car . 7 x . ac p̄ti 7 di
midia falina . vIII . denar . T.R.E. uał xvI . fol .
m̄ fimiliter.

348 b

In ead Draitone ħƀ Wluui ep̄s . I . car tre ad glđ .
Tra ad . I . car . Ħ fuit S Benedicti de Ramefy . teftiñ
hōuṁ de Wapentac . q̇ dicunt fe nefcire p que ep̄s
eā tenuerit . Ibi hŧ cõm . A . II . borđ . 7 vIII . acs p̄ti .
7 I . falina de xvI . denar . T.R.E. uał . III . fol . m̄ . II . fol .

DRAITONE HVND .

ꝝ In ipfa DRAITONE . ħƀ *Stalr* Radulf . vIII . car tre 7 II . bou .
ad glđ . Tra ad . vIII . car . Ħ tra . ē Soca in ipfa uilla .
Ibi hŧ m̄ . A . cõm . vI . uiłł 7 vI . foch . 7 I . borđ . hñtes
v . car . Ibi . IIII . falinæ 7 dim . vI . folid . 7 xL . ac
p̄ti . T.R.E. uał Draitone cū omibȝ adjacentibȝ
xxx . liƀ . m̄ Lxx . liƀ . Tailla . xx . liƀ . CHIRCHET WAP .

★ ꝝ In Donninctune BEREW huj ꝝ . v . car tre 7 vI .
bou ad glđ . Tra ad tnđ car 7 bou . Ibi hŧ cõm . A .
III . car in dñio . 7 xxvI . uiłł cū . v . car . 7 Ix . faliñ
xII . fol . 7 Lx . acs p̄ti . VLMERESTIG WAPENT

In Weranghe Soca in Draitone . x . car træ ad glđ .
Tra ad . v . car . Ibi . vII . foch hñt . I . car .

In Dõninctune . ħƀ Rađ
vI . bõ tre ad glđ ꝑ ꝝ .
Tra . vI . bob . Ibi sŧ . IIII .
uiłti 7 III . borđ cū dim
car . 7 II . ac p̄ti . 7 II . falinæ
7 de xxxII . den .

Valuit 7 uał . xx . fol .

57 M. In HARROWBY [and] HORBLING Vitharr had 1 carucate of land taxable. Land for 1 plough and 2 oxen. Godric, the Count's man, has ½ plough in lordship;
> 4 villagers who have 5 ploughing oxen.
> 2 mills, 10s; meadow, 10 acres.
Value before 1066, 12s; now 16s.

58 M. In DRAYTON hundred Greifi had 6 bovates of land taxable. Land for 6 oxen. Toli, the Count's man, has 1 plough in lordship;
> 4 villagers and 4 smallholders with 1 plough.
> Meadow, 10 acres; ½ salt-house, 8d.
Value before 1066, 16s; now the same.

59 Also in DRAYTON Bishop Wulfwige had 1 carucate of land taxable. 348 b Land for 1 plough. It was St. Benedict's of Ramsey's according to the witness of men of the Wapentake who state they do not know through whom the Bishop held it. Count Alan has
> 2 smallholders.
> Meadow, 8 acres; 1 salt-house at 16d.
Value before 1066, 3s; now 2s.

DRAYTON hundred

60 M. In DRAYTON itself Ralph the Constable had 8 carucates of land and 2 bovates taxable. Land for 8 ploughs. This land is a jurisdiction of the village itself. Now Count Alan has
> 6 villagers, 6 Freemen and 1 smallholder who have 5 ploughs.
> 4½ salt-houses, 6s; meadow, 40 acres.
Value before 1066 of Drayton with all that was attached to it, £30; now £70. Exactions £20.

KIRTON Wapentake

61 In DONINGTON, an outlier of this manor, 5 carucates of land and 6 bovates taxable. Land for as many ploughs and oxen. Count Alan has 3 ploughs in lordship;
> 26 villagers with 5 ploughs.
> 9 salt-houses, 12s; meadow, 60 acres.

62 M. In DONINGTON Ralph had 6 bovates of land taxable as a manor. Land for 6 oxen.
> 4 villagers and 3 smallholders with ½ plough.
> Meadow, 2 acres; 2 salt-houses at 32d.
The value was and is 20s.

WOLMERSTY Wapentake

63 In WRANGLE, a jurisdiction of Drayton, 10 carucates of land taxable. Land for 5 ploughs.
> 7 Freemen have 1 plough.

In Leche . Soca Drait . XII . car̄ tre ad glđ . Tra

ad . X . car̄ . Ibi . XXX.II . foch 7 XXX . uilł 7 XV . borđ

hn̄t XI . car̄. 7 XXVI . falinas . 7 XXXIIII . ac̄s p̄ti.

De hac Soca hn̄t . II . hŏes comitis . II . carucatas.

7 ibi . II . car̄. 7 I . borđ . 7 XV . falinas . 7 X . uilł . cū

I . car̄.   *LEVRETVNE . HVND.*

In Leuretune Soca Drait . XII . car̄ træ ad glđ.

Tra ad totiđ car̄ . Ibi XXV . foch 7 XV . uilł 7 XXIIII .

borđ hn̄t XII . car̄ . Ibi p̄br 7 æccła . 7 LX . ac̄ p̄ti.

De hac Soca hn̄t . II . hŏes comitis . II . car̄ træ 7 III . boū.

7 Ibi hn̄t . III . car̄ arantes.   *TOFT HVND.*

In Toft Soca Drait . III . car̄ træ ad glđ . Tra ad . III . car̄.

Ibi . XVII . foch hn̄t . V . car̄ 7 dim̄ . 7 XX . ac̄s p̄ti.

In Schirebec Berew *HUNDRET* Drait . II . car̄ tre ad glđ.

7 In ead IX . car̄ tre 7 VI . boū ad glđ . Soca.

in Drait . Tra ad . VIII . car̄ . Ibi . XIX . foch 7 XIII.

uilł hn̄t . VIII . car̄ . Ipfe com̄ . I . car̄ in dn̄io . Ibi

. II . æcclæ 7 II . p̄bri . 7 II . pifcinæ . X . foliđ . 7 XL . ac̄ p̄ti.

In Wibertune *HUNDRET.* Soca Drait . IX . car tre 7 III . boū

ađ glđ . Tra ad . XII . car̄ 7 dim̄ . Ibi XXX.IIII . foch

hn̄t . XI . car̄ . Ibi æccła . XII . ac̄ p̄ti . *FRANETON . H'ð.*

In Wibertune hf . X.
boū tr̄æ ad glđ . Tra ē
. XIII . car̄ . Edelric tenuit
Valuit 7 ual . XX . fol.

In Franetone Berew Drait . VII . car̄ tre 7 VI.

boū ad glđ . Tra ad . X . car̄ . Ibi hŧ A . com̄ in dn̄io

II . car̄ . 7 XII . foch 7 XVI . uilł 7 II . borđ hn̄tes . VIII .

car̄ . Ibi XV . falinæ de XX . fol . 7 C . ac̄ p̄ti.

LEAKE hundred

64 In LEAKE, a jurisdiction [of] Drayton, 12 carucates of land
taxable. Land for 10 ploughs.
32 Freemen, 30 villagers and 15 smallholders have 11
ploughs and
26 salt-houses; meadow, 34 acres.
Of this jurisdiction two of the Count's men have 2 carucates;
2 ploughs there and
1 smallholder; 15 salt-houses; 10 villagers with 1 plough.

LEVERTON hundred

65 In LEVERTON, a jurisdiction [of] Drayton, 12 carucates of land
taxable. Land for as many ploughs.
25 Freemen, 15 villagers and 24 smallholders have 12 ploughs.
A priest and a church; meadow, 60 acres.
Of this jurisdiction two of the Count's men have 2 carucates
of land and 3 bovates. They have 3 ploughs which plough.

(Fish)TOFT hundred

66 In (Fish)TOFT, a jurisdiction [of] Drayton, 3 carucates of land
taxable. Land for 3 ploughs.
17 Freemen have 5½ ploughs and
meadow, 20 acres.

67 In SKIRBECK hundred, an outlier [of] Drayton, 2 carucates of
land taxable. Also in it 9 carucates of land and 6 bovates taxable.
A jurisdiction of Drayton. Land for 8 ploughs.
19 Freemen and 13(?) villagers have 8 ploughs.
The Count himself [has] 1 plough in lordship.
2 churches and 2 priests; 2 fish-ponds, 10s; meadow, 40 acres.

68 In WYBERTON hundred, a jurisdiction [of] Drayton, 9 carucates
of land and 3 bovates taxable. Land for 12½ ploughs.
34 Freemen have 11 ploughs.
A church; meadow, 12 acres.

69 In WYBERTON he has 10 bovates of land taxable. Land for 13
ploughs. Aethelric held it.
The value was and is 20s.

FRAMPTON hundred

70 In FRAMPTON, an outlier [of] Drayton, 7 carucates of land and 6
bovates taxable. Land for 10 ploughs. Count Alan has in lordship
2 ploughs;
12 Freemen, 16 villagers and 2 smallholders who have 8 ploughs.
15 salt-houses at 20s; meadow, 100 acres.

In Cherchetune Soca Drait . x . car̄ træ . 7 i . boū

348 c

7 tcia pars uni boū ad glđ . Tra ad . xii . car̄ . Ibi
.A. com̄ hī xxx . foch 7 xvi . borđ hn̄tes . x . car̄.
7 ii . falinæ . xvi . denar̄ . Ibi æccła . 7 lx . ac̄ p̄ti.

S̃ In Reschintone Soca . xii . car̄ træ ad glđ . Tra totiđ car̄.
Ibi . xx . foch . 7 xii . borđ . hn̄t . vi . car̄ . 7 xxx . ac̄ p̄ti.

S̃ In Alfgare . Soca Drait . x . car̄ tre 7 v . boū . ad glđ.
Tra ad . ix . car̄ . Ibi xl . ii . foch hn̄t . vi . car̄ . 7 v .
ac̄s p̄ti.   RICHE Hᴏ

S̃ In RICHE Soca Drait . x . car̄ tre ad glđ . Tra ad . x .
car̄ . Ibi xxx . v . foch 7 xxviii . borđ . hn̄t . vii . car̄.
7 xii . ac̄ p̄ti.   BICHERE Hᴏ.

S̃ In BICHERE Soca Drait . v . car̄ træ 7 vii . boū ad
glđ . Tra ad totiđ car̄ 7 boū . Ibi xix . foch 7 xviii .
uiłł 7 i . borđ hn̄tes . v . car̄ . Ibi æccła 7 xx . faline
xxx . foliđ . 7 xx ac̄ p̄ti.   HVND

S̃ In Gofebtechirche . Soca Drait . iii . car̄ træ 7 ii .
boū ad glđ . Tra ad . iii . car̄ 7 ii . boū.
De hac tra hī Vłbt . vi . bouatas . Ibi . i . car̄ . 7 ii .
uiłł 7 x . borđ . cū . i . car̄ . 7 vi . ac̄s p̄ti . 7 ii . faline
xii . denar̄ . Aliæ . ii . carucate 7 iiii . boū funt in Soca
Drait . Sex bouatas ten̄ Adeftan . 7 focā habuit
Radulf . 7 he . vi . ualuer̄ . T.R.E. iiii . fol . m̄ xl . fol.

Svᴅ S̃ In Tric . Soca Drait . dimiđ car̄ tre ad glđ . Tra ad
ᴋᴇᴅɪɴɢ iiii . boū . Ibi . i . borđ . 7 lx . ac̄ p̄ti.

S̃ In Burch Soca Drait . i . car̄ 7 dim̄ ad glđ . Tra ad xii .
boū . Ibi . iii . foch 7 ii . uiłł 7 iii . borđ . hn̄t . i . car̄ 7 dim̄.

71   In KIRTON hundred, a jurisdiction [of] Drayton, 10 carucates of
      land and 1 bovate and the third part of 1 bovate taxable. Land   348 c
      for 12 ploughs. Count Alan has
         30 Freemen and 16 smallholders who have 10 ploughs.
         2 salt-houses, 16d. A church; meadow, 60 acres.

72 S. In 'RISKENTON' hundred, a jurisdiction, 12 carucates of land taxable.
      Land for as many ploughs.
         29 Freemen and 12 smallholders have 6 ploughs.
         Meadow, 30 acres.

73 S. In ALGAR (kirk) hundred, a jurisdiction [of] Drayton, 10 carucates
      of land and 5 bovates taxable. Land for 9 ploughs.
         42 Freemen have 6 ploughs and
         meadow, 5 acres.

   RICHE hundred
74 S. In *RICHE*, a jurisdiction [of] Drayton, 10 carucates of land
      taxable. Land for 10 ploughs.
         35 Freemen and 28 smallholders have 7 ploughs.
         Meadow, 12 acres.

   BICKER hundred
75 S. In BICKER, a jurisdiction [of] Drayton, 5 carucates of land and 7
      bovates taxable. Land for as many ploughs and oxen.
         19 Freemen, 18 villagers and 1 smallholder who have 5 ploughs.
         A church and a priest; 20 salt-houses, 30s; meadow, 20 acres.

76 S. In GOSBERTON hundred, a jurisdiction [of] Drayton, 3 carucates
      of land and 2 bovates taxable. Land for 3 ploughs and 2 oxen.
      Of this land Wulfbert has 6 bovates; 1 plough there.
         2 villagers and 10 smallholders with 1 plough.
         Meadow, 6 acres; 2 salt-houses, 12d.
      The other 2 carucates and 4 bovates are in the jurisdiction
      [of] Drayton.
      Aethelstan held 6 bovates and Earl Ralph had the jurisdiction.
      Value before 1066 of these 6 (bovates), 4s; now 40s.

SOUTH RIDING

77 S. In *TRIC*, a jurisdiction [of] Drayton, ½ carucate of land taxable.
      Land for 4 oxen.
         1 smallholder.
         Meadow, 60 acres.

78 S. In BURGH (le Marsh), a jurisdiction [of] Drayton, 1½ carucates
      taxable. Land for 12 oxen.
         3 Freemen, 2 villagers and 3 smallholders have 1½ ploughs.

§ In Herdetorp Soca . Drait . 1 . bouata tre ad glđ . Tra
ad . 1 . boū . Ibi . 11 . uiłł . araꝫ . 11 . bob . 7 xx . ac ꝑti.

ⓜ In eađ *HARDETORP* . ħɓ Elnod . 1 . car træ ad glđ .
Tra ad . 1 . car . Ibi Eudo ħo com ħt . 111 . focħ . cū dim car .
7 c . acs ꝑti . T.R.E. uał . xx . foł . m̄ . 11 . foł 7 viii . denar .

HVND § In Calnodefbi Soca huj ⓜ . 11 . boū tre ad glđ . Tra
ad . 111 . boū . Ibi . 11 . uiłł ħnt dimid car . 7 c . ac marefc .

§ In Hacɓdinghā . Soca alia . vi . boū tre ad glđ . Tra
ad . ix . boū . Ibi Eudo ħo comitis . 1111 . focħ 7 11 . uiłł
ħntes . 1 . car . 7 xxx . acs ꝑti . *ELLEHO WAPENT.*

ɓ In Holobech 7 Copolade . ħɓ Algar . 1 . car tre ad
glđ . Tra . vi . boū . Ber in Flec . Alan⁹ ħt . ꝧ miniſtri
regis clam ad oꝑ regis . Ibi fuꝫ . 111 . uiłł . cū . 111 . bob in car .

§ Ibidē ħɓ Agar⁹ xiii . car træ 7 vi . boū ad glđ . Tra
ix . car 7 11 . boū . Soca in Gadenay . De hac tra ħt
Alan . v . car . Landric tenet de eo . Ibi ħt . 11 . car .
7 xxix . uiłł cū . v . car . 7 qᵗ xx . acs ꝑti . Valet . viii . liɓ
H̄ deracinata . ē ad opus regis .

348 d

. HYLLE WAP.
ⓜ In *HACBERDINGHA* . ħɓ Holchetel dim car træ ad glđ .
Tra ad . 1 . car . Ibi ħt Eudo ħo com xvi . acs ꝑti . De
hac tra funt xxx . ac foca in Bizebi . Pciū ej in alijs ⓜ .
CALSVAD WAPENT.

ⓜ In *MALTEBI* . Brocles ħɓ . vi . boū tre ad glđ . Tra ad
vi . boues . Ibi Eudo fub comite ħt . 111 focħ . 7 1111 . uiłł cū
. 1 . car . 7 xx . acs ꝑti . T.R.E. uał . x . foł . m̄ fimilit .

79 S. In ADDLETHORPE, a jurisdiction [of] Drayton, 1 bovate of land taxable. Land for 1 ox.
>2 villagers plough with 2 oxen.
>Meadow, 20 acres.

80 M. Also in ADDLETHORPE Alnoth had 1 carucate of land taxable. Land for 1 plough. Eudo, the Count's man, has
>3 Freemen with ½ plough; and
>meadow, 100 acres.

Value before 1066, 20s; now 2s 8d.

81 S. In CANDLESBY hundred, a jurisdiction of this manor, 2 bovates of land taxable. Land for 3 oxen.
>2 villagers have ½ plough.
>Marsh, 100 acres.

82 S. In HAGWORTHINGHAM, another jurisdiction, 6 bovates of land taxable. Land for 9 oxen. Eudo, the Count's man, [has]
>4 Freemen and 2 villagers who have 1 plough and
>meadow, 30 acres.

ELLOE Wapentake

83 B. In HOLBEACH and WHAPLODE Earl Algar had 1 carucate of land taxable. Land for 6 oxen. An outlier of Fleet. Count Alan has it, but the King's officers claim it for the King's use.
>3 villagers with 3 oxen in a plough.

84 S. There also Earl Algar had 13 carucates of land and 6 bovates taxable. Land for 9 ploughs and 2 oxen. A jurisdiction of Gedney. Of this land Count Alan has 5 carucates. Landric holds from him. He has 2 ploughs.
>29 villagers with 5 ploughs.
>Meadow, 80 acres.

Value £8.

It is adjudged for the King's use.

HILL Wapentake   348 d

85 M. In HAGWORTHINGHAM Holmketill had ½ carucate of land taxable. Land for 1 plough. Eudo, the Count's man, has
>>meadow, 16 acres.
>Of this land 30 acres are a jurisdiction of Beesby.
>Its assessment is in other manors.

CALCEWATH Wapentake

86 M. In MALTBY (le Marsh) Broklauss had 6 bovates of land taxable. Land for 6 oxen. Eudo has under the Count
>3 Freemen and 5 villagers with 1 plough; and
>meadow, 20 acres.

Value before 1066, 10s; now the same.

In Strobi Soca in Lecheburne . 11 . boū trǣ 7 dim̄ ad glđ.

Tra ad . v . boū . lbi . 11 . focħ hn̄t dim̄ caŕ . 7 x . acs p̄ti.

CHIRCHETONE WAP̄.

ꟲIn CHIRCHETVNE . ħƀ Edric . x . boū tre ād glđ . Tra

ad . 1 . caŕ 7 v . boū . Ibi Toli hō comitis . hŧ . 1 . caŕ . 7 1111.

BICHE   uiłł hn̄t . 1 . caŕ . 7 v111 . ac̄ p̄ti . T.R.E . uał . xl . foł . m̄

HVND   ꟲIn STEVENINGE . ħƀ Aldene . 111 . caŕ trǣ   ⟨xx . foł.

ad glđ . Tra ad . 111 . caŕ . Ibi Goisfrid hō comitis hŧ

11 . caŕ . 7 v111 . uiłł hn̄tes dimid caŕ . 7 v1 . faliñ . v111.

Dunninc folid . 7 l . acs p̄ti . T.R.E . uał xx . foł . m̄ fimilɩ̄.

hūnd   ꟲIn QVEDHAVERINGE . ħƀ Turchil . 1 . caŕ tre ad glđ.

Tra ad . 1 . caŕ . cū faca 7 foca . p̄t . 11 . bouatas . fup

q̄s comes hŧ foca . Hanc trā tenet Guert hō comitis.

, fed hōēs de Wapentac nefciuɲ p q̄ē . Ibi . 111 . uiłł.

WANEB   7 v1 . ac̄ p̄ti . 7 11 . faline . x11 . denaŕ . T.R.E . uał . x . foł.
WAP̄

ꟲIn STOCHE . ħƀ Radulf . 111 . caŕ trǣ ad glđ.   ⟨ m̄ fimił.

Tra ad . 111 . caŕ . Ibi Colegri hō cōm hŧ . 11 . caŕ ađ aulā.

7 v11 . uiłł 7 1 . borđ cū . 11 . caŕ . 7 11 . moliñ . v11 . foł.

7 1111 . denaŕ . 7 xxx . ac̄ p̄ti . 7 cxl ac̄ filue paſtił.

7 v1 . p̄tic . T.R.E . uał . xxx . foł . m̄ . lx . foł.

ꟲIn NORTHNICHE . ħƀ Siuuard . 1111 . caŕ tre ad glđ.

k   Tra ad . 11 . caŕ . Ibi Colegri hō comitis hŧ . 1 . caŕ . 7 11 .

uiłł arantes . 11 . boƀ . 7 1 . moliñ . v . folid . 7 łx . v1 . ac̄

p̄ti . T.R.E . uał xx . foł . m̄ fimił.

Sortebrañ.
calūniat   ★

In STRUBBY, a jurisdiction of Legbourne, 2½ bovates of land taxable. Land for 5 oxen.
>2 Freemen have ½ plough and
>meadow, 10 acres.

KIRTON Wapentake

88 M. In KIRTON Eadric had 10 bovates of land taxable. Land for 1 plough and 5 oxen. Toli, the Count's man, has 1 plough.
>4 villagers have 1 plough.
>Meadow, 8 acres.
Value before 1066, 40s; now 20s.

BICKER hundred

89 M. In 'STENNING' Halfdan had 3 carucates of land taxable. Land for 3 ploughs. Geoffrey [of] Tournai, the Count's man, has 2 ploughs.
>8 villagers who have ½ plough.
>6 salt-houses, 8s; meadow, 50 acres.
Value before 1066, 20s; now the same.

DONINGTON hundred

90 M. In QUADRING Thorketill had 1 carucate of land taxable. Land for 1 plough with full jurisdiction except for 2 bovates over which the Count has jurisdiction. Gyrthr, the Count's man, holds this land, but the men of the Wapentake do not know through whom.
>3 villagers.
>Meadow, 6 acres; 2 salt-houses, 12d.
Value before 1066, 10s; now the same.

WINNIBRIGGS Wapentake

91 M. In (South) STOKE Ralph the Constable had 3 carucates of land taxable. Land for 3 ploughs. Kolgrimr, the Count's man, has 2 ploughs at the Hall;
>7 villagers and 1 smallholder with 2 ploughs.
>2 mills, 7s 4d; meadow, 30 acres; woodland pasture, 140 acres and 6 perches.
Value before 1066, 30s; now 60s.

92 M. In NORTH HYKEHAM hundred Siward had 4 carucates of land taxable. Land for 2 ploughs. Kolgrimr, the Count's man, has 1 plough.
>2 villagers who plough with 2 oxen.
>1 mill, 5s; meadow, 26 acres.
Value before 1066, 20s; now the same.
>Svartbrandr claims it.

k

Ⓜ In *MVNDEBI*. ħɓ Arnui. III . cař tre ad glđ . Tra

ad IIII . cař . Ibi Eudo ħõ comitis ħř . III . cař. 7 XVI . uiłł

7 VIII . borđ ħñt . I . cař 7 dim̃ . 7 cc . aĉ p̃ti.

In Clacheſbi BEREW̃ huj ⁹ Ⓜ . ħř . A . cõm XV . aĉs træ.

CALSVAD In Telageſtorp . Soᴄᴀ|. III . bou træ ad glđ . Tra ad . III .
WAP In Mundebi

boues . Ibi . V . ſocħ 7 . I . borđ . ħñt dim̃ cař . 7 XXX . aĉ p̃ti.

Ⓜ In *MVNDEBI*
.VI. *HACBERDINGHA*. Ormchetel Siuert Elric Suen Suaue

Holmchethel . ħɓr VIII . cař træ ad gld . Tra ad XI . cař

7 V . boues . Ibi Eudo ħõ comitis ħř in dñio . III . cař.

7 XL . uiłł . 7 IIII . ſocħ 7 XII . bờrđ . ħñtes . V . cař 7 VI . boŭ

arantes . 7 ccc . X . aĉ p̃ti . T.R.E . uał hi . VII . manerii

X . liɓ . M̊ . XVI . liɓ .   *HOTOT HVND*

Ş In *SVĐtone* . I . boŭ træ ad glđ . Ibi . II . uiłł ħñt . XX . aĉs p̃ti.

Soca in Cõbreuorde.

.XIII. ## TERRA HVGONIS COMITIS.

Ⓜ In *GRAΛ* . HÃ̄ . habuit Harold . II . caruĉ tre ſine głdo.
cõm ⁹

Tra ad . VI . cař . Duæ bouate in Soᴄᴀ . de hac tra.

Ibi ħř Hugo comes . IIII . cař in dñio . 7 XLVI . uiłł . 7 VIII .

borđ . 7 I . ſocħ . ħñtes . VIII . cař . Ibi p̃br 7 æccła . 7 I . moliñ

VIII . ſolid . 7 ccc . aĉs p̃ti . Vna leṽ 7 I . q̃ẕ lg̃ . 7 I . leṽ łať.

T.R.E . uał XL . liɓ 7 dimid̃ marká auri . m̃ . LX . liɓ.

Tailla . LXX . liɓ.

I In Lecheburne Soᴄᴀ . X . cař træ ad glđ . Tra ad XII .
VIII
cař . Ibi . XXXI . ſocħ 7 XVIII . uiłł 7 XI . borđ . ħñtes . XVI .

cař . 7 XL . aĉs p̃ti . 7 q̃ter XX . aĉs ſiłuæ paſt p loca.

MUMBY hundred

93 M. In MUMBY Earnwine had 3 carucates of land taxable. Land for 4 ploughs. Eudo, the Count's man, has 3 ploughs.
16 villagers and 8 smallholders have 1½ ploughs.
Meadow, 200 acres.

94 In CLAXBY, an outlier of this manor, Count Alan has 15 acres of land.

CALCEWATH Wapentake

95 In THEDDLETHORPE, a jurisdiction of Mumby, 3 bovates of land taxable. Land for 3 oxen.
5 Freemen and 1 smallholder have ½ plough.
Meadow, 30 acres.

96 6 In HAGWORTHINGHAM MUMBY Ormketill, Sigfrothr, Aelfric, Sveinn,
M. Svafi and Holmketill had 8 carucates of land taxable. Land for 11 ploughs and 5 oxen. Eudo, the Count's man, has in lordship 3 ploughs;
40 villagers, 4 Freemen and 12 smallholders who have 5 ploughs and 6 ploughing oxen.
Meadow, 310 acres.
Value before 1066 of these 7 manors £10; now £16.

HUTTOFT hundred

97 S. In SUTTON (le Marsh) 1 bovate of land taxable.
2 villagers have
meadow, 20 acres.
A jurisdiction of Cumberworth.

13   LAND OF EARL HUGH   349 a

1 M. In GREETHAM Earl Harold had 2 carucates of land without tax.
Land for 6 ploughs. 2 bovates of this land in a jurisdiction.
Earl Hugh has 4 carucates in lordship;
46 villagers, 8 smallholders and 1 Freeman who have 8 ploughs.
A priest and a church; 1 mill, 8s; meadow, 300 acres.
[It is] 1 league and 1 furlong long and 1 league wide.
Value before 1066 £40 and ½ mark of gold; now £60.
Exactions £70.

2 In LEGBOURNE, a jurisdiction, 10 carucates of land taxable. Land for 12 ploughs.
31 Freemen, 18 villagers and 19(?) smallholders who have 16 ploughs and
meadow, 40 acres; woodland, pasture in places, 80 acres.

In Suabi 7 Elgelo 7 Toreſbi 7 Clactorp 7 Totele . Soca.
xii . car̅ tr̅æ ad gl̅d . Tra ad . xviii . car̅ . Ibi xlvi . focħ
7 xx.ii . uilł . 7 xxxviii . borđ . h̅n̅tes . xxx.i . car̅ . 7 vi.
molini . de . iiii . lib . 7 xvi . denar̅ . 7 xx . ac̅ p̅ti . 7 ſexcent̅
ac̅s ſiluæ paſtilis.

In Widerne 7 Abi 7 Hage 7 Caleſbi . Soca . vii . car̅ tr̅æ
7 dm̅ ad gld . Tra ad vi . car̅ 7 dim . Ibi . xvii . focħ.
7 x . uilł h̅n̅t . vi . car̅ 7 dimid . 7 xvi . ac̅s p̅ti . 7 q̅t xx
7 xii . ac̅ ſiluæ paſtił 7 minutæ.

In Sutrebi 7 Dalbi 7 Driſtorp . Soca . xv . car̅ tr̅æ ad
gl̅d . Tra ad xvi . car̅ . Ibi xlvii . focħ . 7 viii . uilł . 7 xi.
borđ . h̅n̅tes . xi . car̅ . In Dalbi h̅t com̅ . i . car̅ in d̅n̅io.
7 ii . ecclas . 7 q̅t xx . ac̅s p̅ti.

In Fortintone . 7 Aſchebi . 7 Bretoſt . 7 Langene . Soca.
xviii . car̅ tr̅æ 7 dim̅ ad gld̅ . Tra ad xviii . car̅ . Ibi n̅c̅
xlix . focħ . 7 xxvi . uilł . 7 xx.ii . borđ . h̅n̅t . xviii . car̅.
Ibi . iii . æcclæ . 7 ſexcent̅ 7 xx . ac̅s p̅ti.

In Wenflet 7 Haghe 7 Caleſbi . 7 Tedlageſtorp . 7 Malb̅torp.
Soca . xx . car̅ tr̅æ . 7 ii . bou̅ ad gld̅ . Tra ad totid̅ car̅.
Ibi q̅ter xx . 7 iii . focħ . 7 xxxiii . uilł . 7 xxxv . borđ.
h̅n̅t . xviii . car̅ 7 dim̅ . 7 decies . c . ac̅s p̅ti . 7 xx . ſalinas
x . ſolido₂ . 7 q̅t xx . ac̅s ſiluæ minutæ.

In Hotot 7 Torulueſbi 7 Sutune 7 Druiſtorp 7 Billeſbi
7 Marcheſbi . Soca . xviii . caruc̅ tr̅æ ad gld̅ . Tra ad
xx . car̅ . Ibi . lxix . focħ . 7 xix . uilł . 7 xxiii . borđ . h̅n̅t
xvi . car̅ . 7 ſeptingent̅ 7 q̅t xx . ac̅s p̅ti.

HÏLLE WAPENTAC.

In Langetune 7 Hacberdinch̅a 7 Salmundebi 7 Tedforde
7 Brincle . 7 Winzebi 7 Clacheſbi . Soca . xxix . caruc̅
tr̅æ ad gld . Tra ad . xxx.iii . car̅ . Ibi . cl . focħ . 7 xx . borđ.
7 xii . uilł . h̅n̅tes xxx.ix . car̅ . 7 ix . molin . de . xx . ſol.
7 ccc . 7 l . ac̅s p̅ti . Om̅nis ħ tra uel Soca . p̅tin ad Grandh̅a.

3   In SWABY, BELLEAU, (South) THORESBY, CLAYTHORPE and TOTHILL, a jurisdiction, 12 carucates of land taxable. Land for 18 ploughs.
     46 Freemen, 22 villagers and 38 smallholders who have 31 ploughs.
     6 mills at £4 16d; meadow, 20 acres; woodland pasture, 600 acres.

4   In WITHERN, ABY, HAUGH and CALCEBY, a jurisdiction, 7 carucates of land *and a half* taxable. Land for 6½ ploughs.
     17 Freemen and 10 villagers have 6½ ploughs and
     meadow, 16 acres; woodland pasture and underwood, 92 acres.

5   In SUTTERBY, DALBY and DEXTHORPE, a jurisdiction, 15 carucates of land taxable. Land for 16 ploughs.
     47 Freemen, 8 villagers and 11 smallholders who have 11 ploughs.
     In Dalby the Earl has 1 plough in lordship and
     2 churches; meadow, 80 acres.

6   In FORDINGTON, ASHBY (by Partney), BRATOFT and *LANGENE*, a jurisdiction, 18½ carucates of land taxable. Land for 18 ploughs.
     Now 49 Freemen, 26 villagers and 22 smallholders have 18 ploughs.
     3 churches; meadow, 620 acres.

7   In WAINFLEET, HAUGH, CALCEBY, THEDDLETHORPE and MABLETHORPE, a jurisdiction, 20 carucates of land and 2 bovates taxable. Land for as many ploughs.
     83 Freemen, 33 villagers and 35 smallholders have 18½ ploughs and
     meadow, 1000 acres; 20 salt-houses, 10s; underwood, 80 acres.

8   In HUTTOFT, THURLBY, SUTTON (le Marsh), TRUSTHORPE, BILSBY and MARKBY, a jurisdiction, 18 carucates of land taxable. Land for 20 ploughs.
     69 Freemen, 19 villagers and 23 smallholders have 16 ploughs and
     meadow, 780 acres.

HILL Wapentake
9   In LANGTON, HAGWORTHINGHAM, SALMONBY, TETFORD, BRINKHILL, WINCEBY and CLAXBY (Pluckacre), a jurisdiction, 29 carucates of land taxable. Land for 33 ploughs.
     150 Freemen, 20 smallholders and 12 villagers who have 39 ploughs.
     9 mills at 20s; meadow, 350 acres.
All this land or jurisdiction belongs to Greetham.

Simul ad glđ . cxxxɪ . car̄ . Tra ad . cxl . ɪɪɪɪ . car̄ . Sochi . ccc .

lxx . vɪ . Vitti . cxlvɪɪɪ . Borđ . clxvɪɪɪ . hn̄tes . clvɪ . car̄ .

In *HALTONE* . habuit Harold . vɪɪɪ . car̄ tre ad

glđ . Tra ad . vɪ . car̄ . De hac tra . ſunt . ɪɪɪɪ . car̄ in Soca .

Nc̄ hab Comes Hugo -7 Witts fili Nigelli de eo .

In dn̄io . ɪɪɪɪ . car̄ . 7 ɪɪɪ . uitt 7 ɪx . borđ . 7 xɪɪɪɪ . ſoch .

hn̄tes . ɪɪ . car̄ . 7 xxx . ac̄s p̄ti . T.R.E. uat xɪx . lib̄ . m̄

x . lib̄ . Tailla . v . lib̄ .

In Walecote BEREW̄ huj ō̄ . ɪɪɪ . bou tre ad glđ .

Tra ad ɪɪɪ . boues .

In Wintrintune Soca . ɪɪɪɪ . car̄ tre ad glđ . Tra ad

ɪɪɪɪ . car̄ . Ibi xvɪ . ſoch 7 vɪɪ . borđ hn̄t . ɪɪ . car̄ 7 dim̄ .

In Colebi Soca . xv . bou tre ad glđ . Tra ad . ɪɪ . car̄ .

Ibi . ɪɪɪ . ſoch . ɪ . boue arant . 7 ɪx . ac̄ p̄ti .

In Hedebi Soca . ɪɪɪ . car̄ tre ad glđ . Tra ad . ɪɪ . car̄ .

Ibi nc̄ . ɪx . ſoch 7 ɪ . borđ hn̄t . ɪɪ . car̄ . 7 q̄ter xx . ac̄s p̄ti .

7 xx . ac̄s ſiluæ minutæ .

In Tedulfbi . Soca . x . car̄ tre 7 dim̄ ad glđ . Tra ad ɪx car̄ .

Ibi nc̄ . xvɪ . ſoch 7 xv . borđ . hn̄t . ɪɪɪɪ . car̄ 7 dim̄ . 7 L .

ac̄s p̄ti . 7 lxx ac̄s ſilue minutæ .

In Cropeſbi 7 Cuneſbi Soca . vɪ . car̄ tre 7 vɪ . bou ad glđ .

Tra ad . vɪ . car̄ 7 vɪ . boues . Ibi nc̄ xxv . ſoch 7 x . borđ .

hn̄t . vɪ . car̄ . 7 q̄ter xx . ac̄s p̄ti .

NORT REDING

ō̄ In *BERNODEBI* . hb̄ Harold . vɪ . car̄ tre ad glđ .

Tra ad . xɪɪ . car̄ . Tres carucatæ ſunt in Soca .

Ibi Witts hō comitis . H . ht̄ . ɪɪɪ . car̄ in dn̄io . 7 ɪɪɪɪ .

uitt . 7 lx . ſoch 7 x . borđ . hn̄tes . vɪɪ . car̄ 7 dimid̄ .

T.R.E . uat xɪɪɪɪ . lib̄ . m̄ . xx . lib̄ . Tailla . x . lib̄ .

In Bertone 7 Bechebi 7 Wirichebi . 7 Sumertebi .

7 Haburne . 7 ɪɪ . partes uni bou . ad glđ . Tra ad vɪɪ . car̄ .

Altogether 131 carucates taxable. Land for 144 ploughs. 376
Freemen, 148 villagers and 168 smallholders who have 156 ploughs.

10 In (West) HALTON Earl Harold had 8 carucates of land taxable.
Land for 6 ploughs. Of this land 4 carucates are in a jurisdiction.
Now Earl Hugh has it, and William son of Nigel from him. In
lordship 4 ploughs;
> 3 villagers, 9 smallholders and 14 Freemen who have 2
> ploughs and
> meadow, 30 acres.
Value before 1066 £19; now £10. Exactions £5.

11 In WALCOT, an outlier of this manor, 3 bovates of land taxable.
Land for 3 oxen.

12 In WINTERTON, a jurisdiction, 4 carucates of land taxable.
Land for 4 ploughs.
> 16 Freemen and 7 smallholders have 2½ ploughs.

13 In COLEBY, a jurisdiction, 15 bovates of land taxable. Land for 2
ploughs.
> 3 Freemen plough with 1 ox.
> Meadow, 9 acres.

14 In 'HAYTHBY', a jurisdiction, 3 carucates of land taxable. Land
for 2 ploughs.
> Now 9 Freemen and 1 smallholder have 2 ploughs and
> meadow, 80 acres; underwood, 20 acres.

15 In THEALBY, a jurisdiction, 10½ carucates of land taxable. Land
for 9 ploughs.
> Now 16 Freemen and 15 smallholders have 4½ ploughs and
> meadow, 50 acres; underwood, 70 acres.

16 In CROSBY and (Great) 'CONESBY', a jurisdiction, 6 carucates of
land and 6 bovates taxable. Land for 6 ploughs and 6 oxen.
> Now 25 Freemen and 10 smallholders have 6 ploughs and
> meadow, 80 acres.

NORTH RIDING

17 M. In BARNETBY (le Wold) Earl Harold had 6 carucates of land
taxable. Land for 12 ploughs. 3 carucates are in a jurisdiction.
William, Earl H(ugh)'s man, has 3 ploughs in lordship;
> 4 villagers, 60 Freemen and 10 smallholders who have 7½
> ploughs.
Value before 1066 £14; now £20. Exactions £10.

18 In BARTON (upon Humber) 2 bovates, BIGBY 1 carucate, WORLABY
2 carucates, SOMERBY ½ carucate, and HABROUGH 1 bovate and 2
parts of 1 bovate taxable. Land for 7 ploughs.

Ibi xxx.vi.foch.7 i.uilt.hñtes.iiii.caɍ 7 dim̃.7 xL

acs p̃ti.Ħ Soca p̃tiñ ad Bernodebi.

Itē in Lobingehā.7 Irebi 7 Ribi ⁱⁱⁱⁱ·ᶜ'⁷·ᵗ·ᵇ⁵ ᵗ·ᶜ'⁷ᵈⁱᵐ ⁱⁱⁱⁱ·ᶜ'⁷ᵈⁱᵐ Simul ad gld.x.

caruc̃ træ.7 i.bou.Tra ad xx.caɍ 7 ii.bou.Soca

in Bernodebi.Ibi.L.ii.foch 7 xi.uilt.7 vii.bord.

hñtes xi.caɍ.7 cccxv.acs p̃ti.

In Ribi ht Erneis hō comitis.ii.caɍ in dñio.Illā Socā

tenet ipfe de comite.Alias teneɴ Wilt Radulf 7 Aze

linus hōcs comitis.

In FVGELESTOV.ħb Godric.vi.bou tre ad gld.Tra

ad xi.bou.Ibi Rozelin hō cō ht.i.caɍ.7 vii.uilt.

7 i.bord.cū.i.caɍ.7 c.acs p̃ti.T.R.E.uat xx.fot.

m̃.xL.fot.

349 c

꜀In HAMINGEBI.ħb Lābecarl.vi.bou træ ad gld.

Tra ad.vi.bou.Ibi Baldric hō comit ht.i.caɍ.7 ii.

uilt.7 ii.bord.7 vii.foch hñtes.ii.caɍ.7 dim̃ moliñ

vii.folid.7 xxx.acs p̃ti.T.R.E.uat xxx.fot.m̃.xxv.fot.

In Buchehale 7 Horfitone Soca huj ꝏ.ix.bou

træ ad gld.Tra ad.i.caɍ 7 ii.bou.Ibi.x.foch.7 iii.

bord hñt.ii.caɍ.7 Lx.ii.acs p̃ti.7 xx.acs filuæ paſt

SVD ẼEDING ₤p̃ loca.

꜀In STAINTVNE.ħb Godric.iii.caɍ træ ad gld.Tra

ad.iiii.caɍ.Dim̃ carucata fochoƶ.Ibi Osbñ hō cō

ht.ii.caɍ.7 v.uilt.7 iiii.bord.7 iiii.foch.cū.ii.caɍ.

7 i.moliñ.xii.denaɍ.7 q̃t xx.ac p̃ti.7 cxL.acs filuæ

minutæ.T.R.E.uat.iii.lib.m̃ fimilit.   ₤vi.bou.

In Rerefbi BEREꝯ huj ꝏ.vi.bou tre ad gld.Tra ad

꜀In BOLINTONE.ħb Lābecarl.iii.bou tre 7 dim̃

ad gld.Tra ad.i.caɍ.Ibi Colfuan hō comit ht.i.caɍ.

7 ii.uilt.7 iii.bord.hñtes dim̃ caɍ.7 x.acs p̃ti.7 cLx

acs filuæ minutæ.T.R.E.uat.xx.fot.m̃ fimilit.

36 Freemen and 1 villager who have 4½ ploughs and
meadow, 40 acres.
This jurisdiction belongs to Barnetby (le Wold).

19 Also in *LOBINGEHAM* 4 carucates and 1 bovate, IRBY (upon Humber)
1½ carucates, and RIBY 4½ carucates. Altogether 10 carucates of
land and 1 bovate taxable. Land for 20 ploughs and 2 oxen. A
jurisdiction of Barnetby (le Wold).
   52 Freemen, 11 villagers and 7 smallholders who have 11
      ploughs and
   meadow, 315 acres.

20 In RIBY Erneis, the Earl's man, has 2 ploughs in lordship. He
holds that jurisdiction himself from the Earl. William, Ralph and
Azelin, the Earl's men, hold the others.

21 In FULSTOW Godric had 6 bovates of land taxable. Land for 11
oxen. Rozelin, the Earl's man, has 1 plough.
   7 villagers and 1 smallholder with 1 plough.
   Meadow, 100 acres.
Value before 1066, 20s; now 40s.

22 M. In HEMINGBY Lambakarl had 6 bovates of land taxable. Land for 6   349 c
oxen. Baldric, the Earl's man, has 1 plough.
   2 villagers, 2 smallholders and 7 Freemen who have 2 ploughs.
   ½ mill, 7s; meadow, 30 acres.
Value before 1066, 30s; now 25s.

23 In BUCKNALL and HORSINGTON, a jurisdiction of this manor, 9
bovates of land taxable. Land for 1 plough and 2 oxen.
   10 Freemen and 3 smallholders have 2 ploughs and
   meadow, 62 acres; woodland, pasture in places, 20 acres.

SOUTH RIDING

24 M. In STAINTON (by Langworth) Godric had 3 carucates of land
taxable. Land for 4 ploughs. ½ carucate [is] the Freemen's.
Osbern, the Earl's man, has 2 ploughs.
   5 villagers, 4 smallholders and 4 Freemen with 2 ploughs.
   1 mill, 12d; meadow, 80 acres; underwood, 140 acres.
Value before 1066 £3; now the same.

25 In REASBY, an outlier of this manor, 6 bovates of land taxable.
Land for 6 oxen.

26 M. In BULLINGTON Lambakarl had 3½ bovates of land taxable. Land
for 1 plough. Kolsveinn, the Earl's man, has 1 plough.
   2 villagers and 3 smallholders who have ½ plough and
   meadow, 10 acres; underwood, 160 acres.
Value before 1066, 20s; now the same.

In Cuningeſbi . Inland in Tedintone . 1 . boū trǽ ad glđ.

Ibi . 1 . uilłs arat . 11 . bob . 7 1 . piſcaria . xxx . denař . 7 11.

ač p̃ti . 7 xx . ačs ſiluæ.

⊗ In TADEWELLE . ħɓ Harold . v . car trǽ ad glđ.

Tra ad xx . car̄ . Duæ carucate in Soca . Ibi ħt Hugo

vi . car̄ in dn̄io . 7 xii . uilł . 7 1111 . borđ . 7 xx . 1111 . ſocħ.

hn̄tes . 111 . car̄ . Ibi æccła . 7 1 . molin̄ xvi . denař . 7 v111 . ač

p̃ti . 7 q̃ter . xx . ač ſiluæ paſtił . T.R.E. uał . xv . liɓ . m̃

xx . liɓ . Tailla . c . ſoł.

In Halintun 7 Radreſbi 7 Maltebi . Soca huj . ⊗ . 1x.
  ⁷ Cheleſturne.

car trǽ ad gld . Tra ad . 1x . car̄ . Ibi xli . ſocħ 7 xx . uilł
  7 11.boū   7 dı̄m

hn̄t . vi . car̄ . 7 x . ačs p̃ti.

⊗ In ROCHELAND . ħɓ Godric . 1 . car tre ad glđ . Tra ad

111 . car̄ . Ibi Briſard hō comit ħt . 1 . car̄ . 7 vi . uilł . 7 111.

borđ . cū . 1 . car̄ . Ibi æccła 7 1 . molin̄ . 11 . ſolid . 7 xxx . ač p̃ti.

T.R.E. uał . 1111 . liɓ . m̃ . xl . ſoł.

⊗ In FARFORDE . ħɓ Lābecarl . 1 . car trǽ 7 dim̄ ad glđ . Tra

ad . 11 . car̄ . In Soca . 1 . bouata . Ibi Baldric hō com̄ ħt

✳ 1 . car̄ . 7 x . uilł 7 11 . ſocħ 7 vi . borđ cū . 11 . car̄ . Ibi æccła

.111. 7 1 . molin̄ . 111 . ſolid . 7 v111 . ač p̃ti . T.R.E. uał . 111 . liɓ m̃ ſimił.

⊗ In WELLE . ħɓr Allef . Edric 7 Godric . 11 . car tre ad glđ?
                                            ⁷ una bouata min'.

Tra ad . 111 . car̄ . In Soca dimid bouata . Ibi Oſɓn hō com̄ ħt

111 . car̄ . 7 v111 . uilł . 7 11 . ſocħ . cū . 1 . car̄ . 7 1 . ſalina . 7 xxx.
                                                              1111

ačs p̃ti . 7 v . ačs ſiluæ minutæ . T.R.E. uał . c . ſoł . m̃ . 1111 . liɓ . Taila . v . ſoł.

✳ In Oxecūbe . Soca in Farforde . 1 . car trǽ 7 dim̄ ad glđ . Tra

ad . 11 . car̄ . Ibi x11 . ſocħ 7 1 . uilł hn̄t . 11 . car̄ . 7 lx . ačs p̃ti.

⌐ T.R.E. 7 m̃ . xl . ſoł.

27   In CONINGSBY, *inland* of Toynton, 1 bovate of land taxable.
        1 villager ploughs with 2 oxen.
        1 fishery, 30d; meadow, 2 acres; woodland, 20 acres.

28 M. In TATHWELL Earl Harold had 5 carucates of land taxable. Land
        for 20 ploughs. 2 carucates in a jurisdiction. Earl Hugh has 6
        ploughs in lordship;
          12 villagers, 4 smallholders and 24 Freemen who have 3 ploughs.
          A church; 1 mill, 16d; meadow, 8 acres; woodland pasture,
            80 acres.
        Value before 1066 £15; now £20. Exactions 100s.

29   In HALLINGTON, KELSTERN, RAITHBY and MALTBY, a jurisdiction of
        this manor, 9 carucates of land and 2 bovates taxable. Land for
        9½ ploughs.
          41 Freemen and 20 villagers have 6 ploughs and
          meadow, 10 acres.

30 M. In RUCKLAND Godric had 1 carucate of land taxable. Land for 3
        ploughs. Brisard, the Earl's man, has 1 plough.
          6 villagers and 3 smallholders with 1 plough.
          A church; 1 mill, 2s; meadow, 30 acres.
        Value before 1066 £4; now 40s.

31 M. In FARFORTH Lambakarl had 1½ carucates of land taxable. Land
        for 2 ploughs. In a jurisdiction 1 bovate. Baldric, the Earl's man,
Z·   has 1 plough.
          10 villagers, 2 Freemen and 6 smallholders with 2 ploughs.
          A church; 1 mill, 3s; meadow, 8 acres.
        Value before 1066 £3; now the same.

13,32 is added at the foot of col. 349c, after the next entry, and is directed by transposition signs to its correct place in the text.

33 3 In (Maiden)WELL Aleifr, Eadric and Godric had 2 carucates of
  M. land, less 1 bovate, taxable. Land for 3 ploughs. In a jurisdiction
        ½ bovate. Osbern, the Earl's man, has 3 ploughs.
          8 villagers and 2 Freemen with 1 plough.
          1 salt-house; meadow, 34 acres; underwood, 5 acres.
        Value before 1066, 100s; now £4. Exactions 5s.

13,32, added and directed by transposition signs to its correct place.

Z 32 In OXCOMBE, a jurisdiction of Farforth, 1½ carucates of land
        taxable. Land for 2 ploughs.
          12 Freemen and 1 villager have 2 ploughs and
          meadow, 60 acres.
         Value before 1066 and now, 40s.

Ⓜ Iɴ *WADINTVNE* . ħƀ Harold . xxiiii . caͬ tͬe ad glđ.

Ťra ad totiđ caͬ . In Soc ᴀ . ɪx . caͬucatæ . 7 ɪɪ . bouatæ.

Ibi ħⱦ coͫ Hugo . ɪɪɪɪ . caͬ in đñio . 7 xv . uiⱦ . 7 ɪx . borđ.

7 xxɪɪɪɪ . focħ . ħñtes xɪ . caͬ . Ibi æccła 7 pƀr . 7 ɪɪ . moliñ

de xɪ . foliđ . 7 cᴄʟxx . aͨ ƥti . T.R.E . uaⱦ . c . liƀ . ɪɪɪɪ . liƀ.

min . ᵯ xx . liƀ . Tailla . x . liƀ.

Iɴ Medriceſham Bᴇʀᴇ̃ẇ huj Ⓜ . vɪɪɪ . caͬ tͬe 7 dĩ

ad glđ . Ťra ad . ɪɪɪɪ . caͬ 7 ɪɪ . boues . Ibi ħⱦ coͫ . ɪɪ . caͬ.

7 x . uiⱦ 7 vɪ . borđ . cũ . ɪɪ . caͬ . 7 ɪ . miliñ . vɪɪɪ . foliđ . 7

nonaᵹ
cxc . aͨs ƥti . 7 cxx . aͨs filuæ minutæ.

Iɴ Timbrelund . Bᴇʀᴇ̃ẇ . vɪ . bou tͬe ad glđ . Ťra ad . ɪɪɪɪ.

bou . Ibi . ɪɪ . borđ ħñt dĩ caͬ . 7 ʟ . aͨs filuæ minutæ

Iɴ Hermodeſtune Soc ᴀ de Wadintone . xx . caͬ tͬe

7 dĩ ad glđ . Ťra ad totiđ caͬ . Ibi xxxvɪɪɪ . focħ 7 xɪ.

borđ ħñt . x . caͬ . Ibi æccła 7 pƀr . 7 ɪ . piſcaria redđ

ʟ̃xxv . anguiⱦ.

Ⓜ Iũ *EXEWELLE* . ħƀ Harold . ɪɪ . caͬ tͬæ ad glđ . Ťra ad . vɪ.

caͬ . Ibi Gozelin ħõ comit . H . ħⱦ . ɪɪ . caͬ . 7 xɪɪɪ . uiⱦ . 7 ɪɪ.

borđ . ħñtes . v . caͬ . 7 xvɪ . aͨ ƥti . T.R.E . uaⱦ . c . foliđ.

ᵯ . vɪ . liƀ.

★ Ⓜ Iɴ *FVLNODEBI LOBI* . ħƀ Harold . ɪɪ . caͬ tͬe ad glđ . Ťra ad . ɪɪɪ.

caͬ . Ibi Baldric ħõ comit ħⱦ . ɪ . caͬ . 7 ɪx . focħ . 7 v . uiⱦ

7 ɪɪɪɪ . borđ ħñtes . ɪ . caͬ 7 dĩ . 7 ʟx . aͨ ƥti . T.R.E . uaⱦ

xʟ . fot . ᵯ similiⱦ . Pƀr cjđ uillæ ħⱦ . ɪɪ . de rege bou tͬæ ad glđ . 7 xɪɪ . aͨs ͬpti

Ⓜ Iɴ *ORMESBI* . ħƀ . Godric . ɪɪɪ . caͬ tͬe ad glđ . Ťra ad

ɪɪɪɪ . caͬ . Ibi Hugo ħõ comitis ħⱦ . ɪɪ . caͬ . 7 vɪɪ . uiⱦ.

7 ɪ . borđ . 7 xɪ . focħ ħñtes . ɪɪ . caͬ . 7 ɪ . moliñ xxxɪɪ . den.

7 q̃ter xx . aͨ ƥti . T.R.E . uaⱦ . ʟxx . fot . ᵯ . ɪɪɪɪ . liƀ.

Ⓜ Iɴ *CHETELESBI* . ħƀ Godric . ɪɪɪ . caͬ tͬe ad glđ . Ťra

ad . ɪɪɪɪ . caͬ . Ibi Hugo ħõ coͫ ħⱦ . ɪɪɪ . caͬ . 7 vɪ . uiⱦ . 7 ɪ.

borđ . 7 xɪ . focħ . ħñtes . ɪɪ . caͬ 7 dimiđ . 7 ɪ . molđ . xxxɪɪ.

denaͬ . 7 ʟx . aͨs ƥti . T.R.E . uaⱦ . ɪɪɪɪ . liƀ . ᵯ . c . fot.

34 M. In WADDINGTON Earl Harold had 24 carucates of land taxable. 349 d
Land for as many ploughs. In a jurisdiction 9 carucates of land
and 2 bovates. Earl Hugh has 4 ploughs in lordship;
15 villagers, 9 smallholders and 24 Freemen who have 11 ploughs.
A church and a priest; 2 mills at 11s; meadow, 270 acres.
Value before 1066 £100 less £4; now £20. Exactions £10.

35 In METHERINGHAM, an outlier of this manor, 8½ carucates of land
taxable. Land for 4 ploughs and 2 oxen. The Earl has 2 ploughs.
10 villagers and 6 smallholders with 2 ploughs.
1 mill, 8s; meadow, 190 acres; underwood, 120 acres.

36 In TIMBERLAND, an outlier, 6 bovates of land taxable. Land for 4
oxen.
2 smallholders have ½ plough and
underwood, 50 acres.

37 In HARMSTON, a jurisdiction of Waddington, 20½ carucates of land
taxable. Land for as many ploughs.
38 Freemen and 11 smallholders have 10 ploughs.
A church and a priest; 1 fishery pays 75,000 eels.

38 M. In ASHWELL Earl Harold had 2 carucates of land taxable. Land for
6 ploughs. Jocelyn, Earl H(ugh)'s man, has 2 ploughs.
13 villagers and 2 smallholders who have 5 ploughs.
Meadow, 16 acres.
Value before 1066, 100s; now £6.

39 M. In FULLETBY Earl Harold had 2 carucates of land taxable. Land
for 3 ploughs. Baldric, the Earl's man, has 1 plough.
9 Freemen, 5 villagers and 4 smallholders who have 1½ ploughs.
Meadow, 60 acres.
Value before 1066, 40s; now the same.

40 A priest of this village has from the King 2 bovates of land
taxable and
meadow, 12 acres.

41 M. In (South) ORMSBY Godric had 3 carucates of land taxable. Land
for 4 ploughs. Hugh, the Earl's man, has 2 ploughs.
7 villagers, 1 smallholder and 11 Freemen who have 2 ploughs.
1 mill, 32d; meadow, 80 acres.
Value before 1066, 70s; now £4.

42 M. In KETSBY Godric had 3 carucates of land taxable. Land for 4
ploughs. Hugh, the Earl's man, has 3 ploughs.
6 villagers, 1 smallholder and 11 Freemen who have 2½ ploughs.
1 mill, 32d; meadow, 60 acres.
Value before 1066 £4; now 100s.

In Walmeſgar Soc huj ꝏ̄ .una caruc̄ træ ad glđ.

.ɪɪɪ.̃ Tra ad . xɪɪɪɪ . bou.

ꝏ̄ In HECHᾶ . h̄br Elueua Godric 7 Edric . ɪɪ . car̄ træ
ad glđ . Tra ad . vɪ . car̄ . Ibi monachi S̃ Seueri hn̄t
ɪɪɪ . car̄.7 xxɪx . uiƚƚ.7 ɪɪɪ . borđ . cū . vɪ . car̄.7 xLvɪ.
ac̄s p̄ti.7 ſiluæ p loca past . ɪ . leu lḡ.7 ɪɪɪ . q̃ɀ̃ lat̄.
T.R.E. uaƚ . vɪ . liƀ . m̄ . vɪɪɪ . liƀ.

ꝏ̄ In NEVBERIE . hƀ Godric . ɪɪɪ . car̄ træ ad glđ . Tra ad
ɪɪɪ . car̄ . Ibi Osƀn hō comitis hƚ . ɪɪ . car̄.7 xɪɪɪ . uiƚƚ.7 ɪɪ.
borđ.cū . ɪɪ . car̄.7 cxx . ac̄s p̄ti.7 q̃ngent ac̄s ſiluæ past.
T.R.E. uaƚ . Lx . ſoƚ . m̄ . c . ſoƚ.

350 a

.XIIII   TERRA IVONIS TAILLGEBOSC.

ꝏ̄ In TATENAI habuer̄ Turgiſle 7 Suen . ɪɪɪɪ . caruc̄ træ
ad glđ . Tra ad . vɪɪɪ . car̄ . In Soc A . ɪ . car 7 ɪɪ . bou.7 ɪɪɪ . parᵗ ᶜⁱᵃ
ɪɪ . bou . de hac tra . Nc̄ Ivo tailleboſc hƚ ibi in dn̄io
vɪ . car̄.7 xxv . uiƚƚ.7 vɪɪ . borđ.7 xɪɪ . ſoch . hn̄tes vɪ . car̄.
Ibi . ɪ . molin̄ . xvɪ . ſoliđ.7 xɪɪɪ . ſaline . xɪɪ . ſoliđ.7 cxL . ac̄
p̄ti . T.R.E. uaƚ . x . liƀ . m̄ . xx . liƀ . Tailla xx . liƀ.

In Holtone Soc A huj ꝏ̄ . ɪɪ . car̄ tre ad glđ . Tra ad . ɪɪɪɪ.
car̄ . Ibi . xɪɪɪɪ . ſoch hn̄t . ɪɪɪ . car̄ . Vaƚ . xL . ſoƚ.

ꝏ̄ Ibidē hƀ Esƀn . ɪ . car̄ tre ad glđ . Tra ad . ɪɪ . car̄ . Ibi Her
mer hō Iuon hƚ . v . uiƚƚ 7 ɪɪ . borđ . arantes . v . bob.
Ibi ſeđ molini.7 xɪɪɪɪ . ac̄ p̄ti . T.R.E.7 m̄ uaƚ . xL . ſoƚ.

In Humbreſtone . Soc A de Tatenai . vɪ . car̄ tre ad glđ.
Tra ad . xɪɪ . car̄ . Ibi . Lxvɪɪ . ſoch . hn̄t xvɪɪɪ . car̄.7 cc.

ꝏ̄ In CLEIA . hƀ Gribold . ɪɪ . bou tre 7 ɪɪ . part ⸗ ac̄s p̄ti.
uni bou . ad glđ . Tra ad dim̄ car̄ . Ibi Wimund hō Ju
hƚ dim̄ car̄.7 xvɪ . ac̄s p̄ti . T.R.E. uaƚ xx . ſoƚ . m̄ x . ſoƚ.

43   In WALMSGATE, a jurisdiction of this manor, 1 carucate of land taxable. Land for 14 oxen.

44 3   In HAUGHAM Aelfgifu, Godric and Eadric had 2 carucates of land
M.   taxable. Land for 6 ploughs. The monks of St. Sever's have 3 ploughs.
      29 villagers and 3 smallholders with 6 ploughs.
      Meadow, 46 acres; woodland, pasture in places, 1 league long
         and 3 furlongs wide.
Value before 1066 £6; now £8.

45 M.   In NEWBALL Godric had 3 carucates of land taxable. Land for 3
      ploughs. Osbern, the Earl's man, has 2 ploughs.
      13 villagers and 2 smallholders with 2 ploughs.
      Meadow, 120 acres; woodland pasture, 500 acres.
Value before 1066, 60s; now 100s.

14   LAND OF IVO TALLBOYS   350 a

1 2   In TETNEY Thorgils and Sveinn had 4 carucates of land taxable.
M.   Land for 8 ploughs. In a jurisdiction 1 carucate, 2 bovates and
      the third part of 2 bovates of this land. Now Ivo Tallboys has in
      lordship there 6 ploughs;
      25 villagers, 7 smallholders and 12 Freemen who have 6 ploughs.
      1 mill, 16s; 13 salt-houses, 12s; meadow, 140 acres.
Value before 1066 £10; now £20. Exactions £20.

2   In HOLTON (le Clay), a jurisdiction of this manor, 2 carucates of
      land taxable. Land for 4 ploughs.
      14 Freemen have 3 ploughs.
Value 40s.

3 M.   There also Esbjorn had 1 carucate of land taxable. Land for 2
      ploughs. Hermer, Ivo's man, has
      5 villagers and 2 smallholders who plough with 5 oxen.
      A mill site; meadow, 14 acres.
Value before 1066 and now, 40s.

4   In HUMBERSTONE, a jurisdiction of Tetney, 6 carucates of land
      taxable. Land for 12 ploughs.
      67 Freemen have 18 ploughs and
      meadow, 200 acres.

5 M.   In CLEE Grimbald had 2 bovates of land and 2 parts of 1 bovate
      taxable. Land for ½ plough. Wigmund, Ivo's man, has ½ plough and
      meadow, 16 acres.
Value before 1066, 20s; now 10s.

M In *TERNESCROV*. hb Grinchel. v. bou trae ad gld.
Tra ad. x. boues. Ibi Wimund ht. i. car. 7 v. uill. cu
uno boue. 7 xii. acs pti. T.R.E. ual 7 m. xx. sol.

WALESCROS WAPENTAC.

In Wisilingha. ht Iuo dim car tre. de Soca Eriz.
M In *CLACHESBI* 7 *NORMANESBI*. hb Goduin. x. bou
tre ad gld. Tra ad ii. car 7 dimid.
.III. M Ibide habuer Godric Siuuard Vlchel 7 Goduin
xii. bou tre ad gld. 7 i. tosta cu saca 7 soca. Tra ad. iii. car.
Ibi Hugo ho Iuonis ht. ii. car. 7 xlviii. soch. 7 iiii. bord.
cu. vi. car. Ibi. ii. aecclae. 7 c. ac pti. 7 xl. ac siluae minutae.
T.R.E. ual. xl. sol. m. iiii. lib. Tailla. iiii. lib.
In Osgotebi 7 Tauelebi. Inland .ii. bo 7 Soca .i. bo huj M. iii. bou
tre ad gld. Tra ad. vi. boues. Ibi. iiii. soch 7 i. uills arant
vi. bob. 7 i. molin ibi. iii. solid. 7 iii. ac pti.
M In *CLACHESBI*. hb Aluuin. iii. bou tre ad gld. Tra
ad. vi. bou. Ibi Goisfrid ho Iuon ht. i. car. 7 ii. uill
n arant. 7 i. molin. ii. solid. 7 xiii. ac pti. 7 vi. ac siluae
minute. T.R.E. ual. xv. sol. m. xiii. solid.
M In *TORGREBI*. hb Grimbald. ii. bou tre ad gld. Tra
ad. v. bou. Ibi Odo ho Iuon ht. i. car. 7 ii. uill. 7 iii.es
partes uni molini. v. solid. 7 ix. acs pti. T.R.E. ual. xx.
sol. m xxx. solid.
M In *WALESBI* 7 Otesbi. hb Gribold. i. car trae ad gld.
Tra ad. ii. car. Ibi Goisfrid ho Iuon ht. i. car. 7 xx.
uill. cu. ii. car. 7 i. molin. xvi. denar. 7 xx. acs pti.

350 b
7 v. acs siluae minutae. T.R.E. ual. xl. sol. m simil. Tailla. x. sol.
M In *TORESWE*. hb Gribold. ii. bou trae ad gld. Tra
ad. vi. bou. Ibi Odo ho Iuon ht. i. uill. i. boue arant.
7 xv. ac pti 7 dim. T.R.E. ual. xx. sol. m ix. sol 7 iiii.
denar.

6 M. In THRUNSCOE Grimketill had 5 bovates of land taxable. Land for 10 oxen. Wigmund has 1 plough.
　　5 villagers with 1 ox.
　　Meadow, 12 acres.
Value before 1066 and now, 20s.

WALSHCROFT Wapentake
7　In (North) WILLINGHAM Ivo has ½ carucate of land of the jurisdiction of Eirikr.

8 M. In CLAXBY and NORMANBY (le Wold) Godwine had 10 bovates of land taxable. Land for 2½ ploughs.

9 3 There also Godric, Siward, Ulfketill and Godwine had 12 bovates
M. of land taxable and 1 plot with full jurisdiction. Land for 3 ploughs. Hugh, Ivo's man, has 2 ploughs.
　　48 Freemen and 4 smallholders with 6 ploughs.
　　2 churches; meadow, 100 acres; underwood, 40 acres.
Value before 1066, 40s; now £4. Exactions £4.

10　In OSGODBY and TEALBY *inland*, 2 bovates, and a jurisdiction, 1 bovate, of this manor: 3 bovates of land taxable. Land for 6 oxen.
　　4 Freemen and 1 villager plough with 6 oxen.
　　1 mill there, 3s; meadow, 3 acres.

11 M. In CLAXBY Alwine had 3 bovates of land taxable. Land for 6 oxen. Geoffrey, Ivo's man, has 1 plough.
　　2 villagers who do not plough.
　　1 mill, 2s; meadow, 13 acres; underwood, 6 acres.
Value before 1066, 15s; now 13s.

12 M. In THORGANBY Grimbald had 2 bovates of land taxable. Land for 5 oxen. Odo, Ivo's man, has 1 plough.
　　2 villagers.
　　3 parts of 1 mill, 5s; meadow, 9 acres.
Value before 1066, 20s; now 30s.

13 M. In WALESBY and OTBY Grimbald had 1 carucate of land taxable. Land for 2 ploughs. Geoffrey, Ivo's man, has 1 plough.
　　20 villagers with 2 ploughs.
　　1 mill, 16d; meadow, 20 acres; underwood, 5 acres.
Value before 1066, 40s; now the same. Exactions 10s.

350 b

14 M. In THORESWAY Grimbald had 2 bovates of land taxable. Land for 6 oxen. Odo, Ivo's man, has
　　1 villager who ploughs with 1 ox.
　　Meadow, 15½ acres.
Value before 1066, 20s; now 9s 4d.

ꝏ In *Crosbi*. hƀ Siuuard . v . bou̅ t̅re ad gld̅.
Tra ad . ii . car̅ . In Soca . v . ac̅ træ . Ibi Odo ho̅ Iuonis
ht̅ . i . car̅ 7 dim̅ . 7 vi . uill 7 i . bord cu̅ . i . car̅ . 7 iii . molin̅
viii . folid . 7 xviii . ac̅ p̅ti . T.R.E. ual . xxx . fol . m̅ xl . fol.

ꝏ In *Blisvrg*. hƀ Gamel . v . bou̅ 7 dim̅ ad gld̅ . T̅ra
ad . xi . boues . Ibi Nigell ho̅ Iuo̅n ht̅ . ii . car̅ . 7 vii . uill
7 v . bord . cu̅ . i . car̅ . 7 i . molin̅ . xii . denar̅ . 7 xx . ac̅s p̅ti.
T.R.E. ual xxvi . fol . 7 viii . den . m̅ . l . fol . Tailla . xx . fol.

ꝏ In *Glantia*. hƀ Turgifle . iii . car̅ t̅re ad gld̅ . T̅ra
ad . iiii . car̅ . In Soca . ii . caruc̅ t̅re 7 ii . bou̅ de hac t̅ra.
Ibi Rainfrid ho̅ Iuo̅n ht̅ . ii . car̅ . 7 ii . uill 7 xiii . bord.
7 xix . foch cu̅ . ii . car̅ 7 dim̅ . 7 q̅t xx . 7 x . ac̅s p̅ti.
T.R.E. ual . xxx . fol . m̅ . lx . fol . Tailla . xx . fol.

ꝏ In *Normanebi*. hƀ Code . v . car̅ t̅ræ ad gld̅ . T̅ra
ad . viii . car̅ . In Soca . i . car̅ 7 dimidia . Ibi ht̅ Iuo m̅
iiii . car̅ . 7 xv . uill 7 xiiii . foch hn̅tes . v . car̅ . Ibi æccla
7 pƀr . 7 ii . molin̅ . v . folid 7 iiii . denar̅ . 7 lxvii . ac̅ p̅ti
7 dim̅ . T.R.E. ual . l . fol . m̅ . c . fol . Tailla . xx . fol.
In Efnetrebi Soca huj ꝏ . i . bou̅ t̅ræ . Ibi . iii . foch . vi.
bob arant . 7 xl . ac̅ p̅ti.

ꝏ In *Ovnebi*. hƀ Code . iiii . bou̅ t̅ræ ad gld̅ . T̅ra ad dim̅ car̅.
Ibi Petrus ho̅ Iuo̅n ht̅ . i . car̅ . 7 ii . uill . 7 x . ac̅s p̅ti.
T.R.E. ual . x . fol . m̅ . xx . fol
Ibid ht̅ Iuo . i . bo̅ t̅ræ de foca . R . ep̅i.

ꝏ In *Svmertebi* . vii . bou̅ t̅ræ ad gld̅ . Tra ad . vii . bou̅.
Ibi ht̅ Iuo . i . bord 7 xx . ac̅s filuæ past . T.R.E. ual . xx . fol.

ꝏ In *Tonestale* . hƀ . Gamel . ii . car̅ t̅ræ ad ⌠m̅ . v . fol.
gld̅ . T̅ra ad . ii . car̅ 7 dim̅ . In Soca . x . bou̅ iftius t̅ræ.
Ibi ht̅ Iuo . ii . car̅ in dn̅io . 7 ii . uill 7 xi . foch 7 i . bord
cu̅ . ii . car̅ . Ibi æccla 7 pƀr . 7 i . molin̅ . ii . folid . 7 vii . ac̅
p̅ti . T.R.E. ual . xl . fol . m̅ . iiii . liƀ.

15 M. In CROXBY Siward had 5 bovates of land taxable. Land for 2 ploughs. In a jurisdiction 5 acres of land. Odo, Ivo's man, has 1½ ploughs.
   6 villagers and 1 smallholder with 1 plough.
   3 mills, 8s; meadow, 18 acres.
Value before 1066, 30s; now 40s.

16 M. In BLYBOROUGH Gamall had 5½ bovates taxable. Land for 11 oxen. Nigel, Ivo's man, has 2 ploughs.
   7 villagers and 5 smallholders with 1 plough.
   1 mill, 12d; meadow, 20 acres.
Value before 1066, 26s 8d; now 50s. Exactions 20s.

17 M. In GLENTHAM Thorgils had 3 carucates of land taxable. Land for 4 ploughs. In a jurisdiction 2 carucates of land and 2 bovates of this land. Rainfrid, Ivo's man, has 2 ploughs.
   2 villagers, 13 smallholders and 19 Freemen with 2½ ploughs.
   Meadow, 90 acres.
Value before 1066, 30s; now 60s. Exactions 20s.

18 M. In NORMANBY (-by-Spital) Koddi had 5 carucates of land taxable. Land for 8 ploughs. In a jurisdiction 1½ carucates. Now Ivo has 4 ploughs.
   15 villagers and 14 Freemen who have 5 ploughs.
   A church and a priest; 2 mills, 5s 4d; meadow, 67½ acres.
Value before 1066, 50s; now 100s. Exactions 20s.

19 In SNITTERBY, a jurisdiction of this manor, 1 bovate of land.
   3 Freemen who plough with 6 oxen.
   Meadow, 40 acres.

20 M. In OWMBY (-by-Spital) Koddi had 4 bovates of land taxable. Land for ½ plough. Peter, Ivo's man, has 1 plough.
   2 villagers.
   Meadow, 10 acres.
Value before 1066, 10s; now 20s.

21 There also Ivo has 1 bovate of land of the jurisdiction of Bishop Remigius.

22 M. In SOMERBY 7 bovates of land taxable. Land for 7 oxen. Ivo has
   1 smallholder and
   woodland pasture, 20 acres.
Value before 1066, 20s; now 5s.

23 M. In 'DUNSTALL' Gamall had 2 carucates of land taxable. Land for 2½ ploughs. In a jurisdiction 10 bovates of this land. Ivo has 2 ploughs in lordship;
   2 villagers, 11 Freemen and 1 smallholder with 2 ploughs.
   A church and a priest; 1 mill, 2s; meadow, 7 acres.
Value before 1066, 40s; now £4.

ⓂIn *MORTVNE*.h̄b Gamel.III.bou træ ad glđ.Tra ad
VI.bou.Ibi h̄r Iuo.IIII.uill.II.bobȝ arant.7 x.ac̄s p̄ti.
Moræ 7 minuta filua:dim̄ lev l̄g.7 dim̄ lat̄.T.R.E.ual
.IIII.fol.m̄.x.fol.

ⓂIn *SCOTONE*.h̄b Gamel.II.car træ 7 dim̄ ad glđ.Tra
ad.II.car 7 dim̄.In SocA.dim̄ caruc de hac tra.Ibi Gozel
h̄o Iuon h̄r.II.car.7 xv.uill.7 III.borđ.7 vi.foch.cū
.II.car.7 xxx.I.ac̄ p̄ti.7 xvIII.ac̄ filuæ min̄.7 feđ molini.
T.R.E.ual.xxx.fol.m̄.L.fol.Tailla.x.fol.

MANELINDE WAPENTAC.

ⓂIn *HIBOLDESTOV* h̄b Gamel.I.car tre 7 dim̄ ad glđ.
Tra ad.III.car.Ibi h̄r Iuo.IIII.car.7 xvIII.uill.7 II.
borđ.cū.II.car.7 I.molin̄.v.folid.7 cxI.ac̄s p̄ti.
7 Lx.ac̄s filuæ minutæ.T.R.E.ual.c.fol.m̄.c.fol.
Tailla.xx.folid.

ⓂIn *GAMELSTORP* [Hilboldeftou].h̄b Vlgar.II.bou træ.Hanc h̄r
in c̄abio p̄ una bou.7 II.pifcar de Crul.Ibi.I.car.
T.R.E.7 m̄.x.fol.

ⒷIn *STRAITONE* 7 Scallebi.Inland.III.bou træ ad
glđ.Ibi un̄ h̄o Iuon.I.car 7 I.uill.T.R.E.ual.v.fol.
7 IIII.den.m̄ xx.fol.

ⓂIn *ALCHEBARGE*.h̄b Wills malet.v.car træ
ad glđ.Tra ad.vi.car.In SocA.III.car de hac tra.
Ibi h̄r Iuo.III.car.7 vIII.uill.7 xx.foch.cū.v.car.
T.R.E.ual.c.fol.m̄.IIII.lib.Tailla.xL.fol.

ⓂIn *SAXEBI*.h̄br Siuuard:IIII.car træ ad glđ.Tra ad.vII.
car|Ibi Roger h̄o Iuon h̄r.II.car.7 vIII.uill.7 II.
foch cū.III.car.7 III.pifcar.III.folid.T.R.E.ual.IIII.
lib.m̄.L.fol.Tailla.x.fol.

24 M. In MORTON Gamall had 3 bovates of land taxable. Land for 6
oxen. Ivo has
> 4 villagers who plough with 2 oxen; and
> meadow, 10 acres; moors and underwood ½ league long and
> ½ wide.

Value before 1066, 4s; now 10s.

25 M. In SCOTTON Gamall had 2½ carucates of land taxable. Land for
2½ ploughs. In a jurisdiction ½ carucate of this land. Jocelyn,
Ivo's man, has 2 ploughs.
> 15 villagers, 3 smallholders and 6 Freemen with 2 ploughs.
> Meadow, 31 acres; underwood, 18 acres; a mill site.

Value before 1066, 30s; now 50s. Exactions 10s.

MANLEY Wapentake   350 c

26 2 In HIBALDSTOW Gamall had 1½ carucates of land taxable. Land
M. for 3 ploughs. Ivo has 4 ploughs.
> 18 villagers and 2 smallholders with 2 ploughs.
> 1 mill, 5s; meadow, 111 acres; underwood, 60 acres.

Value before 1066, 100s; now 100s. Exactions 20s.

27 M. In HIBALDSTOW [and] GAINSTHORPE Wulfgar had 2 bovates of land.
He has this in exchange for 1 bovate and 2 fisheries of Crowle.
1 plough.
Value before 1066 and now, 10s.

28 B. In STURTON and SCAWBY, *inland*, 3 bovates of land taxable. One of
Ivo's men has 1 plough.
> 1 villager.

Value before 1066, 5s 4d; now 20s.

29 M. In ALKBOROUGH William Malet had 5 carucates of land taxable.
Land for 6 ploughs. In a jurisdiction 3 carucates of this land.
Ivo has 3 ploughs.
> 8 villagers and 20 Freemen with 5 ploughs.

Value before 1066, 100s; now £4. Exactions 40s.

30 2 In SAXBY (All Saints) Siward and Thorgils had 4 carucates of land
M. taxable. Land for 7½ ploughs. Roger, Ivo's man, has 2 ploughs.
> 8 villagers and 2 Freemen with 3 ploughs.
> 3 fisheries, 3s.

Value before 1066 £4; now 50s. Exactions 10s.

.III.

ω In *CHELVINGEHOV* . Briford . Siuuard 7 Turgis . II . car̄
træ 7 VII . bou ad glđ . Tra ad . III . car̄ . In SOCA . I . caruc̄
7 I . bouata 7 II . toftæ . Ibi Odo hō Iuōn hȳ . III . car̄.
7 IIII . uilt 7 XIX . foch cū . III . car̄ . 7 dimid molin̄ . IIII .
folidoᵹ . 7 CCXII . ac̄ p̄ti . T.R.E . ual . V . lib̄ . m̄ . III . lib̄ .

ω In *LINBERGE* . hb̄ Aluuin . IX . bou træ ⎰ Tailla . XX . fol.
ad glđ . Tra ad . IIII . car̄ . In SOCA . una bou de hac tra .
Ibi Nigell hō Iuōn hȳ . III . car̄ . 7 I . uilt . T.R.E . ual . X.L .
fol . m̄ LX . fol .

ω In *NEVHVSE* . hb̄ Aluuin . V . bou træ ad glđ . Tra ad . X .
boues . Ibi Roger hō Iuōn hȳ . I . car̄ . 7 VI . uilt . cū . I . car̄ .
7 I . molin̄ . II . folid . 7 XXX . ac̄s p̄ti . T.R.E . ual . XXII . fol .

ω In *IRIBI* . hb̄ . Seuuard . I . car̄ træ ad glđ .   ⎰ m̄ XL . fol .
Tra ad . II . car̄ . Ibi Odo hō Iuōn hȳ . I . car̄ . 7 V . uilt . 7 X
bord arantes . III . bob . T.R.E . ual X . fol 7 VIII . den̄ . m̄ . XX . s̄ .
In *HOCTVNE* hȳt Iuo . I . car̄ træ ad glđ . in Efcabio . Tra
ad . II . car̄ . Ibi . c̄ . I . car̄ . Odo hȳ . 7 ualet XV . fol .   Ƴ
In *HABVRNE* hb̄ Turgis . III . bou 7 tciā parte bou ad
glđ . SOCA in Haltune . Wafta . c̄ .

ω In *BROCHELESBI* . hb̄ Aluuin . III . bou træ ad glđ . Tra
ad . I . car̄ . Vna bou in SOCA . Ibi Nigell hō Iuōn hȳ
II . foch cū . II . bob arantes . T.R.E . ual . XVI . fol . m̄ . III . fol .
Ƴ SOCA In Wade . II . bou ad glđ . Tra . II . bou . Ibi . IIII . uilt 7 I . foch
⎰ hn̄t dim̄ car̄ .
⎱ 7 . V . ac̄s p̄ti .

350 d

ω In *CABVRNE* . hb̄ Vnlof . I . car̄ træ 7 III . bou ad glđ .
Tra ad . III . car̄ . Ibi Roger hō Iuōn hȳ . II . car̄ . 7 III . uilt
7 V . bord 7 XI . foch cū . II . car̄ 7 dim̄ . 7 c . ac̄s p̄ti . T.R.E .
ual . XXX . fol . m̄ LX . fol . Tailla . XX . fol .

31 3 In KILLINGHOLME Beorhtfrith, Siward and Thorgils [had] 2
M. carucates of land and 7 bovates taxable. Land for 3 ploughs. In a
jurisdiction 1 carucate, 1 bovate and 2 plots. Odo, Ivo's man,
has 3 ploughs.
   4 villagers and 19 Freemen with 3 ploughs.
   ½ mill, 3s; meadow, 212 acres.
Value before 1066 £5; now £3. Exactions 20s.

32 M. In (Little) LIMBER Alwine had 9 bovates of land taxable. Land for
4 ploughs. In a jurisdiction 1 bovate of this land. Nigel, Ivo's man,
has 3 ploughs.
   L villager.
Value before 1066, 40s; now 60s.

33 M. In NEWSHAM Alwine had 5 bovates of land taxable. Land for 10
oxen. Roger, Ivo's man, has 1 plough.
   6 villagers with 1 plough.
   1 mill, 2s; meadow, 30 acres.
Value before 1066, 22s; now 40s.

34 M. In IRBY (upon Humber) Siward had 1 carucate of land taxable.
Land for 2 ploughs. Odo, Ivo's man, has 1 plough.
   5 villagers and 10 smallholders who plough with 3 oxen.
Value before 1066, 10s 8d; now 20s.

35 In HOLTON (le Moor) Ivo has 1 carucate of land taxable, in
exchange. Land for 2 ploughs. 1 plough; Odo has it.
Value 15s.

*14,36 is added at the foot of col. 350c (after 14,38) and is directed by transposition signs to
its correct place in the text.*

37 In HABROUGH Thorgils had 3 bovates and the third part of a bovate
taxable. A jurisdiction of (East) Halton. It is waste.

38 M. In BROCKLESBY Alwine had 3 bovates of land taxable. Land for 1
plough. 1 bovate in a jurisdiction. Nigel, Ivo's man, has
   2 Freemen who plough with 2 oxen.
Value before 1066, 16s; now 3s.

14,36, directed by transposition signs to its correct place.
Jurisdiction:

36 S. In WAITHE 2 bovates taxable. Land for 2 oxen.
   4 villagers and 1 Freeman have ½ plough and
   meadow, 5 acres.

39 M. In CABOURN Wulfnoth had 1 carucate of land and 3 bovates taxable.   350 d
Land for 3 ploughs. Roger, Ivo's man, has 2 ploughs.
   3 villagers, 5 smallholders and 11 Freemen with 2½ ploughs.
   Meadow, 100 acres.
Value before 1066, 30s; now 60s. Exactions 20s.

₰ In *CVCVALT*. ħɓ Aluuin . 1 . bou træ 7 dim ad glđ . Tra ad
dim car̄ . Ibi Gozelin hō Iuon ħt . 1 . car̄ . T.R.E . ual . xx .

₰ In *REBVRNE* . ħɓ Gamel . 1 . car̄ træ   ⨍ fot . m̄ xvi . fot .
7 dim bou ad glđ . Tra ad . 1 . car̄ 7 dim bou . Ibi Petrus
hō Iuon ħt . 1 . car̄ . 7 v . uilt . 7 1 . foch 7 1 . borđ cū . 1 . car̄ .
7 xxiiii . ac̄s p̄ti . T.R.E . ual . xxi . fot . m̄ . xxx . fot .
Tailla . x . fot .   ⨍ cū . 1 . boue . 7 viii . ac̄ p̄ti . Valet . v . fot .

₰ Ibidē ħɓ Aldene . iii . bou træ ad glđ . Ibi ħt Iuo . 1 . uilt

₰ In *WESTLEDEBI* . ħɓ Harold . vii . bou træ ad gld .
Tra ad . xiiii . bou . Ibi ħt Odo hō Iuon . dim car̄ . 7 ii .
uilt 7 ii . borđ cū dim car̄ . 7 xx . ac̄s p̄ti . T.R.E . ual . xx . fot .

₰ In *LOBINGEHA* ħɓ Aluuin . vi . bou tre ad glđ . ⨍ m̄ . xvi . fot .
Tra ad . xii . bou . Ibi Odo hō Iuon ħt . 1 . borđ . cū . 1 . bou arant .
7 xxx . ac̄s p̄ti . T.R.E . ual . xx . fot . m̄ xii . fot .

₰ In *CHELEBI* . ħɓ Aluuin . ii . bou tre ad glđ . Tra ad . iiii .
bou . Ibi ħt Nigel hō Iuon dim car̄ . 7 ii . uilt 7 1 . borđ .
uno boue arantes . Ibi feđ molini . 7 xxvii . ac̄ p̄ti . T.R.E .
ual . x . fot . m̄ . xx . fot .   *HAWARDESHOV WAPENT.*

₰ In *BELTESFORD* . ħɓ Stori . vi . car̄ træ ad glđ .
Tra ad . viii . car̄ . De hac tra . ii . car̄ in foca . Ibi ħt Iuo
v . car̄ in dn̄io . 7 ix . uilt . 7 xv . borđ . 7 xlv .
foch . hn̄tes . ix . car̄ . Ibi . ii . molini de . xviii . fot 7 viii .
denar̄ . 7 ccc.lx . ac̄s p̄ti . 7 iii . ac̄ filuæ minute . Vna
leu lḡ . 7 1 . lat̄ . T.R.E . ual . xv . liɓ . m̄ xxxiii . liɓ . Tailla
xxvii . liɓ .   Soca hvjvs·manerii .

In Colchefbi . iii . car̄ tre ad glđ . Tra . iii . carucarū .
Ibi . xvi . foch 7 ii . uilt . hn̄t . vi . car̄ . 7 1 . moliñ . iiii . folid .
7 p̄ɓr & æccła . 7 cxx . ac̄ p̄ti .

40 M. In CUXWOLD Alwine had 1½ bovates of land taxable. Land for ½ plough. Jocelyn, Ivo's man, has 1 plough.
Value before 1066, 20s; now 16s.

41 M. In REDBOURNE Gamall had 1 carucate of land and ½ bovate taxable. Land for 1 plough and ½ ox. Peter, Ivo's man, has 1 plough.
5 villagers, 1 Freeman and 1 smallholder with 1 plough.
Meadow, 24 acres.
Value before 1066, 21s; now 30s. Exactions 10s.

42 M. There also Halfdan had 3 bovates of land taxable. Ivo has
1 villager with 1 ox.
Meadow, 8 acres.
Value 5s.

43 M. In 'WESTLABY' Harold had 7 bovates of land taxable. Land for 14 oxen. Odo, Ivo's man, has ½ plough.
2 villagers and 2 smallholders with ½ plough.
Meadow, 20 acres.
Value before 1066, 20s; now 16s.

44 M. In *LOBINGEHAM* Alwine had 6 bovates of land taxable. Land for 12 oxen. Odo, Ivo's man, has
1 smallholder who ploughs with 1 ox; and
meadow, 30 acres.
Value before 1066, 20s; now 12s.

45 M. In KEELBY Alwine had 2 bovates of land taxable. Land for 4 oxen. Nigel, Ivo's man, has ½ plough.
2 villagers and 1 smallholder who plough with 1 ox.
A mill site; meadow, 27 acres.
Value before 1066, 10s; now 20s.

HAVERSTOE Wapentake
46 M. In BELCHFORD Stori had 6 carucates of land taxable. Land for 8 ploughs. Of this land 2 carucates in a jurisdiction. Ivo has 5 ploughs in lordship;
9 villagers, 15 smallholders and 45 Freemen who have 9 ploughs.
2 mills at 18s 8d; meadow, 360 acres; underwood, 3 acres.
[It is] 1 league long and 1 wide.
Value before 1066 £15; now £33. Exactions £27.

Jurisdiction of this manor:
47 In GOULCEBY 3 carucates of land taxable. Land for 3 ploughs.
16 Freemen and 2 villagers have 6 ploughs.
1 mill, 4s; a priest and a church; meadow, 120 acres.

In Hamingebi.iii.car.ad glđ.Tra.iii.c̄ru.Ibi.xx,ii.
foch 7 vii.uilt 7 vi.borđ.hñt.vii.car.7 cxx.ac̄ p̄ti.
In Scamelefbi.vi.car tre ad glđ.Tra.vii.car.Ibi hĩ
Iuo.i.car.7 xxvii.foch.7 xi.uilt 7 iii.borđ hñt.v.
car.7 cc.xl.ac̄ p̄ti.
In Calcheuuelle.i.car træ 7 dim̄ ad glđ.Tra ad tntđ.
Ibi.xii.foch 7 i.uilt hñt.ii.car.7 lx.ac̄s p̄ti.
In Duninctune.vi.car træ ad glđ.Tra.viii.car.Ibi
hĩ Iuo.iii.çar.7 xxviii.foch.7 vi.borđ.hñt.vi.car.
7 ii.molin̄.xvii.fot 7.iiii.den.7 cc.xl.ac̄ p̄ti.
In Stangehou.iii.car træ ad glđ.Tra.iii.car.Ibi
hĩ Iuo.ii.car.7 xxiii.foch.7 v.uilt.hñt,iiii,car.

7 cxx.ac̄ p̄ti.7 xx.ac̄ filuæ minutæ.
In Eftrebi.iii.car træ ad glđ.Tra.iii.car.Ibi.ix.foch
7 ii.uilt 7 vii.borđ hñtes.iii.car.7 cxx.ac̄s p̄ti.
In duob̄ mentinghes.vii.car tre ad glđ.7 v.boũ.
7 v.pars bouatæ ad glđ.Tra arabit duplex.Ibi hĩ
Iuo.ii.car in dño.7 xxvii.foch 7 x.uilt 7 xx.borđ
hñtes.ix.car.7 cc.lx.ac̄ p̄ti.7 c.ac̄ filuæ paftilis.
7 decies.c.7 x.ac̄ filuæ minutæ.
In Stigefuuald.ii.car tre 7 ii.boũ ad glđ.Tra.ii.car.
7 ii.boũ.Ibi.x.foch 7 iii.uilt 7 iiii.borđ hñt.iii.car.
7 xl.ac̄ p̄ti.7 qt xx ac̄ filuæ paft.
In Horfintone.i.car tre ad glđ.Tra ad.i.car.Ibi.iiii.
uilt 7 iiii.foch hñt.i.car.7 l.ac̄ p̄ti.7 xxv.ac̄ filuæ
In Burgrede 7 Turlai.i.car træ 7 ii boũ.   ⎰minutæ
7 tcia pars boũ ad glđ.Tra arab ad tntđ.Ibi.ix.foch
ⱦ hñt.iii.car.7 clxxv.ac̄ p̄ti.7 clxxx.ac̄ filuæ paftil.
7 q̄ngentæ ac̄ filuæ minutæ.

48 In HEMINGBY 3 carucates taxable. Land for 3 ploughs.
22 Freemen, 7 villagers and 6 smallholders have 7 ploughs.
Meadow, 120 acres.

49 In SCAMBLESBY 6 carucates of land taxable. Land for 7 ploughs.
Ivo has 1 plough.
27 Freemen, 11 villagers and 3 smallholders have 5 ploughs.
Meadow, 240 acres.

50 In CAWKWELL 1½ carucates of land taxable. Land for as much.
12 Freemen and 1 villager have 2 ploughs and
meadow, 60 acres.

51 In DONINGTON (on Bain) 6 carucates of land taxable. Land for 8
ploughs. Ivo has 3 ploughs.
28 Freemen and 6 smallholders have 6 ploughs.
2 mills, 17s 4d; meadow, 240 acres.

52 In STENIGOT 3 carucates of land taxable. Land for 3 ploughs.
Ivo has 2 ploughs.
23 Freemen and 5 villagers have 4 ploughs.
Meadow, 120 acres; underwood, 20 acres.   351 a

53 In ASTERBY 3 carucates of land taxable. Land for 3 ploughs.
9 Freemen, 2 villagers and 7 smallholders who have 3
ploughs and
meadow, 120 acres.

54 In the two MINTINGS 7 carucates of land taxable and 5 bovates
and the fifth part of a bovate taxable. Twice as much arable land.
Ivo has 2 ploughs in lordship;
27 Freemen, 10 villagers and 20 smallholders who have 9 ploughs.
Meadow, 260 acres; woodland pasture, 100 acres; underwood,
1010 acres.

55 In STIXWOULD 2 carucates of land and 2 bovates taxable. Land for
2 ploughs and 2 oxen.
10 Freemen, 3 villagers and 4 smallholders have 3 ploughs.
Meadow, 40 acres; woodland pasture, 80 acres.

56 In HORSINGTON 1 carucate of land taxable. Land for 1 plough.
4 villagers and 4 Freemen have 1 plough.
Meadow, 50 acres; underwood, 25 acres.

57 In 'BURRETH' and 'THORLEY' 1 carucate of land and 3 bovates and
the third part of a bovate taxable. Arable land for as much.
9 Freemen have 3 ploughs.
Meadow, 175 acres; woodland pasture, 180 acres; underwood,
500 acres.

ᴍ In *BOLINTONE* . h̄b Lābe . v . boú træ ad glđ . Ťra
ɪɪ . caŕ . Ibi h̄t Odo h̄o Iuon̄ . ɪ . caŕ . ⁊ xɪɪɪ . uiłł . ⁊ ɪ . uiłł
⁊ ɪɪ . borđ . cū . ɪ . caŕ . ⁊ v . ac̄ p̄ti . ⁊ q̄t xx . ac̄ siluæ min̄ .
T.R.E . uał xvɪ . soł . m̄ xx . soł . Tailla . x . soł .

ᴍ In *BENINGVRDE* h̄b Siuuard . ɪɪɪ . caŕ træ ad glđ . Ťra
ad . vɪ . caŕ . De hac t̄ra . dim̄ caŕ in soca . Ibi Odō h̄o Iuon̄
h̄t . ɪɪɪ . caŕ . ⁊ xɪ . uiłł ⁊ x . borđ . ⁊ xvɪɪɪ . socħ . hn̄tes
vɪ . caŕ . ⁊ cxʟ . ac̄ p̄ti . T.R.E . uał . ɪɪɪɪ . lib̄ . m̄ . v . lib̄ .
Tailla . xx . soł .

ᴍ In *CHINETORP* . h̄b Bertor . ɪɪ . boú ⁊ dim̄ ⁊ t̄cia pars
dimidiæ boú ad glđ . Ťra arab duplex . Ibi h̄t Odo . ɪɪ .
uiłł . arantes . ɪɪ . bob . ⁊ v . ac̄ p̄ti . ⁊ q̄t xx . ac̄ siluæ past
p loca . T.R.E . uał . x . soł . m̄ similit̄ . In Strubi . ɪɪ . bō ad glđ .

ᴍ In *LVDESFORDE* . h̄b Turold . v . boú tre ad glđ . Ťra
. x . boú . Ibi h̄t Odo . ɪ . caŕ . ⁊ vɪɪɪ . uiłł cū . ɪ . caŕ . ⁊ ɪ . molđ
xɪɪ . den . ⁊ x . ac̄s p̄ti . T.R.E . uał xʟ . soł . m̄ . xxx . soł .

ᴍ In *ELLINGETONE* h̄b Gamel . ɪɪ . caŕ træ ad glđ . Ťra
ad . ɪɪ . caŕ . Ibi Walter h̄o Iuon̄ h̄t . ɪɪ . caŕ . ⁊ ɪɪɪɪ . uiłł .
⁊ vɪ . socħ ⁊ ɪɪɪ . borđ cū . ɪ . caŕ . ⁊ ɪ . molin̄ . vɪɪɪ . solido₂ .
⁊ xxx . ac̄ p̄ti . ⁊ xxx . ac̄ siluæ minutæ . ⁊ æcclā . T.R.E .
uał . xʟ . soł . m̄ . ʟx . soł .

ᴍ In *WIDVN* . h̄b Aluuin . ɪɪ . caŕ træ ad glđ . Ťra . ɪɪɪ . caŕ .
Ibi Wimund h̄o Iuon̄ h̄t . ɪɪ . caŕ . ⁊ ɪɪɪɪ . uiłł ⁊ ɪɪɪɪ .
socħ cū . ɪ . caŕ . ⁊ vɪɪɪ . ac̄ p̄ti . T.R.E . uał xʟ . soł . m̄
similit̄ . Tailla . xx . solidos .

351 b

ᴍ In *ORMESBI* . h̄b Aluuin . ɪɪ . caŕ tre ⁊ ɪɪ . boú ad glđ .
Ťra . ɪɪɪ . caŕ ⁊ dim̄ . Ibi Wimund h̄o Iuon̄ h̄t . ɪɪ . caŕ .
⁊ xɪɪɪ . socħ ⁊ ɪɪ . uiłł cū . ɪɪ . caŕ . ⁊ xvɪ . ac̄ p̄ti . ⁊ vɪɪɪ .
ac̄ siluæ minutæ . T.R.E . uał . ʟ . soł . m̄ xʟ . soł . Tailla
𝄍 xx . soł .

58 M. In BULLINGTON Lambi had 5 bovates of land taxable. Land for 2 ploughs. Odo, Ivo's man, has 1 plough.
13 villagers, 1 villager and 2 smallholders with 1 plough.
Meadow, 5 acres; underwood, 80 acres.
Value before 1066, 16s; now 20s. Exactions 10s.

59 2 In BENNIWORTH Siward and Thorgautr had 3½ carucates of land
M. taxable. Land for 6 ploughs. Of this land ½ carucate in a jurisdiction. Odo, Ivo's man, has 3 ploughs.
11 villagers, 10 smallholders and 18 Freemen who have 6 ploughs.
Meadow, 140 acres.
Value before 1066 £4; now £5. Exactions 20s.

60 M. In KINGTHORPE Bergthorr had 2½ bovates and the third part of ½ bovate taxable. Twice as much arable land. Odo has
2 villagers who plough with 2 oxen.
Meadow, 5 acres; woodland, pasture in places, 80 acres.
Value before 1066, 10s; now the same.

61 In STRUBBY 2 bovates taxable.

62 M. In LUDFORD Thoraldr had 5 bovates of land taxable. Land for 10 oxen. Odo has 1 plough.
8 villagers with 1 plough.
1 mill, 12d; meadow, 10 acres.
Value before 1066, 40s; now 30s.

63 M. In EDLINGTON Gamall had 2 carucates of land taxable. Land for 2 ploughs. Walter, Ivo's man, has 2 ploughs.
4 villagers, 6 Freemen and 3 smallholders with 1 plough.
1 mill, 8s; meadow, 30 acres; underwood, 30 acres; a church.
Value before 1066, 40s; now 60s.

64 2 In WYHAM Alwine had 2 carucates of land taxable. Land for 3
M. ploughs. Wigmund, Ivo's man, has 2 ploughs.
4 villagers and 4 Freemen with 1 plough.
Meadow, 8 acres.
Value before 1066, 40s; now the same. Exactions 20s.

65 M. In (North) ORMSBY Alwine had 2 carucates of land and 2 bovates   351 b
taxable. Land for 3½ ploughs. Wigmund, Ivo's man, has 2 ploughs.
13 Freemen and 2 villagers with 2 ploughs.
Meadow, 16 acres; underwood, 8 acres.
Value before 1066, 50s; now 40s. Exactions 20s.

Ṁ In *BOLINBROC* . hb Stori . II . caɼ tꝛæ ad glđ . Tꝛa
.II . caɼ . In SOCA . I . caɼ de hac tꝛa . Ibi hɪ Iuo modo
.II . caɼ ꝛ7 XII . uiłł 7 VIII . borđ . 7 XII . focħ ; cū . III . caɼ.
Ibi æccła . 7 mercatū nouū . 7 III . molini . x . folidoꝛ.
7 LXX . aɔ ꝑti . T.R.E . uał XXX . liḃ . m̃ . XL . liḃ . Tailla.
q̃ter . XX . liḃ . cū om̃ibꝛ adjacentibꝛ . SOCA HVJ MAN.
In Harebi . IIII . caɼ tꝛe ad glđ . Tꝛa . IIII . caɼ . Ibi . XXX.III.
focħ 7 V . uiłł 7 V . borđ hn̄t . IIII . caɼ . 7 c . aɔ ꝑti.
In Melingefbi . VI . caɼ tꝛe ad glđ . Tꝛa . VI . caɼ . Ibi
XXX.VI . focħ ꝛ7 VIII . uiłł 7 IIII . borđ hn̄t . VI . caɼ . 7 XL . aɔ ꝑti.
In Afgerebi . III . caɼ tꝛe ad glđ . Tꝛa . III . caɼ . Ibi . XX.
focħ 7 II . uiłł . hn̄t . III . caɼ . 7 q̃t XX . acs ꝑti.
In Endrebi . V . caɼ tꝛe ad glđ . Tꝛa . V . caɼ . Ibi . XXIIII.
focħ 7 V . borđ . hn̄t . V . caɼ . 7 c . acs ꝑti.
In Radebi . III . caɼ tꝛe 7 VII . boū ad glđ . Tꝛa ad tntđ c̃ 7 b̃.
Ibi XVIII . uiłł 7 III . uiłł 7 V . borđ . hn̄t . IIII . caɼ . Ibi æccła
7 molin̄ . XII . folid . 7 XL . aɔ ꝑti.
In Hundelbi . IIII . caɼ tꝛe ad glđ . Tꝛa . IIII . caɼ . Ibi . XXV.
focħ 7 XII . uiłł hn̄t . IIII . caɼ . Ibi æccła 7 molin̄ . V . folid.
7 q̃t XX . aɔ ꝑti . In hac tꝛa hb Tor . IIII . acs tꝛe quæ
ptinent ad Spilefbi Ṁ epi đunelm̃.
In Haltūn 7 Stepi . IX . caɼ tꝛæ ad glđ . Tꝛa . IX . caɼ.
Ibi hɪ Iuo . I . caɼ . 7 LVIII . focħ 7 IIII . uiłł cū . IX . caɼ.
Ibi eccła 7 IIII . molini . XXIIII . folid . 7 cxx . aɔ ꝑti
In Torp . II . caɼ tꝛe 7 V . boū ad glđ . Tꝛa ad totid . c̃ 7 b̃.
Ibi XVIII . focħ 7 VIII . uiłł hn̄t . III . caɼ . Ibi æccła . 7 cc.LXXX.
In Totintun . III . caɼ tꝛæ ad glđ . Tꝛa . III . caɼ.   ⎰ aɔ ꝑti.
Ibi XIIII . uiłł 7 XIII . focħ hn̄t . III . caɼ . Ibi æccła . 7 XXX.
aɔ ꝑti . 7 V . aɔ 7 dim̃ filue minutæ.

66 M. In BOLINGBROKE Stori had 2 carucates of land taxable. Land for 2 ploughs. In a jurisdiction 1 carucate of this land. Now Ivo has 2 ploughs.
　　12 villagers, 8 smallholders and 12 Freemen with 3 ploughs.
　　A church; a new market; 3 mills, 10s; meadow, 70 acres.
Value before 1066 £30; now £40. Exactions £80, with all that is attached.

Jurisdiction of this manor:

67　In HAREBY 4 carucates of land taxable. Land for 4 ploughs.
　　33 Freemen, 5 villagers and 5 smallholders have 4 ploughs.
　　Meadow, 100 acres.

68　In MININGSBY 6 carucates of land taxable. Land for 6 ploughs.
　　36 Freemen, 8 villagers and 4 smallholders have 6 ploughs.
　　Meadow, 40 acres.

69　In ASGARBY 3 carucates of land taxable. Land for 3 ploughs.
　　20 Freemen and 2 villagers have 3 ploughs and
　　meadow, 80 acres.

70　In (Mavis) ENDERBY 5 carucates of land taxable. Land for 5 ploughs.
　　24 Freemen and 5 smallholders have 5 ploughs and
　　meadow, 100 acres.

71　In RAITHBY 3 carucates of land and 7 bovates taxable. Land for as many ploughs and oxen.
　　18 villagers, 3 villagers and 5 smallholders have 4 ploughs.
　　A church; a mill, 12s; meadow, 40 acres.

72　In HUNDLEBY 4 carucates of land taxable. Land for 4 ploughs.
　　25 Freemen and 12 villagers have 4 ploughs.
　　A church; a mill, 5s; meadow, 80 acres.
　　On this land Thorr had 4 acres of land which belong to the Bishop of Durham's manor, Spilsby.

73　In HALTON (Holegate) and (Little) STEEPING 9 carucates of land taxable. Land for 9 ploughs. Ivo has 1 plough.
　　58 Freemen and 4 villagers with 9 ploughs.
　　A church; 4 mills, 24s; meadow, 120 acres.

74　In THORPE (St. Peter) 2 carucates of land and 5 bovates taxable. Land for as many ploughs and oxen.
　　18 Freemen and 8 villagers have 3 ploughs.
　　A church; meadow, 280 acres.

75　In TOYNTON (All Saints) 3 carucates of land taxable. Land for 3 ploughs.
　　14 villagers and 13 Freemen have 3 ploughs.
　　A church; meadow, 30 acres; underwood, 5½ acres.

In Stichenai . iii . car̄ træ ad glđ . Tra . iii . car̄ . Ibi . xxxiii.
focħ 7 v . uiłł hn̄t . iii . car̄ . Ibi æccła 7 xl . ac̄ p̄ti.

In Sibolci . vi . car̄ træ ad glđ . Tra . vi . car̄ . Ibi . li . focħ
7 xvi . uiłł 7 x . borđ . hn̄t . vi . car̄ . Ipfe Iuo hr̄ ibi . i . car̄.
7 æccła . 7 c.xx . ac̄ p̄ti.

In Stichesforde . ii . car̄ træ 7 dim̄ ad glđ . Tra ad totiđ . c̄

Ibi xxviii . focħ 7 ii . uiłł hn̄t . iii . car̄ . Ibi æccła . 7 xxx . ac̄ p̄ti.

In Eftrecale . iiii . car̄ træ 7 dim̄ ad glđ . Tra ad totiđ car̄.

Ibi hr̄ Iuo . i . car̄ . 7 vii . focħ 7 xii . uiłł . 7 iiii . borđ.
cū . iiii . car̄ 7 dim̄ . Ibi dimiđ æccła . 7 xx . ac̄ p̄ti.

351 c

Ibi ħb Sūmerled Man 7 ualeb xx . fot . T.R.E. m̄ fimił.

In Weftrecale . iiii . car̄ tre ad glđ . Tra . v . car̄ . Ibi . xxxv.
focħ 7 viii . uiłł 7 vi . borđ hn̄t . vi . car̄ . 7 c . ac̄s p̄ti.

In Totintun . v . car̄ 7 ii . bou tre ad glđ . Tra . vi . car̄.
Ibi . xl . focħ 7 vii . uiłł 7 iii . borđ hn̄t . vi . car̄ . Ibi æccła
7 lxx . ac̄ p̄ti . 7 x . ac̄ fiłuæ minutæ.

In Hagenebi . ii . car̄ tre 7 v . bou ađ glđ . Tra ad totiđ
car̄ 7 bou . Ibi . xiiii . focħ 7 iiii . uiłł 7 ii . borđ . hn̄t . iii . car̄.

In Cherchebi 7 Refuefbi . xii . car̄ træ ad glđ ℔7 lxx.iii.ac̄ p̄ti.
Tra . xii . car̄ . Ibi . l.iiii . focħ 7 xiiii . uiłł hn̄t xii . car̄.

Ibi hr̄ Iuo . i . car̄ . 7 ii . æcclas . 7 clxxx . ac̄s p̄ti.

Totū ⋈ cū omib3 | adjacentib3 . vi . lev łḡ . 7 vi . łat.

⋈ In ARCHINTONE . ħb Efbern . iiii . car̄ træ ad glđ . Tra
viii . car̄ . De hac tra . ii . car̄ 7 dim̄ in Soca . Ibi Goisfriđ
hō Iuon hr̄ . ii . car̄ . 7 xix . focħ 7 v . uiłł cū . iii . car̄.
Ibi dimiđ æccła . 7 dim̄ feđ molini . 7 lx . ac̄ p̄ti . T.R.E . uał
lx . fot . m̄ . vi . łib . Tailla . xl . fot.

76 In STICKNEY 3 carucates of land taxable. Land for 3 ploughs.
    33 Freemen and 5 villagers have 3 ploughs.
    A church; meadow, 40 acres.

77 In SIBSEY 6 carucates of land taxable. Land for 6 ploughs.
    51 Freemen, 16 villagers and 10 smallholders have 6 ploughs.
    Ivo himself has 1 plough there.
    A church; meadow, 120 acres.

78 In STICKFORD 2½ carucates of land taxable. Land for as many
    ploughs.
    28 Freemen and 2 villagers have 3 ploughs.
    A church; meadow, 30 acres.

79 In EAST KEAL 4½ carucates of land taxable. Land for as many
    ploughs. Ivo has 1 plough.
    7 Freemen, 12 villagers and 4 smallholders with 4½ ploughs.
    ½ church; meadow, 20 acres.
    Sumarlithi had a manor there; value before 1066, 20s; now   351 c
    the same.

80 In WEST KEAL 4 carucates of land taxable. Land for 5 ploughs.
    35 Freemen, 8 villagers and 6 smallholders have 6 ploughs and
    meadow, 100 acres.

81 In TOYNTON (St. Peter) 5 carucates and 2 bovates of land taxable.
    Land for 6 ploughs.
    40 Freemen, 7 villagers and 3 smallholders have 6 ploughs.
    A church; meadow, 70 acres; underwood, 10 acres.

82 In HAGNABY 2 carucates of land and 5 bovates taxable. Land for
    as many ploughs and oxen.
    14 Freemen, 4 villagers and 2 smallholders have 3 ploughs.
    Meadow, 73 acres.

83 In (East) KIRKBY and REVESBY 12 carucates of land taxable. Land
    for 12 ploughs.
    54 Freemen and 14 villagers have 12 ploughs.
    Ivo has 1 plough and
    2 churches; meadow, 180 acres.
  The whole manor with all that is attached to it [is] 6 leagues long
  and 6 wide.

84 M. In ELKINGTON Esbjorn had 4 carucates of land taxable. Land for 8
    ploughs. Of this land 2½ carucates in a jurisdiction. Geoffrey,
    Ivo's man, has 2 ploughs.
    19 Freemen and 5 villagers with 3 ploughs.
    ½ church; ½ mill site; meadow, 60 acres.
  Value before 1066, 60s; now £6. Exactions 40s.

In Grimeſbi.Soca.ı.car̂ ꞇre 7 dim ad glđ.Tra.ıı.car̂.

Ibi h̅t Goıſfrid.ı.car̂.7 v.uiłł 7 vı.ſoch cū.ı.car̂.7 x.ac̄

B̅In Lodebẏ.vıı.bou ꞇre ad glđ.Tra ad.ı.car̂ 7 dim. Sꝑti⸱

7 S̄ʳ Inland in Hundebi.7 Soca in Clacheſbi.Ibi.vııı.uiłł

7 ııı.borđ.h̅n̅t.ı.car̂.7 xv.ac̄s p̅ti⸱

ꝳIn BRVNE.h̅б Seuuen.ııı.bou ꞇre ad glđ.Tra.ııı.bou.

Ibi Odo h̅o Iuon h̅t.ııı.uiłł 7 ı.borđ.cū dım̄ car̂.7 vı⸱

parꞇē molini.xx.denar̂.7 ııı.piſcin̄.vııı.den̄.7 7 ııı.ac̄s

p̅ti.7 dim̄.7 xv.ac̄s ſiluæ minutæ.T.R.E.uał.vı.ſoł.m̂.x.ſoł⸱

In BREZBI 7 Sapreꞇone.ı.car̂ ꞇræ ad glđ.Tra ad.ı.car̂.

Soca in Bergebi.Ibi.ıı.uiłł 7 ı.borđ.h̅n̅t.ı.car̂.7 xvı.

ac̄s p̅ti.7 xxx.ac̄s ſiluæ paſt.7 v.ac̄s ſiluæ minutæ.

In Hundinꞇone.ıx.car̂ ꞇre ad glđ.Tra ad.ıx.car̂.Soca

in Bergebi.Ibi h̅t Iuo.ıı.car̂.7 xvı.uiłł 7 ıııı.borđ.7 x⸱

ſoch.h̅nꞇes.ııı.car̂ 7 dimid.Ibi æccła 7 pбr.7 ſeđ molin̄.

7 cv.ac̄s p̅ti.T.R.E.uał.vı.liб.m̂.v.liб.Tailla xx.ſoł.

In Barcheſtone.x.bou ꞇre ad glđ.Tra.x.bou.Soca

in Hundindune.Ibi.ı.car̂ in dn̅io.7 ı.ſoch 7 ı.uiłł 7 ııı.

borđ.cū.ı.car̂.7 xııı.ac̄ p̅ti.

In Sideſtan.ıı.bou ꞇre ad glđ.Soca Hundinꞇone.Waſta.ē.

ꝳIn CHINETORP.h̅бr Berꞇor 7 Torul.vıı.bou 7 dimid.

7 ꞇciā parꞇē dimiđ bou ad glđ.Tra arabił ad duplū.

Ibi Odo h̅o Iuon h̅t.ı.car̂.7 x.uiłł.cū.ı.car̂.7 xv.ac̄

p̅ti.7 q̄t xx.ac̄ ſiluæ paſt p̄ loca.T.R.E.uał.ʟ.ſoł.m̂

Sxʟ.ſoł.

351 d

ꝳIn Wiueleſtorp.h̅бr ⁷ᴮᵒˡᵉ Bernac ˣˣ.ıı.car̂ ꞇræ ad glđ.Tra.ıııı.car̂.

De hac ꞇra.ıı.car̂.in Soca.Ibi Odo h̅o Iuon.ı.car̂.7 x.ſoch

7 x.uiłł.h̅nꞇes.ıı.car̂ 7 dimiđ.7 ⁱⁱⁱ.molin̄.xx.ᵗⁱſolid.7 xʟ.

ac̄s p̅ti.7 xıı.ac̄s ſiluæ minutæ.T.R.E.uał.xʟ.ſoł.m̂

ʟxxx.ſoł.m̂ xxx.ſoł.

85 In (Little) GRIMSBY, a jurisdiction, 1½ carucates of land taxable. Land for 2 ploughs. Geoffrey has 1 plough.
5 villagers and 6 Freemen with 1 plough.
Meadow, 10 acres.

86 B. In SLOOTHBY 7 bovates of land taxable. Land for 1½ ploughs.
& S. *Inland*, 6 bovates, of Hanby and a jurisdiction, 1 bovate, of Claxby.
8 villagers and 3 smallholders have 1 plough and meadow, 15 acres.

87 M. In BOURNE Sveinn had 3(?) bovates of land taxable. Land for 3 oxen. Odo, Ivo's man, has
3 villagers and 1 smallholder with ½ plough; and the sixth part of a mill, 20d; 3 fish-ponds, 8d; meadow, 3½ acres; underwood, 15 acres.
Value before 1066, 6s; now 10s.

88 In BRACEBY and SAPPERTON 1 carucate of land taxable. Land for 1 plough. A jurisdiction of Barrowby.
2 villagers and 1 smallholder have 1 plough and meadow, 16 acres; woodland pasture, 30 acres; underwood, 5 acres.

89 In HONINGTON 9 carucates of land taxable. Land for 9 ploughs. A jurisdiction of Barrowby. Ivo has 2 ploughs.
16 villagers, 4 smallholders and 10 Freemen who have 3½ ploughs.
A church and a priest; a mill site; meadow, 105 acres.
Value before 1066 £6; now £5. Exactions 20s.

90 In BARKSTON 10 bovates of land taxable. Land for 10 oxen. A jurisdiction of Honington. 1 plough in lordship;
1 Freeman, 1 villager and 3 smallholders with 1 plough.
Meadow, 13 acres.

91 In SYSTON 2 bovates of land taxable. A jurisdiction [of] Honington. It is waste.

92 M. In KINGTHORPE Bergthorr and Thorulfr had 7½ bovates and the third part of ½ bovate taxable. Twice as much arable land. Odo, Ivo's man, has 1 plough.
10 villagers with 1 plough.
Meadow, 15 acres; woodland, pasture in places, 80 acres.
Value before 1066, 50s; now 40s.

93 M. In WILSTHORPE Beornheah and Boli had 4 carucates of land taxable. Land for 4 ploughs. Of this land 2 carucates in a jurisdiction. Odo, Ivo's man, [has] 1 plough.
10 Freemen and 10 villagers who have 2½ ploughs.
2 mills, 20s; meadow, 40 acres; underwood, 12 acres.
Value before 1066, 40s; now 80s; now 30s.

351 d

In Opeſtorp ⹁ ıı ⹁ boū tre ad glđ ⹁ Tra ⹁ ıı ⹁ boū ⹁ Ibi ⹁ ıı ⹁ ſocħ
cū dimiđ caꝛ ⹁ 7 ıııı ⹁ ač p̄ti.

ↀ In *BERTVNE* 7 Torp ⹁ ħb ⹁ xıııı ⹁ boū træ ad glđ ⹁ Tra
ad ⹁ xıııı ⹁ boū ⹁ Ibi Azor ħo Iuon ħt ⹁ ııı ⹁ uiłł 7 ıı ⹁ borđ.
cū ⹁ ıı ⹁ caꝛ ⹁ 7 ccc ⹁ ačs ſiluæ minutæ ⹁ 7 xııı ⹁ ačs p̄ti ⹁ T.R.E.
ual ⹁ xxx ⹁ ſoł ⹁ m̄ ⹁ xx ⹁ ſoł ⹁ Ħ jacet in Bergebi.
In Helperichā ⹁ vı ⹁ boū tre ad glđ ⹁ Tra ⹁ vı ⹁ boū ⹁ Soca
in Wiueleſtorp ⹁ Ibi ⹁ ııı ⹁ ſocħ 7 ı ⹁ borđ ⹁ cū ⹁ ı ⹁ caꝛ ⹁ 7 ı ⹁ ač p̄ti.

ↀ In *SPALLINGE* ⹁ ħb Algar ⹁ ıx ⹁ caꝛ træ ad glđ ⹁ Tra
ad totiđ caꝛ ⹁ Ibi ħt Iuo ⹁ ıııı ⹁ caꝛ in dn̄io ⹁ 7 xl ⹁ uiłł.
7 xxx.ııı ⹁ borđ ⹁ hn̄tes ⹁ xııı ⹁ caꝛ ⹁ Ibi mercatū ⹁ 7 vı ⹁ piſ
cariæ ⹁ xxx ⹁ ſoliđ ⹁ 7 de ſalinis xx ⹁ ſoł ⹁ 7 ſilua alnoꝛ
vııı ⹁ ſoliđ ⹁ T.R.E. ual ⹁ xx.ııı ⹁ liƀ ⹁ 7 ıı ⹁ ſoł 7 vııı ⹁ den ⹁ m̄ ⹁ xxx.
liƀ ⹁ Tailla ⹁ xxx ⹁ liƀ.
In Tite ⹁ ııı ⹁ caꝛ træ 7 ıı ⹁ boū ad glđ ⹁ Tra ⹁ ıı ⹁ caꝛ ⹁ Berew
in Spallinge ⹁ Ibi ⹁ ıx ⹁ uiłł ⹁ 7 ı ⹁ borđ hn̄t ⹁ ııı ⹁ caꝛ ⹁ Ibi ħt
Iuo ⹁ ıı ⹁ caꝛ in dn̄io ⹁ 7 æcclam
In Picebech Soca ⹁ x ⹁ caꝛ tre ad glđ ⹁ Tra ⹁ x ⹁ caꝛ ⹁ Ibi ⹁ xx.ıı.
ſocħ ⹁ 7 7 xvı ⹁ uiłł 7 xıı ⹁ borđ ⹁ hn̄t ⹁ ıx ⹁ caꝛ ⹁ 7 piscariæ ⹁ ı̄ ⹁ 7 ꝺ ⹁ anguił.
In Weſtune 7 Multune ⹁ Soca ⹁ x ⹁ caꝛ tre 7 ı ⹁ boū ad glđ.
Tra totiđ c 7 b ⹁ Ibi ⹁ xx.vı ⹁ ſocħ 7 xxx.ı ⹁ uiłł 7 xx ⹁ borđ.
hn̄t ⹁ xx ⹁ carucas.
In Waletone 7 Bodebi ⹁ ıı ⹁ caꝛ træ 7 ıı ⹁ boū ad glđ ⹁ Tra
ııı ⹁ carucarū ⹁ Soca in Hunbia ⹁ Ibi ⹁ vıı ⹁ ſocħ 7 ⹁ uiłł
7 v ⹁ borđ hn̄t ⹁ ıııı ⹁ caꝛ ⹁ 7 ı ⹁ moliñ ⹁ ıı ⹁ ſoliđ ⹁ W . . . đ ħt.

Jurisdiction:
94   In OBTHORPE 2 bovates of land taxable. Land for 2 oxen.
       2 Freemen with ½ plough.
       Meadow, 4 acres.

95 M. In BURTON (Coggles) and (Bassing)THORPE he had 14 bovates of
       land taxable. Land for 14 oxen. Atsurr, Ivo's man, has
         3 villagers and 2 smallholders with 2 ploughs; and
         underwood, 300 acres; meadow, 13 acres.
       Value before 1066, 30s; now 20s.
       This lies in Barrowby.

96   In HELPRINGHAM 6 bovates of land taxable. Land for 6 oxen.
       A jurisdiction of Wilsthorpe.
         3 Freemen and 1 smallholder with 1 plough.
       Meadow, 1 acre.

97 M. In SPALDING Earl Algar had 9 carucates of land taxable. Land for
       as many ploughs. Ivo has 4 ploughs in lordship;
         40 villagers and 33 smallholders who have 13 ploughs.
         A market, 40s; 6 fisheries, 30s; from salt-houses, 20s;
           a wood of alders, 8s.
       Value before 1066 £23 2s 8d; now £30. Exactions £30.

98   In TYDD (St. Mary) 3 carucates of land and 2 bovates taxable.
       Land for 2 ploughs. An outlier of Spalding.
         9 villagers and 1 smallholder have 3 ploughs.
         Ivo has 2 ploughs in lordship and
         a church.

99   In PINCHBECK, a jurisdiction, 10 carucates of land taxable. Land
       for 10 ploughs.
         22 Freemen, 16 villagers and 12 smallholders have 9 ploughs.
         4 fisheries, 1500 eels.

100   In WESTON and MOULTON, a jurisdiction, 10 carucates of land and
       1 bovate taxable. Land for as many ploughs and oxen.
         26 Freemen, 31 villagers and 20 smallholders have 20 ploughs.

101   In WELTON (le Marsh) and BOOTHBY 2 carucates of land and 2
       bovates taxable. Land for 3 ploughs. A jurisdiction of Hanby.
         7 Freemen, [2?] villagers and 5 smallholders have 4 ploughs.
         1 mill, 2s.
         W(igmu)nd has it.

XV. TERRA WILLI DE WARENE.

Ⓜ In *CARLETVNE* . hb Harold . v . cař træ ad glđ . Tra . vii.
cař . Ibi Aldelin hõ Wiłłi de Warena hĩ . iii . cař in dñio.
7 xxi . focħ de . ii . cař huj tre . 7 xi . uiłł 7 vi . borđ . cũ . v.
cař . Ibi pbr 7 æccła . 7 l . ač pti . T.R.E . uał . vi . liƀ . m̃ . x . liƀ.

Ⓑ In Beningtone . ii . cař træ 7 ii . bou ad glđ . Tra . iii . cař.
7 S⁷ x.boū Inland 7 Soca ejđ Ⓜ . Ibi . i . cař in dñio . 7 iii . focħ
7 i . borđ hñt . i . cař . 7 xx . ač̃s pti.

352 a
XVI. TERRA ROGERIJ PICTAVENSIS.

Ⓜ In *RIBI* . hb Stanchil xii . bou tre ad glđ . Tra ad . iii . cař.
Ibi Ernuin hõ Rogerij pict̃au hĩ . i . cař . 7 v . uiłł . 7 v.
focħ . cũ . i . cař . 7 xii . ač̃s pti . T.R.E . uał xxx . foł . m̃ fimił

Ⓜ In *SVALVN* . hbr Stanchil : i . cař træ   � Tailla . x . foł.
ad glđ . Tra . ii . cař . Ibi Wimund hõ Rog hĩ dim̃ cař.
7 iii . uiłł 7 iii . focħ cũ . i . cař . T.R.E . uał . xl . foł . m̃ xx . foł.

k Ⓜ In *RASE* . iii . bou træ ad glđ . Tra . vii . bou . Ibi Mainard
hõ Rog hĩ . iiii . uiłł . cũ dim̃ cař . T.R.E . uał x . foł . m̃ xx.ii.

Ⓜ In *COLESI* hb Ernui . iii . cař tre ad glđ . Tra . vi .   〈 foł.
cař . Ibi Roger hõ Rog pict hĩ . i . cař 7 dim̃ . 7 iiii . uiłł
7 vi . borđ . 7 xx . focħ . hñtes . iii . cař . T.R.E . uał . c . foł . m̃ . lx.

In *TORENTVN* hb Grimbold . ii . bou træ ad glđ . Tra . vi.
bou . Ibi hĩ Rog pict . i . cař . 7 i . uiłł . T.R.E . uał . x . foł . m̃ . v.

k Ibidē hĩ Roger . xi . bou træ ad glđ . Tra . xiiii . bou
7 ccc . lx . iiii . ač̃s pti.

15   LAND OF WILLIAM OF WARENNE

1 M. In CARLTON (Scroop) Earl Harold had 5 carucates of land taxable.
Land for 7 ploughs. Aldelin, William of Warenne's man, has 3
ploughs in lordship;
> 21 Freemen on 2 carucates of this land; 11 villagers and 6
> smallholders with 5 ploughs.
A priest and a church; meadow, 50 acres.
Value before 1066 £6; now £10.

2 B. In (Long) BENNINGTON 2 carucates of land and 2 bovates taxable.
& S. Land for 3 ploughs. *Inland*, 10 bovates, and a jurisdiction, 1
carucate, also of this manor. 1 plough in lordship.
> 3 Freemen and 1 smallholder have 1 plough and
> meadow, 20 acres.

16   LAND OF ROGER OF POITOU   352 a

1 M. In RIBY Steinketill had 12 bovates of land taxable. Land for 3
ploughs. Earnwine, Roger of Poitou's man, has 1 plough.
> 5 villagers and 5 Freemen with 1 plough.
> Meadow, 12 acres.
Value before 1066, 30s; now the same. Exactions 10s.

2 M. In SWALLOW Steinketill and Earnwine had 1 carucate of land
taxable. Land for 2 ploughs. Wigmund, Roger's man, has ½ plough.
> 3 villagers and 3 Freemen with 1 plough.
Value before 1066, 40s; now 20s.

K   3 M. In (Middle) RASEN 3 bovates of land taxable. Land for 7 oxen.
Mainard, Roger's man, has
> 4 villagers with ½ plough.
Value before 1066, 10s; now 22s.

4 M. In (South) KELSEY Earnwine had 3 carucates of land taxable.
Land for 6 ploughs. Roger, Roger of Poitou's man, has 1½ ploughs.
> 4 villagers, 6 smallholders and 20 Freemen who have 3 ploughs.
Value before 1066, 100s; now 60[s].

5   In THORNTON (le Moor) Grimbald had 2 bovates of land taxable.
Land for 6 oxen. Roger of Poitou has 1 plough.
> 1 villager.
Value before 1066, 10s; now 5[s].

K   6   There also Roger has 11 bovates of land taxable. Land for 14 oxen.
> Meadow, 364 acres.

꘎ In *HOCTVN*. h̄b Ernui dim̄ car̄ træ ad gl̄d . Tra . i . car̄.
Ibi Rog h̄o Rog pict h̄t . i . car̄ . 7 iiii . foch . cū dim̄ car̄.
7 v . ac̄s p̄ti . T.R.E. & m̄ . ual . x . fol.

k ꘎ In *DRESBI*. h̄b Ernui . i . car̄ træ 7 dim̄ ad gt̄ . Tra . iii . car̄.
h̄ tra jacet in æccta de Wingehā . Ibi . ii . bord araj̄ . ii . bob.
Ibi LXX.vi . ac̄ p̄ti . Rog pict h̄t . T.R.E. ual̄ . xxx . fol . m̄ x . fol.

꘎ In *OSGOTEBI* h̄b Ingemund . ii . bou træ 7 dim̄ ad gl̄d.
Tra . v . bou . Ibi Goisfrid h̄o Rog h̄t . iiii . uil̄t . 7 . i . bord.
7 i . foch cū dim̄ car̄ . 7 i . molin . iii . fol de q̄ Rem ep̄s h̄t
focā . 7 xx . ac̄s p̄ti . T.R.E. ual̄ xx . fol . m̄ . v . fol.

꘎ In *TAVELESBI*. h̄br Suuen 7 Brinot . i . car̄ træ 7 dim̄
ad gl̄d . Tra . ii . car̄ 7 dim̄ . Ibi Roger h̄o Rog pict h̄t
. i . car̄ . 7 iiii . uil̄t 7 v . bord . 7 iii . foch . arantes . v . bob.
Ibi . iiii . molini . xvi . fol 7 iiii . denar̄ . 7 LXX.viii . ac̄ p̄ti.
SocA HVj ꘎ . In Rase.   In Osgotebi In Walesbi In
Otebi ad gl̄d . iii . car̄ træ 7 i . bou 7 dim̄ . Tra . vii . caruc̄.
Ibi XL.i . fochi h̄ntes . iiii . car̄ . 7 LX . ac̄s p̄ti . 7 i . molin
iii . folido₹ .

꘎ In *HAINTONE* . h̄b Oudon . ix . bou træ ad gl̄d . Tra . ii . car̄
7 ii . bou . Ibi Acun h̄o Rog h̄t . i . car̄ . 7 viii . uil̄t . 7 ii . bord.
cū . i . car̄ 7 dim̄ . 7 LX . ac̄s p̄ti . T.R.E. ual̄ . xxx . fol . m̄ . xL . fol.
In Strubi . SocA huj ꘎ . ii . bou træ ad gld̄ . Tra . iiii . bou.
Ibi . i . foch 7 . ii . bord . arant . ii . bob.

7 M. In HOLTON (le Moor) Earnwine had ½ carucate of land taxable.
Land for 1 plough. Roger, Roger of Poitou's man, has 1 plough.
    4 Freemen with ½ plough.
    Meadow, 5 acres.
Value before 1066 and now, 10s.

K 8 M. In OWERSBY Earnwine had 1½ carucates of land taxable. Land for
3 ploughs. This land lies in (the lands of) the church of Winghale.
    2 smallholders plough with 2 oxen.
    Meadow, 76 acres.
    Roger of Poitou has it.
Value before 1066, 30s; now 10s.

9 M. In OSGODBY Ingimundr had 2½ bovates of land taxable. Land for
5 oxen. Geoffrey, Roger's man, has
    4 villagers, 1 smallholder and 1 Freeman with ½ plough.
    1 mill, 3s, of which Bishop Remigius has the jurisdiction;
      meadow, 20 acres.
Value before 1066, 20s; now 5s.

10 2 In TEALBY Sveinn and Beorhtnoth had 1½ carucates of land
  M. taxable. Land for 2½ ploughs. Roger, Roger of Poitou's man, has
1 plough.
    4 villagers, 5 smallholders and 3 Freemen who plough with
      5 oxen.
    4 mills, 16s 4d; meadow, 78 acres.

Jurisdiction of this manor:
11   In (Market) RASEN 8½ bovates, in OSGODBY 1 bovate, in WALESBY
1 carucate, in OTBY 1 carucate: 3 carucates of land and 1½
bovates taxable. Land for 7 ploughs.
    41 Freemen who have 4 ploughs and
    meadow, 60 acres; 1 mill, 3s.

12 M. In HAINTON Authunn had 9 bovates of land taxable. Land for 2
ploughs and 2 oxen. Hakon, Roger's man, has 1 plough.
    8 villagers and 2 smallholders with 1½ ploughs.
    Meadow, 60 acres.
Value before 1066, 30s; now 40s.

13   In STRUBBY, a jurisdiction of this manor, 2 bovates of land
taxable. Land for 4 oxen.
    1 Freeman and 2 smallholders plough with 2 oxen.

ᵐ̃In *HAINTONE*.hɓr Clac 7 Sendi.ı.caᵏ 7 dim̃ bou ad
glð.Ťra ad.ıı.caᵏ.Ibi Alɓt hõ Roǧ hᵗ.ı.caᵏ.7 ııı.uiℓℓ.
arantes.ııı.boɓ.7 ℓıııı.aᵏs p̃ti.T.R.E.uaℓ.ℓ.foℓ.m̃.ℓx.s̃

✝In Barcuurde 7 **Sutrei**.Inland 7 Sͦoca huj ᵐ̃ ad glð.
    Ibi.vı.foch 7 ıı.uiℓℓ hñt.ıı.caᵏ.Ibi.ı.pifcaᵏ.7 xvı.aᵏ p̃ti.
                                        ⌐7 xx.aᵏ filuæ past.

352 b

ᵐ̃In *BECHELINGE*.hɓ Alric.ıı.boū tre ad glð.Ťra ıııı.boū.
    Ibi.ııı.uiℓℓ 7 ıııı.borð.arant.ııı.boɓȝ.Ibi.ıııı.aᵏ p̃ti.
    T.R.E.uaℓ.x.foℓ.m̃.xx.foℓ.
    In Terintone Socᴀ.v.bou træ ad glð.Ťra.x.boū.
    Ibi.ııı.foch 7 ııı.uiℓℓ.7 ı.borð.hñt.ı.caᵏ.7 ı.boū arant.
                                        ⌐7 vııı.aᵏs p̃ti.

WESŘEDING.

ᵐ̃In *SVARDESFORDE*.hɓ Vlchil.ııı.boū tre ad glð.Ťra
    ıııı.boū.Nc̃ Mainarð 7 Turalð hñt de Rogeᵏ.7 Wafta.c̃.
    Ibi.xvı.aᵏ p̃ti.T.R.E.uaℓ.x.foℓ.
ᵐ̃In *ŦORP*.hɓ.Sperri.vı.boū træ ad glð.Ťra.ı.caᵏ.7 Frane
    7 Alnoð.vı.caᵏ træ ad glð.Ťra.ıı.caᵏ.Ibi hᵗ Roǧ pict
    ıııı.uiℓℓ 7 vııı.foch hñtes.ıııı.caᵏ.Ipfe.v.boū arantes.
    7 xxıııı.aᵏs p̃ti.T.R.E.uaℓ.ıııı.lib.m̃.ℓx.foℓ.Tailla.x.foℓ.

    In Hagetone.ııı.bͦ ad glð
    Soca in Snereforde.

★ In *WARTON.*
    In Tunec.ı.caᵏ 7 dimið ad glð.Ťra.ıı.caᵏ.Inland
    7 Soca.Ibi.vı.foch 7 ıııı.uiℓℓ 7 ı.borð.hñt.ı.caᵏ 7 dimið.
    7 xx.aᵏs p̃ti.Siluæ past.ı.lev lǧ.7 ð.lat.
    In Toneftele.ı.caᵏ tre 7 ıı.boū ad glð.Ťra xıı.boū.Inland
    7 Soca.Ibi.ı.uiℓℓ 7 ı.foch cū dimið caᵏ.Iuo hᵗ.ıı.bouat.
    7 redð focā.

14 2 In HAINTON Klakkr and Sjundi had 1 carucate and ½ bovate
M. taxable. Land for 2 ploughs. Albert, Roger's man, has 1 plough.
   3 villagers who plough with 3 oxen.
   Meadow, 54 acres.
   Value before 1066, 50s; now 60s.

16,15–16 are entered after 14,34 in the opposite column and are directed by transposition signs to their correct place in the text.

17 In BARKWITH and SOUTHREY *inland*, 2 bovates, and a jurisdiction, 3 bovates, of this manor taxable.
   6 Freemen and 2 villagers have 2 ploughs.
   1 fishery; meadow, 16 acres; woodland pasture, 20 acres.

18 M. In BECKERING Aelfric had 2 bovates of land taxable. Land for   352 b
4 oxen.
   3 villagers and 4 smallholders plough with 3 oxen.
   Meadow, 3 acres.
Value before 1066, 10s; now 20s.

19 In (West) TORRINGTON, a jurisdiction, 5 bovates of land taxable. Land for 10 oxen.
   3 Freemen, 3 villagers and 1 smallholder have 1 plough and
      1 ploughing ox and
   meadow, 8 acres.

WEST RIDING

20 M. In SNARFORD Ulfketill had 3 bovates of land taxable. Land for 4 oxen. Now Mainard and Thoraldr have them from Roger. It is waste.
   Meadow, 16 acres.
Value before 1066, 10s.

21 In HACKTHORN 3 bovates taxable. A jurisdiction of Snarford.

22 3 In (Nor)THORPE Sperrir had 6 bovates of land taxable. Land for 1
M. plough. And Frani and Alnoth [had] 6 carucates of land taxable. Land for 2 ploughs. Roger of Poitou has
   4 villagers and 8 Freemen who have 3 ploughs. He himself
      [has] 5 ploughing oxen and
   meadow, 24 acres.
Value before 1066 £4; now 60s. Exactions 10s.

23 In 'THONOCK' [and] in WHARTON 1½ carucates taxable. Land for 2 ploughs. *Inland* and a jurisdiction.
   6 Freemen, 4 villagers and 1 smallholder have 1½ ploughs and
   meadow, 20 acres; woodland pasture, 1 league long and ½ wide.

24 In 'DUNSTALL' 1 carucate of land and 2 bovates taxable. Land for 12 oxen. *Inland*, 4 bovates, and a jurisdiction, 6 bovates.
   1 villager and 1 Freeman with ½ plough.
   Ivo has 2 bovates and pays jurisdiction.

⁊ In altero Torp . II . bou træ ad gld . Inland in Torp
supiori M . Rog pict nil ht ibi. ⁊ In Loletorp . dim car ad gld . Soca. ★

M In *TORP* . hb Godric . I . car tre 7 dim ad gld . Tra . II . car.
Ibi Rog ho Rog pict ht . II . car . 7 I . uilt . 7 VI . bord . II . ob
bob arantes . T.R.E . uat XL . sol . m . XX . sol.

k M In *LASTONE* hb Suuen . I . car træ 7 dim ad gld . Tra . II . car.
Ibi Blancard ho Rog pict ht . I . car . 7 III . uilt . III . ob . bob
arant . 7 dim molin . XII . den . 7 dim piscaria . II . solidoz.
7 XV . ac pti . T.R.E . uat . XXX . sol . m XX . sol.

In Scotone . II . bou træ ad gld . SOCA de Lestone.

M In ead *LASTONE* . hb Leduin . X . bou træ ad gld . Tra . XII.
bou . Ibi . V . soch hnt . VI . bou arantes . 7 VIII . acs pti . T.R.E.
uat . XXX . sol . m . X . sol. ⁊ In Blitone . II . bou træ ad gld . Soca . huj M

M In *STANTONE* . hb Gamel . VI . bou tre ad gld . Tra . VI . bou.
Ibi Rog ho Rog ht dim car . 7 VI . uilt cu . I . car . 7 XVI
ac pti . T.R.E . uat . XX . sol . m . X . sol.

M In *ELESHAM* . hb Wills . IX . bou træ ad gld . Tra . II . car
7 dim . Ibi Ernui ho Rog ht . I . car . 7 V . uilt 7 I . bord . arant
. II . ob . bob . 7 LX . ac pti . T.R.E . uat LX . sol . m XX . sol . Tailla . X . s.

In Catenai Inland huj M . V . bou træ 7 III . partes . I . bou
ad gld . Ibi . V . uilt hnt . I . car.

† In Blasebi . sunt . II . bouatæ . de silua quæ jacet in Haintun.

In Sisse SOCA in Haintune . II . car træ 7 dim . 7 dim bouata
ad gld . Tra . III . car . Ibi . XXX . soch hnt . III . car . 7 CCCXX . acs pti.

M In *ALDVLVEBI* . hb Grichil . V . bou tre ad gld . Tra . I . car.
Ibi Blancard ho Rog pict ht dim car . 7 V . uilt 7 IIII . bord.

25   In the other ('South)THORPE' 2 bovates of land taxable. *Inland* of the above manor, Northorpe. Roger of Poitou has nothing there.

26   In YAWTHORPE ½ carucate taxable. A jurisdiction.

27 M.   In (Nor)THORPE Godric had 1½ carucates of land taxable. Land for 2 ploughs. Roger, Roger of Poitou's man, has 2 ploughs.
     1 villager and 6 smallholders who plough with 2 oxen.
Value before 1066, 40s; now 20s.

28 M.   In LAUGHTON Sveinn had 1½ carucates of land taxable. Land for 2
K   ploughs. Blancard, Roger of Poitou's man, has 1 plough.
     3 villagers who plough with 3 oxen.
     ½ mill, 12d; ½ fishery, 2s; meadow, 15 acres.
Value before 1066, 30s; now 20s.

29   In SCOTTON 2 bovates of land taxable. A jurisdiction of Laughton.

30 M.   Also in LAUGHTON Leodwine had 10 bovates of land taxable. Land for 12 oxen.
     5 Freemen have 6 ploughing oxen and
     meadow, 8 acres.
Value before 1066, 30s; now 10s.

31   In BLYTON 2 bovates of land taxable. A jurisdiction of this manor.

32 M.   In STAINTON Gamall had 6 bovates of land taxable. Land for 6 oxen. Roger, Roger's man, has ½ plough.
     6 villagers with 1 plough.
     Meadow, 16 acres.
Value before 1066, 20s; now 10s.

33 M.   In ELSHAM William had 9 bovates of land taxable. Land for 2½ ploughs. Earnwine, Roger's man, has 1 plough.
     5 villagers and 1 smallholder who plough with 2 oxen.
     Meadow, 60 acres.
Value before 1066, 60s; now 20s. Exactions 10s.

34   In CADNEY, *inland* of this manor, 5 bovates of land and 3 parts of 1 bovate taxable.
     5 villagers have 1 plough.

16,15–16, directed by transposition signs to their correct place in the text.
15   In BLEASBY 2 bovates of woodland which lies in Hainton.

16   In SIXHILLS, a jurisdiction of Hainton, 2½ carucates of land and ½ bovate taxable. Land for 3 ploughs.
     30 Freemen have 3 ploughs and
     meadow, 320 acres.

35 M.   In AUDLEBY Grimketill had 5 bovates of land taxable. Land for 1 plough. Blancard, Roger of Poitou's man, has ½ plough.
     5 villagers and 4 smallholders.

In CATEFI . ħƀr Godric 7 Siuuard . IIII . boū tre ⁷ᵈⁱᵐ⁹
ad glđ . Ťra . I . caŕ . Ibi ħť Rog m̄ dim̄ caŕ . 7 II . uilł
7 I . focħ cū . I . caŕ . 7 x . ačs p̄ti . T.R.E. ual . xxx . fol.
m̄ fimiliť . In Wicħā . dimiđ boū tre . Inland Catebi.

In Welletune . dim̄ caŕ træ ad glđ . Ťra XII . boū.
Soca huj̉ m̄ . Ibi . IIII . focħ 7 III . uilł ħ̄nt . I . caŕ 7 dim̄.
7 II . partes uni fed molini.

m̄ In LECHEBVRNE . ħƀ Hambe . I . caŕ træ ad glđ.
Ťra . I . caŕ 7 dim̄ . Ibi Girard hō Rog ħť . VIII . focħ
7 XI . borđ cū . I . caŕ . 7 xx . ačs p̄ti . 7 cxL.II . ačs filuæ
minutæ . T.R.E. ual . xxx . fol . m̄ . xx . fol.
In Sūmercotes . III . parⁱˢ uni carucatæ . ad glđ . Ťra ad
dim̄ caŕ . Ibi . III . focħ arant . II . boƀʒ.

m̄ In INGEHA . ħƀ Aluui . IIII . bou tre ad glđ . Ťra . VI . boū.
Ibi ħť Rog . III . focħ 7 II . borđ 7 I . uilł . cū . I . caŕ . 7 x . ačs
p̄ti . T.R.E. ual x . fol . m̄ fimil . Mainard tenet.
In Cotes . I . boū træ ad glđ . Inland in Ingeħā.

m̄ In FILINGEHA . ħƀ Turgot . II . caŕ træ 7 I . bou ad glđ . Ťra
III . caŕ 7 dimiđ . Ibi Anfchitil hō Rog ħť . II . caŕ . 7 IX . focħ
7 II . uilł . cū . II . caŕ 7 dim̄ . 7 q̄t xx . ač p̄ti . T.R.E. ual . xxx . fol.
m̄ XL . fol . Tailla . x . fol.

m̄ In NETELTONE . ħƀ Grichil . v . bou tre ad glđ . Ťra . II . caŕ.
Ibi Blancard hō Rog ħť . v . uilł 7 IIII . borđ . 7 I . focħ cū . I .
caŕ . 7 II . molinos . x . folid . 7 xL . ačs p̄ti . T.R.E. ual . xL . fol.

m̄ In CROCESTONE . ħƀ Afchil . VI . bou træ ad gld ⌐ m̄ xxx . fol.
Ťra . XII . boū . Ibi Anfchitil hō Rog ħť . I . caŕ . 7 v . uilł
7 VII . focħ . cū . I . caŕ . T.R.E. ual xL . fol . m̄ fimiliť.

36 2 In (South) 'CADEBY' Godric and Siward had 4½ bovates of land
M. taxable. Land for 1 plough. Now Roger has ½ plough.
    2 villagers and 1 Freeman with 1 plough.
    Meadow, 10 acres.
Value before 1066, 30s; now the same.

37 In (East) WYKEHAM ½ bovate of land. *Inland* [of] (South) Cadeby.

38 In WELTON (le Wold) ½ carucate of land taxable. Land for 12 oxen.
A jurisdiction of this manor.
    4 Freemen and 3 villagers have 1½ ploughs.
    2 parts of 1 mill site.

39 M. In LEGBOURNE Ambi had 1 carucate of land taxable. Land for 1½
ploughs. Gerard, Roger's man, has
    8 Freemen and 11 smallholders with 1 plough.
    Meadow, 20 acres; underwood, 142 acres.
Value before 1066, 30s; now 20s.

40 In SOMERCOTES 3 parts of 1 carucate taxable. Land for ½ plough.
    3 Freemen plough with 2 oxen.

41 M. In INGHAM Alwige had 4 bovates of land taxable. Land for 6 oxen.
Roger has
    3 Freemen, 2 smallholders and 1 villager with 1 plough.
    Meadow, 10 acres.
Value before 1066, 10s; now the same.
    Mainard holds it.

42 In COATES 1 bovate of land taxable. *Inland* of Ingham.

43 M. In FILLINGHAM Thorgautr had 2 carucates of land and 1 bovate
taxable. Land for 3½ ploughs. Asketill, Roger's man, has 2 ploughs.
    9 Freemen and 2 villagers with 2½ ploughs.
    Meadow, 80 acres.
Value before 1066, 30s; now 40s. Exactions 10s.

44 M. In NETTLETON Grimketill had 5 bovates of land taxable. Land for
2 ploughs. Blancard, Roger's man, has
    5 villagers, 4 smallholders and 1 Freeman with 1 plough; and
    2 mills, 10s; meadow, 40 acres.
Value before 1066, 40s; now 30s.

45 M. In CROXTON Asketill had 6 bovates of land taxable. Land for 12
oxen. Asketill, Roger's man, has 1 plough.
    5 villagers and 7 Freemen with 1 plough.
Value before 1066, 40s; now the same.

ꝏ In *Blochesha*. ħƀ Turuer . ix . caꝛ́ trӕ 7 v . boū ad glđ.
Tra totid caꝛ 7 boū . Ibi ħꞃ Rog pict . i . caꝛ in dñio . 7 xviii₁ ⁷⁷ᵈⁱⁱ̃·
ſocħ 7 ii . uiłł hñtes . v . caꝛ́ . 7 xiii . acˢ p̃ti . T.R.E. uał . iiii.
liƀ . m̂ . iii . liƀ.

ꝏ̃ In *Canevvic* 7 Bragebruge . ħƀ Strui . ii . caꝛ́ tre ad
glđ . Tra . ii . caꝛ́ . Ibi Ernuin hō Rog ħꞃ . i . caꝛ́ . 7 iiii . ſocħ
7 v . uiłł 7 i . borđ , arantes . vi . boƀ . Ibi ӕccła 7 pƀr . 7 xl
ac̃ p̃ti . 7 ii . piſcaꝛ . ii . ſolid . T.R.E. uał . xxx . ſoł . m̂ xl . ſoł.
Ibidē . i . caꝛ́ tre ad glđ . Tra . i . caꝛ́ . In Branzuic jacet₁

ꝏ̃ In *Aclei* . ħƀ Archilbar xiii . boū trӕ ad glđ . Tra . x . boū.
Ibi . v . uiłł . 7 xvi . ac̃ p̃ti . T.R.E. 7 m̂ uał . xx . ſoł.
In Haneurde . iii boū trӕ ad glđ . Tra . i . caꝛ́ . Soca in Sner
teforde . Ibi Turold ħꞃ . i . ſocħ 7 ii . borđ . arantes . ii . boƀ.

.XVII. ## Terra Rogerij De Bvsli.

ꝏ̃ In *Grentewelle* ħƀ Suuen . iii₁ caꝛ́ trӕ ad glđ.
Tra . v . caꝛ́ . Ibi Turold hō Rogerij de buſli ħꞃ
iii . caꝛ́ . 7 xv . uiłł 7 vi . borđ cū . iiii . caꝛ́ . Ibi ӕccła
7 pƀr . 7 ii₁ piſcaꝛ xv . den . 7 i . moliñ . v . ſolidoꝗ.
7 xvi . ac̃ p̃ti . T.R.E. uał . viii . liƀ . m̂ ſimiłr.

ꝏ̃ In *Aplebi* 7 *Risebi* 7 Saleclif ħƀ Gamel . ix . caꝛ́
trӕ 7 v . boū ad glđ . Tra xix . caꝛ́ 7 ii₁ boū . Ibi ħꞃ
Rogeꝛ de buſli in dñio . iiii . caꝛ́ . 7 xxxi . uiłł . 7 ii.
borđ . cū . vi . caꝛ́ . 7 xxxi . ſocħ cū . vi . caꝛ́ . Ibi ӕccła
7 pƀr . Silua paſt dim leū lḡ . 7 i . q̃ꝗ łaꞇ . 7 xx . ac̃
p̃ti . T.R.E. uał viii . liƀ . m̂ . x . liƀ . Tailla . iii . liƀ₁
In Sanꝗtone Soca . i . caꝛ́ tre ad glđ . Tra . i . caꝛ́₁
Ibi . xii . ſocħ hñꞇ . ii . caꝛ́ . 7 vi . acˢ p̃ti.

46 M. In BLOXHOLM Thorfrothr had 9 carucates of land and 5 bovates taxable. Land for as many ploughs and oxen. Roger of Poitou has 1½ ploughs in lordship;
    18 Freemen and 2 villagers who have 5 ploughs and meadow, 13 acres.
Value before 1066 £4; now £3.

47 M. In CANWICK and BRACEBRIDGE Strui had 2 carucates of land taxable. Land for 2 ploughs. Earnwine, Roger's man, has 1 plough.
    4 Freemen, 5 villagers and 1 smallholder who plough with 6 oxen.
A church and a priest; meadow, 40 acres; 2 fisheries, 2s.
Value before 1066, 30s; now 40s.

48 There also 1 carucate of land taxable. Land for 1 plough. It lies in *Branzuic*.

49 M. In EAGLE Arnketill Barn had 13 bovates of land taxable. Land for 10 oxen.
    5 villagers.
    Meadow, 16 acres.
Value before 1066 and now, 20s.

50 In (Cold) HANWORTH 3 bovates of land taxable. Land for 1 plough. A jurisdiction of Snarford. Thoraldr the priest has
    1 Freeman and 2 smallholders who plough with 2 oxen.

17   LAND OF ROGER OF BULLY   352 d

1 M. In 'GREETWELL' Sveinn had 3 carucates of land taxable. Land for 5 ploughs. Thoraldr, Roger of Bully's man, has 3 ploughs.
    15 villagers and 6 smallholders with 4 ploughs.
    A church and a priest; 2 fisheries, 15d; 1 mill, 5s; meadow, 16 acres.
Value before 1066 £8; now the same.

2 M. In APPLEBY, RISBY and 'SAWCLIFFE' Gamall had 9 carucates of land and 5 bovates taxable. Land for 19 ploughs and 2 oxen. Roger of Bully has in lordship 4 ploughs;
    31 villagers and 2 smallholders with 6 ploughs;
      31 Freemen with 6 ploughs.
    A church and a priest; woodland pasture ½ league long and 1 furlong wide; meadow, 20 acres.
Value before 1066 £8; now £10. Exactions £3.

3 In SANTON, a jurisdiction, 1 carucate of land taxable. Land for 1 plough.
    12 Freemen have 2 ploughs and meadow, 6 acres.

TERRA ROBERTI DE TODENI.

ᴍ **I**n *ENGLEBI*. h̅b Tur̄got . ɪɪɪɪ . car̄ træ ad gl̅d . Tra . ɪɪɪɪ .
car̄ . Ibi Bereng de Rot̅b̅to de Todeni h̅t . ɪɪ . car̄ .
7 ᴠɪɪɪ . uilł cū . ɪɪ . car̄ . 7 c q̅t xx . ac̅s p̅ti . Siluæ paſtil
ᴠɪ . q̄ꝗ l̅g . 7 ɪɪɪ . lat̄ . T.R.E. ual̄ . ᴠɪɪɪ . lib̅ . m̅ x̷ . lib̅.
Tailla . xʟ . ſoł.   De hac tra . ɪ . car̄ 7 dim in Socᴀ
In Broxholme x . car̄ tre ad gl̅d . Tra . x . car̄ . Socᴀ
7 In̅land . Ibi . ɪ . car̄ in dn̅io . 7 xx.ɪɪɪɪ . ſoch̅ . 7 ɪɪ . uilł .
cū . ᴠɪɪɪ . car̄ 7 dimid . Ibi æccła . 7 cc . ac̅ p̅ti .

ᴍ **I**n *ESETORP* . h̅b Tur̄got . ɪɪ . car̄ træ ad gl̅d . Tra . ɪɪɪ . car̄,
Ibi Bereng de Rob̅ . h̅t . ɪ . car̄ 7 dim . 7 xɪɪ . uilł . 7 ɪɪ .
ſoch̅ . cū . ɪɪɪ . car̄ . 7 ʟx . ac̅s p̅ti . 7 xxx.ɪɪɪ . ac̅s ſiluæ paſt .
T.R.E. ual̄ . xʟ . ſoł . m̅ ſimił . Tailla . x . ſoł . ⌠ Socᴀ dim car̄ .

ᴍ **I**n *BRANZBI* . h̅b Tur̄got . ɪɪ . car̄ træ ad gl̅d . Tra . ɪɪ . car̄ .
Ibi De Rob̅to Bereng h̅t . ɪ . 7 ᴠɪ . uilł 7 ɪɪɪ . ſoch̅ cū
una car̄ 7 dim . 7 xɪɪɪɪ . ac̅s p̅ti . 7 ʟ . ac̅s ſiluæ minutæ .
T.R.E. ual̄ . ʟx . ſoł . m̅ . ʟ . ※

ᴍ **I**n *CORINGEHA* . h̅b Tur̄got . ɪɪ . car̄ tre ad gl̅d . Tra
ɪɪ . car̄ . Ibi de Rob̅to Bereng h̅t . ɪ . car̄ . 7 ᴠ . uilł 7 ɪɪɪ .
bor̄d . cū . ɪ . car̄ 7 dim . Silue paſt ᴠ . q̄ꝗ l̅g . 7 ᴠ . lat̄ .
T.R.E. ual̄ . ʟ . ſoł . m̅ . xxx .

※In Burtone . ɪ . car̄ tre ad gl̅d . Tra . ɪ . car̄ . Inlant Branzbi . Ibi . ɪɪ .
⌠ bor̄d . hn̅t . ɪ . car̄ .

353 a

ᴍ **I**n *BINNIBROC* . h̅b Tur̄got . ᴠɪɪɪ . car̄ tre 7 . ɪɪɪɪ . bou
7 dim ad gl̅d . Tra . xxɪɪɪɪ . car̄ . Nc̅ h̅t Rob de Todeni.
7 Berg de illo . In dn̅io . ɪɪɪɪ . car̄ . 7 ᴠɪ . uilł 7 ɪɪɪɪ . bor̄d .
7 xʟ.ɪɪɪɪ . ſoch̅ cū . ᴠɪɪɪ . car̄ . Ibi æccła 7 pb̅r . 7 ɪɪ . molin
xx . ſolid . 7 c . ac̅ p̅ti . T.R.E. ual̄ ᴠɪɪ . lib̅ . m̅ . xᴠ . lib̅ .
Tailla . x . lib̅ . De hac tra . ɪɪɪɪ . car̄ 7 ɪɪɪɪ . bo̅ 7 dim S̅ Soch̅ .

1 M. In INGLEBY Thorgautr Lagr had 4 carucates of land taxable. Land
for 4 ploughs. Berengar has 2 ploughs from Robert of Tosny.
5 Freemen and 8 villagers with 2 ploughs.
Meadow, 180 acres; woodland pasture, 6 furlongs long and
3 wide.
Value before 1066 £8; now £10. Exactions 40s.
Of this land 1½ carucates in a jurisdiction.

2 In BROXHOLME 10 carucates of land taxable. Land for 10 ploughs.
A jurisdiction, 9 carucates, and *inland*, 1 carucate. 1 plough in
lordship;
24 Freemen and 2 villagers with 8½ ploughs.
A church; meadow, 200 acres.

3 M. In (Busling)THORPE Thorgautr had 2 carucates of land taxable.
Land for 3 ploughs. Berengar has 1½ ploughs from Robert.
12 villagers and 2 Freemen with 3 ploughs.
Meadow, 60 acres; woodland pasture, 33 acres.
Value before 1066, 40s; now the same. Exactions 10s.
A jurisdiction, ½ carucate.

4 M. In BRANSBY Thorgautr had 2 carucates of land taxable. Land for 2
ploughs. Berengar has 1 from Robert.
6 villagers and 3 Freemen with 1½ ploughs.
Meadow, 14 acres; underwood, 50 acres.
Value before 1066, 60s; now 50[s].   ⋇

*18,5 is added at the foot of col. 352d (after 18,6) and is directed by transposition signs to
its correct place in the text.*

6 M. In CORRINGHAM Thorgautr had 2 carucates of land taxable. Land
for 2 ploughs. Berengar has 1 plough from Robert.
5 villagers and 3 smallholders with 1½ ploughs.
Woodland pasture 5 furlongs long and 5 wide.
Value before 1066, 50s; now 30[s].

18,5, directed by transposition signs to its correct place.

⋇ 5 In BURTON 1 carucate of land taxable. Land for 1 plough. *Inland*
[of] Bransby.
2 smallholders have 1 plough.

7 M. In BINBROOK Thorgautr Lagr had 8 carucates of land and 4½   353 a
bovates taxable. Land for 24 ploughs. Now Robert of Tosny has
it, and Berengar from him. In lordship 4 ploughs;
6 villagers, 4 smallholders and 44 Freemen with 8 ploughs.
A church and a priest; 2 mills, 20s; meadow, 100 acres.
Value before 1066 £7; now £15. Exactions £10.
Of this land 4 carucates and 4½ bovates are the Freemen's.

ʂ In Ludeburg. VIII . caꞃ́ tꞃǽ ad glđ . Tꞃa . XII . caꞃ́ . Soca
fupioris ᴍ̃ . Ibi hᵵ Bereng . III . caꞃ́ . 7 XXXVIII . focħ
cū . V . caꞃ́ . 7 cc . aĉs p̃ti.

ʂ In Fodrebi 7 Turgrebi . V . caꞃ́ tꞃǽ 7 V . boū ad glđ . Tꞃa
IX . caꞃ́ . Ibi hᵵ Berg . I . caꞃ́ . 7 XXXIII . focħ . 7 II . borđ.
cū . VI . caꞃ́ . 7 cxx . aĉs p̃ti . 7 IIII . faliñ . II . folid.

ʂ In Croſbi . I . caꞃ́ tꞃǽ ad glđ . Tꞃa . III . caꞃ́ . Ibi . XIIII . focħ
7 IIII . borđ . hñt . III . caꞃ́ . 7 III . aĉs p̃ti.

ᴍ̃ In OFFINTVNE . ħɓ Erneber . II . caꞃ́ tre ad glđ . Tꞃa . II.
caꞃ́ . Ibi . hᵵ Roɓt de Todeni . II . caꞃ́ . 7 VIII . uiᵽ . 7 II . borđ.
cū . II . caꞃ́ . 7 X . aĉs p̃ti . T.R.E . 7 m̃ . uaᵽ . XL . foᵵ . Tailla . X . ꞩ

ᴍ̃ In TALINTVNE . ħɓr Aluuiñ 7 Erneber . V . caꞃ́ tꞃǽ
7 dim̃ ad glđ . Tꞃa totiđ . caꞃ́ . Ibi Wiᵽs 7 Roger hões
Roɓti hñt . I . caꞃ́ 7 dim̃ . 7 V . uiᵽ cū . I . caꞃ́ . 7 XVII . aĉs
p̃ti . T.R.E . uaᵵ XL . foᵵ . m̃ . XXX.

ᴍ̃ In GRITEFORDE . ħɓ Turgot . V . caꞃ́ tꞃǽ 7 dim̃ ad glđ.
Tꞃa totiđ caꞃ́ . Ibi Berg de Roɓto hᵵ . II . caꞃ́ . 7 X . uiᵽ.
7 X . focħ 7 II . borđ . cū . III . caꞃ́ 7 dim̃ . 7 II . moliñ . X . folid.
7 LX . aĉs p̃ti . 7 XX . aĉs filuǽ past p loca . T.R.E . uaᵵ
VIII . liɓ . m̃ . IX . liɓ . Tailla . III . liɓ.

ʂ In Breſeburc 7 Barnetone . V . caꞃ́ tꞃǽ 7 dim̃ ad glđ . Tꞃa
totiđ caꞃ́ . Ibi . XVII . focħ 7 VI . uiᵽ hñt . V . caꞃ́ 7 dim̃.
7 XL . aĉs p̃ti.

ᴍ̃ In RINGESDVNE . ħɓr Aſlac 7 Dane . IIII . caꞃ́ tꞃǽ . 7 VII.
boū 7 II . partes uni boū ad glđ . Tꞃa totiđ c̃ 7 boū.
Ibi Iuo hō Roɓti hᵵ . II . caꞃ́ . 7 IX . uiᵽ 7 VI . focħ . 7 I.
borđ . cū . I . caꞃ́ 7 dim̃ . 7 XLVI . aĉs p̃ti . 7 c.xx . aĉs filuǽ
minutǽ . 7 tciã parte̅ ǽcclǽ . T.R.E . uaᵵ . L . foᵵ . m̃ . LX.

8. S. In LUDBOROUGH 8 carucates of land taxable. Land for 12 ploughs. A jurisdiction of the above manor. Berengar has 3 ploughs.
    38 Freemen with 5 ploughs.
    Meadow, 200 acres.

9 S. In FOTHERBY 4 carucates and 5 bovates, and THORGANBY, 1 carucate: 5 carucates of land and 5 bovates taxable. Land for 9 ploughs. Berengar has 1 plough.
    33 Freemen and 2 smallholders with 6 ploughs.
    Meadow, 120 acres; 4 salt-houses, 2s.

10 S. In CROXBY 1 carucate of land taxable. Land for 3 ploughs.
    14 Freemen and 4 smallholders have 3 ploughs and
    meadow, 3 acres.

11 M. In UFFINGTON Arnbjorn had 2 carucates of land taxable. Land for 2 ploughs. Robert of Tosny has 2 ploughs.
    8 villagers and 2 smallholders with 2 ploughs.
    Meadow, 10 acres.
Value before 1066 and now, 40s. Exactions 10s.

12 2 In TALLINGTON Alwine and Arnbjorn had 5½ carucates of land
M. taxable. Land for as many ploughs. William and Roger, Robert's men, have 1½ ploughs.
    5 villagers with 1 plough.
    Meadow, 17 acres.
Value before 1066, 40s; now 30[s].

13 M. In GREATFORD Thorgautr Lagr had 5½ carucates of land taxable. Land for as many ploughs. Berengar has 2 ploughs from Robert.
    10 villagers, 10 Freemen and 2 smallholders with 3½ ploughs.
    2 mills, 10s; meadow, 60 acres; woodland, pasture in places,
    20 acres.
Value before 1066 £8; now £9. Exactions £3.

14 S. In BRACEBOROUGH and 'BANTHORPE' 5½ carucates of land taxable. Land for as many ploughs.
    17 Freemen and 6 villagers have 5½ ploughs and
    meadow, 40 acres.

15 M. In 'RINGSTONE' Aslakr and Dena had 4 carucates of land and 7 bovates and 2 parts of 1 bovate taxable. Land for as many ploughs and oxen. Ivo, Robert's man, has 2 ploughs.
    9 villagers, 6 Freemen and 1 smallholder with 1½ ploughs; and
    meadow, 46 acres; underwood, 120 acres; the third part of a
    church.
Value before 1066, 50s; now 60[s].

In CHERCHEBI . II . boᷓu̅ træ ad gld . Tᷓra . II . boū . Ibi . II . uilt
arant . III . boᷣb . 7 II . ac̅ p̃ti . 7 xL . ac̅ filuæ minutæ . Inland.

ꟳ In GREIBI . h̅ᷓb Erneᷣb . II . car træ 7 II . bou ad gld . Tᷓra
totiᷓd caᷓr 7 boū . Ibi Gunfrid ho Rob̅ti h̅t . III . soc̅h . 7 I . bord.ᷓ
arant̑ . II . boᷣb . Ibi . xI . ac̅ p̃ti . 7 ccIx . ac̅ filuæ past̑ . T.R.E.
ual̅ . IIII . liƀ . m̅ xL . fot.

ꟳ In SCACHETORP . h̅b Erneber x . boᷓu̅ træᷓ ad gld̅ . Tᷓra to
tiᷓd boū . Nc̅ . e̅ waf̅tū . T.R.E.ual̅ . c . fot . m̅ utcunq̨ x . Sot.

353 b

ꟳ In ASLACHEBI . h̅b Erneber . vI . caᷓr træᷓ 7 dim̅ bou̅
ad gld̅ . Tᷓra totiᷓd caȓ . Nc̅ h̅t Rob̅t ibi . vII . uilt . 7 I.
bord̅ . h̅ntes . II . caᷓr . 7 xL . ac̅s p̃ti . 7 xx.IIII . ac̅s filuæ
minutæ . De duab car h̅t Gist de gand Socā in Fulchingehā.

ꟳ In AVETORP . h̅b Erneber . II . caᷓr træᷓ 7 dim̅ ad gld̅ . Tᷓra
III . caᷓr . Ibi h̅t Gunfrid h̅o Rob̅ti dim̅ caᷓr . 7 IIII . foc̅h.
7 I . bord̅ . cū . I . caᷓr . Ibi . xII . ac̅ p̃ti . 7 cxxx . ac̅s p̃ti . T.R.E.
ual̅ . vI . liƀ . m̅ . xL . fot . Tailla . xx . fot.

§ In Loᷓctone . v . boᷓu̅ træ 7 tcia pars . I . bou̅ . ad gld̅.
Tᷓra totiᷓd boū . Ibi . xI . foc̅h h̅nt . I . caȓ . 7 dimiᷓd æcclam.
7 vIII . ac̅s filuæ minutæ.

§ In Aflachebi . vI . boᷓu̅ tre 7 dim̅ ad gld̅ . Tᷓra . I . caruc̅.
Ibi . vI . foc̅h h̅nt . II . caᷓr . 7 vI . ac̅s p̃ti . 7 xII . ac̅s filuæ min̅.

§ In Sepingehā . I . caᷓr træᷓ ad gld̅ . Tᷓra . I . caᷓr . Ibi . IIII.
foc̅h h̅nt . I . caᷓr . 7 x . ac̅s p̃ti . 7 vI . ac̅s filuæ minutæ.

ꟳ In RIPESLAI . h̅b Tori . vIII . caᷓr tre ad gld̅ . Tᷓra . Ix.car̅.
Ibi h̅t Iuo h̅o Rob̅ti . II . caᷓr . 7 II . uilt . 7 xxIx . foc̅h . cū
vIII . caᷓr 7 dimid . Ibi æccta . 7 cxx . ac̅ filuæ paftit.
7 ccccL . ac̅ filuæ minutæ . T.R.E.ual̅ . vI . liƀ . m̅ . c . fot.
Tailla . xL . fot . SocA . vI . bouatarū.

16 In KIRKBY (Underwood) 2 bovates of land taxable. Land for 2 oxen.
2 villagers plough with 3 oxen.
Meadow, 2 acres; underwood, 40 acres.
Inland.

17 M. In (West) GRABY Arnbjorn had 2 carucates of land and 2 bovates
taxable. Land for as many ploughs and oxen. Gunfrid, Robert's
man, has 2 ploughs.
3 Freemen and 1 smallholder who plough with 2 oxen.
Meadow, 11 acres; woodland pasture, 209 acres.
Value before 1066 £4; now 40s.

18 M. In SCOTTLETHORPE Arnbjorn had 10 bovates of land taxable. Land
for as many oxen. Now it is waste.
Value before 1066, 100s; now, at the most, 10s.

19 M. In ASLACKBY Arnbjorn had 6 carucates of land and ½ bovate   353 b
taxable. Land for as many ploughs. Now Robert has there
7 villagers and 1 smallholder who have 2 ploughs and
meadow, 40 acres; underwood, 24 acres.
Of 2 carucates Gilbert of Ghent has the jurisdiction in
Folkingham.

20 M. In 'AVETHORPE' Arnbjorn had 2½ carucates of land taxable. Land
for 3 ploughs. Gunfrid, Robert's man, has ½ plough.
4 Freemen and 1 smallholder with 1 plough.
Meadow, 12 acres; meadow, 130 acres.
Value before 1066 £6; now 40s. Exactions 20s.

21 S. In LAUGHTON 5 bovates of land and the third part of 1 bovate
taxable. Land for as many oxen.
11 Freemen have 1 plough and
½ church; underwood, 8 acres.

22 S. In ASLACKBY 6½ bovates of land taxable. Land for 1 plough.
6 Freemen have 2 ploughs and
meadow, 6 acres; underwood, 12 acres.

23 S. In 'SEMPRINGHAM' 1 carucate of land taxable. Land for 1 plough.
4 Freemen have 1 plough and
meadow, 10 acres; underwood, 6 acres.

24 M. In ROPSLEY Thorir had 8 carucates of land taxable. Land for 9
ploughs. Ivo, Robert's man, has 2 ploughs.
2 villagers and 29 Freemen with 8½ ploughs.
A church; woodland pasture, 120 acres; underwood, 450 acres.
Value before 1066 £6; now 100s. Exactions 40s.
A jurisdiction of 6 bovates.

ᴔ In *DENTVNE* uel Huuelle . ħb . Eddiua . vi . car̄ ꞌꞌ træ
ad gld̄ . Tra totid̄ē car̄ꞌ . Ibi ħt̄ Roꝟt in dñio . iii . car̄.
7 xiii . uiłł . cū . iiii . car̄ . T.R.E. uał . iiii . liƀ . 7 v . ſoł . 7 ii . den̄ꞌ.
m̄ . c . ſoł . Tailla . xx . ſoł.
In Hungretune . vi . car̄ ꞌꞌ træ ad gld̄ꞌ . Tra . vi . car̄ꞌ . Inland . ē.
Ibi . xiii . uiłł hn̄t . vi . car̄ . 7 l . ac̄s p̄ti . 7 lxxxvii . ac̄s
ſiluæ minutæ . H̄ ſilua . ē in Soca de granthā.

ᴔ In *VLESTANETORP* . ħb Leuric . iiii . car̄ ꞌꞌ tre ad gld̄.
Tra totid car̄ꞌ . Ibi ħt̄ Roꝟt in dñio . i . car̄ . 7 vi . uiłł
7 iii . bord̄ . 7 viii . ſoch hn̄tes . iii . car̄ . 7 iii . molin̄ . xv . ſolid̄.
.ii. T.R.E. 7 m̄ uał . xl . ſoł.
ᴔ Ibid̄ē . ħb̄r Goduin 7 Archel . iiii . car̄ ꞌꞌ tre ad gld̄ꞌ . Tra
totid̄ . car̄ꞌ . Ibi ħt̄ Roꝟt . i . molin̄ 7 dimid̄ . viii . ſoł 7 vi . den̄.
7 xi . uiłł cū . i . car̄ . Ibi æccła 7 p̄ƀr . hn̄s dim car̄ huj̄ træ.
Ibi xxx . ac̄ p̄ti . 7 iii . uirgate . T.R.E. 7 m̄ uał . xl . ſoł.

ᴔ In *ABVRNE* . ħb Turgot xii . car̄ ꞌꞌ træ ad gld̄ꞌ . Tra totid̄
car̄ꞌ . Ibi de Roꝟto ħt̄ Berenḡ . in dñio . ii . car̄ . 7 xiiii.
uiłł 7 iiii . bord̄ . 7 i . ſoch . cū . iiii . car̄ . Ibi æccła 7 p̄ƀr.
7 i . molin̄ . xx . ſolid̄ . 7 i . piſcar̄ mille anguiłłr̄ . 7 c . ac̄s
p̄ti . T.R.E. uał . v . liƀ . m̄ . vi . liƀ.

353 c
In Hadinctone . iii . car̄ ꞌꞌ træ 7 dim̄ ad gld̄ꞌ . Tra . ii . car̄.
Berew̄ in Aburne . Ibi . ii . uiłł hn̄t . dim̄ car̄ꞌ . 7 vi . ac̄
p̄ti . 7 iii . ac̄ ſiluæ minutæ.
ᴔ In *ADELINCTVNE* . ħb Goduin . iii . car̄ ꞌꞌ træ ad gld̄.
Tra . vi . car̄ꞌ . Ibi ħt̄ Roꝟt in dñio . ii . car̄ . 7 xiiii . ſoch.
7 v . uiłł . 7 v . bord̄ cū . iiii . car̄ . Ibi æccła . 7 cxl . ac̄s p̄ti.
Ibi ħt̄ Warin̄ ho ej̄ . i . car̄ . 7 i . bord̄ . hn̄s . ii . bou ꞌꞌ træ.
T.R.E. uał . iii . liƀ . m̄ vi . liƀ.

353 b, c

25 M. In DENTON or WYVILLE Eadgifu had 6 carucates of land taxable.
Land for as many ploughs. Robert has in lordship 3 ploughs;
13 villagers with 4 ploughs.
Value before 1066 £4 5s 4d; now 100s. Exactions 20s.

26 In HUNGERTON 6 carucates of land taxable. Land for 6 ploughs.
It is *inland*.
13 villagers have 6 ploughs and
meadow, 50 acres; underwood, 87 acres. This wood is in the
jurisdiction of Grantham.

27 M. In WOOLSTHORPE Leofric had 4 carucates of land taxable. Land for
as many ploughs. Robert has in lordship 1 plough;
6 villagers, 3 smallholders and 8 Freemen who have 3 ploughs.
3 mills, 15s.
Value before 1066 and now, 40s.

28 2 There also Godwine and Arnketill had 4 carucates of land taxable.
M. Land for as many ploughs. Robert has
1½ mills, 8s 6d.
11 villagers with 1 plough.
A church and a priest who has ½ carucate of this land.
Meadow, 30 acres and 3 virgates.
Value before 1066 and now, 40s.

29 M. In AUBOURN Thorgautr Lagr had 12 carucates of land taxable.
Land for as many ploughs. Berengar has in lordship 2 ploughs
from Robert;
14 villagers, 4 smallholders and 1 Freeman with 4 ploughs.
A church and a priest; 1 mill, 20s; 1 fishery, 1000 eels;
meadow, 100 acres.
Value before 1066 £5; now £6.

30 In HADDINGTON 3½ carucates of land taxable. Land for 2 ploughs.   353 c
An outlier of Aubourn.
2 villagers have ½ plough.
Meadow, 6 acres; underwood, 3 acres.

31 M. In ALLINGTON Godwine had 3 carucates of land taxable. Land for
6 ploughs. Robert has in lordship 2 ploughs;
14 Freemen, 5 villagers and 5 smallholders with 4 ploughs.
A church; meadow, 140 acres.
Warin, his man, has 1 carucate.
1 smallholder who has 2 bovates of land.
Value before 1066 £3; now £6.

ᴔ In *Nortchime* . ħɓ Mere . vɪ . caʀ ꞇ tre ad gld́ .

Tra . vɪɪɪ . caʀ . Ibi Iuo hō Roɓti . ħꞇ . ɪɪɪ . caʀ . 7 xɪɪ . uiłł .

7 ɪɪ . borđ . cū . ɪɪɪɪ . caʀ . 7 ʟvɪ . aćs p̄ti . 7 xxx . aćs filuæ

paſt . T.R.E. uał . ɪɪɪ . liɓ 7 ꞇ xɪɪɪ . ſoł . ṁ . vɪɪ . liɓ.

.XIX. ## TERRA BERENGARIJ DE TODENI.

ᴔ In *Adelingetone* . ħɓr Vlfchetel 7 Goduin . vɪ . caʀ

ꞇ træ ad gld́ . Tra . v . caʀ . Ibi Berenger ħꞇ . ɪ . caʀ . 7 xɪɪɪɪ .

ſoch . 7 v . uiłł 7 v . borđ . hn̄tes . ɪɪɪɪ . caʀ . Ibi æccła . hn̄s

diṁ caʀ huj træ . 7 cxʟ . ać p̄ti . T.R.E. uał . ɪɪɪ . liɓ . ṁ . vɪ . liɓ.

.XX. ## TERRA ILBERTI DE LACI.

ᴔ In *Dvneha* . ħɓ Alrich . ɪɪ . caʀ træ ad gld́ . Tra . ɪɪ . caʀ .

Nc ħꞇ Ilɓt de Laci . De eo miles ej . in dn̄io . ɪ . caʀ . 7 ɪɪ . ſoch .

7 ɪɪ . uiłł . cū . ɪ . caʀ . 7 xvɪɪ . aćs p̄ti . T.R.E. uał xx . ſoł . ṁ . xvɪ .

Ɓ In Scotorne . vɪɪ . bou træ ad gld́ . Tra . ɪx . bou ⌐ Tailla . ɪɪɪɪ . ſoł .

Ș In Stou . diṁ caʀ tre ad gld́ . Tra diṁ caʀ . Inland 7 Soca .

ᴔ In *Welingeha* . ħɓ Deincora xɪɪ . bou træ ad gld́ . Tra

xɪɪ . bou . In hac tra manet un miles Ilɓti . T.R.E. 7 ṁ uał

⌐ xx . ſoł .

.XXI. ## TERRA HENRICI DE FERRERES.

ᴔ In *Witenai* . ħɓ Seubar xɪɪ . caʀ tre ad gld́ . Tra . vɪɪɪ .

caʀ . Ibi Safuualo hō Henrici ħꞇ . ɪɪ . caʀ . 7 x . uiłł . 7 ɪɪɪɪ .

borđ . 7 xxx . ſoch . hn̄tes . v . caʀ . 7 ccc . ać p̄ti . T.R.E. uał . x . liɓ .

ṁ . vɪɪ . liɓ . Tailla . ɪɪɪ . liɓ . ⌐ 7 Waſta . ē .

Ɓ In Wintrintone . ɪɪ . bou træ ad gld́ . Tra . ɪɪ . bou . Inland . ē .

32 M. In NORTH KYME Merra had 6 carucates of land taxable. Land for 8 ploughs. Ivo, Robert's man, has 3 ploughs.
    12 villagers and 2 smallholders with 4 ploughs.
    Meadow, 56 acres; woodland pasture, 30 acres.
Value before 1066 £3 13s 8d; now £7.

19   LAND OF BERENGAR OF TOSNY

1 2 M. In ALLINGTON Ulfketill and Godwine had 6 carucates of land taxable. Land for 5 ploughs. Berengar of Tosny has 1 plough.
    14 Freemen, 5 villagers and 5 smallholders who have 4 ploughs.
    A church which has ½ carucate of this land; meadow, 140 acres.
Value before 1066 £3; now £6.

20   LAND OF ILBERT OF LACY

1 M. In DUNHOLME Aelfric had 2 carucates of land taxable. Land for 2 ploughs. Now Ilbert of Lacy has them. A man-at-arms of his [has] in lordship 1 plough from him;
    2 Freemen and 2 villagers with 1 plough.
    Meadow, 17 acres.
Value before 1066, 20s; now 16[s]. Exactions 4s.

2 B. In SCOTHERN 7 bovates of land taxable. Land for 9 oxen.

3 S. In STOW (St. Mary) ½ carucate of land taxable. Land for ½ plough. *Inland* and a jurisdiction.

4 In WILLINGHAM (by Stow) Deincora had 12 bovates of land taxable. Land for 12 oxen. One of Ilbert's men-at-arms lives on this land.
Value before 1066 and now, 20s.

21   LAND OF HENRY OF FERRERS

1 M. In WHITTON Siward Barn had 12 carucates of land taxable. Land for 8 ploughs. Saswalo, Henry's man, has 2 ploughs.
    10 villagers, 4 smallholders and 30 Freemen who have 5 ploughs.
    Meadow, 300 acres.
Value before 1066 £10; now £7. Exactions £3.

2 B. In WINTERTON 2 bovates of land taxable. Land for 2 oxen. It is *inland* and waste.

.XXII.

TERRA WILLI DE PERCI.

ᚱ In *IMVNGEHA*.ħɓ Aluuin.iiii.car tre.7 i.bou 7 dim
ad glđ.Tra.viii.car.Ibi hт Witts de pci in dnio
iiii.car.7 xii.uitt 7 xiiii.borđ.7 xiii.foċħ hnтes
iiii.car.7 qt xx.aċs pti.T.R.E.uat.viii.liɓ.m̊ fimilit.
Tailla.xl.fot. ⌐ In Lenefbi.dim bou tre ad glđ.Soca.

ᚱ In *ABVRNE*.ħɓ Alcude.vi.bou tre ad glđ.Tra.xii.
bou.Ibi Norman hõ Witti hт dim car.7 ii.uitt.7 iiii.
borđ.7 v.foċħ cũ.i.car 7 ii.boɓ arant.7 lx.aċs pti.
T.R.E.uat.xiiii.fot.m̊ xx.fot.Tailla.iiii.fot.

ᛋ In Lobingeha.i.bou træ 7 dim ad glđ.Tra.iii.bou.
Ibi.i.foċħ.cũ.ii.boɓ aranɟS.7 xx.aꞓ pti.

In *TORENTONE*.ħɓ Aluuine.ii.car træ 7 vi.bou ad glđ.
✝ Tra.iiii.car.Ibi xii.foċħ 7 iii.borđ 7 ii.uitt.cũ.i.car
7 dimid.Et fup has.xi.bouatas træ hт Rog pict.xi.
bou fimilit ficuti Witts.q̓s idē W.debet haɓe teſtim
houm de Wapent.Ibi.ccc.lxiiii.aꞓ pti.Soca ĩ Orefbi.

ᚱ In *ORESBI*.ħɓ Aluuine.vii.bou træ 7 ii.partes
uni bou ad glđ.Tra.ii.car.Ibi Witts in dnio hт.ii.car
7 iii.uitt 7 x.foċħ cũ.i.car.Ibi æccta 7 pɓr.7 i.molin
iii.folid.7 qt xx.aꞓ pti.T.R.E.uat xl.fot.m̊.l.fot.

ᚱ In *CABVRNE*.ħɓ Grinchil.i.car træ ⌐ Tailla.x.fot.
ad glđ.Tra.ii.car.Ibi Norman hõ Witti hт.i.car.
7 i.uitt 7 i.borđ.7 xii.aċs pti in Chetfi.T.R.E.uat.xxx.
fot.m̊.xxvi fot.

In Cucualt.i.bou træ ad glđ.Intand In Caburne.

1 2   In IMMINGHAM Alwine had 4 carucates of land and 1½ bovates
M.   taxable. Land for 8 ploughs. William of Percy has in lordship 4
ploughs;
    12 villagers, 14 smallholders and 13 Freemen who have 4
      ploughs and
    meadow, 80 acres.
Value before 1066 £8; now the same. Exactions 40s.

2   In LACEBY ½ bovate of land taxable. A jurisdiction.

3 M.   In HABROUGH Alcude had 6 bovates of land taxable. Land for 12
oxen. Norman, William's man, has ½ plough.
    2 villagers, 4 smallholders and 5 Freemen who plough with
      1 plough and 2 oxen.
    Meadow, 60 acres.
Value before 1066, 14s; now 20s. Exactions 4s.

4 S.   In *LOBINGEHAM* 1½ bovates of land taxable. Land for 3 oxen.
    1 Freeman who ploughs with 2 oxen.
    Meadow, 20 acres.

5   In THORNTON (le Moor) Alwine had 2 carucates of land and 6
bovates taxable. Land for 4 ploughs.
    12 Freemen, 3 smallholders and 2 villagers with 1½ ploughs.
And besides these 11 bovates of land Roger of Poitou, just like
William, similarly has 11 bovates which this William ought to
have according to the witness of the men of the Wapentake.
    Meadow, 364 acres.
A jurisdiction of Owersby.

*22,6 is entered at the foot of col. 353d (in the middle of 22,16), and is directed by
transposition signs to its correct place in the text.*

7 M.   In OWERSBY Alwine had 7 bovates of land and 2 parts of 1 bovate
taxable. Land for 2 ploughs. William has in lordship 2 ploughs;
    3 villagers and 10 Freemen with 1 plough.
    A church and a priest; 1 mill, 3s; meadow, 80 acres.
Value before 1066, 40s; now 50s. Exactions 10s.

8 M.   In CABOURN Grimketill had 1 carucate of land taxable. Land for 2
ploughs. Norman, William's man, has 1 plough.
    1 villager and 1 smallholder.
    Meadow, 12 acres in (North) Kelsey.
Value before 1066, 30s; now 26s.

9   In CUXWOLD 1 bovate of land taxable. *Inland* of Cabourn.

ᴍ In *WICHINGEBI*. ħɓ Turgot . ɪɪ . caɍ træ ad glđ . Tra ɪɪɪ . caɍ.
Ibi Osɓn hō Wiłłi ħⲦ . ɪɪ . caɍ . ⁊ vɪɪɪ . uiłł ⁊ ɪɪ . foch . cū . ɪɪ.
caɍ . ⁊ xv . aćs p̄ti . Silua minuta . ɪ . lev łḡ . ⁊ v . q̊ʒ łaⳏ.
T.R.E. ⁊ m̃ uał ɪɪɪ . łiɓ.   Soca Huj ᴍ.

§ In Weſtledebi . ɪx . bou tre ad glđ . Tra . xvɪɪɪ . boū . Ibi
Radulf⁹ hō Wiłłi . ħⲦ . vɪ . foch . cū . ɪɪ . caɍ . ⁊ xxx . aćs p̄ti.

§ In Bechelinge . ɪ . bou træ ⁊ dim̃ ad glđ . Tra . ɪɪɪ . boū . Ibi
Roɓt⁹ hō Wiłłi . ħⲦ ɪ . foch . ⁊ ɪ . borđ . arant . ɪɪ . boɓ⁹ . ⁊ ɪ . ać p̄ti.

§ In Rerefbi . dim̃ caɍ træ ad glđ . Tra . ɪɪɪɪ . boū . Ibi Norman
hō Wiłłi ħⲦ . ɪ . foch cū dim̃ caɍ . ⁊ x . ać p̄ti.

§ In Sneleſlunt . ɪɪɪɪ . boū tre ad glđ . Tra . ɪ . caɍ . Ibi Waldin⁹
hō Wiłłi ħⲦ . ɪɪɪ . foch cū . ɪ . caɍ . ⁊ vɪ . ać p̄ti . ⁊ vɪ . ać filuæ min⁹.

§ In Rerefbi . ɪɪɪɪ . bou tre ad glđ . Tra . ɪɪɪɪ . boū . In Sneleſlunt ⌐jacet.

ᴍ In *STAINFELDE* . ħɓ Siuuard⁹ . ɪ . caɍ træ ⁊ dim̃ ad glđ . Tra . ɪ . c̄.
Ibi ħⲦ Wiłłs . ɪ . caɍ . ⁊ vɪɪɪ . uiłł . ⁊ vɪ . borđ . ⁊ ɪɪɪɪ . foch.
cū . ɪɪɪɪ . caɍ . ⁊ xL . aćs p̄ti . ⁊ cc.Lx.ɪɪɪɪ . ać filuæ paſtił.

† In Bernetebi . ɪɪ . bou tre ad glđ . Tra . ɪɪɪɪ . boɓ . Waſta . ē . Inland
                                            ⌐ in Torentune.

T.R.E . uał . xxx . foł . m̃ . Lx . foł.

§ Ibid ħɓ Tona . ɪ . caɍ træ ⁊ dim̃ ad glđ . Soca in Berlinge.
Ibi ħⲦ Wiłł . ɪɪɪɪ . foch ⁊ ɪ . borđ . cū . ɪɪ . caɍ . ⁊ xx . aćs p̄ti.
⁊ cxvɪɪ . aćs filuæ paſtił.

10 M. In WICKENBY Thorgautr had 2 carucates of land taxable. Land for
3 ploughs. Osbern, William's man, has 2 ploughs.
8 villagers and 2 Freemen with 2 ploughs.
Meadow, 15 acres; underwood 1 league long and 5 furlongs
wide.
Value before 1066 and now £3.

Jurisdiction of this manor:
11 S. In 'WESTLABY' 9 bovates of land taxable. Land for 18 oxen. Ralph,
William's man, has
6 Freemen with 2 ploughs; and
meadow, 30 acres.

12 S. In BECKERING 1½ bovates of land taxable. Land for 3 oxen.
Robert, William's man, has
1 Freeman and 1 smallholder; they plough with 2 oxen.
Meadow, 1 acre.

13 S. In REASBY ½ carucate of land taxable. Land for 4 oxen. Norman,
William's man, has
1 Freeman with ½ plough.
Meadow, 10 acres.

14 S. In SNELLAND 4 bovates of land taxable. Land for 1 plough. Waldin,
William's man, has
3 Freemen with 1 plough.
Meadow, 6 acres; underwood, 6 acres.

15 S. In REASBY 4 bovates of land taxable. Land for 4 oxen. It lies in
Snelland.

16 M. In STAINFIELD Siward had 1½ carucates of land taxable. Land for
1 plough. William has 1 plough.
8 villagers, 6 smallholders and 4 Freemen with 4 ploughs.
Meadow, 40 acres; woodland pasture, 264 acres.
22,16 continues after 22,6.

22,6, added but directed by transposition signs to its correct place.
—€6 In BARNETBY (le Wold) 2 bovates of land taxable. Land for 4 oxen.
It is waste. *Inland* of Thornton (le Moor).

22,16 continued
(16) Value before 1066, 30s; now 60s. 354 a

17 S. There also Tonni had 1½ carucates of land taxable. A jurisdiction
of Barlings. William has
4 Freemen and 1 smallholder with 2 ploughs; and
meadow, 20 acres; woodland pasture, 117 acres.

§ Iɴ Apeleia . vii . bou̅ tra̅ ad gℓđ . Tra . xii . bou̅ . Ibi . x .
ſocħ hn̅t . iii . caɼ . 7 xv . ać̅s p̊ti . 7 cx . ać̅s ſiluæ minut̅ .

§ Ibiđ ħƀ Tona . vii . bou̅ tre ad gℓđ . Tra . xii . bou̅ . Socᴀ in
Berlinge . Ibi ħꜧ Wiℓℓs . x . ſocħ cu̅ . iii . caɼ . 7 x . ać̅s p̊ti .
7 cx . ać̅s ſiluæ minutæ .

§ Ibiđe̅ ħƀ Aluric . ii . bou̅ tra̅ ad gℓđ . Socᴀ in Bolintone .
Ibi ħꜧ Wiℓℓs . ii . ſocħ cu̅ . i . boue arant̅ .

ℳ Iɴ *Lᴠᴅᴇꜰᴏʀᴅᴇ* . ħƀ Alſi . i . caɼ tre 7 vi . bou̅ ad gℓđ . Tra
ℳ iii . caɼ 7 dim̅ . 7 Ibiđe̅ ħƀr Wilac 7 Siuuard . iii . caɼ
tra̅ ad gℓđ . Tra . vi . caɼ . Ibi ħꜧ Wiℓℓs de p̄ci . in dn̅io
iii . caɼ 7 dim̅ . 7 xxviii . uiℓℓ 7 viii . ſocħ cu̅ . iiii . caɼ . ʟx .
ać̅s p̊ti . T.R.E . 7 m̅ uaℓ . iiii . liƀ . Tailla . xx . ſoℓ .
Ibiđ ħƀ Tona . ii . bou̅ tre ad gℓđ . Tra . iiii . bou̅ . Socᴀ in
Badeburg . Waſta . e̅ . Ibi . iiii . ać̅ p̊ti .

ℳ Iɴ *Cʜᴇᴠʀᴇᴍᴏɴᴛ* . ħƀ Elſi . iii . caɼ tre ad gℓđ . Tra . vi .
caɼ . Ibi ħꜧ Wiℓℓs in dn̅io . iiii . caɼ . 7 xviii . uiℓℓ . 7 iiii .
borđ . 7 ii . ſocħ . hn̅tes . iiii . caɼ . Ibi æccℓa . 7 i . moliñ . ii .
ſoℓiđ . 7 xx . ać̅s p̊ti . T.R.E . uaℓ . iii . liƀ . m̅ . iiii .

ℳ Iɴ *Gʀɪᴍᴇꜱʙɪ* . ħƀ Alric . i . caɼ tra̅ 7 ii . bou̅ ad gℓđ .
Tra . iii . caɼ . Ibi Fulco ho̅ Wiℓℓi . ħꜧ . i . caɼ . 7 iii . uiℓℓ
7 v . ſocħ cu̅ . i . caɼ . Ibi æccℓa . 7 xi . ać̅ p̊ti . 7 i . ſalina . vi .
denaɼ . T.R.E . uaℓ xxx . ſoℓ . m̅ xx.v . ſoℓ . Tailla . v . ſoℓ .

.iiii.
ℳ Iɴ *Cᴏᴠᴇɴʜᴀ̅* ħƀr Alſi 7 Chetel 7 Turuer . iii . caɼ tre
7 dim̅ ad gℓđ . Tra . iiii . caɼ . Ibi ħꜧ Wiℓℓs . in dn̅io . iii . caɼ .
7 xviii . uiℓℓ 7 xvii . ſocħ . cu̅ . v . caɼ 7 dimid . 7 v . ſalinas
ii . ſoℓiđ . 7 cʟ . ać̅s p̊ti . T.R.E . uaℓ cx . ſoℓ . m̅ iiii . liƀ . Tailla
ꬵ xxx . ſoℓ .

18 S. In APLEY 7 bovates of land taxable. Land for 12 oxen.
10 Freemen have 3 ploughs and
meadow, 15 acres; underwood, 110 acres.

19 S. There also Tonni had 7 bovates of land taxable. Land for 12
K oxen. A jurisdiction of Barlings. William has
10 Freemen with 3 ploughs; and
meadow, 10 acres; underwood, 110 acres.

20 S. There also Aelfric had 2 bovates of land taxable. A jurisdiction
K of Bullington. William has
2 Freemen who plough with 1 ox.

21 M. In LUDFORD Alsige had 1 carucate of land and 6 bovates taxable.
Land for 3½ ploughs.

22 2 There also Vigleikr and Siward had 3 carucates of land taxable.
M. Land for 6 ploughs. William of Percy has in lordship 3½ ploughs;
28 villagers and 8 Freemen with 4 ploughs.
Meadow, 60 acres.
Value before 1066 and now £4. Exactions 20s.

23 There also Tonni had 2 bovates of land taxable. Land for 4 oxen.
A jurisdiction of Baumber. It is waste.
Meadow, 4 acres.

24 M. In KIRMOND (le Mire) Alsige had 3 carucates of land taxable. Land
for 6 ploughs. William has in lordship 4 ploughs;
18 villagers, 4 smallholders and 2 Freemen who have 4 ploughs.
A church; 1 mill, 2s; meadow, 20 acres.
Value before 1066 £3; now [£] 4.

25 M. In (Little) GRIMSBY Aelfric had 1 carucate of land and 2 bovates
taxable. Land for 3 ploughs. Fulco, William's man, has 1 plough.
3 villagers and 5 Freemen with 1 plough.
A church; meadow, 11 acres; 1 salt-house, 6d.
Value before 1066, 30s; now 25s. Exactions 5s.

26 3 In COVENHAM Alsige, Ketill and Thorfrothr had 3½ carucates of
M. land taxable. Land for 4 ploughs. William has in lordship 3 ploughs;
18 villagers and 17 Freemen with 5½ ploughs.
5 salt-houses, 2s; meadow, 150 acres.
Value before 1066, 110s; now £4. Exactions 30s.

Chetel 7 Turuer frs fuer.7 p̄ morte patris sui
trā diuiser.Ita tam̄ ut Chetel faciens seruitiū regis ha
beret adjutoriū Turuer fris sui.Terrā Chetel hb Wills
de rege.trā aut Turuer emit isde Wills ab Anschitillo
q̄dā coquo.T.R.Willi.

In ALCHINTON.hb Ælsi.VIII.car tre ad glt̄.Tra.XVI.
car.Ibi Fulco hō Willi ht.II.car.7 XXX.VIII.soch cū
VII.car.7 dim̄.Ibi æccta.7 moliñ.III.solid.7 sedes alteri
mol.7 XX.ac̄ p̄ti.T.R.E.ual.III.lib.m̄.IIII.Tailla XL.sot.
Sex car 7 dim̄ de hac tra sunt soch.

SIn Germundtorp.III.bou tre 7 dim̄ ad glt̄.Tra totid bou.
Soca i Couenhā.Ibi.III.soch hūt.I.car.7 L.ac̄s p̄ti.

SIn Houten Soca i Lagesbi.x.bou tre ad glt̄.Tra.II.car

354 b

Ibi Eurard hō Willi ht.VI.soch 7 IIII.uillt.7 II.bord.
cū.II.car.7 XXX.ac̄s p̄ti.

In RISTONE 7 CARLETONE.hb Alfi.III.car træ ad glt̄.
Tra.IIII.car.Ibi Osbn hō Willi ht.II.car.7 IIII.uillt.
7 IIII.bord.7 XVIII.soch.cū.IIII.car.Ibi æccta.7 II.moliñ
v.solid.7 XXX.ac̄ p̄ti.7 c.ac̄ siluæ pastit.T.R.E.7 modo
ualet.XL.sot.Tailla.XX.sot.Medietas de hac tra.ē soch.

In ENGLEBI.hb Gunneuuate.II.car træ 7 II.bou ad
glt̄.Tra totid cr 7 bou.Ibi ht Wills.I.car.7 v.uillt.
7 I.soch cū dim̄ car.Ibi pbr.7 L.ac̄ p̄ti.7 L ac̄ siluæ miñ
T.R.E.ual.XX.sot.m̄.XXV.Tailla.v.sot.

Ketill and Thorfrothr were brothers and after the death of their father they divided the land; in such a way, however, that Ketill, while doing the King's service, should have the help of his brother, Thorfrothr. William of Percy had Ketill's and Alsige's land from the King; but this William bought Thorfrothr's land from Asketill, a cook, after 1066.

Ý

22,27 is added after 22,28 and is directed by transposition signs to its correct place in the text.

28 M. In ELKINGTON Alsige had 8 carucates of land taxable. Land for 16 ploughs. Fulco, William's man, has 2 ploughs.
    38 Freemen with 7½ ploughs.
    A church; a mill, 3s; the site of another mill; meadow, 20 acres.
Value before 1066 £3; now [£] 4. Exactions 40s.
6½ carucates of this land are the Freemen's.

22,27, directed by transposition signs to its correct place.

Ý 27 S. In GRAINTHORPE 3½ bovates of land taxable. Land for as many oxen. A jurisdiction of Covenham.
    3 Freemen have 1 plough and
    meadow, 50 acres.

22,36, misplaced and directed by transposition signs to its correct place in the text.

ʌ 36 S. In 'HOLTHAM', a jurisdiction of Legsby, 10 bovates of land taxable. Land for 2 ploughs. Evrard, William's man, has   354 b
    6 Freemen, 4 villagers and 2 smallholders with 2 ploughs and meadow, 30 acres.

29 M. In (North) RESTON and (Little) CARLTON Alsige had 3 carucates of land taxable. Land for 4 ploughs. Osbern, William's man, has 2 ploughs.
    4 villagers, 4 smallholders and 18 Freemen with 4 ploughs.
    A church; 2 mills, 5s; meadow, 30 acres; woodland pasture, 100 acres.
Value before 1066 and value now, 40s. Exactions 20s.
Half of this land is the Freemen's.

30 M. In INGLEBY Gunnhvatr had 2 carucates of land and 2 bovates taxable. Land for as many ploughs and oxen. William has 1 plough.
    5 villagers and 1 Freeman with ½ plough.
    A priest; meadow, 50 acres; underwood, 50 acres.
Value before 1066, 20s; now 25[s]. Exactions 5s.

ᚹIn *ODENEBI*.ħƀ Grinchel.ɪɪ.car̄ træ ⁊ ɪɪɪ.bou ad glđ.

Tra.ɪɪɪɪ.car̄.⁊ vɪ.boū.Ibi Wills hō Willi hɼ.ɪɪɪ.car̄.

⁊ vɪɪ.uill ⁊ xɪ.soch cū.ɪɪɪ.çar̄.⁊ ɪ.moliñ.ɪɪ.soliđ.⁊ xL.

ac̄s p̄ti.T.R.E.ual.xL.sol.m̄.Lx.Tailla.xx.sol.

De hac tra.ɪx.bouatæ in Soca.

ᚹIn *STAINTON*.ħƀ Grinchel.ɪɪɪɪ.boū træ ad glđ.Tra

xɪɪ.boū.Ibi Alulf hō Willi.hɼ.ɪɪ.car̄.⁊ vɪ.uill cū.ɪ.

car̄.⁊ ɪ.mol xɪɪ.deñ.⁊ xxvɪ.ac̄ p̄ti.T.R.E.ual xxx.sol.

ᚹIn *FODREBI*.ħƀ Sberne dim̄ car̄ træ ad glđ.   ⌐m̄.L.

Tra.xɪɪ.boū.Fulco hō Willi hɼ eā ⁊ colit.Ibi.ɪɪɪɪ.ac̄ p̄ti.

T.R.E.ual.x.sol.m̄.ɪɪɪ.sol.

ᚹIn *WIGHINGESBI*.ħƀ Godric.v.boū tre ad glđ.Tra

vɪɪ.boū.Ibi Roƀt hō Willi hɼ.ɪ.car̄.⁊ ɪ.uill cū.ɪ.boue.

⁊ x.ac̄s p̄ti.T.R.E.⁊ m̄ ual.xx.sol.

ᚹIn *LAGESBI*.ħƀ Alsi.ɪ.car̄ træ ad glđ.Tra.ɪɪ.car̄.Ibi

Eurard hō Willi hɼ.ɪɪ.car̄.⁊ vɪ.uill.⁊ ɪ.borđ.cū.ɪ.car̄.

⁊ ɪ.moliñ.vɪ.denar̄.⁊ xɪɪ.ac̄ p̄ti.⁊ xɪɪ.ac̄ siluæ pastil p̄ loca.

ᛈ T.R.E.ual xxx.sol.m̄.xL.

§ Ibiđ.ɪɪɪɪ.boū træ ad glđ.Soca ī Waragebi.Wasta.ē.

§ In Sūmertebi.ħƀ Salecoc.ɪɪ.car̄ træ ⁊ dim̄ ad glđ.

Tra.v.car̄.Soca in Brune.Ibi.xɪɪɪɪ.soch hñt.v.car̄.

⁊ q̄t xx.ac̄s p̄ti.⁊ xx.ac̄s siluæ minutæ.

TERRA GISLEBERTI TISON.

ᚹIn *FEREBI*.ħƀ Goduin.ɪɪ.car̄ træ ⁊ vɪɪ.boū.⁊ vɪɪɪ.

part boū ad glđ.Tra.ɪɪɪɪ.car̄.Ibi Anschitillus hō

Gisleƀti tison hɼ.ɪ.car̄ ⁊ vɪ.soch.de.ɪx.boū huj træ.

⁊ xvɪɪ.uill hñtes.ɪɪɪɪ.car̄ ⁊ dim̄.Ibi æccła.⁊ ɪ.moliñ

x.soliđ.⁊ ɪ.passagiū.Lx.soliđ.⁊ ccx.ac̄s p̄ti.T.R.E.

ual vɪɪɪ.liƀ.m̄ similit.

31 M. In OWMBY Grimketill had 2 carucates of land and 3 bovates taxable. Land for 4 ploughs and 6 oxen. William, William's man, has 3 ploughs.
>7 villagers and 11 Freemen with 3 ploughs.
>1 mill, 2s; meadow, 40 acres.

Value before 1066, 40s; now 60[s]. Exactions 20s.
Of this land 9 bovates in a jurisdiction.

32 M. In STAINTON (le Vale) Grimketill had 4 bovates of land taxable. Land for 12 oxen. Aethelwulf, William's man, has 2 ploughs.
>6 villagers with 1 plough.
>1 mill, 12d; meadow, 26 acres.

Value before 1066, 30s; now 50[s].

33 M. In FOTHERBY Esbjorn had ½ carucate of land taxable. Land for 12 oxen. Fulco, William's man, has it and cultivates it.
>Meadow, 4 acres.

Value before 1066, 10s; now 3s.

34 M. In WICKENBY Godric had 5 bovates of land taxable. Land for 7 oxen. Robert, William's man, has 1 plough.
>1 villager with 1 ox.
>Meadow, 10 acres.

Value before 1066 and now, 20s.

35 M. In LEGSBY Alsige had 1 carucate of land taxable. Land for 2 ploughs. Evrard, William's man, has 2 ploughs.
>6 villagers and 1 smallholder with 1 plough.
>1 mill, 6d; meadow, 12 acres; woodland, pasture in places, 12 acres.

Λ   Value before 1066, 30s; now 40[s].

22,36 is added at the foot of col. 354a and the top of 354b (after 22,27) and is directed by transposition signs to its correct place in the text.

37 S. There also 4 bovates of land taxable. A jurisdiction of Wragby. It is waste.

38 S. In SOMERBY Salecoc had 2½ carucates of land taxable. Land for 5 ploughs. A jurisdiction of Burnham.
>14 Freemen have 5 ploughs and
>meadow, 80 acres; underwood, 20 acres.

23   LAND OF GILBERT TISON

1 M. In (South) FERRIBY Godwine had 2 carucates of land and 7 bovates and the eighth part of a bovate taxable. Land for 4 ploughs. Asketill, Gilbert Tison's man, has 1 plough.
>6 Freemen on 9 bovates of this land; 17 villagers who have 4½ ploughs.
>A church; 1 mill, 10s; 1 ferry, 60s; meadow, 210 acres.

Value before 1066 £8; now the same.

.XXIIII.   TERRA GISLEBERTI DE GAND.

⓯ In SCANTONE . hɓ Vlf fenifc . vi . car træ 7 dim ad
gld . Tra . x . car . Ibi hɼ Giflebt de Gand . iiii . car
in dnio . 7 xvi . uilt 7 xii . foch 7 vi . bord . cū . vii . car.
Ibi æccla 7 pɓr . 7 i . molin . ii . folid . 7 clxvi . ac pti . T.R.E.
uat . vi . liɓ . m̂ . viii . liɓ . Tailla . iiii . liɓ.

Ɓ In Rifun . i . car 7 dim ad gld . Tra . i . car 7 dim . BER in Scant.
Ibi hɼ Colsuan . i . car . 7 i . molin . xii . den . 7 xxxvi . acs pti.
hō Giflebti

Š In Burtone . iii . car træ ad gld . Tra . ii . car . Ibi xi . foch
7 ix . bord cū . iii . car .   Ɩaran . v . boɓ . 7 iiii . ac pti.

Š In Carletone . vi . bou tre ad gld . Tra totid boɓ . Ibi . ii . foch

⓯ In VVILINGEHA . hɓ Vlf . xiiii . bou tre ad gld . Tra
totid boɓ . Ibi hɼ Giflebt . ii . car . 7 xii . uilt . 7 i . foch cū
ii . car . Ibi æccla 7 pɓr . 7 ii . pifcar xxx.ii . denar . 7 xl . acs
pti . T.R.E. uat . c . fot . m̂ . iiii . liɓ .   ƖSOCA de Scanton.

Š In Brotulbi 7 Torp . iii . car træ ad gld . Tra . iii . car . Ibi . v .
foch 7 ii . bord hnt . iii . car 7 ii . boues . 7 viii . ac pti . ItE

Š In Torp 7 Æftorp . v . car træ 7 ii . bou ad gld . Tra . vi . car.
Ibi . x . foch . 7 i . bord cū . iii . car 7 dim . Ibi un hō Gifleɓ.
hɼ . vi . foch . 7 v . bord cū . i . car . 7 e . i . ac pti.

Ɓ In Netelha . ii . bou træ ad gld . Inland ī Wilingeha.
In Stou . Vlf . iiii . toftæ cū faca 7 foca . In Scantone.

⓯ In APLEBI 7 Rifebi 7 Saleclif . hɓ Vlf . ii . car træ
ad gld . Tra . iiii . car . Ibi Roɓt hō Giflebti . hɼ . ii .
car . 7 x . uilt . 7 ii . bord cū . ii . car . Ibi pɓr 7 æccla.
7 xii . ac pti . T.R.E. uat . l . fot . m̂ . xl . Tailla . x . fot.

Ɓ In Roxebi . ii . bou træ ad gld . Tra . iii . bou . Ibi . i . uilts.
hɼ . ii . bou.

1 M. In SCAMPTON Ulfr Fenman had 6½ carucates of land taxable. Land
for 10 ploughs. Gilbert of Ghent has 4 ploughs in lordship;
16 villagers, 12 Freemen and 6 smallholders with 7 ploughs.
A church and a priest; 1 mill, 2s; meadow, 166 acres.
Value before 1066 £6; now £8. Exactions £4.

2 B. In RISEHOLME 1½ carucates taxable. Land for 1½ ploughs. An
outlier of Scampton. Kolsveinn, Gilbert's man, has 1 plough.
1 mill, 12d; meadow, 36 acres.

3 S. In BURTON 3 carucates of land taxable. Land for 2 ploughs.
11 Freemen and 9 smallholders with 3 ploughs.

4 S. In (Middle) 'CARLTON' 6 bovates of land taxable. Land for as
many oxen.
2 Freemen plough with 5 oxen.
Meadow, 4 acres.

5 M. In (Cherry) WILLINGHAM Ulfr had 14 bovates of land taxable.
Land for as many oxen. Gilbert has 2 ploughs.
12 villagers and 1 Freeman with 2 ploughs.
A church and a priest; 2 fisheries, 32d; meadow, 40 acres.
Value before 1066, 100s; now £4.

Jurisdiction of Scampton:
6 S. In BRATTLEBY and THORPE (le Fallows) 3 carucates of land taxable.
Land for 3 ploughs.
5 Freemen and 2 smallholders have 3 ploughs and 2 oxen and
meadow, 8 acres.

7 S. Also in THORPE (le Fallows) and AISTHORPE 5 carucates of land
and 2 bovates taxable. Land for 6 ploughs.
10 Freemen and 1 smallholder with 3½ ploughs.
One of Gilbert's men has
6 Freemen and 5 smallholders with 1 plough.
Meadow, 101 acres.

8 B. In NETTLEHAM 2 bovates of land taxable. *Inland* of (Cherry)
Willingham.

9 In STOW (St. Mary) Ulfr [had] 4 plots with full jurisdiction. In
Scampton.

10 M. In APPLEBY, RISBY and 'SAWCLIFFE' Ulfr had 2 carucates of land
taxable. Land for 4 ploughs. Robert, Gilbert's man, has 2 ploughs.
10 villagers and 2 smallholders with 2 ploughs.
A priest and a church; meadow, 12 acres.
Value before 1066, 50s; now 40[s]. Exactions 10s.

11 B. In ROXBY 2 bovates of land taxable. Land for 3 oxen.
1 villager has 2 oxen.

ᴍ Iɴ *WINTRINGEHĀ*.hᵬ Vlf.xɪɪ.caᷞ tre ad glᵭ.Tᷞa
totiᵭ caᷞ.Ibi Roᵬt hõ Gisleᵬti hᷠ.ɪɪɪɪ.eaᷞ in dñio.
7 xʟ.viʬ.7 v.socħ 7 x.borᵭ.cū.vɪɪ.caᷞ.Ibi pᵬr
7 æccla.7 ɪɪɪ.mot xxx.vɪɪ.sot 7 ɪɪɪɪ.deñ.7 ɪ.passagiū
xɪɪɪ.solid.7 sedes piscariæ.T.R.E.uat 7 m̃.x.liᵬ.Tailla.xʟ.s̃

ᴍ Iɴ *BERTONE*.hᵬ Vlf xɪɪɪ.caᷞ tre ad glᵭ.Tᷞa.xxvɪɪ.
caᷞ.Ibi hᷠ Gisleᵬt.vɪɪ.caᷞ in dñio.7 ʟxɪɪɪ.uiʬ 7 xvɪ.
borᵭ cū.ɪx.caᷞ.7 xʟ.ɪɪ.socħ 7 ʟxvɪɪ.borᵭ.cū.x.caᷞ.
Ibi æccla 7 pᵬr.7 ɪɪ.moliñ.xʟ.solid.7 ɪ.mercatū 7 passa
giū de.ɪɪɪɪ.liᵬ.

s̃ Iɴ *FEREBI*.ɪɪɪ.caᷞ tre ad glᵭ.ɪ.boᷣ miñ.7 vɪɪɪ.pars uni
boᷣ ad glᵭ.Soca de Bertone.Tᷞa:v.caᷞ 7 dimiᵭ.Ibi m̃
xxx.ɪɪɪɪ.socħ 7 xɪɪɪ.borᵭ cū.vɪɪɪ.caᷞ.7 ɪ.passagiū.ɪɪɪ.liᵬ.
7 ccx.aᷝs p̃ti.7 cclx aᷝs maresc.T.R.E.uat xxx.vɪɪɪ.liᵬ.
7 xvɪ.sot.m̃ xxx.liᵬ.Tailla.x.liᵬ.

✝Iɴ Sudtone.ɪɪ.boᷣ træ ad glᵭ.Tᷞa.ɪɪɪ.boᵬ.Ibi hᷠ Gisleᵬt gregē ouiū.

354 d

s̃ Iɴ Horchetou.ɪɪɪɪ.caᷞ tre ad glᵭ.Tᷞa.vɪɪ.caᷞ.Soca 7 Inlanᵭ
in Bertone.Ibi hᷠ Gisleᵬt.ɪ.caᷞ 7 dimiᵭ.7 vɪɪ.uiʬ.7 xx.
socħ.cū.vɪɪɪ.caᷞ 7 dimiᵭ.
Iɴ Langetone hᷠ Gisleᵬt.cxʟ.aᷝs siluæ past.

ᴍ Iɴ *BARDENAI*.hᵬ Vlf.ɪɪ.caᷞ tre ad glᵭ.Tᷞa.ɪɪɪ.caᷞ.
Ibi hᷠ Gisleᵬt.ɪ.caᷞ:7 xvɪ.uiʬ 7 v.borᵭ.7 vɪ.socħ
cū.ɪɪ.caᷞ.7 ɪ.mot.vɪɪɪ.solid.7 v.piscaᷞ.v.sot 7 ɪɪɪɪ.deñ.
7 xx.aᷝs p̃ti.7 q̃ngent aᷝ siluæ past.T.R.E.7 m̃.uat
xx.liᵬ.Tailla.xxx.liᵬ.

s̃ Iɴ Osgotebi Soca huj̃ ᴍ.ɪɪ.caᷞ tre ad glᵭ.Tᷞa.ɪɪɪ.caᷞ.
Ibi.xvɪ.socħ hñt.ɪɪɪ.caᷞ.7 ʟx.aᷝ p̃ti.7 ccxʟ.aᷝ siluæ
pastit p̃ loca.

12 M. In WINTERINGHAM Ulfr had 12 carucates of land taxable. Land for
as many ploughs. Robert, Gilbert's man, has 4 ploughs in lordship;
40 villagers, 5 Freemen and 10 smallholders with 7 ploughs.
A priest and a church; 3 mills, 37s 4d; 1 ferry, 13s; a site of
a fishery.
Value before 1066 and now £10. Exactions 40s.

13 M. In BARTON (upon Humber) Ulfr had 13 carucates of land taxable.
Land for 27 ploughs. Gilbert has 7 ploughs in lordship;
63 villagers and 16 smallholders with 9 ploughs.
42 Freemen and 67 smallholders with 10 ploughs.
A church and a priest; 2 mills, 40s; 1 market; a ferry at £4.

14 S. In (South) FERRIBY 3 carucates of land taxable, less 1 bovate, and
the eighth part of 1 bovate taxable. A jurisdiction of Barton
(upon Humber). Land for 5½ ploughs.
Now 34 Freemen and 13 smallholders with 8 ploughs.
1 ferry, £3; meadow, 210 acres; marsh, 260 acres.
Value before 1066 £38 16s; now £30. Exactions £10.

*24,21, added at the foot of col. 354c and directed by transposition signs to its correct place
in the text.*

21 In *SUDTONE* 2 bovates of land taxable. Land for 3 oxen. Gilbert
has a flock of sheep.

15 S. In HORKSTOW 4 carucates of land taxable. Land for 7 ploughs.   354 d
A jurisdiction and *inland* of Barton (upon Humber). Gilbert has
1½ ploughs.
7 villagers and 20 Freemen with 8½ ploughs.

16 In LANGTON (by Wragby) Gilbert has 140 acres of woodland
pasture.

17 M. In BARDNEY Ulfr had 2 carucates of land taxable. Land for 3
ploughs. Gilbert has 1 plough.
16 villagers, 5 smallholders and 6 Freemen with 2 ploughs.
1 mill, 8s; 5 fisheries, 5s 4d; meadow, 20 acres; woodland
pasture, 500 acres.
Value before 1066 and now £20. Exactions £30.

18 S. In 'OSGODBY', a jurisdiction of this manor, 2 carucates of land
taxable. Land for 3 ploughs.
16 Freemen have 3 ploughs.
Meadow, 60 acres; woodland, pasture in places, 240 acres.

ẞ In Sutreie . Inland in Wilingehā . II . bou træ ad glđ.
Ibi . III . uiłł . VI . boƀ arant . 7 I . piſcar . 7 IIII . ađ p̃ti . 7 xx
ađ ſiluæ paſtilis.

ꝳ In *BADEBVRG* . ħƀ . ħƀ Vlf XII . car træ ad glđ . Tra
x . car . Ibi ħ̃ Giſleƀt . v . car . 7 XXI . uiłł . 7 VI . borđ.
7 xx . ſocħ 7 XVI . borđ eoꝝ . Int om̃s . VII . car . 7 I . molin
VIII . ſolid . 7 CXL ađs ſiluæ paſtił . T.R.E . uał . x . liƀ.
✝ m̃ XII . liƀ . Tailla . III . liƀ . De hac tra . VI . car in SOCA.

ꝳ In *ELLINGETONE* ħƀ Vlf . x . car træ ad glđ . Tra x . car.
Ibi Egbert ħo Giſleƀti ħ̃ . IIII . car . 7 xxv . ſocħ . 7 VII.
uiłł 7 XIIII . borđ . cū . VI . car . 7 I . molin . XVI . ſolidoꝝ.
7 q̃t xx 7 x . ađ p̃ti . 7 CCX . ađ ſiluæ minutæ . T.R.E.
uał x . liƀ . m̃ XI . liƀ . Tailla . III . liƀ.

ẞ In Sanctone Inland in Riſebi . I . bou træ ad glđ . Waſta . ē.

ꝳ In *LVZEBI* . ħƀ Tonne . III . car træ ad glđ . Tra . IIII . car.
Ibi Wiłłs ħo Giſleƀti ħ̃ . v . car . 7 XVII . ſocħ 7 VIII . uiłł.
ħ̃tes . IX . car . Ibi æccła 7 pƀr . 7 I . molin . III . ſolid.
7 c q̃t xx . ađ p̃ti . T.R.E . uał . XIIII . liƀ . m̃ . x . liƀ . Tailla . c . ſolid.

ꝳ In *EDEHA* ħƀ Vlf . XII . car træ ad glđ . Tra . XII . car.
Ibi ħ̃ Giſleƀt . v . car . 7 XXXII . uiłł . 7 XXIIII . ſocħ.
7 IIII . borđ . cū . IX . car . 7 XXIX . ađs p̃ti . 7 CCCC . ađs ſiluæ
paſtił p̃ loca . T.R.E . uał x . liƀ . m̃ XVIII . liƀ . Tailla . VI . liƀ.

ẞ In Offran . BEREW . III . car træ 7 dim̃ ad glđ . Tra . v . car.
Ibi II . car in dñio . 7 v . uiłł cū . III . car . 7 q̃t xx . ađ p̃ti.
7 CXX . ađ ſiluæ minutæ.

ẞ In Bacſtune BER . II . car træ ad glđ . Tra . II . car . Ibi Iuo
ħo Giſleƀti ħ̃ dim̃ car . 7 VIII . ſocħ de . I . car huj tre.
7 IIII . uiłł 7 III . borđ . cū . II . car . 7 XL . ađs p̃ti . Valet . L . ſoł.

19 B. In SOUTHREY, *inland* of (Cherry) Willingham, 2 bovates of land taxable.
>3 villagers who plough with 6 oxen.
>1 fishery; meadow, 4 acres; woodland pasture, 20 acres.

20 M. In BAUMBER Ulfr had 12 carucates of land taxable. Land for 10 ploughs. Gilbert has 5 ploughs.
>21 villagers, 6 smallholders, 20 Freemen and their 16 smallholders; between them 7 ploughs.
>1 mill, 8s; woodland pasture, 140 acres.
>Value before 1066 £10; now £12. Exactions £3.
>Of this land 6 carucates in a jurisdiction.

24,21 is entered at the foot of col. 354c (after 24,14) and is directed by transposition signs to its correct place in the text.

22 M. In EDLINGTON Ulfr had 10 carucates of land taxable. Land for 10 ploughs. Ecbeorht, Gilbert's man, has 4 ploughs.
>25 Freemen, 7 villagers and 14 smallholders with 6 ploughs.
>1 mill, 16s; meadow, 90 acres; underwood, 210 acres.
>Value before 1066 £10; now £11. Exactions £3.

23 B. In SANTON, *inland* of Risby, 1 bovate of land taxable. It is waste.

24 M. In LUSBY Tonni had 3 carucates of land taxable. Land for 4 ploughs. William, Gilbert's man, has 5 ploughs.
>17 Freemen and 8 villagers who have 9 ploughs.
>A church and a priest; 1 mill, 3s; meadow, 180 acres.
>Value before 1066 £14; now £10. Exactions 100s.

25 M. In EDENHAM Ulfr had 12 carucates of land taxable. Land for 12 ploughs. Gilbert has 5 ploughs.
>32 villagers, 24 Freemen and 4 smallholders with 9 ploughs.
>Meadow, 29 acres; woodland, pasture in places, 400 acres.
>Value before 1066 £10; now £18. Exactions £6.

26 B. In *OFFRAN*, an outlier, 3½ carucates of land taxable. Land for 5 ploughs. 2 ploughs in lordship;
>5 villagers with 3 ploughs.
>Meadow, 80 acres; underwood, 120 acres.

27 B. In BASTON, an outlier, 2 carucates of land taxable. Land for 2 ploughs. Ivo, Gilbert's man, has ½ plough.
>8 Freemen on 1 carucate of this land; 4 villagers and 3 smallholders with 2 ploughs.
>Meadow, 40 acres.
>Value 50s.

§ In Griteford . II . bou tre ad glđ . Soca . Ibi . IIII . soch cū . I . car.

§ In Berchā . dim car træ ad glđ . Tra . IIII . bob . Soca in Edehā.
Ibi . IIII . soch arant . II . bob . 7 ualet . VIII . sot.

★ § In Braseborg 7 Barnetorpi . dimid car ad glđ . Tra . IIII . bou.

§ In Opetcrp . XIII . bou træ ad glđ . Tra totiđ bou . Ibi . XVII .
soch hūt . III . car . 7 XX . ac pti . 7 XX . ac siluæ past.

§ In Withā 7 Mannetcrp 7 Totf| Lund . VIII . car træ 7 tcia
pars uni car . Tra totiđ car . Ibi . XLV . soch 7 X . borđ
hūt . X . car . Ibi æccla . 7 XL . ac pti . 7 XL . ac siluæ pastit.
7 I . molin . XX . solid . De hac tra tenet Bereuuold . I . car
træ . 7 ibi hŧ . I . car . 7 I . mot . XII . solid . 7 II ; uitt . 7 IIII . borđ.
cū dim car . T.R.E . ual . XX . sot . m̄ . XL.

§ In Carlebi . XV . bou tre ad glđ . Ibi . VIII . soch 7 I . borđ
hūt . II . car . T.R.E . ual . XX . sot . m̄ similit . Tailla . VII . sot.
Hanc trā hŧ Iuo 7 Bereuuold sub eo . 7 ipse ibi dim car ⌐ car.

§ In Eftou . VI . bou træ 7 dim ad glđ . Ibi . V . soch hūt dim

§ In Berchā . dim car tre ad glđ . Tra . IIII . bob . Soca in Casuic.

ᄶ In CRANEWELLE . hŧ Vlf . XII . car træ ad glđ . Tra
totiđ car . Ibi Goisfrid hō Gistebti . hŧ . I . car in dñio.
7 XX.I . soch de . IX . car huj tre . 7 II . uitt 7 V . borđ
cū . VIII . car . 7 XXIX . acs pti . Tra arab . XXII . q̃ɀ lg.
7 VII . 7 dim lat . Pascua . X . q̃ɀ lg . 7 VII . 7 dim lat.
T.R.E . ual . c . sot . m̄ . VII . lib.

ᄶ In TORP . hŧ Tunne . III . car træ 7 III . bou ad glđ . Tra
IIII . car . Ibi hŧ Gistebt . V . car . 7 VIII . uitt . cū . II . car.
Ibi pbr 7 æccla . 7 CXX . ac pti . T.R.E . ual . XVIII . lib.
m̄ . XX.V . lib.

28 S. In GREATFORD 2 bovates of land taxable. A jurisdiction.
4 Freemen with 1 plough.

29 S. In BARHOLM ½ carucate of land taxable. Land for 4 oxen. A
jurisdiction of Edenham.
4 Freemen who plough with 2 oxen.
Value 8s.

30 S. In BRACEBOROUGH and 'BANTHORPE' ½ carucate taxable. Land for 4   355 a
oxen.

31 S. In OBTHORPE 13 bovates of land taxable. Land for as many oxen.
17 Freemen have 3 ploughs.
Meadow, 20 acres; woodland pasture, 20 acres.

32 S. In WITHAM (on the Hill), MANTHORPE, TOFT and LOUND 8 carucates
of land and the third part of 1 carucate. Land for as many ploughs.
45 Freemen and 10 smallholders have 10 ploughs.
A church; meadow, 40 acres; woodland pasture, 40 acres;
1 mill, 20s.
Of this land Berewold holds 1 carucate of land and has 1 plough.
1 mill, 12s.
2 villagers and 4 smallholders with ½ plough.
Value before 1066, 20s; now 40[s].

33 S. In CARLBY 15 bovates of land taxable.
8 Freemen and 1 smallholder have 2 ploughs.
Value before 1066, 20s; now the same. Exactions 7s.
Ivo has this land, and Berewold under him, and himself [has]
½ plough there.

34 S. In 'STOWE' 6½ bovates of land taxable.
5 Freemen have ½ plough.

35 S. In BARHOLM ½ carucate of land taxable. Land for 4 oxen.
A jurisdiction of Casewick.

36 M. In CRANWELL Ulfr had 12 carucates of land taxable. Land for as
many ploughs. Geoffrey, Gilbert's man, has 1 plough in lordship;
21 Freemen on 9 carucates of this land; 2 villagers and 5
smallholders with 8 ploughs.
Meadow, 29 acres; arable land 22 furlongs long and 7½ wide;
pastureland 10 furlongs long and 7½ wide.
Value before 1066, 100s; now £7.

37 M. In (Culver)THORPE Tonni had 3 carucates of land and 3 bovates
taxable. Land for 4 ploughs. Gilbert has 5 ploughs.
8 villagers with 2 ploughs.
A priest and a church; meadow, 120 acres.
Value before 1066 £18; now £25.

★ §̃ In Ouſtorp 7 Lereſbi . iii . car̃ træ ad glð . Tra . ii . car̃ . Ibi . ix
   ſoch 7 ix . borð hñt . iiii . car̃ . Ibi æcc̃la 7 p̃br . 7 xx.iiii . ac̃
   p̃ti . 7 xx . ac̃ ſiluæ minutæ.

§̃ In Huuelle . i . car̃ 7 dim̃ boũ . Tra . i . car̃ . Ibi . iii . ſoch hñt
   . i . car̃ 7 ii . boũ arant . 7 viii . ac̃s p̃ti.

B §̃ In Hechintune Inland 7 Soca . viii . car̃ træ ad glð . Tra
7 §̃ totid car̃ . Ibi hñ in dñio Giſlebt . ii . car̃ . 7 xx.ii . ſoch.
   7 vii . uill 7 xv . borð cũ . viii . car̃ . Ihi p̃r
   7 æcc̃la . 7 c . ac̃ p̃ti . 7 iii . piſcar̃ . v . ſolid . 7 . iiii . denar̃.

§̃ In Hale . viii . car̃ 7 dim̃ ad glð . Tra . x . car̃ . Ibi . xxx.
   viii . ſoch hñt . xii . car̃ . Ibi hñ Radulf hõ Giſlebti
   . iii . car̃ in dñio . Soca   ſ Grethã . 7 x . ac̃ p̃ti.

§̃ In Habdinghã . vi . boũ træ ad glð . Tra . x . boũ . Soca in
B Ibið . i . car̃ træ ad glð . Tra . xii . boũ . Berĕ in Luzebi.
   Ibi in dñio . i . car̃ . 7 i . uill 7 i . borð cũ uno boue araŋs.
   7 xx . ac̃ p̃ti . 7 i . molin̄ xii . den.

§̃ Ibið . i . car̃ træ ad glð . Tra . ii . car̃ . Soca in Luzebi.
   Ibi . ii . borð . cũ . i . boue . 7 xxx . ac̃ p̃ti.

355 b   Soca in Bardenai.

§̃ In Partone . Soca . v . car̃ træ ad glð . Tra totid car̃.
   Ibi hñ Giſlebt . xvii . ſoch . 7 xxvii . borð . cũ . v . car̃.
   Ibi . ē mercatũ . x . ſolid . 7 c . ac̃ p̃ti.

§̃ In Scheueldebi . vi . car̃ tre ad glð . Tra . vi . car̃ . Ibi hñ
   Giſlebt . iii . car̃ in dñio . 7 æcc̃lam . 7 ii . molin xiii . ſolid.
   7 xl . ac̃s p̃ti . Ibi inuenit xxviii . ſoch . 7 ix . borð . cũ . ix . car̃.

§̃ In Screnbi . iiii . car̃ træ 7 dim̃ ad glð . Tra . iiii . car̃ . Ibi
   xv . ſoch 7 viii . borð cũ . v . car̃ . 7 c . ac̃ p̃ti . 7 una æcc̃la.

Jurisdiction of this manor:

38 S. In EAST THORPE and EWERBY 3 carucates of land taxable. Land
for 2 ploughs.
9 Freemen and 9 smallholders have 4 ploughs.
A church and a priest; meadow, 24 acres; underwood, 20 acres.

39 S. In HOWELL 1 carucate and ½ bovate. Land for 1 plough.
3 Freemen have 1 plough and 2 ploughing oxen and
meadow, 8 acres.

40 B. In HECKINGTON *inland*, 3 carucates, and a jurisdiction, 5 carucates:
& S. 8 carucates of land taxable. Land for as many ploughs. Gilbert
has in lordship 2 ploughs;
22 Freemen, 7 villagers and 15 smallholders with 8 ploughs.
A priest and a church; meadow, 100 acres; 3 fisheries, 5s 4d.

41 S. In HALE 8½ carucates taxable. Land for 10 ploughs.
38 Freemen have 12 ploughs.
Ralph, Gilbert's man, has 3 ploughs in lordship.
A jurisdiction.

42 S. In HAGWORTHINGHAM 6 bovates of land taxable. Land for 10 oxen.
A jurisdiction of Greetham.
Meadow, 10 acres.

43 B. There also 1 carucate of land taxable. Land for 12 oxen. An
outlier of Lusby. In lordship 1 plough;
1 villager and 1 smallholder who ploughs(?) with 1 ox.
Meadow, 20 acres; 1 mill, 12d.

44 S. There also 1 carucate of land taxable. Land for 2 ploughs. A
jurisdiction of Lusby.
2 smallholders with 1 ox.
Meadow, 30 acres.

Jurisdiction of Bardney: 355 b

45 S. In PARTNEY, a jurisdiction, 5 carucates of land taxable. Land for
as many ploughs. Gilbert has
17 Freemen and 27 smallholders with 5 ploughs.
A market, 10s; meadow, 100 acres.

46 S. In SKENDLEBY 6 carucates of land taxable. Land for 6 ploughs.
Gilbert has 3 ploughs in lordship and
a church; 2 mills, 13s; meadow, 40 acres. He found there
28 Freemen and 9 smallholders with 9 ploughs.

47 S. In SCREMBY 4½ carucates of land taxable. Land for 4 ploughs.
15 Freemen and 8 smallholders with 5 ploughs.
Meadow, 100 acres; 1 church.

§ In Stepinge . xi . car̄ træ 7 dim̄ ad gld̄ . T̄ra totid car̄.

Ibi . lxi . socħ . 7 xi . bord̄ . hn̄t . x ː car̄ . 7 ii ː æcclas . 7 q̄t xx . ac̄

§ In Calnodesbi . i . car̄ tre ad gld̄ . T̄ra . i . car̄. ⨍ p̄ti.

Ibi . xiii . socħi . 7 vi . bord̄ . hn̄t . ii . car̄.

§ In Burg . viii . car̄ tre ad gld̄ . T̄ra . viii . car̄ . Ibi . xx . i.

socħ . 7 xi . uiłł . 7 iii . bord̄ . hn̄t vi . car̄ . 7 i . æccła . 7 d . ac̄ p̄ti.

§ In Herdetorp . iiii . car̄ tre 7 ii . bou ad gld̄ . T̄ra totid car̄.

Ibi . xviii . socħ 7 xvii ː uiłł . hn̄t ː iiii . car̄ . 7 xl . ac̄ . p̄ti. .cccc

B̄ In Wemflet . i . bou træ ad gld̄ . Wasta . ē . Inland . est.

§ In Haberdingħā . ħt Gozelin fili Lanbti unā æcclam ː

ː7 dim̄ car̄ træ . ad gld̄ ː unde Gislebt ħt socā. de gand 9

Ꝏ In *WILGEBI* . ħb Tunne . ii . car̄ træ ad gld̄ . T̄ra . iiii . car̄.

Ibi Roger ħō Gislebti ħt . ii . car̄ . Ibi . iiii . socħ de dim̄

car̄ træ hn̄t . ii . car̄ . 7 xl . ac̄s p̄ti ː 7 xl . ac̄s matefc . 7 cxx.

ac̄ filuæ past . 7 lx . ac̄ filuæ minutæ ː T.R.E . uał . iiii . lib.

B̄ In Mundebi . BEREW . ii . bou træ ad gld̄ .   ⨍ m̄ . viii . lib.

T̄ra . iii . bob . Ibi ħt . Gislebt . i . uiłł cū uno boue arans.

★ B̄ Ibidē BER . ii . bou træ ad gld̄ . T̄ra . vi . bob . Ibi . vi . uiłł.

7 viii . bord̄ . cū . i . car̄ . 7 xxx . ac̄ p̄ti . Dn̄s q̄t xx . ac̄s p̄ti. ti

B̄ In Haroldestorp . i . car̄ tre ad gld̄ . T̄ra . ii . car̄ . Ibi . iiii.

socħ de dimid car̄ træ . 7 ii . uiłł 7 ii . bord̄ . cū ˌ vi . bob arañ.

Ibi Roḡ ħt . i . car̄ . 7 xxx . ac̄ marefch.

B̄ In Slodebi . iii . bou træ ad gld̄ . T̄ra . vi ˌ bob . Ibi ħt Roḡ

. ii . uiłł . iii . bobȝ arantes . 7 x . ac̄s marefch.

B̄ In Wilgebi . iii . bou træ cū faca 7 foca . ad gld̄ . T̄ra . v . bcb.

Ibi . ē una æccła ħn̄s dimid car̄ ː T.R.E . xx . fot . m̄ . x . fot. Υ

48 S. In (Great) STEEPING 11½ carucates of land taxable. Land for as many ploughs.
    61 Freemen and 11 smallholders have 10 ploughs and 2 churches; meadow, 80 acres.

49 S. In CANDLESBY 1 carucate of land taxable. Land for 1 plough.
    13 Freemen and 6 smallholders have 2 ploughs.

50 S. In BURGH (le Marsh) 8 carucates of land taxable. Land for 8 ploughs.
    21 Freemen, 11 villagers and 3 smallholders have 6 ploughs.
    1 church; meadow, 500 acres.

51 S. In ADDLETHORPE 4 carucates of land and 2 bovates taxable. Land for as many ploughs.
    18 Freemen and 17 villagers have 4 ploughs.
    Meadow, 440 acres.

52 B. In WAINFLEET 1 bovate of land taxable. It is waste. It is *inland*.

53 S. In HAGWORTHINGHAM Jocelyn son of Lambert has 1 church and ½ carucate of land taxable over which Gilbert of Ghent has jurisdiction.

54 M. In WILLOUGHBY Tonni had 2 carucates of land taxable. Land for 4 ploughs. Roger, Gilbert's man, has 2 ploughs.
    4 Freemen on ½ carucate of land have 2 ploughs and
    meadow, 40 acres; marsh, 40 acres; woodland pasture, 120 acres; underwood, 60 acres.
    Value before 1066 £4; now £8.

55 B. In MUMBY, an outlier, 2 bovates of land taxable. Land for 3 oxen. Gilbert has
    1 villager who ploughs with 1 ox.

56 B. There also, an outlier, 4 bovates of land taxable. Land for 6 oxen.
    6 villagers and 8 smallholders with 1 plough.
    Meadow, 30 acres. The lord [has] 80 acres of meadow.

57 B. In HASTHORPE 1 carucate of land taxable. Land for 2 ploughs.
    4 Freemen on ½ carucate of land; 2 villagers and 2 smallholders plough with 6 oxen.
    Roger has 1 plough.
    Marsh, 30 acres.

58 B. In SLOOTHBY 3 bovates of land taxable. Land for 6 oxen. Roger has 2 villagers who plough with 3 oxen; and
    marsh, 10 acres.

59 B. In WILLOUGHBY 3 bovates of land with full jurisdiction, taxable. Land for 5 oxen.
    1 church which has ½ carucate.
    Value before 1066, 20s; now 10s.

24,60 is added at the foot of col. 355b (in the middle of 24,62) and is directed by transposition signs to its correct place in the text.

ⓜ In *CLACHESBI* . h̄b Tonne . vi . boū trǽ ad glđ . Tra . xii .
boū . Ibi Rademer h̄o Gifleḃti h̄t . ii . car . 7 vi . uill
cū . i . car . Ibi filuæ minutæ fexcentæ 7 lx . acræ .
T.R.E . 7 m̄ ual . viii . liḃ .
In eađ uilla h̄t Gifleḃt q̄ter . xx . ac̄s filuæ minutæ .
7 alias . cxx . ac̄s filuæ minutæ . De tribʒ partibʒ har̄ ac̄rū .
h̄t Wido de credun focam .
Ḃ In Slodebi . Inland de Clachefbi . dim car̄ træ ad glđ .

Ⲩ In Waletune 7 Bodebi . i . car̄ trǽ ad glđ . Tra . i . car̄ . Soca i Wilgebi .

355 c

Tra . i . carucæ . Ibi . vi . uill 7 i . borđ cū . i . car̄ . 7 lx . ac̄ p̄ti .
Ṣ In Befebi Soca . iii . car̄ træ ad glđ . Tra totiđ car̄ . Ibi .
xx . fock 7 viii . borđ h̄nt . v . car̄ 7 dim 7 q̄t xx 7 x . ac̄
p̄ti . 7 clxxx . ac̄ filuæ minutæ .
Ṣ In Maltefbi . ii . car̄ træ 7 vi . boū ad glđ . Tra . iii . car̄ .
Ibi xiiii . fock h̄nt . ii . car̄ . 7 lx . ac̄s p̄ti . 7 v . ac̄s filuæ min .
Ḃ In Salebi dim car̄ træ ad glđ . Tra . iiii . bob . Ibi . ii . uill
uno boue arantes . 7 x . ac̄ p̄ti . 7 xxx . ac̄ filuæ minutæ .
Ṣ In Widerne . iii . car̄ træ 7 dim ad glđ . Tra . iiii . car̄ . Ibi h̄o
Gifleḃti Rauemer h̄t . ii . car̄ . 7 xx . fock 7 xiii . uill cu . iii .
car̄ . 7 i . molin̄ . xv . folid . 7 c q̄t xx . ac̄s p̄ti . Ibi pḃr 7 æccla . [Soca . e . H . F . baldri .]
Ṣ In Strobi . ii . boū 7 dim ad glđ . Tra . v . boū . Ibi . ii . uill h̄nt
dim car̄ . 7 x . ac̄s p̄ti .
ⓜ In *WELLE* . h̄b Tonne . i . car̄ træ ad glđ . Tra . iii . car̄ .
Ibi Rauemer h̄o Gifleḃti h̄t . ii . car̄ . 7 iiii . foch đe . ii .
boū huj tre . 7 xii . uill cū . i . car̄ . 7 i . molin̄ . xv . folid .
7 i . ac̄ p̄ti 7 dimiđ . 7 xxii . ac̄ filuæ . T.R.E . ual viii . liḃ . m̄ . vii . lḃ .

61 M. In CLAXBY Tonni had 6 bovates of land taxable. Land for 12
oxen. Rademer, Gilbert's man, has 2 ploughs.
6 villagers with 1 plough.
Underwood, 660 acres.
Value before 1066 and now, £8.
Also in the village Gilbert has 80 acres of underwood, and
another 120 acres of underwood. Of three parts of these acres
Guy of Craon has the jurisdiction.

62 B. In SLOOTHBY, *inland* of Claxby, ½ carucate of land taxable.
24,62 *continues after* 24,60

24,60, *directed by transposition signs to its correct place.*
60 In WELTON (le Marsh) and BOOTHBY 1 carucate of land taxable.
Land for 1 plough. A jurisdiction of Willoughby.

24,62 continued
(62) Land for 1 plough. 355 c
6 villagers and 1 smallholder with 1 plough.
Meadow, 60 acres.

63 S. In BEESBY, a jurisdiction, 3 carucates of land taxable. Land for as
many ploughs.
20 Freemen and 8 smallholders have 5½ ploughs.
Meadow, 90 acres; underwood, 180 acres.

64 S. In MALTBY (le Marsh) 2 carucates of land and 6 bovates taxable.
Land for 3 ploughs.
14 Freemen have 2 ploughs and
meadow, 60 acres; underwood, 5 acres.

65 B. In SALEBY ½ carucate of land taxable. Land for 4 oxen.
2 villagers who plough with 1 ox.
Meadow, 10 acres; underwood, 30 acres.

66 S. In WITHERN 3½ carucates of land taxable. Land for 4 ploughs.
Gilbert's man, Ravemer, has 2 ploughs.
20 Freemen and 13 villagers with 3 ploughs.
1 mill, 15s; meadow, 180 acres. A priest and a church.
The jurisdiction is H(ugh) son of Baldric's.

67 S. In STRUBBY 2½ bovates taxable. Land for 5 oxen.
2 villagers have ½ plough and
meadow, 10 acres.

68 M. In WELL Tonni had 1 carucate of land taxable. Land for 3 ploughs.
Ravemer, Gilbert's man, has 2 ploughs.
4 Freemen on 2 bovates of this land; 12 villagers with 1 plough.
1 mill, 15s; meadow, 1½ acres; woodland, 22 acres.
Value before 1066 £8; now £7.

Ŝ In Vleſbi.ii.bou̅ tre ad gł̄d Tra.iiii.bou̅.Ibi.i.ſocħ cū.i.car̄.

Ŝ In Alforde.vi.bou̅ tre 7 dim̄ ad gł̄d.Tra xii.bou̅.Ibi
ii.ſocħ 7 iii.uiłł 7 i.borđ.cū.i.car̄.7 x.ac̄ p̄ti.

Ḃ In Maltetorp.dim̄ car̄ træ ad gł̄d.Tra.i.car̄.Ibi.iiii.
uiłł hn̄t.i.car̄.7 xx.ac̄s p̄ti.

ⒸⒽ In _ASCHEBI_.ħ̄b Siuuard.i.car̄ 7 dim̄ ad gł̄d.Tra.ii.car̄.
Ibi Roger hō Giſłebti ħ̄.ii.car̄.7 v.uiłł 7 v.borđ.cū
dim̄.car̄.7 c.ac̄s p̄ti.7 vi.ac̄s ſiluæ minutæ.T.R.E.uał
xxx.ſoł.m̄.xl.Tailla.iii.ſoliđ.

ⒸⒽ In _DRIBI_.ħ̄b Siuuard.v.car̄ træ 7 dim̄ ad gł̄d.Tra
v.car̄.Ibi Iuo hō Giſłebti ħ̄ in dn̄io.iiii.car̄.7 vii.
ſocħ de.ii.car̄ tre.7 iii.uiłł 7 v.borđ.iii.car̄.7 i.moł
xii.den̄.7 lx.ac̄s p̄ti.T.R.E.uał.vi.lib̄.m̄.c.ſoł.Tailla.

ⒸⒽ In _CROFT_.ħ̄b Odincarl.ii.car̄ træ 7 ii.bou̅ ⌐xx.ſoł.
ad gł̄d.Tra.ii.car̄ 7 ii.bou̅.Ibi Radułł hō Giſłebti
ħ̄.ii.car̄.7 ix.ſocħ.7 iii.uiłł 7 iii.borđ cū.iii.car̄.7 i.
ſalina.vi.den̄.7 cxx.ac̄ p̄ti.T.R.E.uał xx.ſoł.m̄.iiii.lib̄.

Ḃ In Wemflet _BEREW_.ii.bou̅ træ ad gł̄d.Ibi.vi.uiłł cum
ii.bob̄.7 vi.ſalinæ.iii.ſoliđ.

ⒸⒽ In _CHIME_.ħ̄b Tunne.xiiii.bou̅ træ ad gł̄d.Tra.i.car̄ 7 dim̄.
Ibi Egbriħt hō Giſłebti ħ̄ dim̄ car̄.7 vi.uiłł cū dim̄ car̄.
7 i.ac̄ p̄ti.7 q̄t xx 7 ii.ac̄s ſiluæ min̄.7 iii.piſcar̄.ii.ſoliđ.
T.R.E.uał.xx.ſoł.m̄.xl.

In Mortun 7 Hermodeſtorp.ii.car̄ træ 7 dim̄.7 iiii.part uni
car̄.7 iiii.part.i.bouatæ.ad gł̄d.Tra totiđ c 7 b.SocA in Edeħa.

355 d
Ibi fuer̄.xiiii.ſocħ 7 v.borđ.cū.iii.car̄.Ibi ſunt.xl.v.
ac̄ p̄ti.7 xl.ac̄ ſiluæ past.

69 S. In ULCEBY 2 bovates of land taxable. Land for 4 oxen.
    1 Freeman with 1 plough.

70 S. In ALFORD 6½ bovates of land taxable. Land for 12 oxen.
    2 Freemen, 3 villagers and 1 smallholder with 1 plough.
    Meadow, 10 acres.

71 B. In MABLETHORPE ½ carucate of land taxable. Land for 1 plough.
    4 villagers have 1 plough and
    meadow, 20 acres.

72 M. In (West) ASHBY Siward had 1½ carucates taxable. Land for 2
ploughs. Roger, Gilbert's man, has 2 ploughs.
    5 villagers and 5 smallholders with ½ plough.
    Meadow, 100 acres; underwood, 6 acres.
Value before 1066, 30s; now 40[s]. Exactions 3s.

73 M. In DRIBY Siward had 5½ carucates of land taxable. Land for 5
ploughs. Ivo, Gilbert's man, has in lordship 4 ploughs;
    7 Freemen on 2 carucates of land; 3 villagers and 5 smallholders
      [with] 3 ploughs.
    1 mill, 12d; meadow, 60 acres.
Value before 1066 £6; now 100s. Exactions 20s.

74 M. In CROFT Othenkarl had 2 carucates of land and 2 bovates taxable.
Land for 2 ploughs and 2 oxen. Ralph, Gilbert's man, has 2 ploughs.
    9 Freemen, 3 villagers and 3 smallholders with 3 ploughs.
    1 salt-house, 6d; meadow, 120 acres.
Value before 1066, 20s; now £4.

75 B. In WAINFLEET, an outlier, 2 bovates of land taxable.
    6 villagers with 2 oxen.
    6 salt-houses, 3s.

76 M. In (South) KYME Tonni had 14 bovates of land taxable. Land for
1½ ploughs. Ecbeorht, Gilbert's man, has ½ plough.
    6 villagers with ½ plough.
    Meadow, 1 acre; underwood, 82 acres; 3 fisheries, 2s.
Value before 1066, 20s; now 40[s].

77   In MORTON and HANTHORPE 2½ carucates of land, the fourth part
of 1 carucate and the fourth part of 1 bovate taxable. Land for as
many ploughs and oxen. A jurisdiction of Edenham.
    There were 14 Freemen and 5 smallholders with 3 ploughs.   355 d
    There are
    meadow, 45 acres; woodland pasture, 40 acres.

r ⊕ In HOLM . ħƀ Vlf . xii . car̄ træ in dn̄io . 7 xii . car̄ træ soca
ad glđ . Tra totiđ car̄ . Ibi ħ Gisleƀt . iiii . car̄ in dn̄io .
7 xxviii . soch . 7 xxviii . uilt . 7 iii . borđ . hn̄tes xiiii . car̄ .
Ibi . ii . pƀri 7 ii . æcclæ . 7 i . molin̄ . xiii . sot 7 iiii . den̄ . T.R.E.
ual . x . liƀ . m̄ simit . Tailla . iii . liƀ .
In Wilgebi ħ Gisleƀt . iiii . parte æcclæ . soca in Wardebi .

⊕ In BVRGELAI . ħƀ Vlf . ii . car̄ tre ad glđ . Tra . vii . car̄ .
Ibi ħ Goisfriđ ħo Gisleƀti . ii . car̄ . 7 xxx . uilt . 7 vii .
borđ . cū . iiii . car̄ . 7 xxx . ac̄ pti . Siluæ . i . leu lḡ . 7 iii . q̃ƶ
lat̄ . T.R.E . ual . iiii . liƀ . m̄ c . sot .

⊕ In BODEBI . ħƀ Siuuate . v . car̄ træ ad glđ . Tra . v . car̄
Ibi Roger ħo Gisleƀti ħ . i . car̄ in dn̄io . 7 iiii . uilt . 7 ii .
borđ 7 xii . soch de . iii . car̄ huj̄ tre . hn̄tes . iii . car̄ .
Ibi æccła . 7 vi . ac̄ pti . 7 xl . ac̄ siluæ past . 7 lx . ac̄ siluæ
minutæ . T.R.E . ual . lx . sot . m̄ similit . De . iii . bouatis
7 dimidia huj̄ træ . redđ Wido de Credun soca .

⊕ In FOLCHINGEHA . ħƀ Vlf . xii . car̄ træ ad glđ .
Tra totiđ car̄ . Ibi ħ Gisleƀt in dn̄io . v . car̄ . 7 xxiiii .
uilt 7 v . soch 7 ix . borđ cū . vii . car̄ . Ibi æccła . 7 i . molin̄
x . solid . 7 viii . den̄ . 7 c . ac̄ pti . 7 q̃t xx . ac̄ siluæ min̄ .
T.R.E . ual . l . liƀ . m̄ xl . liƀ . Tailla . l . liƀ .

ƀ In Craneuuelle Inland huj̄ ⊕ . i . car̄ træ 7 dim ad glđ .
De hac tra ħƀ Azor soca . Ibi Goisfriđ ħo Gisleƀti ħ vi . uilt
7 i . borđ . cū . i . car̄ . 7 xvii . ac̄s pti 7 dim . T.R.E . xx . sot . m̄ x .
SOCA HVJ̄ MAN .

S In Hondintone . iii . car̄ tre ad glđ . Tra . iii . car̄ . Ibi Fulbt
ħo Gisleƀti ħ . xii . soch 7 i . borđ . cū . iii . car̄ . 7 xxx . v . ac̄s

S In Asedebi . v . car̄ tre ad glđ . Tra . vii . car̄ . ⌐ pti . lx . s .
Ibi . xviii . soch 7 iii . borđ hn̄t . vi . car̄ . 7 xl . ac̄s pti . 7 xxx .
ac̄s siluæ min̄ .

ɪ 78 M. In 'HOLME' Ulfr had 12 carucates of land in lordship and 12 carucates of land, a jurisdiction, taxable. Land for as many ploughs. Gilbert has 4 ploughs in lordship;
28 Freemen, 28 villagers and 3 smallholders who have 14 ploughs.
2 priests and 2 churches; 1 mill, 13s 4d.
Value before 1066 £10; now the same. Exactions £3.

79 In (Scott) WILLOUGHBY Gilbert has the fourth part of a church, a jurisdiction of Aswarby.

80 M. In BURLEY Ulfr had 2 carucates of land taxable. Land for 7 ploughs. Geoffrey, Gilbert's man, has 2 ploughs.
30 villagers and 7 smallholders with 4 ploughs.
Meadow, 30 acres; woodland 1 league long and 3 furlongs wide.
Value before 1066 £4; now 100s.

81 M. In BOOTHBY (Pagnell) Sighvatr had 5 carucates of land taxable. Land for 5 ploughs. Roger, Gilbert's man, has 1 plough in lordship;
4 villagers, 2 smallholders and 12 Freemen on 3 carucates of this land who have 3 ploughs.
A church; meadow, 6 acres; woodland pasture, 40 acres; underwood, 60 acres.
Value before 1066, 60s; now the same.
From 3½ bovates of this land Guy of Craon pays jurisdiction.

82 M. In FOLKINGHAM Ulfr had 12 carucates of land taxable. Land for as many ploughs. Gilbert has in lordship 5 ploughs;
24 villagers, 5 Freemen and 9 smallholders with 7 ploughs.
A church; 1 mill, 10s 8d; meadow, 100 acres; underwood, 80 acres.
Value before 1066 £50; now £40. Exactions £50.

83 B. In CRANWELL, *inland* of this manor, 1½ carucates of land taxable. Of this land Atsurr had the jurisdiction. Geoffrey, Gilbert's man, has
6 villagers and 1 smallholder with 1 plough; and meadow, 17½ acres.
Value before 1066, 20s; now 10[s].

Jurisdiction of this manor:

84 S. In HONINGTON 3 carucates of land taxable. Land for 3 ploughs. Fulbert, Gilbert's man, has
12 Freemen and 1 smallholder with 3 ploughs; and meadow, 35 acres.
[Value] 60s.

85 S. In OASBY 5 carucates of land taxable. Land for 7 ploughs.
18 Freemen and 3 smallholders have 6 ploughs and meadow, 40 acres; underwood, 30 acres.

ş In Lauintone. IIII. car̄ træ ad glđ. 7 III. pars. I. car̄. Tra. v. c̄
ad glđ. Ibi hŧ Azelin hõ Gisleḃti. II. car̄ in dñio. 7 x. uilt
7 III. borđ. cū. III. car̄. 7 xxx. ac̄s p̄ti. Valet. c. fol.

ş In Picheuuorde. II. car̄ træ 7 dim boū ad glđ. Tra. II. car̄
7 dim. Ibi Gist hŧ xxi. foch cū. IIII. car̄. 7 xvi. ac̄s p̄ti.
7 L. ac̄s filuæ minutæ. 7 xx. ac̄s filuæ paſt.

ş In Hazebi. I. car̄ tre ad glđ. Tra. xii. boū. Ibi xiii. foch
7 v. borđ hñt. III. car̄. 7 v. ac̄s p̄ti.

ş In Denbelbi. I. car̄ træ ad glđ. Tra. xii. boū. Ibi. xx. foch
7 III. borđ hñt. III. car̄. 7 xviii. ac̄s p̄ti. 7 xii. ac̄s filuæ min.

ş In Esḃnebi. IIII. car̄ tre ad glđ. Tra. v. car̄ 7 dimiđ.

Ibi xvi. foch 7 viii. borđ hñt viii. car̄. 7 I. æccła ibi. ē.

§ In Trichingehā. I. car̄ tre ad glđ. Tra. I. car̄. Ibi. ē forū
reddeſ xL. fol. 7 xi. foch 7 viii. borđ.

ş In Stou. v. car̄ træ 7 dim ad glđ. Tra totiđ car̄. Ibi Roḃt
hõ Gisleḃti hŧ xxi. foch 7 xiiii. borđ hñtes. v. car̄.
Ibi. I. car̄ in dñio. 7 I. æccła. 7 xvi. ac̄ p̄ti. p̄ciū. c. folid.

ş In Walecote. IIII. car̄ træ ad glđ. Tra. v. car̄. Ibi xxii. foch
7 IIII. borđ 7 dim æccła. 7 xx. vi. ac̄ p̄ti.

§ In Bellingeburg hŧ Gisleḃt foca fup dim caruc træ.

§ In Berchetorp. xv. boū tre ad glđ. Tra. II. car̄. Ibi. viii.
foch 7 viii. borđ hñt. III. car̄. 7 xxvii. ac̄s p̄ti.

ş In Loctone. IIII. car̄ træ ad glđ. Tra. IIII. car̄. Ibi. xiiii.
foch 7 IIII. borđ. hñt. III. car̄ 7 dim. 7 IX. ac̄s p̄ti. 7 XIII. ac̄s
£ filuæ min.

86 S. In (Little) ʻLAVINGTON' 4 carucates of land taxable and the third part of 1 carucate taxable. Land for 5 ploughs. Azelin, Gilbert's man, has 2 ploughs in lordship;
>10 villagers and 3 smallholders with 3 ploughs.
>Meadow, 30 acres.

Value 100s.

87 S. In PICKWORTH 2 carucates of land and ½ bovate taxable. Land for 2½ ploughs. Gilbert has
>21 Freemen with 4 ploughs; and
>meadow, 16 acres; underwood, 50 acres; woodland pasture, 20 acres.

88 S. In HACEBY 1 carucate of land taxable. Land for 12 oxen.
>13 Freemen and 5 smallholders have 3 ploughs and meadow, 5 acres.

89 S. In DEMBLEBY 1 carucate of land taxable. Land for 12 oxen.
>20 Freemen and 3 smallholders have 3 ploughs and meadow, 18 acres; underwood, 12 acres.

90 S. In OSBOURNBY 4 carucates of land taxable. Land for 5½ ploughs.
>16 Freemen and 8 smallholders have 8 ploughs.   356 a
>1 church is there.

91 S. In THREEKINGHAM 1 carucate of land taxable. Land for 1 plough.
>A market-place which pays 40s.
>11 Freemen and 8 smallholders.

92 S. In ʻSTOW' 5½ carucates of land taxable. Land for as many ploughs. Robert, Gilbert's man, has
>21 Freemen and 14 smallholders who have 5 ploughs.
>1 plough in lordship.
>1 church; meadow, 16 acres.

Assessment, 100s.

93 S. In WALCOT 4 carucates of land taxable. Land for 5 ploughs.
>22 Freemen and 4 smallholders.
>½ church; meadow, 26 acres.

94 S. In BILLINGBOROUGH Gilbert has jurisdiction over ½ carucate of land.

95 S. In BIRTHORPE 15 bovates of land taxable. Land for 2 ploughs.
>8 Freemen and 8 smallholders have 3 ploughs and meadow, 27 acres.

96 S. In LAUGHTON 4 carucates of land taxable. Land for 4 ploughs.
>14 Freemen and 4 smallholders have 3½ ploughs and meadow, 9 acres; underwood, 13 acres.

§ In Aslachebi 7 Spingeha . iii . car̃ tre
  7 ii . boũ ad gld̃ . Tra . iii . car̃ 7 dim̃ . Ibi . xiii . focħ
  7 i . bord̃ hñtes . iii . car̃ . 7 dim̃ æccla 7 vi . pars alteri æcclæ
  7 xxiiii . ac̃s p̃ti . 7 xl . ac̃ filuæ minutæ.

§ In Pochinton . ii . car̃ træ 7 ii . boũ ad gld̃ . Tra totid c 7 b.
  Ibi . xvi . focħ hñt . vi . car̃ . 7 xxx . ii . ac̃ p̃·i . 7 xl . ac̃ filuæ

§ In Goldefbi . iii . car̃ tre 7 i . boũ ad gld̃ . Tra . iii . car̃ .
  Ibi xvii . focħ 7 ii . bord̃ hñt . v . car̃ . 7 xx . v . ac̃s p̃ti .
  7 c . ac̃s filuæ miñ.

§ In Hag 7 Brandune . iii . car̃ træ 7 iii . boũ ad gld̃ . Tra . v .
  car̃ . Ibi . xiii . focħ hñt . vi . car̃ . 7 vi . ac̃s p̃ti . Hoc totũ
  tenet Derinc de Giflebto . 7 ħt ibi dim̃ car in dñio . Valet . xl . s.

§ In Chirchebi . vii . car̃ træ ad gld̃ . Tra . v . car̃ . Ibi xxx . i .
  focħ . 7 vi . bord̃ . hñt . vi . car̃ .

§ In Wilgebi . v . car̃ træ ad gld̃ . Tra . x . car̃ . Ibi . xx . ix . focħ
  7 i . bord̃ hñt . vi . car̃ . Ibi p̃br 7 æccla . 7 cxl . ac̃ p̃ti . 7 xx

§ In Afuuardebi . iiii . car̃ træ 7 dim̃ . 7 i . boũ ad gld̃ . ∫ iiii . ac̃ p̃ti .
  Tra . ix . car̃ . Ibi . xl . i . focħ 7 iii . bord̃ hñt xviii . car̃ .
  Ibi p̃br 7 æccla . 7 ii . partes uni æcclæ . 7 c qt xx ac̃ p̃ti .
  De hac tra ħt Radulf p̃br . iii . car̃ 7 dim̃ . 7 Ibi ħt . iiii . car̃

§ In Scredintune . x . car̃ tre 7 dim̃ ad gld̃ . Tra . ix . ∫ in dñio .
  car̃ . Ibi xl . focħ 7 i . uill hñt . xiiii . car̃ . Ibi p̃br & æccla .

§ In Helperinchã 7 Burton . v . car̃ træ   ∫ 7 xx . i . ac̃ p̃ti .
  7 ii . boũ ad gld̃ . Tra . viii . car̃ . Ibi xxxv . focħ . 7 vii . bord̃
  hñt . x . car̃ . 7 xxvi . ac̃ p̃ti .

97 S. In ASLACKBY, ½ carucate, and 'SEMPRINGHAM', 2 carucates and 6 bovates: 3 carucates of land and 2 bovates taxable. Land for 3½ ploughs.

    13 Freemen and 1 smallholder who have 3 ploughs.

    ½ church and the sixth part of another church; meadow, 24 acres; underwood, 40 acres.

98 S. In POINTON 2 carucates of land and 2 bovates taxable. Land for as many ploughs and oxen.

    16 Freemen have 6 ploughs.

    Meadow, 32 acres; underwood, 40 acres.

99 S. In INGOLDSBY 3 carucates of land and 1 bovate taxable. Land for 3 ploughs.

    17 Freemen and 2 smallholders have 5 ploughs and meadow, 25 acres; underwood, 100 acres.

100 S. In HOUGH (on the Hill) and BRANDON 3 carucates of land and 3 bovates taxable. Land for 5 ploughs.

    13 Freemen have 6 ploughs and meadow, 6 acres.

    Dering holds the whole of this from Gilbert and has ½ plough there in lordship.

    Value 40s.

101 S. In KIRKBY (la Thorpe) 7 carucates of land taxable. Land for 5 ploughs.

    31 Freemen and 6 smallholders have 6 ploughs.

102 S. In (Silk) WILLOUGHBY 5 carucates of land taxable. Land for 10 ploughs.

    29 Freemen and 1 smallholder have 6 ploughs.

    A priest and a church; meadow, 140 acres; meadow, 24 acres.

103 S. In ASWARBY 4½ carucates of land and 1 bovate taxable. Land for 9 ploughs.

    41 Freemen and 3 smallholders have 18 ploughs.

    A priest and a church and 2 parts of 1 church; meadow, 180 acres.

    Ralph the priest has 3½ carucates of this land. He has 4 ploughs in lordship.

104 S. In SCREDINGTON 10½ carucates of land taxable. Land for 9 ploughs.

    40 Freemen and 1 villager have 14 ploughs.

    A priest and a church; meadow, 21 acres.

105 S. In HELPRINGHAM, 3 carucates and 2 bovates, and BURTON (Pedwardine), 2 carucates: 5 carucates of land and 2 bovates taxable. Land for 8 ploughs.

    35 Freemen and 7 smallholders have 10 ploughs.

    Meadow, 26 acres.

TERRA HUGONIS FILIJ BALDRICI.

ↁ In *BVNDEBI*. ħbr Grinchel 7 Merdo 7 Aldene 7 alij. IIII.
taini. III. car̅ træ ad glđ. Tra. VI. car̅. Ibi Hugo. f. Baldri
ħt. III. car̅ in dn̅io. 7 XIIII. uiłt 7 VII. borđ. cū. IIII. car̅.
T.R.E. uał. IIII. lib. m̅. VI. Tailla. xx. fot. Socħ. III. bou huj træ.

ↁ In *VLVRICEBI*. ħb Grinchel dim car̅ træ ad glđ. Tra
. I. car̅. Ibi Radulf ħo Hug ħt. I. car̅. 7 II. uiłt. hn̅tes
II. bou in car̅. T.R.E. 7 m̅. xx. fot uał.

ↁ In *LINBERGE* ħbr Siuuard 7 Vlf. II. car̅ tre 7 dim̅
ad glđ. Tra. v. car̅ 7 dim̅. Ibi ħt Hugo. f. B. II. car̅.
7 x. uiłt 7 IIII. borđ. 7 xx. focħ de. v. bou huj træ.
Int om̅s. IIII. car̅. 7 II. bō in car̅. T.R.E. uał c. fot. m̅
fimił. Tailla. xx. fot.

In Caburne. dim̅ bou træ. Soca in Linberge.

ↁ In *CHERNITONE*. ħb Tope. II. bou træ ad glđ. Tra
II. car̅. Ibi Hamelin ħo Hug ħt. I. car̅. 7 v. uiłt
7 VIII. borđ. 7 x. focħ cū. I. car̅. hn̅tes. XVIII. toft.
T.R.E. uał xL. fot. m̅. xxx. Tailla. x. fot.

ↁ In *CROCESTONE*. ħb Siuuard. x. bou træ ad glđ.
Tra. II. car̅ 7 dim̅. Ibi Hamelin ħo Hug. I. car̅.
7 VI. uiłt. 7 III. borđ. 7 II. focħ cū. I. car 7 dim̅. SOCA. I. bou.
Ibi. VIII. ac̅ p̅ti. T.R.E. 7 m̅ uał. xL. fot.

ↁ In *STALINEVRG*. ħbr Siuuard 7 Gamel 7 Vlchil
. I. car̅ træ ad glđ. Tra. II. car̅. Ibi ħt Hugo. I. car̅. 7 II.
focħ de. v. toft. 7 II. uiłt. 7 I. borđ. 7 II. molin̅ 7 dim̅. x. fot.
7 II. falin̅ 7 dim̅. II. fot. 7 cc. ac̅ p̅ti. T.R.E. 7 m̅. xxx. fot. uał.

ↁ In *STAINTONE*. ħb Bertor. I. car̅ træ ad glđ. Tra
III. car̅. Ibi ħt Hugo. I. car̅. 7 IIII. focħ de. I. bou træ
7 XI. uiłt 7 III. borđ. cū. I. car̅ 7 II. bou in car̅. 7 Lv. ac̅
p̅ti. T.R.E. uał. III. lib. m̅ xL. fot. Tailla. x. fot.

1 6 In BONBY Grimketill, Merdo, Halfdan and three other thanes had
M. 3 carucates of land taxable. Land for 6 ploughs. Hugh son of
Baldric has 3 ploughs in lordship;
14 villagers and 7 smallholders with 4 ploughs.
Value before 1066 £4; now [£] 6. Exactions 20s.
Freemen [have] 3 bovates of this land.

2 M. In WORLABY Grimketill had ½ carucate of land taxable. Land for
1 plough. Ralph, Hugh's man, has 1 plough.
2 villagers who have 2 oxen in a plough.
Value before 1066 and now, 20s.

3 2 In (Great) LIMBER Siward and Ulfr had 2½ carucates of land
M. taxable. Land for 5½ ploughs. Hugh son of Baldric has 2 ploughs.
10 villagers, 4 smallholders and 20 Freemen on 5 bovates of
this land; between them 4 ploughs and 2 oxen in a plough.
Value before 1066, 100s; now the same. Exactions 20s.

4 In CABOURN ½ bovate of land. A jurisdiction of (Great) Limber.

5 M. In KIRMINGTON Topi had 2 bovates of land taxable. Land for 2
ploughs. Hamelin, Hugh's man, has 1 plough.
5 villagers, 8 smallholders and 10 Freemen with 1 plough
who have 18 plots.
Value before 1066, 40s; now 30[s]. Exactions 10s.

6 M. In CROXTON Siward had 10 bovates of land taxable. Land for 2½
ploughs. Hamelin, Hugh's man, [has] 1 plough.
6 villagers, 3 smallholders and 2 Freemen with 1½ ploughs.
A jurisdiction of 1 bovate.
Meadow, 8 acres.
Value before 1066 and now, 40s.

7 M. In STALLINGBOROUGH Siward, Gamall and Ulfketill had 1 carucate
of land taxable. Land for 2 ploughs. Hugh has 1 plough.
2 Freemen on 5 plots; 2 villagers and 1 smallholder.
2½ mills, 10s; 2½ salt-houses, 2s; meadow, 200 acres.
Value before 1066 and now, 30s.

8 M. In STAINTON (le Vale) Bergthorr had 1 carucate of land taxable.
Land for 3 ploughs. Hugh has 1 plough.
4 Freemen on 1 bovate of land; 11 villagers and 3 smallholders
with 1 plough and 2 oxen in a plough.
Meadow, 55 acres.
Value before 1066 £3; now 40s. Exactions 10s.

ꝏ In *CABVRNE* . ħƀ Grinchel . II . car̄ trǣ 7 III . bou̇ 7 dīm̄
ad glđ . Tra . v . car̄ . Ibi hꞇ Hugo . II . car̄ . 7 XII . focħ de . I .
car̄ tre . 7 I . uiłł 7 III . borđ cū . III . car̄ . 7 xx . ac̄s p̊ti .
T.R.E . uał . xxx . fol . m̊ . LX . Tailla . xx . fol .

Ɓ In Cucualt *BEREW* . III . bou̇ trǣ ad glđ . Tra . vI . bou̇ .
Ibi . IIII . uiłł 7 III . focħ cū . I . car̄ .

ꝏ In *CROCESTONE* . ħƀ . Grinchel diṁ car̄ tre ad glđ .
Ṫra . I . car̄ . Ibi Hamelin hō Huġ hꞇ . I . car̄ . IX . focħ
de . II . bou̇ tre . 7 vI . uiłł 7 I . borđ . hñtes . I . car̄ 7 dīm̄ .
7 vIII . ac̄s p̊ti . T.R.E . 7 m̊ uał . XL . fol .

Ş In Toreſbi 7 Aluuoldeſbi . I . bou̇ 7 v . parṫ . I . bou̇ ad glđ .
Ṫra . II . bou̇ . Soca in Caburne . Ibi . II . uiłł 7 II . faline
. II . folidoꝫ . 7 xv . ac̄ p̊ti .

356 c

ꝏ In *TORP* . ħƀr Clac 7 Leuuin̊ . x . bou̇ trǣ ad glđ .
Ṫra . II . car̄ 7 dim̄ . Ibi Giſlebꞇ hō Hug̊ hꞇ . I . car̄ 7 dim̄ .
7 II . focħ de . v . bou̇ tre 7 dīm̄ . 7 xII . uiłł 7 v . borđ .
cū . I . car̄ 7 dim̄ . 7 Lx . ac̄s p̊ti . T.R.E . uał . Lx . fol . m̊ . L .

Ɓ In Bechebi *BER* . v . bou̇ tre 7 dīm̄ ad glđ . ⸍ Tailla . x . ş
Ṫra . I . car̄ . Ibi . I . uiłł 7 I . borđ . hñt . I . boue in car̄ .

ꝏ In *HAMINGEBI* . ħƀ Edric . vI . bou̇ tre ad glđ .
Ṫra . vI . bob . Ibi hꞇ Hugo . II . car̄ . 7 XIII . focħ
de . II . bou̇ tre . 7 IIIí . uiłł cū . II . car̄ . 7 Lx . ac̄s p̊ti .
T.R.E . uał Lx . fol . m̊ . c . Tailla . xx . fol .

Ş In Buchehale . vI . bou̇ trǣ 7 dim̄ ad glđ . Tra totiđ
bob . Ibi . v . focħ 7 II . uiłł hñt . I . car̄ . 7 Lxv . ac̄s
p̊ti . 7 Ix . ac̄s filuǣ paſt 7 minutǣ filuǣ . v . ac̄s .

Ş In Horfintone . II . car̄ trǣ 7 vI . bou̇ 7 dim̄ ad glđ .
Ṫra . III . car̄ . Ibi xvI . focħ 7 II . borđ hñt . III . car̄ .
7 CL.III . ac̄ p̊ti . 7 xv . ac̄ filuǣ miñ .

9 M. In CABOURN Grimketill had 2 carucates of land and 3½ bovates taxable. Land for 5 ploughs. Hugh has 2 ploughs.
12 Freemen on 1 carucate of land; 1 villager and 3 smallholders with 3 ploughs.
Meadow, 20 acres.
Value before 1066, 30s; now 60[s]. Exactions 20s.

10 B. In CUXWOLD, an outlier, 3 bovates of land taxable. Land for 6 oxen.   k
4 villagers and 3 Freemen with 1 plough.

11 M. In CROXTON Grimketill had ½ carucate of land taxable. Land for 1 plough. Hamelin, Hugh's man, has 1 plough.
9 Freemen on 2 bovates of land; 6 villagers and 1 smallholder who have 1½ ploughs and
meadow, 8 acres.
Value before 1066 and now, 40s.

12 S. In (North) THORESBY and 'AUDBY' 1 bovate and 5 parts of 1 bovate taxable. Land for 2 oxen. A jurisdiction of Cabourn.
2 villagers.
2 salt-houses, 2s; meadow, 15 acres.

13 2 In (Kettleby) 'THORPE' Klakkr and Leofwine had 10 bovates of   356 c
M. land taxable. Land for 2½ ploughs. Gilbert, Hugh's man, has 1½ ploughs.
2 Freemen on 5½ bovates of land; 12 villagers and 5 smallholders with 1½ ploughs.
Meadow, 60 acres.
Value before 1066, 60s; now 50[s]. Exactions 10s.

14 B. In BIGBY, an outlier, 5½ bovates of land taxable. Land for 1 plough.
1 villager and 1 smallholder have 1 ox in a plough.

15 M. In HEMINGBY Eadric had 6 bovates of land taxable. Land for 6 oxen. Hugh has 2 ploughs.
13 Freemen on 2 bovates of land; 3 villagers with 2 ploughs.
Meadow, 60 acres.
Value before 1066, 60s; now 100[s]. Exactions 20s.

Jurisdiction:
16 S. In BUCKNALL 6½ bovates of land taxable. Land for as many oxen.
5 Freemen and 2 villagers have 1 plough and
meadow, 65 acres; woodland pasture, 9 acres; underwood, 5 acres.

17 S. In HORSINGTON 2 carucates of land and 6½ bovates taxable. Land for 3 ploughs.
16 Freemen and 2 smallholders have 3 ploughs.
Meadow, 153 acres; underwood, 15 acres.

Ṡ In Ludeforde Soca in Wichā . II . boū træ ad glđ .
Tra . IIII . boū . Ibi . II . focħ hñt dim̄ cař . 7 IIII . ač p̄ti .

Ꝏ In CLACHESBI . ħƀ Dane . I . cař tre ad glđ . Tra . XIIII .
boƀ . Ibi Wido gener Hug . hī . II . cař . 7 I . focħ de
III . boū tre . 7 v . uiłł cū . I . cař 7 dim̄ . Ibi æccła 7 p̄ƀr .
7 I . moliñ . II . folidoꝝ . 7 cxx . ač filuæ miñ . Inde hī Gis
leƀt de gand . II . part . 7 Wido alias tres part . T.R.E.
uał . vIII . liƀ . m̊ . Ix .   SOCA huj Ꝏ
Ṡ In Widerne . vI . boū træ ad glđ . Tra . I . cař . Ibi . vIII .
focħ 7 II . uiłł hñt . II . cař . 7 xII . ačs p̄ti . 7 Lx . ačs filuæ
Ṡ In Endretorp . II . cař tre 7 dim̄ ad glđ . Tra . v . cař � min .
Ibi . xIx . focħ 7 Ix . borđ hñt . IIII . cař . Silua minuta
dimiđ leṽ lḡ . 7 tntđ łaī .
Ṡ In Strobi 7 Malteby . vII . boū træ ad glđ . Tra . xII . boū .
Ibi . v . focħ hñt . v . boū in cař . 7 xxx . ačs p̄ti .
Ṡ In Saleby . II . cař træ ad glđ . Tra . II . cař . Ibi . II . focħ
7 II . uiłł . hñt . II . cař .
Ṡ In Thuorſtorp . II . cař tre ad glđ . Tra . II . cař . Ibi . v .
focħ 7 II . borđ hñt . II . cař 7 dim̄ . 7 xL . ač p̄ti . 7 xL . ač
Ꝏ In SLODEBI . ħƀ Dane . III . boū træ ad glđ . ⌐ filuæ miñ
Tra . I . cař . Ibi Wido gener hug hī . IIII . uiłł 7 III .
borđ . cū dim̄ cař . 7 IIII . ačs p̄ti . T.R.E. uał . xx . fol . m̊ . vI . s .

.XXXVI.   TERRA COLSVAIN.
Ꝏ In BROTVLBI ħƀ Chetel . III . cař tre ad glđ . Tra . III .
cař 7 dim̄ . Ibi hī Colfuan . II . cař in dñio . 7 Ix . focħ
de . vII . boū huj træ . 7 vī uiłł 7 I . borđ . cū . IIII . cář . T.R.E.
uał xL . fol . m̊ Lx . Tailla . xx . fol .

18 S. In LUDFORD, a jurisdiction of (West) 'Wykeham', 2 bovates of land taxable. Land for 4 oxen.
2 Freemen have ½ plough.
Meadow, 4 acres.

19 M. In CLAXBY Dena had 1 carucate of land taxable. Land for 14 oxen.
Guy, Hugh's son-in-law, has 2 ploughs.
1 Freeman on 3 bovates of land; 5 villagers with 1½ ploughs.
A church and a priest; 1 mill, 2s; underwood, 120 acres.
Gilbert of Ghent has 2 parts of this and Guy the other three parts.
Value before 1066 £8; now [£] 9.

Jurisdiction of this manor:
20 S. In WITHERN 6 bovates of land taxable. Land for 1 plough.
8 Freemen and 2 villagers have 2 ploughs and
meadow, 12 acres; underwood, 60 acres.

21 S. In (Wood)THORPE 2½ carucates of land taxable. Land for 5 ploughs.
19 Freemen and 9 smallholders have 4 ploughs.
Underwood ½ league long and as wide.

22 S. In STRUBBY, 5 bovates, and MALTBY (le Marsh), 2 [bovates] : 7
bovates of land taxable. Land for 12 oxen.
5 Freemen have 5 oxen in a plough and
meadow, 30 acres.

23 S. In SALEBY 2 carucates of land taxable. Land for 2 ploughs.
2 Freemen and 2 villagers have 2 ploughs.

24 S. In THORESTHORPE 2 carucates of land taxable. Land for 2 ploughs.
5 Freemen and 2 smallholders have 2½ ploughs.
Meadow, 40 acres; underwood, 40 acres.

25 M. In SLOOTHBY Dena had 3 bovates of land taxable. Land for 1
plough. Guy, Hugh's son-in-law, has
4 villagers and 3 smallholders with ½ plough; and
meadow, 4 acres.
Value before 1066, 20s; now 6s.

[26]   LAND OF KOLSVEINN   356 d

1 M. In BRATTLEBY Ketill had 3 carucates of land taxable. Land for 3½
ploughs. Kolsveinn has 2 ploughs in lordship;
9 Freemen on 7 bovates of this land; 6 villagers and 1
smallholder with 4 ploughs.
Value before 1066, 40s; now 60[s]. Exactions 20s.

ᴔ In RISVN . ħɓ Lepfi . ɪ . caɼ ᷈ tɼæ ad glð . Tɼa . ɪ . caɼ . Ibi ħɼ
Colſuan . ɪɪ . caɼ . 7 ɪɪɪ . uiłł 7 ɪ . borð cū . ɪ . caɼ . 7 ɪ . moliñ
ɪɪ . folið . T.R.E. uał xx . fol . m̄ . ʟx .

ᴔ In FALINGEVRDE . ħɓ Sberne dim̄ caɼ ᷈ tre ad glð . Tɼa
ɪɪɪɪ . boū . Ibi . ɪɪɪ . uiłł Colſuan hn̄t dim̄ caɼ . 7 vɪɪɪ . ačs
p̄ti . T.R.E. x . fol . m̄ . v . 7 ɪɪɪɪ . den .

ᴔ In SCOTSTORNE 7 Holme 7 Sudborc . ħɓ Turulf . ɪɪɪ,
caɼ ᷈ tɼæ 7 v . boū ad glð . Tɼa . ɪɪɪɪ . caɼ . Ibi ħɼ Colſuan . ɪ . caɼ .
7 xɪ . focħ de . ɪɪ . caɼ ᷈ tɼæ 7 dim̄ . 7 ɪ . uiłł 7 ɪ . borð . cū . ɪɪɪ . caɼ .
7 ʟxɪɪɪɪ . ačs p̄ti . T.R.E. uał . xʟ . fol . m̄ . ʟx . Tailla xx . s.
Ibidē ħɓ Godric . ɪɪɪɪ . bō tɼæ 7 dimiđ· ad glð . Tɼa . ɪ . caɼ . Ibi . ɪ . uiłł
7 ɪ . borð hn̄t . ɪɪ . boū in caɼ . T.R.E. 7 m̄ . uał . v . fol .
Ibidē ħɼ Colſuan . ɪ . caɼ ᷈ tɼæ de rege fīc dicit . 7 inde
reddit in fiſcartone Ꞩ Petro de bur c̄ſuetudinē . Ibi ħɼ . ɪ .
moliñ . 7 ɪɪɪ . uiłł cū . ɪ . caɼ . T.R.E. 7 m̄ . x . fol redđ .

ᴔ In BERLINGE . ħɓ Col . vɪ . bou tre ad glð . Tɼa . ɪ . caɼ .
Ibi ħɼ Colſ . ɪ . caɼ . 7 ɪɪɪ . uiłł cū dim̄ caɼ . 7 ɪ . ecčam .
T.R.E. uał . x . fol . m̄ . ɪɪɪɪ . liɓ .

ᵬ In Refan . vɪ . bou tre ad glð . Tɼa . ɪ . caɼ . BEREW̃
Ibi Colſuan . ɪ . caɼ . 7 ɪɪɪɪ . uiłł dim̄ caɼ . 7 xvɪɪɪ . ačs p̄ti .

ᴔ In CAMESLINGEHA᷈ . ħɓr Chenut 7 Elnod 7 Vlchel .
7 Sbern . ɪɪɪɪ . caɼ ᷈ tɼæ 7 dmđ ad glð . Tɼa . v . caɼ . Ibi ħɼ
Colſuan . ɪɪɪɪ . caɼ in dn̄io . 7 vɪɪɪ . focħ de dim̄ caɼ huj᷈ tɼæ .
7 xɪ . uiłł 7 ɪɪ . borð . cū . ɪɪɪ . caɼ . 7 ʟxx . ač᷈ p̄ti . T.R.E.
uał . ɪɪɪ . liɓ . m̄ . ɪɪɪɪ . Tailla . xx . fol .

2 M. In RISEHOLME Leofsige had 1 carucate of land taxable. Land for 1 plough. Kolsveinn has 2 ploughs.
>   3 villagers and 1 smallholder with 1 plough.
>   1 mill, 2s.
Value before 1066, 20s; now 60[s].

3 M. In FALDINGWORTH Esbjorn had ½ carucate of land taxable. Land for 4 oxen.
>   3 villagers of Kolsveinn's have ½ plough and meadow, 8 acres.
Value before 1066, 10s; now 5[s] 4d.

4 M. In SCOTHERN, 'HOLME' and SUDBROOKE Thorulfr had 3 carucates of land and 5 bovates taxable. Land for 4 ploughs. Kolsveinn has 1 plough.
>   11 Freemen on 2½ carucates of land; 1 villager and 1 smallholder with 3 ploughs.
>   Meadow, 64 acres.
Value before 1066, 40s; now 60[s]. Exactions 20s.

5   There also Godric had 4½ bovates of land taxable. Land for 1 plough.
>   1 villager and 1 smallholder have 2 oxen in a plough.
Value before 1066 and now, 5s.

6   There also Kolsveinn has 1 carucate of land from the King as he states, of which he pays the customary dues in Fiskerton to St. Peter's of Peterborough. He has
>   1 mill; 3 villagers with 1 plough.
Before 1066 and now it paid [and pays], 10s.

7 M. In BARLINGS Cola had 6 bovates of land taxable. Land for 1 plough. Kolsveinn has 1 plough and
>   3 villagers with ½ plough; and
>   1 church.
Value before 1066, 10s; now £4.

26,8 is entered in the next col. (after 26,21) and is directed by transposition signs to its correct place in the text.

9 B. In REEPHAM 6 bovates of land taxable. Land for 1 plough. An outlier. Kolsveinn [has] 1 plough.
>   4 villagers [with] ½ plough.
>   Meadow, 18 acres.

10 M. In CAMMERINGHAM Knutr, Alnoth, Ulfketill and Esbjorn had 4½ carucates of land taxable. Land for 5 ploughs. Kolsveinn has 4 ploughs in lordship;
>   8 Freemen on ½ carucate of this land; 11 villagers and 2 smallholders with 3 ploughs.
>   Meadow, 70 acres.
Value before 1066 £3; now [£] 4. Exactions 20s.

꙼In _INGEHĀ_.ħƀr Frane 7 Sūmerled.ı.caꞃ træ ad glđ.

Tra.ı.caꞃ 7 dim.Ibi Roḡ 7 Anſchitil hōēs Colſuan

hñt.ı.caꞃ 7 dim.7 ıııı.uiłł 7 ı.borđ.cū.ııı.boƀ in caꞃ.

7 xvı.ačs p̄ti.T.R.E.uał.ʟ.ſoł.m̃.xxx.Tailla.x.ſoł.

Ŝ In Friſetorp.ııı.caꞃ træ ad glđ.Tra.ııı.caꞃ.Soca in Ingehā.

7 Felingehā.Ibi.x.ſocħ 7 ııı.borđ hñt.ııı.caꞃ.7 ʟ.ačs

p̄ti.7 xx.ačs ſiluæ miñ.

Ŝ In Faldingeurde.ıı.caꞃ træ ad glđ.Tra.ıı.caꞃ 7 dimiđ.

◉ Soca in Figelingehā 7 Splintone 7 ʟagehā.Ibi.ıx.ſocħ.

hñt.ı.caꞃ.7 xxvı.ačs p̄ti.7 ı.ač ſiluæ.

꙼In _HANEVRDE_.ħƀ Frane.vı.ƀō træ ad glđ.Tra.xıı.

boƀ.Ibi Turolđ pƀr ħt.ı.caꞃ.7 vı.uiłł.7 ı.borđ hñtes

.ı.caꞃ.7 x.ačs p̄ti.T.R.E.uał.xx.ſoł.m̃.xxx.

Ɓ In Hagetorne Bᴇʀ.ııı.bou træ ad glđ.

7 ıııı.pars.ı.bou
Tra.ıııı.boƀ

357 a

꙼In eađ _HAGETORNE_.ħƀ Chenut.ııı.bou træ ad glđ.

Tra.ıııı.bou.Ibi ħt Colſuan.ıı.boues in caꞃ.7 vııı.ačs p̄ti.

T.R.E.uał.v.ſoł 7 ıııı.den.m̃ ſimiliꞇ.

꙼In _SCALEBI_ 7 Stratone.ħƀ Turulf.xı.bou træ ad glđ.

Tra.ıı.caꞃ.Ibi ħt Alured hō Colſuan ħt.ı.caꞃ.7 v.

ſocħ de.ı.caꞃ huj tꞃe.7 ııı.uiłł cū.ı.caꞃ 7 dimiđ.

T.R.E.uał x.ſoł.m̃.xx.Tailla.v.ſoł.

Ɓ In Reburne.ıı.bou træ 7 ıııı.part.ı.bouatæ ad glđ.Tra

.v.boƀ 7 dim.Colſuan ħt 7 waſta.ē.

Ŝ In Hiboldeſtou.ꞇcia pars.ıı.bouaꞇ.ad glđ.Soca in Scaꞇ

꙼In _RISVN_ 7 Carlentun ħƀ Alſi dimiđ caꞃ tꞃe ad glđ.

Tra.vı.boƀ.Ibi Matħs hō Colſ ħt.ı.caꞃ.7 ıııı.uiłł

cū dim caꞃ.7 xx.ačs p̄ti.7 ᴄʟx ačs ſiluæ paſt.T.R.E.uał

xv.ſoł.m̃.xxx.

11 M. In INGHAM Frani and Sumarlithi had 1 carucate of land taxable.
Land for 1½ ploughs. Roger and Asketill, Kolsveinn's men,
have 1½ ploughs.
4 villagers and 1 smallholder with 3 oxen in a plough.
Meadow, 16 acres.
Value before 1066, 50s; now 30[s]. Exactions 10s.

26,12 is entered in the next column (after 26,22) and is directed by transposition signs to its correct place in the text.

13 S. In FRIESTHORPE 3 carucates of land taxable. Land for 3 ploughs.
A jurisdiction of Ingham, 7 bovates, and Fillingham, 17 bovates.
10 Freemen and 3 smallholders have 3 ploughs and
meadow, 50 acres; underwood, 20 acres.

26,24, entered here and directed to its correct place by transposition signs.

24 S. In FALDINGWORTH 2 carucates of land taxable. Land for 2½
⊙ ploughs. A jurisdiction of Fillingham, 6 bovates, Spridlington, 1
carucate, and Ingham, 2 bovates.
9 Freemen have 1 plough and
meadow, 26 acres; woodland, 1 acre.

14 M. In (Cold) HANWORTH Frani had 6 bovates of land taxable. Land
for 12 oxen. Thoraldr the priest has 1 plough.
6 villagers and 1 smallholder who have 1 plough and
meadow, 10 acres.
Value before 1066, 20s; now 30[s].

15 B. In HACKTHORN, an outlier, 3 bovates of land taxable and the fourth
part of 1 bovate. Land for 4 oxen.

16 Also in HACKTHORN Knutr had 3 bovates of land taxable. Land   357 a
for 4 oxen. Kolsveinn has 2 oxen in a plough and
meadow, 8 acres.
Value before 1066, 5s 4d; now the same.

17 M. In SCAWBY and STURTON Thorulfr had 11 bovates of land taxable.
Land for 2 ploughs. Alfred, Kolsveinn's man, has 1 plough.
5 Freemen on 1 carucate of this land; 3 villagers with 1½ ploughs.
Value before 1066, 10s; now 20[s]. Exactions 5s.

18 B. In REDBOURNE 2 bovates of land and 4 parts of 1 bovate taxable.
Land for 5½ oxen. Kolsveinn has it. It is waste.

19 S. In HIBALDSTOW the third part of 2 bovates taxable. A jurisdiction
of Scawby.

20 M. In RISEHOLME and (South) CARLTON Alsige had ½ carucate of land
taxable. Land for 6 oxen. Matthew, Kolsveinn's man, has 1 plough.
4 villagers with ½ plough.
Meadow, 20 acres; woodland pasture, 160 acres.
Value before 1066, 15s; now 30[s].

In COCRINTON . hб Elnod . I . boū tre ad glđ . Tra . II . bob.
Ibi hт Matнs dim car . T.R.E . 7 m̄ . III . ſoł.

In BERLINGE hб Oſgot . VI . boū træ ad glđ . Tra . I . car.
Ibi hт Colſ . I . car . 7 II . uiłł 7 III . borđ . cū dimiđ car.
7 XX . acs p̄ti . 7 XX . acs ſilue minutæ . T.R.E . uał XXX . ſoł . m̄ . XL.

In CHEFTESBI hб Aſchil . III . car træ 7 III . boū ad glđ.
Tra totiđ c 7 b . Ibi hт Colſuani hō Adelelm̄ . II . car.
7 IX . uiłł 7 III . borđ . cū . I . car 7 dim̄ . 7 I . moliñ . XVI.
denar . 7 LVIII . acs p̄ti . 7 XL . acs ſiluæ miñ . T.R.E.
7 m̄ uał . XL . ſoł . Taiłla . X . ſoł.

§ In Cotes . II . boū træ ad glđ . Tra . II . boū . SOCA i Ingeh̄ā.

In FILINGEH̄Ā . hбr Frane 7 Elnod 7 Aſchił 7 Elnod
7 Godric . VII . car træ 7 I . boū ad glđ . Tra . XI . car.

Ibi hт Colſuan . IIII . car . 7 XXX . II . ſocн de . IIII . car
huȷ tre 7 dim̄ . 7 XII . uiłł . cū . III . car 7 dim̄ . Ibi æccła
7 CCXL . ac p̄ti . T.R.E . uał . IIII . liб . m̄ . V . Taiłla . XL . ſoł.

In SPERLINCTONE . hбr Ebrarđ 7 II . frs eȷ . II . car træ
7 V . boū 7 dim̄ ad glđ . Tra . III . car . Ibi hт Colſ . II . car.
7 IIII . socн de . I . boū huȷ træ . 7 XVI . uiłł 7 IIII . borđ.
cū . II . car . 7 VIII . acs p̄ti . T.R.E . uał XXI . ſoł . m̄ XL . Taiłla
ƒ X . ſoł.

In OVSTORP . hб Eddiue . III . car træ 7 dim̄ . 7 I . boū
ad glđ . Tra . III . car . Ibi hт Colſ . II . car . 7 VIII . uiłł
cū . I . car . 7 XLIIII . acs p̄ti . 7 XXIII . acs ſiluæ minutæ.
T.R.E . uał . XXX . ſoł . m̄ . LX.

In HECHINTVNE . hбr Turchil 7 Algar . I . car træ 7 VI.
boū ad glđ . Tra . I . car 7 V . boū . Ibi Conded hō Colſ
hт . I . uiłł 7 XVIII . acs p̄ti . T.R.E . uał . XXXVI . ſoł . m̄ XXX . s.

21 In COCKERINGTON Alnoth had 1 bovate of land taxable. Land for 2 oxen. Matthew has ½ plough.
[Value] before 1066 and now, 3s.

26,8, directed by transposition signs to its correct place in the text.

8 M. In BARLINGS Asgautr had 6 bovates of land taxable. Land for 1 plough. Kolsveinn has 1 plough.
2 villagers and 3 smallholders with ½ plough.
Meadow, 20 acres; underwood, 20 acres.
Value before 1066, 30s; now 40[s].

22 M. In KEXBY Asketill had 3 carucates of land and 3½ bovates taxable. Land for as many ploughs and oxen. Aethelhelm, Kolsveinn's man, has 2 ploughs.
9 villagers and 3 smallholders with 1½ ploughs.
1 mill, 16d; meadow, 58 acres; underwood, 40 acres.
Value before 1066 and now, 40s. Exactions 10s.

26,12, directed by transposition signs to its correct place in the text.

12 S. In COATES 2 bovates of land taxable. Land for 2 oxen. A jurisdiction of Ingham.

23 5 M. In FILLINGHAM Frani, Alnoth, Asketill, Alnoth and Godric had 7 carucates of land and 1 bovate taxable. Land for 11 ploughs. Kolsveinn has 4 ploughs.
32 Freemen on 4½ carucates of this land; 12 villagers with 3½ ploughs.
A church; meadow, 240 acres.
Value before 1066 £4; now [£] 5. Exactions 40s.

26,24 is entered in the previous col. (after 26,13) and is directed by transposition signs to its correct place in the text.

25 M. In SPRIDLINGTON Ebrard and his 2 brothers had 2 carucates of land and 5½ bovates taxable. Land for 3 ploughs. Kolsveinn has 2 ploughs.
4 Freemen on 1 bovate of this land; 16 villagers and 4 smallholders with 2 ploughs.
Meadow, 8 acres.
Value before 1066, 21s; now 40[s]. Exactions 10s.

26 M. In EAST THORPE Eadgifu had 3½ carucates of land and 1 bovate taxable. Land for 3 ploughs. Kolsveinn has 2 ploughs.
8 villagers with 1 plough.
Meadow, 44 acres; underwood, 23 acres.
Value before 1066, 30s; now 60[s].

27 2 M. In HECKINGTON Thorketill and Algar had 1 carucate of land and 6 bovates taxable. Land for 1 plough and 5 oxen. Conded, Kolsveinn's man, has
1 villager and
meadow, 18 acres.
Value before 1066, 36s; now 30s.

ƀ In Helperichā . ıı . boú ťre ad glď . Ťra . ıı . boƀ . Ibi . ı . uiłłs
7 ıı . ač ṕti . ĪI ťra pene wałta . ē.

.ıı. In *Hvvelle* Hď . ıı . boú 7 dim̄ ad glď . Ťra . ıı . bō . Soca in Cherchebi.

ᛞ In *Ledvlvetorp* . ħƀr Tor 7 Afchil . v . caŕ ťræ 7 dim̄ ad glď.
Ibi ħť Conded 7 Anchitil hōēs Colš . ıııı . caŕ . 7 vıı . uiłł.
7 . x . borď . 7 . ı . foch cū . ı . caŕ 7 dim̄ . 7 dimiď æccła 7 cū dim̄
pƀro . T.R.E . uał . ıııı . liƀ . m̄ fimił . Tailla . xx . foł.

ᛞ In *Dodintone* . ħƀ Outi . vı . boú ťræ ad glď . Ťra totiď boƀ.
Ibi ħť Colš . ıı . uiłł 7 ıı . borď cū dim̄ caŕ . 7 dim̄ molin̄
. ıııı . foliď . 7 x . ač̄s ṕti . T.R.E . 7 m̄ . uał . x . foł.

Ʂ Ibidē . vı . boú ťræ ad glď . Ťra . vı . boƀ . Soca in Mereſtone.
Ibi . ıı . foch 7 ıı . borď . hn̄t . ıı . boú . Dn̄s dim̄ caŕ . 7 x . ač̄s ṕti.

ᛞ In *Merestone* ħƀ Alfi . ı . caŕ ťræ ad glď . in dn̄io.
7 x . boú ťræ in Soca . Ťra . ııı . caŕ . Ibi Walt hō Colš
ħť . ı . caŕ . 7 ıııı . foch 7 v . borď . cū . ı . caŕ 7 ı . boue . 7 fed
uni moł . 7 xxxıı . ač̄s ṕti . T.R.E . uał . xxx . foł . m̄ . ʟ.

Ʂ In *Hachā* . ıı . caŕ ťræ ad glď . Ťra . xıı . boƀ . Soca i Mereſt.
Ibi . ıııı . foch 7 ı . borď . hn̄t dim̄ caŕ . 7 ıııı . ač̄s ṕti.

ᛞ In *Hachā* . ħƀ Azor . ıı . caŕ ťræ ad glď . Ťra . ııı . caŕ.
Ibi Wiłłs hō Colš ħť . ı . caŕ . 7 v . uiłł 7 v . borď . cū
. ı . caŕ 7 ıı . boƀ . 7 ıı . ač̄s 7 dim̄ ṕti . T.R.E . 7 m̄ . uał . xxx . foł.

ᛞ In *Bolinbvrg* . ħƀ Suen . ıı . caŕ ťræ 7 vıı . boú ad glď.
Ibi Brunel hō Colš ħť . ı . caŕ 7 dim̄ . 7 vııı . uiłł 7 ıı.
borď . cū . ı . caŕ 7 dim̄ . Ibi dim̄ æccła . 7 ı . molin̄ . v . foliď.
7 ıııı . den̄ . 7 xxvıı . ač ṕti . 7 xxvı . ač filuæ minutæ.
T.R.E . uał . xʟ . foł . m̄ . ʟx.

28 B. In HELPRINGHAM 2 bovates of land taxable. Land for 2 oxen.
    1 villager.
    Meadow, 2 acres.
This land is almost waste.

29   In HOWELL hundred 2½ bovates taxable. Land for 2 oxen. A   357 b
jurisdiction of Kirkby (la Thorpe).

30 2 In 'LAYTHORPE' Thorr and Asketill had 5½ carucates of land
  M. taxable. Conded and Asketill, Kolsveinn's men, have 4 ploughs.
    7 villagers, 10 smallholders and 1 Freeman with 1½ ploughs.
    ½ church with ½ priest.
Value before 1066 £4; now the same. Exactions 20s.

31 M. In (Dry) DODDINGTON Auti had 6 bovates of land taxable. Land
for as many oxen. Kolsveinn has
    2 villagers and 2 smallholders with ½ plough; and
    ½ mill, 3s; meadow, 10 acres.
Value before 1066 and now, 10s.

32 S. There also 6 bovates of land taxable. Land for 6 oxen. A
jurisdiction of Marston.
    2 Freemen and 2 smallholders have 2 oxen.
    The lord [has] ½ plough and
    meadow, 10 acres.

33 M. In MARSTON Alsige had 1 carucate of land taxable in lordship and
10 bovates of land in a jurisdiction. Land for 3 ploughs. Walter,
Kolsveinn's man, has 1 plough.
    4 Freemen and 5 smallholders with 1 plough and 1 ox.
    1 mill site; meadow, 32 acres.
Value before 1066, 30s; now 50[s].

34 S. In HOUGHAM 2 carucates of land taxable. Land for 12 oxen. A
jurisdiction of Marston.
    4 Freemen and 1 smallholder have ½ plough and
    meadow, 4 acres.

35 M. In HOUGHAM Atsurr had 2 carucates of land taxable. Land for 3
ploughs. William, Kolsveinn's man, has 1 plough.
    5 villagers and 5 smallholders with 1 plough and 2 oxen.
    Meadow, 2½ acres.
Value before 1066 and now, 30s.

36 M. In BILLINGBOROUGH Sveinn had 2 carucates of land and 7 bovates
taxable. Brunel, Kolsveinn's man, has 1½ ploughs.
    8 villagers and 2 smallholders with 1½ ploughs.
    ½ church; 1 mill, 5s 4d; meadow, 27 acres; underwood, 26 acres.
Value before 1066, 40s; now 60[s].

ᚱIn *VLVESBI* hƀ Alſi . ii . caŕ træ ⁊ i . boú ⁊ dim̄ ad
glđ . Tra . xviii . bob . Ibi Brunel hō Colſ hŧ . i . caŕ
⁊ dim̄ . ⁊ viii . uiłł eū . ii . caŕ . Ibi dim̄ æccła ⁊ i . moliñ
v . ſoliđ . ⁊ iiii . den . T.R.E . ⁊ m̄ . uał . lx . ſoliđ.

Ƨ In Poclintone dim̄ caŕ træ ad glđ . Tra . iiii . boú . Ibi
hŧ Conded hō Colſ . i . caŕ . ⁊ iii . borđ . ⁊ iiii . aćs p̄ti.

Ƨ In Spanebi . ii . caŕ træ ad glđ . Tra . iii . caŕ . Ibi . xii .
ſocħ . hn̄t . ii . caŕ . ⁊ xx . aćs p̄ti.

ᚱIn *NEVTONE* . hƀr Turchil . x . boú ⁷ Goduin træ ad glđ . Tra
. ii . caruć . Ibi Radulf⁹ hō Colſ hŧ . i . caŕ . ⁊ iiii . uiłł
⁊ iiii . borđ . cū dim̄ caŕ . ⁊ xvi ać p̄ti . ⁊ lxxii . ać
ſiluæ minutæ . T.R.E . ⁊ m̄ . lxx . ſoł . Tailla . xx . ſoł.

Ɓ In Vlueſbi . vi . boú træ ⁊ tcia pars . i . boú ad glđ.
Tra . i . caŕ . Inland i Neutone . Ibi m̄ . i . borđ ⁊ ſeđ
uni⁹ molini . ⁊ ix . ać p̄ti.

Ɓ In Trinchigehā . xiiii . bouatæ . ⁊ iii . pars . i . boú
ad glđ . Tra . ii . caŕ ⁊ dim̄ . Inland . Ibi . i . ſocħ . ⁊ v . uiłł
⁊ iii . borđ cū . i . caŕ ⁊ dim̄.

ᚱIn *DELBEBI* . hƀ Gonchel . i . caŕ træ ad glđ . Tra . x . bob.
Ibi Rainalđ⁹ hō Colſ hŧ . i . caŕ . ⁊ iiii . ſocħ ⁊ i . borđ.
cū . i . caŕ . ⁊ xvi . aćs p̄ti . ⁊ xx . aćs ſiluæ miñ . T.R.E . ⁊ m̄
ſ xx . ſoł.

357 c

ᚱIn *SVAVETONE* hƀ Auti . vii . caŕ tre ad glđ . Tra
ix . caŕ . Ibi hŧ Colſuan . iii . caŕ . ⁊ xl . ſocħ de . v . caŕ
huj træ . ⁊ vii . uiłł ⁊ ii . borđ cū . x . caŕ . ⁊ qt xx . aćs
p̄ti . T.R.E . uał . viii . liƀ . m̄ . iiii . Tailla . xl . ſoł.

ᚱIn Eadē villa hƀr Alſi ⁊ Adeſtan . i . caŕ tre ad glđ.
Tra . x . boú . Aluric fŕ eoꝛ habebat ſocā ſup illos
in Hazebi ſolūm in ſeruitio regis . Ibi Colſ hŧ dim̄
caŕ . ⁊ iii . uiłł cū dim̄ caŕ . ⁊ xiii . aćs p̄ti . T.R.E . ⁊ m̄ . x . ſoł.

37 M. In 'OUSEBY' Alsige had 2 carucates of land and 1½ bovates taxable. Land for 18 oxen. Brunel, Kolsveinn's man, has 1½ ploughs.
    8 villagers with 2 ploughs.
    ½ church; 1 mill, 5s 4d.
Value before 1066 and now, 60s.

38 S. In POINTON ½ carucate of land taxable. Land for 4 oxen. Conded, Kolsveinn's man, has 1 plough.
    3 smallholders.
    Meadow, 4 acres.

39 S. In SPANBY 2 carucates of land taxable. Land for 3 ploughs.
    12 Freemen have 2 ploughs and
    meadow, 20 acres.

40 2 In NEWTON Thorketill and Godwine had 10 bovates of land
M. taxable. Land for 2 ploughs. Ralph, Kolsveinn's man, has 1 plough.
    4 villagers and 4 smallholders with ½ plough.
    Meadow, 18 acres; underwood, 72 acres.
[Value] before 1066 and now, 70s. Exactions 20s.

41 B. In 'OUSEBY' 6 bovates of land and the third part of 1 bovate taxable. Land for 1 plough. *Inland* of Newton.
    Now 1 smallholder.
    1 mill site; meadow, 9 acres.

42 B. In THREEKINGHAM 14 bovates and the third part of 1 bovate taxable. Land for 2½ ploughs. *Inland*.
    1 Freemen, 5 villagers and 3 smallholders with 1½ ploughs.

43 M. In DEMBLEBY Gunnketill had 1 carucate of land taxable. Land for 10 oxen. Rainald, Kolsveinn's man, has 1 plough.
    4 Freemen and 1 smallholder with 1 plough.
    Meadow, 16 acres; underwood, 20 acres.
Value before 1066 and now, 20s.

44 M. In SWATON Auti had 7 carucates of land taxable. Land for 9   357 c
ploughs. Kolsveinn has 3 ploughs.
    40 Freemen on 5 carucates of this land; 7 villagers and 2
      smallholders with 10 ploughs.
    Meadow, 80 acres.
Value before 1066 £8; now [£] 4. Exactions 40s.

45 M. Also in this village Alsige and Aethelstan had 1 carucate of land taxable. Land for 10 oxen. Aelfric, their brother, had jurisdiction over them in Haceby but only in the King's service. Kolsveinn has ½ plough.
    3 villagers with ½ plough.
    Meadow, 13 acres.
Value before 1066 and now, 10s.

M̅ In *HORBELINGE* . h̅b̅ Suen . iii . car̅ træ 7 ii . bou ad gl̅d̅.
Tra totid̅ c̅ 7 b̅ . Ibi Mat̅h̅s h̅o Col̅s̅ h̅t̅ . i . car̅ . 7 xi . foc̅h̅
de . i . car̅ huj træ . 7 iii . uil̅t̅ cu̅ . iii . car̅ . 7 xv . ac̅s p̅ti.
T.R.E. 7 m̅ ual . xl . fol . Tailla . xx . fol.

M̅ In *ASEBI* . h̅b̅ Aflac . iii . car̅ træ ad gl̅d̅ . Tra . iiii . car̅.
Ibi Wil̅t̅s h̅o Col̅s̅ h̅t̅ . ix . foc̅h̅ . 7 ii . bord . h̅n̅tes . iiii . car̅.
7 c . ac̅s p̅ti . T.R.E. ual lx . fol . m̅ similit̅ . Tailla . xx . fol.

M̅ In *BERTONE* 7 Billesfelt h̅b̅ Letfled . vi . bou træ
ad gl̅d̅ . Tra . i . car̅ . Ibi Wil̅t̅s h̅o Col̅s̅ h̅t̅ dim̅ car̅ . 7 iii.
uil̅t̅ 7 ii . bord cu̅ dim̅ car̅ . 7 iiii . ac̅ p̅ti . 7 cl . ac̅ filuæ past̅
p loca . T.R.E. ual . xvi . fol . m̅ . xx . fol.

.ii. M̅ In *ASCHEBI* . h̅b̅r Outi 7 Afchil . iii . car̅ træ 7 dim̅ ad gl̅d̅.
Tra . iiii . car̅ . Ibi h̅t̅ Col̅s̅ . i . car̅ 7 dim̅ . 7 xii . uil̅t̅ . 7 ii . foc̅h̅
de . i . bouata huj træ . 7 i . bord . cu̅ . ii . car̅ . 7 xv . ac̅s p̅ti.
T.R.E. ual . l . fol . m̅ . lxx . fol.

M̅ In *NORTCHIME* . h̅b̅ Outi . v . car̅ træ 7 ii . bou ad gl̅d̅.
Tra . ii . car̅ . Ibi h̅t̅ Col̅s̅ . i . car̅ . 7 i . pifcar̅ . viii . den̅.
7 xx . ac̅s p̅ti . 7 v . ac̅s filuæ minutæ . T.R.E. ual . xl . fol.
m̅ . iiii . lib̅.

§ In Weftbi . x . bou tre ad gl̅d̅ . Tra . x . bob̅ . Frifoca i Heidure.
Ibi . i . foc̅h̅ 7 vi . uil̅t̅ h̅n̅t . ii . car̅ . 7 xii . ac̅ p̅ti . 7 l . ac̅
filuæ past̅ p loca.

ß In Euedune . ii . car̅ træ ad gl̅d̅ . Tra . ii . car̅ . Inland in Cher
chebi . Ibi . vi . ac̅ p̅ti . 7 viii . ac̅ filuæ min̅ . 7 xl . ac̅ marefch.

M̅ In *PICHEVORDE* . h̅b̅ Outi . ii . car̅ tre ad gl̅d̅ . Tra . iii . car̅.
hæ duæ carucatæ n̅ fun̅ in numero alicuj hund . neq̅ h̅n̅t
pares in Lincolefcy̅ra . Ibi Wil̅t̅s h̅o Col̅s̅ h̅t̅ . i . car̅ . 7 vi.
uil̅t̅ 7 ii . bord cu̅ . i . car̅ . Ibi p̅b̅r 7 dim̅ æccl̅a . In ifta tra h̅t̅
q̅d̅a̅ francus h̅o . i . car̅ . 7

46 M. In HORBLING Sveinn had 3 carucates of land and 2 bovates taxable. Land for as many ploughs and oxen. Matthew, Kolsveinn's man, has 1 plough.
> 11 Freemen on 1 carucate of this land; 3 villagers with 3 ploughs. Meadow, 15 acres.

Value before 1066 and now, 40s. Exactions 20s.

47 M. In AISBY Aslakr had 3 carucates of land taxable. Land for 4 ploughs. William, Kolsveinn's man, has
> 9 Freemen and 2 smallholders who have 4 ploughs and meadow, 100 acres.

Value before 1066, 60s; now the same. Exactions 20s.

48 M. In BURTON (Coggles) and BITCHFIELD Leodflaed had 6 bovates of land taxable. Land for 1 plough. William, Kolsveinn's man, has ½ plough.
> 3 villagers and 2 smallholders with ½ plough. Meadow, 4 acres; woodland, pasture in places, 150 acres.

Value before 1066, 16s; now 20s.

49 2 M. In ASHBY (de la Launde) Auti and Asketill had 3½ carucates of land taxable. Land for 4 ploughs. Kolsveinn has 1½ ploughs.
> 12 villagers and 2 Freemen on 1 bovate of this land;
>> 1 smallholder with 2 ploughs.

> Meadow, 15 acres.

Value before 1066, 50s; now 70s.

50 M. In NORTH KYME Auti had 5 carucates of land and 2 bovates taxable. Land for 2 ploughs. Kolsveinn has 1 plough.
> 1 fishery, 8d; meadow, 20 acres; underwood, 5 acres.

Value before 1066, 40s; now £4.

51 S. In WESTBY 10 bovates of land taxable. Land for 10 oxen. A free jurisdiction of Heydour.
> 1 Freeman and 6 villagers have 2 ploughs. Meadow, 12 acres; woodland, pasture in places, 50 acres.

52 B. In EVEDON 2 carucates of land taxable. Land for 2 ploughs. *Inland* of Kirkby (la Thorpe).
> Meadow, 6 acres; underwood, 8 acres; marsh, 40 acres.

53 M. In PICKWORTH Auti had 2 carucates of land taxable. Land for 3 ploughs. These 2 carucates are not in the count of any hundred and do not have their like in Lincolnshire. William, Kolsveinn's man, has 1 plough.
> 6 villagers and 2 smallholders with 1 plough. A priest and ½ church.

> On that land a certain freeman has 1 carucate.

In ead uilla . ıı . bou trǣ 7 dimid
funt ad gld . Tra . ııı . boƀʒ 7 dim . Soca in Picheuorde . Ibi . ıı .
uiłł . hnt . ıı . boues . T.R.E. 7 m̅ uał . xl . folid.

.XXVI. TERRA ALVREDI DE LINCOLE.

ꝳ In GOLSE . ħƀ Siuuard . ı . car tre ad gld . Tra . ıı . car
7 dimid . Ibi Radulf hō Aluredi ħt . ı . car . 7 xvı . foch
de . ıı . bou huj tre . 7 vı . uiłł cū . ıı . car . 7 lx . ac̅s p̃ti . T.R.E.
uał . xxx . fol . m̅ . xl . Tailla . x . fol.

ꝳ In HABVRNE . ħƀ Aluuin . v . bou trǣ ad gld . Tra . x . boū .
Ibi Radulf hō Aluredi ħt . ı . car . 7 ı . uiłł 7 ıı . bord .
cū . ıı . boƀ . 7 ı . moliñ . ıı . folid . 7 xxx . ac̅s p̃ti . T.R.E. 7 m̅ . xxx . fol.

ꝳ In COTES . ħƀ Morcar . v . bou trǣ ad gld . Tra . x . boƀ . Ibi
Bernard hō Aluredi . ħt . ıı . uiłł 7 ıı . bord . 7 vııı . foch .
de . ı . bou huj trǣ . cū . ıı . car . 7 c . ac̅s p̃ti . T.R.E. uał xxx .
fol . m̅ xxıııı. ⌐ Soca i Cotes.

Ɓ In Alefbi . dim ƀō trǣ ad gld . Tra . ıı . boƀ . Ibi . ı . uiłłs ħt . ı . bou .

ꝳ In HECHELINGE . ħƀ Morcar . ıı . car ad gld . Tra . ıııı . car .
Ibi Bernard hō Aluredi ħt . ıı . car . 7 xııı . foch de dim car .
huj trǣ . 7 ıı . uiłł 7 ıı . bord . cū . ıı . car 7 dim . 7 dim moliñ
ııı . folid . 7 xxvı . ac̅s p̃ti . T.R.E. uał xl fol . m̅ . l . Tailla . x . fol.

Ɓ In Sualun . ııı . ƀō trǣ ad gld . Tra . vı . boū . Inland huj ꝳ .
Ibi . ı . uiłłs ħt . ı . boue in car.

ꝳ In LINDVDE . ħƀr Wiłłs 7 Grichel 7 Asford . ı . car tre
7 dim ad gld . Tra . ıııı . car . Ibi ħt Alured . ıı . car in dn̅io.

54 Also in this village 2½ bovates of land are taxable. Land for 3½ oxen. A jurisdiction of Pickworth.
   2 villagers have 2 oxen.
   Value before 1066 and now, 40s.

27   LAND OF ALFRED OF LINCOLN   357 d

1 M. In GOXHILL Siward had 1 carucate of land and 2 bovates taxable. Land for 2½ ploughs. Ralph, Alfred's man, has 1 plough.
   16 Freemen on 2 bovates of this land; 6 villagers with 2 ploughs.
   Meadow, 60 acres.
   Value before 1066, 30s; now 40[s]. Exactions 10s.

2 M. In HABROUGH Alwine had 5 bovates of land taxable. Land for 10 oxen. Ralph, Alfred's man, has 1 plough.
   1 villager and 2 smallholders with 2 oxen.
   1 mill, 2s; meadow, 30 acres.
   [Value] before 1066 and now, 30s.

3 M. In (Great) COATES Morcar had 5 bovates of land taxable. Land for 10 oxen. Bernard, Alfred's man, has
   2 villagers, 2 smallholders and 8 Freemen on 1 bovate of this land with 2 ploughs; and
   meadow, 100 acres.
   Value before 1066, 30s; now 24[s].

4 B. In AYLESBY ½ bovate of land taxable. Land for 2 oxen.
   1 villager has 1 ox.
   A jurisdiction of (Great) Coates.

5 M. In HEALING Morcar had 2 carucates of land taxable. Land for 4 ploughs. Bernard, Alfred's man, has 2 ploughs.
   13 Freemen on ½ carucate of this land; 2 villagers and 2 smallholders with 2½ ploughs.
   ½ mill, 3s; meadow, 26 acres.
   Value before 1066, 40s; now 50[s]. Exactions 10s.

6 B. In SWALLOW 3 bovates of land taxable. Land for 6 oxen. *Inland* of this manor.
   1 villager has 1 ox in a plough.

7 2 In LINWOOD William, Grimketill and Asfrothr had 1½ carucates of
M. land taxable. Land for 4 ploughs. Alfred has 2 ploughs in lordship;

7 xx.vilł 7 v.borđ cũ.iiii.caŕ.7 īī.partes molini.ii.soł.

7 cc.7 q̃t xx.ac̃s p̃ti.T.R.E. uał.lxv.soł.m̃ l.soł.Tailla.x.s.

₮ In Rafe.iiii.bou træ ad glđ.Tra xii.boũ. Inland huj c̃õ.

Ibi.iii.uilł hn̄t.ii.bou in caŕ.

§ In altera Rafe.iiii.bou træ 7 dim̃ ad glđ.Tra.i.car

Soca.Ibi.x.focħ hn̄t.i.caŕ.7 i.molin̄ xii.den̄.7 x.ac̃s

c̃õ In *TORESVVE*.ħbr Rolf 7 Code.v.caŕ træ ⟨ p̃ti.

7 vii.bou ad glđ.Tra xiii.caŕ.Ibi hⁱ Alured.ii.caŕ.

7 lvi.focħ.7 v , uilł.cũ.v.caŕ.7 ii.molin̄.iii.folid.

7 xl.ac̃s p̃ti.in foca de Caftre. c̃õ Wilłi de p̃ci.T.R.E.

uał.iiii.lib̃.m̃.c.foł.Tailla.xl.foł.

In Tauelefbi hⁱ Alured.i.molin̄.in foca ep̃i baioc̃.

c̃õ In *CVCVALT*.ħb Leduin.iii.bou træ ad glđ.Tra.vi.bob.

Ibi Gleu hõ Aluredi hⁱ.i.caŕ.7 īī.uilł 7 i.borđ.

T.R.E.7 m̃ uał.xx.foł.

§ In Caburne.i.bou træ ad glđ.Soca ī Cucualt.Ibi.i.uilł

7 i.borđ hn̄t.i.boue in caŕ.

c̃õ In *RODEVVELLE*.ħbr Grinchil 7 Wilłs.iiii.caŕ træ

7.i.bou. ~~7 duas parł.i.bouatæ.~~ ad glđ.Tra.viii.caŕ.

Ibi Gleu hõ Aluredi hⁱ.i.caŕ 7 dim̃.7 xii.focħ de.vii,

bou huj træ.7 vii.uilł.7 i.borđ.cũ.ii.caŕ 7 dim̃.7 ii.

molin̄.iii.folid.7 xlvi.ac̃s p̃ti.7 unã æcctam.T.R.E.

uał.iiii.lib̃.m̃.iii.Tailla.x.foł.

c̃õ In *RODEWELLE*.ħb Torchetel dim̃ caŕ træ ad glđ.Tra.i.caŕ.Ibi hⁱ

Alured.i.focħ 7 ii.borđ.cũ dim̃ caŕ.T.R.E.7 m̃ uał.vi.folid.

In Torefbi 7 Alduluebi.hⁱ Alured.i.falinã in Rodeuuelle.

358 a

§ In Cucualt.i.bou træ ad glđ.Ibi.iii.focħ hn̄t.i.caŕ.

§ In Caburne.ii.bou træ 7 dim̃ ad glđ.Wafta.ē.

20 villagers and 5 smallholders with 4 ploughs; and
2 parts of a mill, 2s; meadow, 280 acres.
Value before 1066, 65s; now 50s. Exactions 10s.

8 B. In (Middle) RASEN 4 bovates of land taxable. Land for 12 oxen.
Inland of this manor.
3 villagers have 2 oxen in a plough.

9 S. In the other RASEN 4½ bovates of land taxable. Land for 1 plough.
A jurisdiction.
10 Freemen have 1 plough and
1 mill, 12d; meadow, 10 acres.

10 2 In THORESWAY Rothulfr and Koddi had 5 carucates of land and 7
M. bovates taxable. Land for 13 ploughs. Alfred has 2 ploughs.
56 Freemen and 5 villagers with 5 ploughs.
2 mills, 3s; meadow, 40 acres in the jurisdiction of Caistor,
William of Percy's manor.
Value before 1066 £4; now 100s. Exactions 40s.

11 In TEALBY Alfred has 1 mill in the Bishop of Bayeux' jurisdiction.

12 M. In CUXWOLD Leodwine had 3 bovates of land taxable. Land for 6
oxen. Gleu, Alfred's man, has 1 plough and
2 villagers and 1 smallholder.
Value before 1066 and now, 20s.

13 S. In CABOURN 1 bovate of land taxable. A jurisdiction of Cuxwold.
1 villager and 1 smallholder have 1 ox in a plough.

14 2 In ROTHWELL Grimketill and William had 4 carucates of land and
M. 1 bovate *and 2 parts of 1 bovate* taxable. Land for 8 ploughs.
Gleu, Alfred's man, has 1½ ploughs and
12 Freemen on 7 bovates of this land; 7 villagers and 1
smallholder with 2½ ploughs; and
2 mills, 3s; meadow, 46 acres; 1 church.
Value before 1066 £4; now [£] 3. Exactions 10s.

15 M. In ROTHWELL Thorketill had ½ carucate of land taxable. Land for
1 plough. Alfred has
1 Freeman and 2 smallholders with ½ plough.
Value before 1066 and now, 6s.

16 In (North) THORESBY and 'AUDBY' Alfred has 1 salt-house in
Rothwell.

17 S. In CUXWOLD 1 bovate of land taxable. 3 Freemen have 1 plough.   358 a

18 S. In CABOURN 2½ bovates of land taxable. It is waste.

ᴍ In *STIGESWALT*. ħƀ Siuuard. vɪ. bou͛ træ͛ ad glđ. Tra. xɪɪ. bob. Ibi ħꝶ idē de Aluredo. ɪɪɪɪ. uiꝶ cū. ɪ. caꝛ. 7 xx. aꞔs p̄ti. 7 xʟ. aꞔs filuæ past͛. T.R.E. 7 m̄. uaꞁ. x. foꞁ.

§ In Terintone ħƀ Rolf. ɪɪɪ. bou͛ træ 7 dim ad glđ. Tra. ɪ. caꝛ. Soca in ipfa uilla. Ibi ħꝶ Gozelin͛ hō Aluredi ɪɪ. foch 7 dimiđ. hn̄tes. ɪɪ. bou 7 dim in caꝛ. 7 xɪ. aꞔs p̄ti.

§ Ibiđ ħƀ Clac. ɪɪɪ. bou͛ tre͛ 7 dim ad glđ. Tra. ɪ. caꝛ. Soca in Haintone. Ibi. ɪɪ. foch 7 dim hn̄t. ɪɪ. bou 7 dim͞ in caruca. Gozeꞁ tenet de Aluredo ·

ᴍ In *ALVINGEHA͛*. ħƀ Edric. v. bou͛ træ͛ 7 dim͞. 7 vɪ. pars uni͛ bou ad glđ. Tra. ɪ. caꝛ 7 dim͞. Ibi Gozeꞁ hō Aluredi ħꝶ. ɪ. caꝛ. 7 v. uiꝶ cū dim͞ caꝛ. Due bou de hac tra͛ funt in Soca. 7 xx. aꞔ p̄ti. T.R.E. uaꞁ xx. foꞁ. m̄. xxx.

§ In Brachenberg. ɪ. bou͛ træ͛ ad glđ. Tra. ɪɪ. bob. Ibi Rannulf͛ hō Alured͛i ħꝶ. ɪ. caꝛ. 7 ɪɪɪɪ. uiꝶ cū dim͞ caꝛ. Soca in Aluinghā. 7 x. aꞔ p̄ti.

ᴍ In ipfa uilla ħƀr Edric 7 Hoch. vɪ. bou͛ træ͛ ad glđ. Tra xɪɪɪɪ. bou͛. Ibi ħꝶ Ran͞n hō Aluredi ħꝶ. ɪ. uiꝶ 7 x. foch cū. ɪɪ. caꝛ. 7 ɪɪɪɪ. part molini. ɪɪ. foliđ. 7 xvɪɪɪ. aꞔ p̄ti. T.R.E. uaꞁ. xvɪ. foꞁ. m̄. xʟ.

ᴍ In *COCRINTONE*. ħƀr Edric 7 Macus. vɪɪ. bou͛ træ͛ ad glđ. Tra. xɪɪɪɪ. bob. Ibi Alured 7 Gozeꞁ hō ej hn̄t dim͞ caꝛ. 7 ɪ. foch de una tofta. 7 ɪɪ. uiꝶ cū dim͞ caꝛ. 7 dim͞ molin͞. ɪɪɪ. foliđ. 7 ʟxx. aꞔ p̄ti. 7 ʟvɪɪɪ. aꞔ filuæ minutæ. T.R.E. uaꞁ xxɪ. foꞁ. m̄. xxx. foꞁ.

ᴍ In *STIVETONE*. ħƀ Elmer. xɪɪɪ. bou͛ træ͛ ad glđ. Tra. ɪɪɪ. ᷓ caꝛ 7 ɪɪ. bou͛. Ibi ħꝶ Alured. ɪɪ. caꝛ. 7 x. foch de dimiđ caꝛ. 7 vɪɪɪ. uiꝶ cū. ɪ. caꝛ. 7 cc. aꞔ filuæ paftiꞁ. T.R.E. uaꞁ. xx. foꞁ. m̄. ʟx. foꞁ.

k

19 M. In STIXWOULD Siward had 6 bovates of land taxable. Land for 12 oxen. He also has from Alfred
    4 villagers with 1 plough; and
      meadow, 20 acres; woodland pasture, 40 acres.
Value before 1066 and now, 10s.

20 S. In TORRINGTON Rothulfr had 3½ bovates of land taxable. Land for 1 plough. A jurisdiction of the village itself. Jocelyn, Alfred's man, has
    2½ Freemen who have 2½ oxen in a plough and
    meadow, 11 acres.

21 S. There also Klakkr had 3½ bovates of land taxable. Land for 1 plough. A jurisdiction of Hainton.
    2½ Freemen have 2½ oxen in a plough.
    Jocelyn holds from Alfred.

22 M. In ALVINGHAM Eadric had 5½ bovates of land and the sixth part of 1 bovate taxable. Land for 1½ ploughs. Jocelyn, Alfred's man, has 1 plough.
    5 villagers with ½ plough.
    2 bovates of this land are in a jurisdiction.
    Meadow, 20 acres.
Value before 1066, 20s; now 30[s].

23 S. In BRACKENBOROUGH 1 bovate of land taxable. Land for 2 oxen. Ranulf, Alfred's man, has 1 plough.
    4 villagers with ½ plough.
    A jurisdiction of Alvingham.
    Meadow, 10 acres.

24 2 In this village Eadric and Hoc had 6 bovates of land taxable.
M. Land for 14 oxen. Ranulf, Alfred's man, has
    1 villager and 10 Freemen with 2 ploughs.
    4 parts of a mill, 2s; meadow, 18 acres.
Value before 1066, 16s; now 40[s].

25 3 In COCKERINGTON Eadric and Maccus had 7 bovates of land taxable.
M. Land for 14 oxen. Alfred and Jocelyn, his man, have ½ plough.
    1 Freeman on 1 plot; 2 villagers with ½ plough.
k   ½ mill, 3s; meadow, 70 acres; underwood, 58 acres.
Value before 1066, 21s; now 30s.

26 M. In STEWTON Aelmer had 13 bovates of land taxable. Land for 3 ploughs and 2 oxen. Alfred has 2 ploughs.
    10 Freemen on ½ carucate of land; 8 villagers with 1 plough.
    Woodland pasture, 200 acres.
Value before 1066, 20s; now 60s.

ꝏ In *CATEBI*. ħƀ Macus. vii. bou͛ t͛re ad glđ . T͛ra . xiiii.
bob . Ibi hͭ Alured. i. caꝛ. 7 i. focħ de. iiii. bou�9 huj t͛ræ.
7 iiii . uilt cū . i . caꝛ. 7 xiii. aĉs p̃ti. T.R.E. ual xxx. fol. m̂.xx.

§ In Grimoldbi. i. bou t͛ræ ad glđ . Soᴄᴀ in Catebi. Alured�9
hͭ . ii . pártes 7 Wilt͛s tcia͛ . Waſt.e͛.

§ In Salflatebi. i. bou t͛ræ ad glđ. T͛ra. i. bou͛ 7 dim̃. Soᴄᴀ in
catebi. Alured hͭ. ii. partes. Wilt͛s tcia͛.

ꝏ In *ᴄᴀᴛᴇʙɪ* *TORP* . ħƀ Rolf. v. bou͛ t͛ræ ad glđ. T͛ra. x. bob. Ibi hͭ
Alured. i. caꝛ. 7 i. focħ de duab͛ bou�9 huj t͛ræ 7 dimiđ.
7 iii. uilt hͭntes. ii. bou͛ in caꝛ. 7 vi. aĉs p̃ti. T.R.E. ual.xxx.
fol. m̂ . lx.   ⌏ Waſta eſt

§ In Wicha͛ dim̃ bou͛ t͛ræ ad glđ. T͛ra. i. bou͛. Soᴄᴀ in Torp.

§ In eođ Wicha͛. v. bo͛ t͛ræ ad glđ. T͛ra. x. bob. Soᴄᴀ in Catebi.
Ibi. v. focħ hͭnt dim̃ caꝛ. 7 x. aĉs p̃ti.

358 b
ꝏ .ɪɪ. In *CHELESTORNE*. ħƀr Rolf 7 Machus. ii. caꝛ t͛ræ
7 vi. bou͛ t͛re ad glđ. T͛ra. v. caꝛ 7 dim̃. Ibi hͭ Alured�9.
.i. caꝛ. 7 ix. focħ de. xv. bou͛ huj t͛ræ. 7 iiii. uilt. cū. ii. caꝛ.
T.R.E. ual. xxx. fol. m̂. xl.

ꝏ In *OFFINTONE*. ħƀ Erneber. vii. caꝛ t͛ræ ad glđ. T͛ra totiđ. caꝛ.
Ibi hͭ Alured�9. ii. caꝛ in dͭnio. 7 xvi. focħ de. iiii. caꝛ huj
✳ t͛ræ. 7 xxxi. uilt. cū. vii. caꝛ. 7 iii. moliñ 7 dim̃ de xl. folid.
Ibi æccla 7 pƀr. 7 c. aĉ p̃ti. T.R.E. ual. vii. liƀ. m̂. xi. Tailla. iii. łƀ.

ꝏ In ead uilla ħƀ Leduin�9. i. caꝛ t͛ræ ad glđ. T͛ra. i. caꝛ.
Ibi hͭ Alured�9. iiii. focħ de. iiii. bou͛ huj t͛ræ. 7 iii. uilt.
cū. i. caꝛ. 7 ix. burgenſes de Stanford redđ. iiii. fol. 7 xx.
aĉs p̃ti. T.R.E. 7 m̂ ual. xxx. folid.

§ In Eſtou. i. bou͛ 7 dim̃ ad glđ. T͛ra. i. bou͛ 7 dim̃. Alured�9
hͭ ibi æcclam una͛ quæ jacet in Offintone.

358 a, b

27 M. In (South) 'CADEBY' Maccus had 7 bovates of land taxable. Land
for 14 oxen. Alfred has 1 plough.
1 Freeman on 4 bovates of this land; 4 villagers with 1 plough.
Meadow, 13 acres.
Value before 1066, 30s; now 20[s].

28 S. In GRIMOLDBY 1 bovate of land taxable. A jurisdiction of (South)
'Cadeby'. Alfred has 2 parts and William the third. It is waste.

29 S. In SALTFLEETBY 1 bovate of land taxable. Land for 1½ oxen.
A jurisdiction of (South) 'Cadeby'. Alfred has 2 parts, William
the third.

30 M. In (Calce)THORPE [and] (South) 'CADEBY' Rothulfr had 5 bovates of
land taxable. Land for 10 oxen. Alfred has 1 plough.
1 Freeman on 2½ bovates of this land; 3 villagers who have
2 oxen in a plough and
meadow, 6 acres.
Value before 1066, 30s; now 60[s].

31 S. In (East) WYKEHAM ½ bovate of land taxable. Land for 1 ox.
A jurisdiction of (Calce)thorpe. It is waste.

32 S. Also in (East) WYKEHAM 5 bovates of land taxable. Land for 10
oxen. A jurisdiction of (South) 'Cadeby'.
5 Freemen have ½ plough and
meadow, 10 acres.

33 2 In KELSTERN Rothulfr and Maccus had 2 carucates of land and 6   358 b
M. bovates taxable. Land for 5½ ploughs. Alfred has 1 plough.
9 Freemen on 15 bovates of this land; 4 villagers with 2 ploughs.
Value before 1066, 30s; now 40[s].

34 M. In UFFINGTON Arnbjorn had 7 carucates of land taxable. Land for
as many ploughs. Alfred has 2 ploughs in lordship;
✳   16 Freemen on 4 carucates of this land; 31 villagers with 7
ploughs.
3½ mills at 40s. A church and a priest; meadow, 100 acres.
Value before 1066 £7; now [£] 11. Exactions £3.

35 M. Also in this village Leodwine had 1 carucate of land taxable.
Land for 1 plough. Alfred has
4 Freemen on 4 bovates of this land; 3 villagers with 1 plough;
9 burgesses of Stamford who pay 4s.
Meadow, 20 acres.
Value before 1066 and now, 30s.

36 S. In 'STOWE' 1½ bovates taxable. Land for 1½ oxen. Alfred has there
1 church which lies in Uffington.

☩ In CASVIC ħб| . vi . bou træ ad glđ . Tra . vi . bob . Ibi Boſo
ħo Aluredi hŧ . i . caŕ . 7 ii . uiłł 7 i . borđ . cū . ii . bob in caŕ.
T.R.E . uał . x . ſoł . m̅ . xx . ſoł.

☩ In TALINTONE . ħб Oluiet . vi . car 7 dimiđ ad glđ.
Tra totiđ caŕ . Ibi hŧ . ii . caŕ . 7 xiiii . ſocħ de . iiii . car træ.
7 ix . uiłł cū . iiii . caŕ . 7 i . moliñ . xii . ſolid . 7 qt xx . ac̅ p̅ti.
T.R.E . uał . iii . liб . m̅ . iiii . Tailla . xx . ſoł.
In Eſtdepinge . iiii . bou . træ ad glđ . Tra dim̅ caŕ . Soca huj ☩ .
Ibi . vi . uiłł 7 ii . borđ hn̅t . i . caŕ 7 dim̅ . 7 xx . ac̅s p̅ti . 7 i . piscaŕ

☩ In CRETONE . ħб Turchil . vi . bou træ 7 iii . parŧ . ii . bou
ad glđ . Tra totiđ bob . Ibi Radulf ħo Aluredi . hŧ dim̅
caŕ . 7 ii . uiłł . 7 ii . ac̅s p̅ti . 7 xxx . ac̅s ſiluæ min . T.R.E . 7 m̅ . xx . ſoł.

☩ In GRENEHA̅ 7 Auuartorp 7 Bolebi . ħб Aldene . ii . caŕ
træ 7 vii . bou ad glđ . Tra totiđ cr 7 b . Ibi hŧ Aluređ
ii . caŕ . 7 iiii . ſocħ de . x . bou huj træ . 7 ii . uiłł cū . ii . caŕ.
7 viii . ac̅s p̅ti . 7 ccc . xx . ac̅s ſiluæ paſt p loca . T.R.E.
uał . xxx . ſoł . m̅ . xl . Tailla . xx . ſoł.

☩ In AIGLESTORP . ħб Siuuard . ii . car tre ad glđ . Tra
ii . caŕ . Ibi hŧ Aluređ . i . caŕ . 7 v . ſocħ de . vi . bou huj
træ . 7 v . uiłł cū . ii . caŕ . 7 xviii . ac̅s p̅ti . 7 ccxl . ac̅s ſiluæ
T.R.E . uał . xxx . ſoł . m̅ . xl . Tailla . xx . ſoł.

☩ In STIGANDEBI . ħб Siuuard . vi . car tre ad glđ . Tra
viii . caŕ . Ibi hŧ Aluređ . ii . caŕ . 7 ii . moliñ . ii . ſoliđ . 7 viii
ac̅s p̅ti 7 dim̅ . 7 xl . ac̅s ſiluæ min . Ibi . iiii . caŕ ejđ træ Soca.
T.R.E . uał . xx . ſoł . m̅ . xl . Tailla . xx . ſoł.

☩ In ROCHESHA̅ ħб Alden . ii . car træ 7 vi . bou ad glđ.
Tra totiđ c 7 b . Ibi Radulf ħo Aluredi . hŧ . i . caŕ
7 dim̅ . 7 viii . uiłł cū . ii . caŕ . 7 xl . ac̅s p̅ti . T.R.E . uał
xl . ſoł . m̅ . l . ſoł.

37 M. In CASEWICK Wulfgeat had 6 bovates of land taxable. Land for 6 oxen. Boso, Alfred's man, has 1 plough.
2 villagers and 1 smallholder with 2 oxen in a plough.
Value before 1066, 10s; now 20s.

38 M. In TALLINGTON Wulfgeat had 6½ carucates of land taxable. Land for as many ploughs. He has 2 ploughs.
14 Freemen on 4 carucates of land; 9 villagers with 4 ploughs.
1 mill, 12s; meadow, 80 acres.
Value before 1066 £3; now [£] 4. Exactions 20s.

39 In EAST DEEPING 4 bovates of land taxable. Land for ½ plough. A jurisdiction of this manor.
6 villagers and 2 smallholders have 1½ ploughs and meadow, 20 acres; 1 fishery, 5d.

40 M. In CREETON Thorketill had 6 bovates of land and 3 parts of 2 bovates taxable. Land for as many oxen. Ralph, Alfred's man, has ½ plough.
2 villagers.
Meadow, 2 acres; underwood, 30 acres.
[Value] before 1066 and now, 20s.

41 M. In IRNHAM, HAWTHORPE and BULBY Halfdan had 2 carucates of land and 7 bovates taxable. Land for as many ploughs and oxen. Alfred has 2 ploughs.
4 Freemen on 10 bovates of this land; 2 villagers with 2 ploughs.
Meadow, 8 acres; woodland, pasture in places, 320 acres.
Value before 1066, 30s; now 40[s]. Exactions 20s.

42 M. In ELSTHORPE Siward had 2 carucates of land taxable. Land for 2 ploughs. Alfred has 1 plough.
5 Freemen on 6 bovates of this land; 5 villagers with 2 ploughs.
Meadow, 18 acres; woodland, 240 acres.
Value before 1066, 30s; now 40[s]. Exactions 20s.

43 M. In STAINBY Siward had 6 carucates of land taxable. Land for 8 ploughs. Alfred has 2 ploughs.
2 mills, 2s; meadow, 8½ acres; underwood, 40 acres.
4 carucates of the same land [is] a jurisdiction.
Value before 1066, 20s; now 40[s]. Exactions 20s.

44 M. In 'ROXHOLM' Halfdan had 2 carucates of land and 6 bovates taxable. Land for as many ploughs and oxen. Ralph, Alfred's man, has 1½ ploughs.
8 villagers with 2 ploughs.
Meadow, 40 acres.
Value before 1066, 40s; now 50s.

ꝼIn *BRANZEWELLE* . ħ Aldene . ii . car træ 7 vi . bou ad
glđ . Tra totid c̄ 7 b . Ibi ħt Alured . iii . uiłł 7 ii . borđ cū
iii . bob ia car . T.R.E. xx . soł . ṁ . x . soł.　　Soca huj ꝼ.

ꞇS In Blocheſhā . ii . car tre 7 iii . bou ad glđ . Tra totid c̄ 7 b .
Ibi . ii . soch cū dim car .

ꝼIn *WIME* ħ Siuuard . iiii . car træ ad glđ . Tra . iiii . car .
Ibi Gleu hō Aluredi ħt . i . car . 7 xi . uiłł 7 iii . borđ .
cū . iii . car . 7 c . acs p̄ti . vi . min . 7 qt xx . acs siluæ past .
T.R.E. uał xl . soł . ṁ . L . Tailla . x . soł . H Soca . ē in Tiſtel

ꝼIn *TISTELTVNE* . ħ Siuuard dim car tre　　　∠tune.
ad glđ . Tra . i . car . Ibi Gleu hō Alurđ ħt . i . car . 7 iii .
uiłł 7 ii . borđ cū đ . car . p̄ciū ej in Wime .　　Soca

ꞇS In alia Tiſteltune . i . car træ ad glđ . Tra . i . car . Ibi . ii .
soch hn̄t iii . bou in car .

ꝼIn *MERESTONE* . ħ Vlſi . i . car tre in dn̄io . 7 i . car
træ in soca . Tra . iii . car . Ibi Walefrid hō Aluredi
ħt . i . car . 7 viii . uiłł 7 ii . borđ . 7 i . soch cū . iii . car .
7 ii . moliñ . viii . solid . 7 xxx.ii . acs p̄ti . T.R.E. uał . xx . soł .

ꝼIn *BRVNE* . ħ Turchil . vi . bou træ　　　∠ṁ xl .
ad glđ . Tra . vi . bob . Ibi Dodiñ hō Aluredi ħt . i . car .
7 ii . uiłł 7 iiii . borđ cū . i . car . 7 tcia part uni molini
iii . solid 7 iiii . den . 7 vi . piscar . xvi . den . 7 vi . acs p̄ti .
7 xxx . acs siluæ past . T.R.E. 7 ṁ . uał . xx . soł .

ꞇB In Torulfbi . dim car træ ad glđ . Tra . iiii . bob . Ibi
iiii . uiłł hn̄t dim car . Inland in Brune .

45 M. In BRAUNCEWELL Halfdan had 2 carucates of land and 6 bovates
taxable. Land for as many ploughs and oxen. Alfred has
 3 villagers and 2 smallholders with 3 oxen in a plough.
[Value] before 1066, 20s; now 10s.

Jurisdiction of this manor:
46 S. In BLOXHOLM 2 carucates of land and 3 bovates taxable. Land for
as many ploughs and oxen.
 2 Freemen with ½ plough.

47 M. In (South) WITHAM Siward had 4 carucates of land taxable. Land
for 4 ploughs. Gleu, Alfred's man, has 1 plough.
 11 villagers and 3 smallholders with 3 ploughs.
 Meadow, 100 acres, less 6; woodland pasture, 80 acres.
Value before 1066, 40s; now 50[s]. Exactions 10s.
 This jurisdiction is in Thistleton.

48 M. In THISTLETON Siward had ½ carucate of land taxable. Land for 1
plough. Gleu, Alfred's man, has 1 plough.
 3 villagers and 2 smallholders with ½ plough.
Its assessment [is] in (South) Witham.

Jurisdiction:
49 S. In another THISTLETON 1 carucate of land taxable. Land for 1
plough.
 2 Freemen have 3 oxen in a plough.

50 M. In MARSTON Wulfsige had 1 carucate of land in lordship and 1
carucate of land in a jurisdiction. Land for 3 ploughs. Walefrid,
Alfred's man, has 1 plough.
 8 villagers, 2 smallholders and 1 Freeman with 3 ploughs.
 2 mills, 8s; meadow, 32 acres.
Value before 1066, 20s; now 40[s].

51 M. In BOURNE Thorketill had 6 bovates of land taxable. Land for 6
oxen. Doding, Alfred's man, has 1 plough and
 2 villagers and 4 smallholders with 1 plough; and
 the third part of 1 mill, 3s 4d; 6 fisheries, 16d; meadow, 6 acres;
 woodland pasture, 30 acres.
Value before 1066 and now, 20s.

52 B. In THURLBY ½ carucate of land taxable. Land for 4 oxen.
 4 villagers have ½ plough.
Inland of Bourne.

ⰗIn *REPINGHALE*.ħƀ Turchil.xv.bou̅ tre.7 ıı.part
uni bou ad glđ.Tra totid̃ bob.Ibi Dodin hõ Aluredi
ħt̃ 'dim̃ car̃.7 vıı.uilt 7 ııı.borđ cũ.ı.car̃ 7 dimiđ.
Ibi pƀr.7 tcia pars æcclæ.7 xx.ac̃s p̃ti.7 lx.ac̃s ſiluæ
minutæ.T.R.E.7 m̃ ual.xxx.ſot.

ⰗIn *CHERCHEBI*.ħƀ Turuert.ı.car̃ træ 7 dim̃ ad glđ.
Tra.xıı.bob.Ibi ħt̃ Alured dim̃ car̃.7 ıııı.ſocħ
de.'ıııı.bou huj træ.7 ıııı.uilt 7 ıı.borđ cũ.ı.car̃.
7 xvı.ac̃s p̃ti.7 lx.ac̃s ſiluæ min.T.R.E.7 m̃.xxx.ſot.

ⰗIbidẽ ħƀ Offran.v.bou træ ad glđ.Tra totid̃ bob.
Ibi iſdẽ Offran ħt̃ de Aluredo.ıı.bou in car̃.7 ıı.uilt.
7 v.ac̃s p̃ti.7 lx.ac̃s ſiluæ miñ.T.R.E.ual.xx.ſot.m̃.x.

ⰗIn *AVETORP*.ħƀ Offran dim̃ car̃ træ ad glđ.Tra
vı.bob.Ibi Suen hõ Aluredi ħt̃.ı.car̃.7 ıı.uilt
7 ı.borđ.7 ıııı.ac̃s p̃ti.T.R.E.ual.v.ſot.m̃ ſimilit.

ⰗIn *STEPINGEHA*.ħƀ Morcar.ıııı.car̃ træ 7 ıı.bou
ad glđ.Tra totid̃ c 7 b.Ibi Gozelin hõ Aluredi
ħt̃.ı.car̃.7 xıııı.ſocħ de.ıı.car̃ 7 dim̃ huj træ.
7 vııı.uilt 7 ıı.borđ.7 ıııı.partẽ uni æcclæ.7 xı.ac̃s p̃ti.
7 vıı.ac̃s ſiluæ miñ.T.R.E.7 m̃ ual.xl.ſot.Ɉailla.xx.ſot.

27

53 M. In RIPPINGALE Thorketill had 15 bovates of land and 2 parts of 1 bovate taxable. Land for as many oxen. Doding, Alfred's man, has ½ plough.
>   7 villagers and 3 smallholders with 1½ ploughs.
>   A priest and the third part of a church; meadow, 20 acres; underwood, 60 acres.
> Value before 1066 and now, 30s.

54 M. In KIRKBY (Underwood) Thorfrothr had 1½ carucates of land taxable. Land for 12 oxen. Alfred has ½ plough.
>   4 Freemen on 4 bovates of this land; 4 villagers and 2 smallholders with 1 plough.
>   Meadow, 16 acres; underwood, 60 acres.
> Value before 1066 and now, 30s.

55 M. There also Osfram had 5 bovates of land taxable. Land for as many oxen. Osfram also has from Alfred 2 oxen in a plough.
>   ˙2 villagers.
>   Meadow, 5 acres; underwood, 60 acres.
> Value before 1066, 20s; now 10[s].

56 M. In 'AVETHORPE' Osfram had ½ carucate of land taxable. Land for 6 oxen. Sveinn, Alfred's man, has 1 plough.
>   2 villagers and 1 smallholder.
>   Meadow, 4 acres.
> Value before 1066, 5s; now the same.

57 M. In 'SEMPRINGHAM' Morcar had 4 carucates of land and 2 bovates taxable. Land for as many ploughs and oxen. Jocelyn, Alfred's man, has 1 plough and
>   14 Freemen on 2½ carucates of this land; 8 villagers and 2 smallholders; and
>   the fourth part of 1 church; meadow, 11 acres; underwood, 7 acres.
> Value before 1066 and now, 40s. Exactions 20s.

ꝳ In *BELLINGEBVRG*. ħƀ Toli . ɪ . caŕ tŕe ad glđ . T́ŕa
.ɪ . caŕ. Ibi ħт Gozeliñ ħõ Aluredi . ɪ . caŕ. 7 ɪɪ . uiħ
7 ɪ . borđ. cū . ɪɪ . boƀ in caŕ. 7 xɪɪɪɪ . ac̃ p̃ti . T.R.E. 7 m̃ . x . foħ.

ꝳ In *BODEBI* 7 S̄umertune ħƀr Aldene . ɪɪɪɪ . caŕ træ
ad glđ . T́ŕa . ɪɪɪɪ caŕ 7 vɪ . boũ. Ibi Gozeliñ ħõ Aluredi
ħт . ɪɪ . caŕ 7 dimiđ. 7 vɪ . foct de . ɪ . caŕ huj træ. 7 ɪɪɪɪ .
uiħ 7 vɪ . borđ cū . ɪɪ . caŕ. 7 ʟv. ac̃ p̃ti . T.R.E. ual̃. xxx.
foħ . m̃ . xʟ.

ꝳ In *HOTOT*. ħƀ Stepi . ɪ . boũ tŕe ad glđ. T́ŕa . ɪ . boũ 7 dim̃.
Ibi Dodo ħõ Aluredi ħт dim̃ caŕ. 7 ɪ . uiħ. 7 xʟ . ac̃s
p̃ti. T.R.E. 7 m̃ ual̃. x . foliđ.

ꝳ Ibidē ħƀ Siuuard . ɪ . boũ træ ad glđ . T́ŕa . ɪ . boũ 7 dim̃.
Ibi Bernarđ ħõ Aluredi ħт . ɪɪ . boũ in caŕ. 7 xʟ ac̃s p̃ti.
T.R.E. 7 m̃ ual̃ . v . foliđ 7 ɪɪɪɪ . deñ.

Ş In Tedlageſtorp. dimiđ caŕ træ ad glđ. T́ŕa . ɪɪɪɪ . boƀ.
Ibi . ɪɪɪɪ . foct 7 ɪ . uiħ hñt . ɪɪ . boũ in caŕ. 7 xʟ ac̃s p̃ti.

Ş In Haburne . ɪ . boũ træ ad glđ. T́ŕa . ɪɪ . boũ. SOCA in
Neuhuſe. Aluređ ħт 7 Waſt . ē.

Ş In Brocheleſbi . ɪ . boũ træ 7 dim̃ ad glđ. T́ŕa . ɪɪɪ . boƀ.
k   SOCA in Neuhuſe. Ibi ħт Aluređ . ɪ . foct cū . ɪɪ . boƀȝ
in caŕ. 7 xɪ . ac̃s p̃ti.

58 M. In BILLINGBOROUGH Toli had 1 carucate of land taxable. Land for 1 plough. Jocelyn, Alfred's man, has 1 plough.
> 2 villagers and 1 smallholder with 2 oxen in a plough.
> Meadow, 14 acres.

[Value] before 1066 and now, 10s.

59 M. In BOOTHBY (Graffoe) and 'SOMERTON' Halfdan and Asfrithr had 4 carucates of land taxable. Land for 4 ploughs and 6 oxen. Jocelyn, Alfred's man, has 2½ ploughs.
> 6 Freemen on 1 carucate of this land; 4 villagers and 6 smallholders with 2 ploughs.
> Meadow, 55 acres.

Value before 1066, 30s; now 40[s].

60 M. In HUTTOFT Stjupi had 1 bovate of land taxable. Land for 1½ oxen. Doda, Alfred's man, has ½ plough.
> 1 villager.
> Meadow, 40 acres.

Value before 1066 and now, 10s.

61 M. There also Siward had 1 bovate of land taxable. Land for 1½ oxen. Bernard, Alfred's man, has 2 oxen in a plough and
> meadow, 40 acres.

Value before 1066 and now, 5s 4d.

62 S. In THEDDLETHORPE ½ carucate of land taxable. Land for 4 oxen.
> 4 Freemen and 1 villager have 2 oxen in a plough and
> meadow, 40 acres.

63 S. In HABROUGH 1 bovate of land taxable. Land for 2 oxen. A jurisdiction of Newsham. Alfred has it. It is waste.

64 S. In BROCKLESBY 1½ bovates of land taxable. Land for 3 oxen. A jurisdiction of Newsham. Alfred has
> 1 Freeman with 2 oxen in a plough; and
> meadow, 11 acres.

k

.XXVIII. TERRA GOZELINI FILIJ LANBERTI.

ⓂIn *BLIBVRG* . ħƀ Toui . vi . bou træ ad glđ . Tra . ii . car.
Ibi Gozelin filius Lanƀti hĩ . ii . car in dñio . 7 i . focħ
de una bou huj træ . 7 viii . uiłł cũ . i . car . 7 xx . aĉs p̃ti.
T.R.E. uał xx . soł . m̃ xxxiii . Tailla . vii . soł.

ⓂIn *GLENTEVVRDE* . ħƀ Godric . vii . bou træ ad glđ.
Tra xii . bob . Ibi Gozeł hĩ . iiii . focħ de . iiii . bou huj
træ . cũ dim̃ car . Anſchitiłł hõ ej hĩ ibi . i . car . 7 xxx.
aĉs p̃ti . T.R.E. uał . x . soł 7 viii . den . m̃ . xx . soł.

ⓂIn *NORMANEBI* 7 Ouneſbi . ħƀ Agemund dim̃ car
tre ad glđ . Tra . iiii . bou . Ibi Colſuan hõ Gozeł hĩ
dim̃ car . 7 i . uiłł . 7 iiii . aĉs p̃ti . T.R.E. uał . viii . soł.
m̃ . x . soliđ. ⌐hĩ Socã . Tra . ix . bou.

Ibidẽ hĩ Gozeł . ix . bou træ ad glđ . unde . Re . ep̃s

ⓂIn *WILINGEHÃ* . ħƀ Aſlac 7 Ernui . v . car træ ad
glđ . 7 tciã part uni car . Tra totiđ car . Ibi hĩ Walo
hõ Gozeł . i . car . 7 v . focħ de . iii . car 7 iii . bou huj træ
7 i . borđ cũ . i . car . T.R.E. uał . lx . soł . m̃ . xl.

ₛIn *STOV* . i . car tre ad glđ . Tra . i . car . SOCA in Wilingehã.
Ibi . iiii . focħ hñt . i . car.

1 M. In BLYBOROUGH Tofi had 6 bovates of land taxable. Land for 2 ploughs. Jocelyn son of Lambert has 2 ploughs in lordship;
 1 Freeman on 1 bovate of this land; 8 villagers with 1 plough.
 Meadow, 20 acres.
Value before 1066, 20s; now 33[s]. Exactions 7s.

2 M. In GLENTWORTH Godric had 7 bovates of land taxable. Land for 12 oxen. Jocelyn has
 4 Freemen on 4 bovates of this land with ½ plough.
 Asketill, his man, has 1 plough there and
 meadow, 30 acres.
Value before 1066, 10s 8d; now 20s.

3 M. In NORMANBY (-by-Spital) and OWMBY (-by-Spital) Agmundr had ½ carucate of land taxable. Land for 4 oxen. Kolsveinn, Jocelyn's man, has ½ plough.
 1 villager.
 Meadow, 4 acres.
Value before 1066, 8s; now 10s.

4 There also Jocelyn has 9 bovates of land taxable of which Bishop Remigius has the jurisdiction. Land for 9 oxen.

5 2 In WILLINGHAM (by Stow) Aslakr and Earnwine had 5 carucates of
M. land taxable and the third part of 1 carucate. Land for as many ploughs. Walo, Jocelyn's man, has 1 plough.
 5 Freemen on 3 carucates and 3 bovates of this land;
  1 smallholder with 1 plough.
Value before 1066, 60s; now 40[s].

6 S. In STOW (St. Mary) 1 carucate of land taxable. Land for 1 plough. A jurisdiction of Willingham (by Stow).
 4 Freemen have 1 plough.

ᴍ. In *INGEHĀ*. ħƀr Alnod 7 Aſlac . ı . cař tre ad glđ . Tra
xɪɪ . boƀ . Ibi Anſchitil hō Gozeł ħŧ . ı . cař . 7 ı . ſocħ de . ıı.
bou huj tre . 7 ı . borđ . cū uno boue in cař . 7 vı . ač̄s p̄ti.
T.R.E. uał . xx . ſoł . m̄ . x . ſoł

ᴍ. In *COTES* . ħƀ Aſlac dim cař træ ad glđ . Tra . ıııı . boƀ.
Ibi . ı . uiłł ħŧ . ı . boū in cař . T.R.E. uał xx . ſoł . m̄ . v.

S Ibidē . ı . bou træ ad glđ . Soca in Ingeħā . Waſta . ē.

S In Eſnetrebi . ı . bou træ ad glđ . Soca in Wadingħā . Waſt

.ıııı. In *HERPESWELLE* . Agemund 7 alij . ıı . fr̄s ħƀr . ıı . cař
7 7 dimidiā tre ad glđ . Tra . ııı . cař . Ibi ħŧ Gozeł . ıı . cař . 7 xııı . uiłł
cū . ııı . cař . 7 dim æcclam . 7 cıx . ač̄s p̄ti . T.R.E. uał . ıx.
ſoliđ . m̄ . ʟ . Tailla . x . ſoł.

ᴍ. In *HAGETORNE* 7 Haneuuorde ħƀr Sighet 7 Briteua
ıı . cař træ 7 ı . boū ad glđ . Tra . ıııı . cař.

S Ibidē . ıııı . bou træ ad glđ . Soca in Herpeſuuelle . 7 aliæ
B . ıı . bou træ ad glđ Inland in Dunebi . Tra uni cař.
Ibi ħŧ Gozeł . ıı . cař in dn̄io . 7 xı . ſocħ de xııı . bou
huj træ . 7 ııı . uiłł 7 xı . borđ . cū . ııı . cař . 7 ı . moliñ
xvı . denar . 7 xʟ . ač̄s p̄ti . T.R.E. 7 m̄ . uał . ʟx . ſoł . Tailla . xx. ti ſoł

ᴍ. In 7 Staintone *WADINGEHĀ* ħƀr Stangrī 7 Agemund . vı . bō
træ ad glđ . Tra . vı . boƀ . Ibi ħŧ Gozeł . ı . cař . 7 xx . uiłł
cū . ı . cař 7 ıı . boƀ in cař . 7 xx . ač̄s p̄ti . T.R.E. uał . xʟ.
ſoł . m̄ xxx . Tailla . x . ſoł.

7 2 In INGHAM Alnoth and Aslakr had 1 carucate of land taxable. Land
M. for 12 oxen. Asketill, Jocelyn's man, has 1 plough.
　　1 Freeman on 2 bovates of this land; 1 smallholder with 1 ox
　　　in a plough.
　　Meadow, 6 acres.
　Value before 1066, 20s; now 10s.

8 M. In COATES Aslakr had ½ carucate of land taxable. Land for 4 oxen.
　　1 villager has 1 ox in a plough.
　　Value before 1066, 20s; now 5[s].

9 S. There also 1 bovate of land taxable. A jurisdiction of Ingham.
　It is waste.

10 S. In SNITTERBY 1 bovate of land taxable. A jurisdiction of
Waddingham. It is waste.

11 4 In HARPSWELL Agmundr and Sigketill and 2 other brothers had
M. 2½ carucates of land taxable. Land for 3 ploughs. Jocelyn has 2
ploughs and
　　13 villagers with 3 ploughs; and
　　½ church; meadow, 109 acres.
　Value before 1066, 9s; now 50[s]. Exactions 10s.

12 2 In HACKTHORN and (Cold) HANWORTH Sigketill and Beorhtgifu had
M. 2 carucates of land and 1 bovate taxable. Land for 4 ploughs.

13 S. There also 4 bovates of land taxable. A jurisdiction of Harpswell.
B. Another 2 bovates of land taxable. *Inland* of Owmby (-by-Spital).
Land for 1 plough. Jocelyn has 2 ploughs in lordship;
　　11 Freemen on 13 bovates of this land; 3 villagers and
　　　11 smallholders with 3 ploughs.
　　1 mill, 16d; meadow, 40 acres.
　Value before 1066 and now, 60s. Exactions 20s.

14 M. In WADDINGHAM and STAINTON Steingrimr and Agmundr had 6
bovates of land taxable. Land for 6 oxen. Jocelyn has 1 plough.
　　20 villagers with 1 plough and 2 oxen in a plough.
　　Meadow, 20 acres.
　Value before 1066, 40s; now 30[s]. Exactions 10s.

.III.

Ⓜ In *REBVRNE*. Agemund 7 Bruhiſe 7 Scule ħbr.VII.

⌐caŕ træ 7 I.bõ ad glđ.

Tra.xIIII.caŕ 7 II.bob.Ibi ħⒸ Gozelin 7 q̅đã hõ ej
III.caŕ in dñio.7 VI.ſocħ de x.bou huj træ.7 xxI.
uiłł.7 IIII.borđ.cũ III.caŕ 7 dim̃.7 I.molin.III.ſoliđ.
7 cxL.aĉs p̃ti.T.R.E.uał.xIII.liƀ.m̃.c.ſoł.Tailla.xx.

Ⓜ In *SCALLEBI* 7 Stratone.ħƀ Agemund xIII.bou træ ad
glđ.Tra.II.caŕ 7 dim̃.Ibi Baldric hõ Gozeł ħ.I.caŕ.
7 VI.ſocħ de.III.bou huj træ.7 I.uiłł 7 III.borđ.cũ.I.caŕ
T.R.E.uał.xx.ſoł.m̃ xxx.Tailla.x.ſoł.

Ⓜ In *BVLESFORDE*.ħƀ Agemund.I.caŕ træ ad glđ.Tra
uni caŕ.Ibi Gozelin 7 q̅đã miles ej hñt.II.caŕ.7 I.ſocħ
7 VI.uiłł 7 IIII.borđ cũ.I.caŕ.7 ſed uni moł.7 æcclam
7 xv.aĉs p̃ti.7 xxx.aĉs ſiluæ min̄.T.R.E.uał.IIII.liƀ.
m̃.xxx.ſoł.Tailla.x.ſoł.   ⌐ũnũ bou.

Ⓑ In Cletħã.II.bou tre ad glđ.Inland huj Ⓜ.Ibi.I.uiłłs ħ
Ⓜ In *RASE*.ħƀ Tor.III.bou tre ad glđ.Tra.v.caŕ.Ibi ħ
Walo hõ Gozeł.II.bou in caŕ.7 I.ſocħ de dim̃ bou huj
træ.7 IIII.uiłł cũ dim̃ caŕ.T.R.E.uał x.ſoł.m̃.xxIIII.

Ⓜ In *TAVELESBI*.ħƀ Edric.I.caŕ tre ad glđ.Tra.xII.
bob.Ibi Godard hõ Gozeł ħ.I.caŕ.7 IIII.ſocħ de
una bou huj tre.7 x.uiłł cũ.I.caŕ 7 dim̃.7 III.molin̄
xvI.ſolid.7 LxI.aĉ p̃ti.T.R.E.uał.Lx.ſoł.m̃ c.Tailla
Ⓢ In Wiuilingeħã.Soca huj Ⓜ.   ⌐Lx.ſoł.
xv.bou træ ad glđ.Tra.III.caŕ 7 dim̃.Ibi.xxvIII.ſocħ
7 x.borđ hñt.II.caŕ 7 dim̃.7 cc.aĉs p̃ti.Ibi ħ Iuo dim̃ caŕ.
Ⓢ In Sũmerlede.I.bou træ ad glđ.Ibi.ē un̄ borđ.
Ⓢ In Clacheſbi 7 Normaneſbi.Ix.bou træ ad glđ.
Tra.II.caŕ 7 II.bou.Ibi.xIIII.ſocħ hñt xI.bou in caŕ.
7 xL.aĉs p̃ti.7 xL.aĉs ſiluæ minutæ.
Ⓢ In Oſgoteſbi.I.bou tre ad glđ.Tra.II.bob.Ibi.I.borđ.

28

15 3 In REDBOURNE Agmundr, Brunhyse and Skuli had 7 carucates of
M. land and 1 bovate taxable. Land for 14 ploughs and 2 oxen.
Jocelyn and a certain man of his have 3 ploughs in lordship;
  6 Freemen on 10 bovates of this land; 21 villagers and
    4 smallholders with 3½ ploughs.
  1 mill, 3s; meadow, 140 acres.
Value before 1066 £13; now 100s. Exactions 20[s].

16 M. In SCAWBY and STURTON Agmundr had 13 bovates of land taxable.
Land for 2½ ploughs. Baldric, Jocelyn's man, has 1 plough.
  6 Freemen on 3 bovates of this land; 1 villager and
    3 smallholders with 1 plough.
Value before 1066, 20s; now 30[s]. Exactions 10s.

17 M. In BOTTESFORD Agmundr had 1 carucate of land taxable. Land for
1 plough. Jocelyn and a certain man-at-arms of his have 2 ploughs
  and 1 Freeman, 6 villagers and 4 smallholders with 1 plough; and
  1 mill site; a church; meadow, 15 acres; underwood, 30 acres.
Value before 1066, £4; now 30s. Exactions 10s.

18 B. In CLEATHAM 2 bovates of land taxable. *Inland* of this manor.
  1 villager has 1 ox.

19 M. In (Middle) RASEN Thorr had 3 bovates of land taxable. Land for
5 ploughs. Walo, Jocelyn's man, has 2 oxen in a plough.
  1 Freeman on ½ bovate of this land; 4 villagers with ½ plough.
Value before 1066, 10s; now 24[s].

20 M. In TEALBY Eirikr had 1 carucate of land taxable. Land for 12 oxen.
Godard, Jocelyn's man, has 1 plough.
  4 Freemen on 1 bovate of this land; 10 villagers with 1½ ploughs.
  3 mills, 16s; meadow, 61 acres.
Value before 1066, 60s; now 100[s]. Exactions 60s.

21 S. In (North) WILLINGHAM, a jurisdiction of this manor, 15 bovates
of land taxable. Land for 3½ ploughs.
  28 Freemen and 10 smallholders have 2½ ploughs and
  meadow, 200 acres.
  Ivo has ½ carucate there.

22 S. In *SUMMERLEDE* 1 bovate of land taxable.
  1 smallholder.

23 S. In CLAXBY and NORMANBY (le Wold) 9 bovates of land taxable.
Land for 2 ploughs and 2 oxen.
  14 Freemen have 11 oxen in a plough and
  meadow, 40 acres; underwood, 40 acres.

24 S. In OSGODBY 1 bovate of land taxable. Land for 2 oxen.
  1 smallholder.

ⴟ In SNELESLVNT . ħɓ Agemund . I . caꝛ tꝛæ ad glđ .

Tꝛa . II . caꝛ . Ibi Rayner hō Gozeł hƚ . I . caꝛ . 7 III . foch

de . II . boủ huj tꝛe . 7 I . uiłt cū dim̄ caꝛ . 7 x . aĉs p̄ti .

7 XIIII . aĉs filuæ min̄ . T.R.E . 7 m̄ . uaƚ . XXX . foƚ .

Ş In Rerefbi . I . caꝛ tꝛæ 7 dim̄ ad glđ . SOCA huj ⴟ

Tꝛa XII . boɓ . Ibi IIII . foch hn̄t . I . caꝛ . 7 v . aĉs p̄ti .

7 x . aĉs filuæ minutæ . De haĉ foca ten̄ W . de p̄ci . IIII . bō

Ş In Sonetorp . VI . boủ tꝛe ad glđ . Tꝛa . I . caꝛ . Ibi . I . foch

7 VI . aꝯ p̄ti .   ⌊foch 7 VI . aꝯ p̄ti .

Ş In Wichingebi . III . boủ tꝛe ad glđ . Tꝛa . v . boɓ . Ibi . IIII .

ⴟ In BLESEBI . ħɓ Agemund . XIIII . boủ tꝛæ 7 dim̄ ad glđ .

Tꝛa . III . caꝛ . Ibi Herman hō Gozeł hƚ . I . caꝛ 7 dim̄ .

7 II . foch de . II . boủ 7 dim̄ huj tꝛæ . 7 II . uiłt 7 II . borđ . cū . I . caꝛ . ⌐7 II . bō

7 CXX . aĉs p̄ti . 7 CXX . aĉs filuæ min̄ . T.R.E . XXII . foƚ . m̄ . XL . foƚ .

Ş In Bechelinge . dim̄ boủ tꝛæ ad glđ . Tꝛa . I . boủ . Ibi . I . foch

                            ⌊aꝛ . I . boue . 7 dim̄ aꝯ p̄ti .

359 c

Ş In Houtone . I . caꝛ tꝛæ ad glđ . Tꝛa . II . caꝛ . Ibi . IIII . foch

cū . IX boɓ in caꝛ . 7 x . aꝯ p̄ti . Herman hƚ Sub Gozeł .

ⴟ In BESEBI 7 Maltebi . ħɓ Agemund . VI . bō tꝛæ ad

glđ . Tꝛa . VI . boɓ . Ibi Eurold hō Gozeł hƚ dim̄ caꝛ .

7 I . foch de . IIII . toftis huj tꝛæ . 7 I . uiłt cū . II . boɓ in caꝛ .

7 æccƚa . T.R.E . 7 m̄ . uaƚ . x . foliđ .

ⴟ In ADREDEBI . ħɓ Lefinc . I . caꝛ tre ad glđ . Tꝛa . XII .

boɓ . Ibi Baldric hō Gozeł hƚ . I . caꝛ . 7 III . foch . 7 v .

uiłt cū . v . caꝛ 7 dim̄ . 7 I . moliñ . II . foliđ . T.R.E . uaƚ . XL

foƚ . m̄ . XXX . foƚ .

25 M. In SNELLAND Agmundr had 1 carucate of land taxable. Land for 2 ploughs. Rainer, Jocelyn's man, has 1 plough.
    3 Freemen on 2 bovates of this land; 1 villager with ½ plough.
    Meadow, 10 acres; underwood, 14 acres.
Value before 1066 and now, 30s.

26 S. In REASBY 1½ carucates of land taxable. A jurisdiction of this manor. Land for 12 oxen.
    4 Freemen have 1 plough and
    meadow, 5 acres; underwood, 10 acres.
    Of this jurisdiction William of Percy holds 4 bovates.

27 S. In SWINTHORPE 6 bovates of land taxable. Land for 1 plough.
    1 Freeman.
    Meadow, 6 acres.

28 S. In WICKENBY 3 bovates of land taxable. Land for 5 oxen.
    4 Freemen.
    Meadow, 6 acres.

29 M. In BLEASBY Agmundr had 14½ bovates of land taxable. Land for 3 ploughs. Herman, Jocelyn's man, has 1½ ploughs.
    2 Freemen on 2½ bovates of this land; 2 villagers and
      2 smallholders with 1 plough and 2 oxen.
    Meadow, 120 acres; underwood, 120 acres.
[Value] before 1066, 22s; now 40s.

30 S. In BECKERING ½ bovate of land taxable. Land for 1 ox.
    1 Freeman ploughs with 1 ox.
    Meadow, ½ acre.

31 S. In HOLTON (cum Beckering) 1 carucate of land taxable. Land for   359 c
2 ploughs.
    4 Freemen with 9 oxen in a plough.
    Meadow, 10 acres.
    Herman has it under Jocelyn.

32 M. In BEESBY and MALTBY (le Marsh) Agmundr had 6 bovates of land taxable. Land for 6 oxen. Eurold, Jocelyn's man, has ½ plough.
    1 Freeman on 4 plots of this land; 1 villager with 2 oxen
      in a plough.
    A church.
Value before 1066 and now, 10s.

33 M. In (Bag) ENDERBY Leysingr had 1 carucate of land taxable.
Land for 12 oxen. Baldric, Jocelyn's man, has 1 plough.
    3 Freemen and 5 villagers with 5½ ploughs.
    1 mill, 2s.
Value before 1066, 40s; now 30s.

In Hacberdingehā hͭ Gozelin.ɪ.moliñ.ɪɪ.ſolidoʒ.

ꝏ In *TEDFORDE*.ħᵬ Britnod.ɪɪ.car̄ træ 7 ɪɪ.boū ad glđ.
Tra.ɪɪɪ.car̄.Ibi Walt hō Gozeł hͭ.ɪ.car̄.7 v.ſocħ
de.vɪ.bou huj træ.7 ɪɪɪ.uiłł cū.ɪ.car̄ 7 dɪ̄m.T.R.E.
uał.xx.ſoł.m̄.xxx.ſoł.   Socᴀ i Hamerigā.

★ ꝏ In *SV̄MERDEBI*.ħᵬ Agemund.ɪ.car̄ tre ad glđ.Tra
xɪɪ.boᵬ.Ibi.v.ſocħ hn̄t.ɪ.car̄ 7 dɪ̄m.7 dim moł.x.den.

ꝏ Ibidē.ħᵬ Snarri.ɪ.car̄ træ ad glđ.Tra.xɪɪ.boᵬ.Ibi
Raẏner hō Gozeł hͭ.vɪ.ſocħ cū.ɪ.car̄.7 dim moliñ
x.denar̄.T.R.E.uał.x.ſoł.m̄.xvɪ.ſoł.

ꝏ In *ANDREBI*.ħᵬ Lefsi.vɪ.boū træ ad glđ.Tra.ɪ.car̄.
Ibi Lanᵬt hō Gozeł hͭ.ɪɪɪ.boū in car̄.7 vɪ.ſocħ 7 ɪ.uiłł
7 ɪ.borđ.cū.ɪ.boue in car̄.T.R.E.uał.vɪɪɪ.ſoł.m̄.x.ſoł.

§ Ibidē.ɪ.bou tre ad glđ.Tra.ɪɪ.boᵬ.Socᴀ in Aſchebi.
Ibi.ɪ.ſocħ 7 ɪ.uiłł hn̄t.ɪ.boū in car̄.   Itē Socᴀ

§ In Marchebi.ɪ.bou træ ad glđ.Ibi.ɪ.ſocħ hͭ.ɪ.boū in car̄.

§ In Wenflet.ɪɪ.bou træ ad glđ.Tra.ɪɪ.boᵬ.Ibi.ɪɪ.uiłł
hn̄t.ɪɪ.boū in car̄.7 xx.aćs p̄ti.7 ɪ.ſalinā.vɪɪɪ.den.

ꝏ In *WIZEBI* 7 Clacheſbi.ħᵬ Agemund.ɪ.car̄ træ ad
glđ.Tra.ɪ.car̄.Ibi Walter hō Gozeł hͭ.ɪ.car̄.7 ɪ.uiłł.
7 ɪ.moliñ.ɪɪɪɪ.ſolid.T.R.E.7 m̄ uał.xx.ſoł.

§ In Waletone 7 Bodebi.ɪɪ.car̄ tre 7 ɪɪ.boū ad glđ.Tra
ɪɪɪ.car̄.Socᴀ in Claſbi.Ibi Raẏner hō Gozeł hͭ
dɪ̄m car̄.7 xɪɪɪɪ.ſocħ hn̄t.ɪɪɪ.car̄.

34 In HAGWORTHINGHAM Jocelyn has 1 mill, 2s.

35 M. In TETFORD Beorhtnoth had 2 carucates of land and 2 bovates
taxable. Land for 3 ploughs. Walter, Jocelyn's man, has 1 plough.
   5 Freemen on 6 bovates of this land; 3 villagers with 1½ ploughs.
Value before 1066, 20s; now 30s.

Jurisdiction of Hameringham:
36 S. In SOMERSBY Agmundr had 1 carucate of land taxable. Land for
12 oxen.
   5 Freemen have 1½ ploughs.
   ½ mill, 10d.

37 M. There also Snarri had 1 carucate of land taxable. Land for 12 oxen.
Rainer, Jocelyn's man, has
   6 Freemen with 1 plough.
   ½ mill, 10d.
Value before 1066, 10s; now 16s.

38 M. In (Bag) ENDERBY Leofsige had 6 bovates of land taxable. Land
for 1 plough. Lambert, Jocelyn's man, has 3 oxen in a plough.
   6 Freemen, 1 villager and 1 smallholder with 1 ox in a plough.
Value before 1066, 8s; now 10s.

39 S. There also 1 bovate of land taxable. Land for 2 oxen.
A jurisdiction of Ashby (Puerorum).
   1 Freeman and 1 villager have 1 ox in a plough.

Also a jurisdiction:
40 S. In MARKBY 1 bovate of land taxable.
   1 Freeman has 1 ox in a plough.

41 S. In WAINFLEET 2 bovates of land taxable. Land for 2 oxen.
   2 villagers have 2 oxen in a plough and
   meadow, 20 acres; 1 salt-house, 8d.

42 M. In WINCEBY and CLAXBY (Pluckacre) Agmundr had 1 carucate of
land taxable. Land for 1 plough. Walter, Jocelyn's man, has 1
plough.
   1 villager.
   1 mill, 4s.
Value before 1066 and now, 20s.

43 S. In WELTON (le Marsh) and BOOTHBY 2 carucates of land and 2
bovates taxable. Land for 3 ploughs. A jurisdiction of Claxby
(Pluckacre). Rainer, Jocelyn's man, has ½ plough.
   14 Freemen have 3 ploughs.